# Oral Transmission and the Dream Narratives of Matthew 1-2

# Oral Transmission and the Dream Narratives of Matthew 1–2

*An Exploration of Matthean Culture Using Memory Techniques*

Alistair N. Shaw

☙PICKWICK *Publications* · Eugene, Oregon

ORAL TRANSMISSION AND THE DREAM NARRATIVES OF MATTHEW 1–2
An Exploration of Matthean Culture Using Memory Techniques

Copyright © 2019 Alistair N. Shaw. All rights reserved. Except for brief quotations in critical publications or reviews, no part of this book may be reproduced in any manner without prior written permission from the publisher. Write: Permissions, Wipf and Stock Publishers, 199 W. 8th Ave., Suite 3, Eugene, OR 97401.

Pickwick Publications
An Imprint of Wipf and Stock Publishers
199 W. 8th Ave., Suite 3
Eugene, OR 97401

www.wipfandstock.com

PAPERBACK ISBN: 978-1-5326-7034-3
HARDCOVER ISBN: 978-1-5326-7035-0
EBOOK ISBN: 978-1-5326-7036-7

*Cataloguing-in-Publication data:*

Names: Shaw, Alistair N., author.

Title: Oral transmission and the dream narratives of Matthew 1–2 : an exploration of Matthean culture using memory techniques / Alistair N. Shaw.

Description: Eugene, OR: Pickwick Publications, 2019. | Includes bibliographical references and index.

Identifiers: ISBN 978-1-5326-7034-3 (paperback). | ISBN 978-1-5326-7035-0 (hardcover). | ISBN 978-1-5326-7036-7 (ebook).

Subjects: LCSH: Bible.—Matthew I–II—Criticism, interpretation, etc. | Oral tradition. | Dreams in the Bible. | Dreams—Religious aspects.

Classification: BS2575.2 S53 2019 (print). | BS2575.2 (ebook).

Manufactured in the U.S.A.                                        09/30/19

To Eilidh,
the first of a new generation

# Contents

*List of Tables* | viii
*Preface* | ix
*Acknowledgments* | xi
*List of Abbreviations* | xii

1. The Problem | 1
2. Orality | 11
3. Memory | 48
4. Methodology | 77
5. Dreams | 100
6. Matthew | 120
7. Comparison of Memory Patterns | 146
8. Conclusion | 222

*Bibliography* | 231
*Author Index* | 249
*Subject Index* | 253
*Ancient Document Index* | 257

# Tables

Table 1: Memory Patterns by Culture | 97

Table 2: Matthew | 144

Table 3: Old Testament | 157

Table 4: Jewish Literature | 174

Table 5: Classical or Hellenistic Historians | 187

Table 6: Classical or Hellenistic Biographers | 196

Table 7: Hellenistic Fiction Writers | 202

Table 8: Artemidorus | 207

Table 9: Old Testament Books | 215

Table 10: Old Testament—Josephus—Jewish—Classical Writers | 218

Table 11: Greek Authors | 219

# Preface

MY INTEREST IN MATTHEW's dream narratives and their implications for his cultural setting was first roused through reading Derek Dodson's PhD thesis for Baylor University, *Reading Dreams: An Audience Critical Approach to the Dreams in the Gospel of Matthew*. He has since produced it in book form with the same title, published by T. & T. Clark International. Although his research was thorough and his arguments rigorous, I found myself questioning his conclusion that Matthew was intentionally writing for a Hellenistic audience. I therefore decided to explore the same area, but coming at it from an entirely different angle, looking at Matthew's source, whether that lay in his own mind or stemmed from material passed on to him by others.

As a result, this monograph is concerned with exploring the cultural background of Matthew's dream narratives and particularly trying to establish whether the literary practice underlying them is closer to that of OT or Greco-Roman literature. This is done through looking at the ways in which the dreams were remembered and transmitted, analyzing the text in search of "memory patterns," devices used in oral and semi-literate societies with the aim of helping people remember a poem or a narrative. Many of these techniques use sound (e.g., alliteration, assonance, and rhythm), but some engage with the structure of the material; occasionally an image might be applied to aid memory. Thereafter dream reports from a variety of other ancient sources are analyzed to reveal the memory patterns which underlie them. Subsequently the results are compared, with attention focused on the few devices which are culturally specific and elsewhere noting the frequency with which devices are used as authors typically express themselves. The outcome is intended to identify the cultural background within which the Matthean dream narratives emerge.

After an introductory chapter, which outlines the problem to be tackled, there are chapters on orality and memory. These are followed by a chapter on methodology, as the method used here in analyzing the dream narratives is new and provides a novel interpretive approach to this section of Matthew. After that come chapters on dreams, Matthew, and a comparison of his text with dream narratives in other literature. Finally a conclusion is offered.

I come to the view that the Matthean narratives have greater affinity with Jewish material and OT in particular than with Greco-Roman literature. The data gathered in the course of my research also allows for other comparisons. Of particular interest are comparisons between the writers of OT and those of Hellenistic background and between Josephus and both the groups just mentioned.

Alistair N. Shaw

January 2019

# Acknowledgments

THIS BOOK IS THE result of five years spent in part-time research at the Department of Theology and Religious Studies at the University of Glasgow. I am indebted to the three people who served as my supervisors and gave much encouragement and support. For the first two years I had Dr. Andrew Adam, who helped me launch this project. For the last two years I had Dr. Sean Adams, who patiently steered me to its completion. I had as second supervisor, Dr. Lisa Hau of the Department of Classics, who gave valuable input with regard to classical literature.

I am also grateful to the trustees of the Hope Trust, who awarded me a John Hope Scholarship and took regular interest in my progress.

Finally, I would like to express my appreciation to my wife, Brenda, for her moral support and the sacrifice made in family time to allow me to purse my studies.

# Abbreviations

In addition to the following, all abbreviations in this monograph are taken from: Billie Jean Collins, et al., *The SBL Handbook of Style: For Ancient Near Eastern, Biblical, and Early Christian Studies* (Atlanta: Society of Biblical Literature Press, 2014).

ACC     *Ancient Christian Commentary on Scripture: Matthew 1–13*. Downers Grove, IL: InterVarsity, 2001

CCL     *Corpus Christianorum*. Series Latina. Turnhout, Belgium: Brepols, 1953–

CGS     *A Companion to Greek Studies*

CS     *Cistercian Studies*. Kalamazoo, MI: Cistercian, 1973–

GCS     *Die griechischen christlichen Schriftsteller*. Berlin: Akademie, 1897–

LAB     Pseudo-Philo. *Liber Antiquitatum Biblicarum*

L & S     Charlton T. Lewis, and Charles Short, *A Latin Dictionary*

LSJ     H. S. Liddell, R. Scott, and H. S. Jones, *A Greek-English Lexicon*

LXX     Septuagint

NPNF     Schaff, et al., eds., *A Select Library of the Nicene and Post-Nicene Fathers of the Christian Church*. 2nd series. 14 vols. 1887–1894. Reprint, Peabody, MA: Hendrickson, 1994

OCCC     *Oxford Companion to Classical Civilization*

OCCL     *Oxford Companion to Classical Literature*

OCD     *Oxford Classical Dictionary*

PG      J. Migne, ed., *Patrologiae cursus completus*. Series Graeca. 166 vols. Paris: Migne, 1857–1886

PL      J.-P. Migne, ed., *Patrologiae cursus completus*. Series Latina. 221 vols. Paris: Migne, 1844–1864

SIG     Wilhelm Dittenberger, ed., *Sylloge Inscriptionum Graecarum*. 4 vols. 3rd ed. Leipzig: Hirzel, 1915–1924

# 1

# The Problem

## Introduction

THE AIM OF THIS monograph is to try and clarify where Matthew stands in relation to his cultural background. The task will be carried out through examination of the dream narratives in the first two chapters of the gospel and comparison of these with dream narratives in the OT, contemporary Jewish writings, as well as Greek and Roman literature.

It is now widely accepted through the writing of Martin Hengel that by the first century CE Judaism was subject to significant Hellenistic influence.[1] This being so, we may expect Matthew to reflect the intermingling of Judaism and Hellenism. What is being proposed here is an attempt to see whether aspects of one of the underlying cultural traditions is more evident in Matthew's work.

Some clarification of terms would be helpful at this stage. "Culture" has a wide range of meanings, but we shall be using it in the sense of "literary practice."[2] Although this may carry wider implications, we shall be drawing our conclusions from the use of devices used in oral and written communication. We have become increasingly aware of just how complex Judaism was in the first century CE. The Qumran scrolls have indicated a real diversity of beliefs and practices. However, there was a common set of Scriptures and it is these that will play an important role here in the representation of Judaism.

It seems that Matthew was aiming his gospel at a readership whose first or only language was Greek, for that is the language of his gospel. It is clear that sufficient numbers of them did not understand Hebrew as to make it necessary for him to render Hebrew expressions such as "Immanuel" into

---

1. Hengel, *Judaism and Hellenism*; Hengel, *'Hellenization' of Judaea*.

2. Others who have approached the issue through literary practice include Kennedy, *New Testament Interpretation*; Kinney, *Hellenistic Dimensions*.

Greek. At 1:23 he quotes Isa 7:14 where the coming child is to be called Ἐμμανουήλ (עִמָּנוּ אֵל). He duly renders this as μεθ' ἡμῶν ὁ Θεός ("God with us").[3] This may suggest that Matthew himself was sufficiently comfortable with Hebrew to make that translation, but we cannot be certain, for it is equally possible that he may have used someone else's translation.[4] We also have the instance of 2:15 where he wants to identify Jesus with Israel as God's son, quoting Hosea 11:1, "Out of Egypt have I called my son." There he carefully avoids the Septuagint rendering: καὶ ἐξ Αἰγύπτου μετεκάλεσα τὰ τέκνα αὐτοῦ ("and out of Egypt have I called his children"). Although it is possible that he used a different Greek translation, no longer extant, it seems to me more likely that he may have rendered himself the Hebrew וממצרים קראתי לבני. If this is correct, it may suggest some Hebraic influence in his background.

The way in which we propose to explore Matthew's cultural background is through an examination of the dream narratives in his account of Jesus's infancy. There are six dreams referred to in Matthew's gospel (Matt 1:20–25; 2:12, 13–15, 19–21, 22; 27:19). They all use the expression κατ' ὄναρ, "in a dream," a phrase that is found nowhere else in NT and indeed not at all in LXX. However, it does occur in classical writings and is frequent in later Greek.[5] The last of Matthew's dreams comes near the end of the gospel at 27:19.[6] It was experienced by Pilate's wife and made such a significant impact upon her that she interrupted her husband's official duties to warn him in relation to "that righteous (δικαίῳ) man." We will concentrate here on the remaining five dreams, which are all to be found in the infancy narrative. Two are narrated in outline without any detail. Both issue warnings, the first at 2:12 urging the Magi not to return to Herod and the second at 2:22 leading Joseph to settle in Galilee. The other three involve an appearance of an angel of the Lord who issues Joseph with

---

3. LXX leaves it as Ἐμμανουήλ at Isa 7:14 without offering a translation. However, at Isa 8:8, 11, the expression μεθ' ἡμῶν ὁ Θεός is used.

4. Some of the leading figures in the patristic period thought that Matthew first wrote his gospel in a Semitic language. Aramaic was suggested by Papias and Eusebius (Eusebius, *History of the Church* 3.24, 39). Hebrew was proposed by Irenaeus of Lyons and Origen (Irenaeus, *Against Heresies* 3.1.1; Eusebius, *History of the Church* 6.25). Most scholars today take the view that the First Gospel was originally written in Greek with little evidence to suggest it was translated from a Semitic predecessor. For example, see France, *Matthew*, 31n2; Davies and Allison, *Matthew*, 1:9–12; Talbert, *Matthew*, 3.

5. E.g., Aristides, *Orationes* 47(23).21 in the second century CE; SIG 1147 in the second or third century CE.

6. This dream will not be examined since it is very brief, being referred to without the detail being narrated, and it possibly belongs to a different source from the other dreams whose cultural background we are seeking to establish.

commands. At 1:20 Joseph is told not to be afraid to take Mary as his wife and to name her child Jesus. In the next two he is told to take the child and his mother with the aim of fleeing to Egypt at 2:13, and of returning to the land of Israel at 2.20. Although the dream references at 2:12 and 2:22 will be taken into account, more attention will be focused on the fuller dream narratives at 1:20–25; 2:13–15, 19–21.

## *The Contribution of Others*

Examination of these narratives has already been carried out by others, most notably Raymond Brown, George Soares Prabhu, Robert Gnuse and Derek Dodson.[7] While the first three see an OT background to the dream narratives, Dodson interprets them in light of the conventions of Greco-Roman literature.

In *The Birth of the Messiah* Brown comprehensively covers the infancy narratives of both Matthew and Luke. He takes the view that the dreams in Matthew may have been inspired by the dreams of Joseph in Genesis 37; 40–41.[8] His argument is based on certain facts: first the father of Jesus was called Joseph and little seems to have been known about him; secondly Joseph was also the name of a famous patriarch in Genesis, who experienced dreams and had an ability to interpret them; furthermore the patriarch Joseph went down to Egypt, as Jesus's father did, and was involved with the Egyptian ruler, the Pharaoh. However, the parallels are not exact. While it is said that an angel appeared, we are told nothing about what Jesus's father saw and so his dreams were largely auditory, while those of the patriarch were visual. The former did not interpret dreams—he simply acted upon their message. The patriarch did not travel to Egypt to escape trouble—he was taken there as a slave, sold by his brothers.[9] The Pharaoh with whom he dealt was a benevolent figure. On the other hand, the father of each Joseph is called Jacob (Gen 35:22–26; Matt 1:16). Moreover, in Genesis 45 Joseph was responsible for Israel travelling to Egypt to escape a crisis, in this case famine. It is not a Joseph typology as such that is being pursued by Matthew, but rather the parallels between the two Josephs play into a Jesus-Israel typology.

---

7. Brown, *Birth of the Messiah*; Prabhu, *Formula Quotations*; Gnuse, "Dream Genre"; Dodson, *Reading Dreams*.

8. Brown, *Birth of the Messiah*, 111–12.

9. Such is the account of Gen 37:25–28. Compare the account of Artapanus, who states that Joseph obtained prior knowledge of the conspiracy by his brothers and requested neighboring Arabs to convey him to Egypt where he was recommended to the king (Artapanus, "On the Jews," quoted in Eusebius, *Praeparatio Evangelica* 9.23.1–4).

Brown himself also recognizes the parallels between Moses and Jesus[10] and their influence upon the narrative of Jesus's infancy.[11]

Soares Prabhu published *The Formula Quotations in the Infancy Narratives of Matthew* in 1976. As the title suggests, his primary concern is Matthew's use of OT quotations. However, he does reflect on the dreams, drawing attention to the resemblance between the Matthean dream narratives and the Elohist dream messages of Genesis.[12] He focuses in particular upon the dream of Jacob at Beersheba at Genesis 46:2–4 in its Septuagintal form and suggests that Matthew used that to model the dream at 2:13–15 and subsequently the other dreams.

In a *Novum Testamentum* article in 1990 Gnuse argues along similar lines to Soares Prabhu.[13] On the basis of a form-critical assessment he maintains that all the patriarchal dreams in Genesis, and not just the one that Soares Prabhu suggests, lie behind Matthew's narrative.[14] One of the problems is that only three of the Genesis narratives (Gen 20:3–8; 31:24; 46:2–4) involve the straightforward reporting of a dream figure's message, as Matthew's do. The other two include symbolic dream material. A verse taken up with describing what the dreamer saw automatically changes the format (Gen 28:12; 31:10). Moreover, all three of Matthew's dream narratives introduce the appearance of the angel in the dream with the word *behold*, a significant feature of his dream reporting pattern. Only one of the five that Gnuse highlights from Genesis (Gen 28:13) introduces the Lord with this word.[15]

There are other difficulties too. Soares Prabhu notes that the dreams of Genesis are more varied and complex than those of the First Gospel and that Matthew lacks the calling of the dreamer by name, a divine self-identification, what is sometimes referred to as *Offenbarungsformel*, a dialogue with the visitor and the covenant assurance at the end. Gnuse acknowledges these differences too, but lays stress on the many points of similarity. We need to consider whether these differences can be lightly laid aside. In Matthew there is no dialogue between Joseph and the angel,

---

10. Brown, *Birth of the Messiah*, 113–14.

11. This is extensively explored and convincingly argued by Allison, particularly with reference to the Infancy Narratives, in Allison, *New Moses*, 140–65.

12. Prabhu, *Formula Quotations*, 223.

13. Gnuse, "Dream Genre," esp. 97.

14. Abimelech (Gen 20:3–8); Jacob (Gen 28:12–16; 31:10–13); Laban (Gen 31:24); Jacob/Israel (Gen 46:2–4).

15. The word *behold* is also used at Genesis 28:12 to introduce the movement of the angels on the ladder. The fact that *behold* is used too at the beginning of God's speech in Genesis 20:3 is of lesser significance as it comes after God's appearance is mentioned.

whereas three out of the five Genesis dreams involve dialogue with God (Gen 20:3–8; 31:10–13; 46:2–4), most notably the one with which Soares Prabhu chooses to work (Gen 46:2–4). Perhaps of greater significance is the lack of self-identification. We cannot dismiss it, as Gnuse does, by saying that there is no need to identify God in Matthew's setting, for the cultural assumption of the audience would be monotheistic.[16] The fact is that it is an angel and not God who appears in Joseph's dreams. Certainly in pre-exilic writing the phrase "angel of the Lord" was used as a vague way of describing God's presence among humans,[17] but in the post-exilic era angels feature as intermediate beings with names and personalities in their own right.[18] By the first century CE when Matthew was writing several different angels were believed to exist.[19] It does seem strange that Joseph is not given some kind of identification for the voice that he hears.[20]

Despite the weaknesses in Gnuse's argument, he does make a valuable theological contribution when he suggests that the Elohist dreams in Genesis assume a transcendent deity and a similar understanding of God is conveyed through Matthew's dream motif.

In 2006 Dodson submitted a PhD thesis to Baylor University entitled, "Reading Dreams: An Audience-Critical Approach to the Dreams in the Gospel of Matthew."[21] As the sub-title suggests, it falls into the category of narrative criticism and adopts the approach of reading the dreams as the authorial audience. He analyses a selection of dream narratives drawn from Greco-Roman histories, biographies and fiction, to reveal their literary functions. Against this background, as well as social practices like divination, he examines the dream reports in Matthew.

Dodson is explicit about his assumption "that Matthew writes to be understood, and that the larger social and literary conventions of his time provide the commonality with his audience upon which communication

---

16. Gnuse, "Dream Genre," 112.

17. E.g., Gen 16:7–12; 22:11–12; Exod 14:19–20; Judg 2:1–4; 6:11–22; 13:3–5, 20–25; 1 Chr 21:18; Ps 34:7.

18. Gabriel is mentioned in Daniel 9:21 and Luke 1:26 and Michael at Daniel 10:13. Raphael is referred to in Enoch 10:4–6 and Uriel in 2 Esdras 4:1; 5:20; 10:26.

19. Of those listed above Uriel is perhaps in doubt as 2 Esdras is post-Second Temple and probably later than Matthew.

20. When Gabriel appeared to Mary (Luke 1:26–38), he did not identify himself. However, that was not a dream. When Gabriel appeared to Daniel (Dan 9:20–27), he did not identify himself. However, Daniel knew him from a previous vision (Dan 8:15–26). Again Gabriel did not identify himself, but he overheard the command, "Gabriel, make this man understand the vision."

21. In 2009 Dodson issued his work in the form of a monograph with the same title. See Dodson, *Reading Dreams*.

takes place."²² We are entitled to ask by whom Matthew wishes to be understood: by a Jewish audience or Greco-Roman or a mixture of both? Dodson appears to assume that it was a Greco-Roman audience. However, if he had examined OT dream narratives as well as, or instead of, Greco-Roman examples and set Matthew's against them, we may wonder whether he would have come up with a different result.

Dodson offers reasons for drawing comparisons with examples from Greco-Roman literature. He points to two elements in Matthew's first dream that resemble features from Greco-Roman dream reporting. There is a brief character sketch of the dreamer in which Joseph is described as δίκαιος ("righteous"). We are also given his mental state: ταῦτα δὲ αὐτοῦ ἐνθυμηθέντος ("he was reflecting upon these things"). This is noteworthy because in the format of Greek dreams there is an initial scene setting that may include the dreamer's mental attitude or emotional condition.²³ The character sketch and mental state in Matthew have to be acknowledged. The adjective δίκαιος does describe Joseph's character,²⁴ but it serves here primarily to explain why he wanted to lay aside his betrothal to Mary, just as the phrase μὴ θέλων αὐτὴν δειγματίσαι ("unwilling to put her to shame") explains why he went about the "divorce" *quietly*. With regard to Joseph's reflection, it bears some resemblance to prayer, which is a common feature in Jewish dream reports.²⁵ John Hanson accepts that the mental state of the dreamer may include prayer.²⁶ It may be that Matthew is here following what he believes to be a Jewish convention, if he saw reflection resembling prayer. Although that convention may have been affected by Hellenistic influence, Matthew's absorption of it may be entirely indirect, if he was already aware of prayer featuring in Jewish dream reports. Alternatively, Joseph's anxious thoughts may simply have to do with the story line. They sum up what has gone before, viz. the fact that Mary was found to be with child and Joseph's own resolve to terminate their relationship. This allows for the use of the genitive absolute construction that introduces each of the dream narratives. In this case the reflection would explain *when* and *why* the angel visited Joseph. Moreover, neither of the features that Dodson highlights appears in the other two dreams, which are narrated in some detail.

---

22. Dodson, *Reading Dreams*, 16.

23. See Hanson, "Dreams and Visions," 1405–413.

24. It could be argued that δίκαιος is deeply Hebraic in meaning. It is used in the description of Zechariah and Elizabeth (Luke 1:6). However, it is also a key word in Greek moral thought.

25. See Dan 9:21; 4 Ezra 3:1–3; 5:121–22; 6:35–37; 1 Enoch 13:7; 2 Baruch 35:1–4; 2 Enoch 69:4; 71:24–25; Josephus, *Ant.* 11.326; Pseudo-Philo, *LAB* 42:2–3.

26. Hanson, "Dreams and Visions," 1407.

Dodson also draws attention to the way in which Matthew presents the angel of the Lord in dreams. Throughout the OT angels appear as messengers in a wide variety of contexts, but rarely in a dream. The messenger in dreams is usually God himself. Since the angel is appearing in dreams to convey the main revelation in Matthew, Dodson suggests that this is largely due to the Greco-Roman tradition of dream *oneiroi*. In the message dreams of Greek literature *oneiroi* are divine messengers sent by the gods; they stand by the head of dreamers and deliver a message. Examples would include the dream figure who visited Agamemnon in the guise of Nestor and Diomedes, son of Tydeus, whose form Athene took, when she visited King Rhesus.[27] Angels came to resemble *oneiroi* in several respects,[28] as both were intermediary figures sent by god(s) to human-beings and spoke messages in dreams in a form that was immediately intelligible. These could be annunciations, encouragement or orders for a certain course of action to be taken, as in Matt 2:13, 19. There are, however, other points of resemblance between the two which are not reflected in Matthew. Like the *oneiros*, the angel might be described as standing beside the dreamer's head. The message might require to be clarified in which case a dialogue would ensue between the dreamer and the *oneiros*. An angel might disguise himself in human form.[29] The appearance of winged creatures which fly is common to the *oneiroi* of Greek tragedy and the angels of early Judaism.[30] So Dodson's argument is that by placing his angel within a dream Matthew was doing something similar to classical writers when they had the *oneiros* figure convey a message in a dream.[31] We cannot deny some influence from Hellenistic culture. However, we may ask whether Matthew's use of the angel involved a conscious adoption of a literary convention or was the influence of Hellenism of a more indirect nature. We need not follow Dodson in seeing the angel as the Greek dream figure. We have observed that Matthew did not embrace all aspects of the *oneiros*. More significantly we note that angels were already appearing in dreams in Hellenistic Judaism, as in Daniel and other apocalyptic texts.[32] It may therefore have seemed natural to Matthew to follow this

---

27. Homer, *Iliad* 2.20; 10.496–97. There are many more examples in the works of Homer. See Homer, *Iliad* 23.62ff; 24.682–89; *Odyssey* 4.795ff; 6.19ff.

28. For features of the resemblance between angels and *oneiroi*, see Flannery-Dailey, *Dreamers, Scribes, and Priests*, 202–3.

29. Just as Oneiros resembled Nestor, so Raphael took on the form of Azarias, son of Ananias, when he met Tobit (Tob 5:4–12).

30. Just as Oedipus speaks of "*a hovering dream*" in Euripides, *Phoenician Women* 1546, so Daniel 9:21 speaks of Gabriel coming to him "*in swift flight.*"

31. See Dodson, *Reading Dreams*, 94, 97, 233–34.

32. E.g., Dan 8:15–27; 9:21; 1 Enoch 72:1; 4 Ezra 2:42–48; 4:1–5:13.

now established practice without being aware or consciously thinking of its Greek origin. If this were the case, we need not see Matthew as aiming his work at a Greco-Roman audience.

Dodson has succeeded in showing that Matthew's dream narratives would have been understood by a Greco-Roman audience and conform to their literary expectations. What is much less clear is whether Matthew deliberately aimed his work at such a readership or it simply fitted their understanding because in his reporting of Joseph's dreams he was following a widespread literary convention.[33] This convention is something which we shall look at in greater detail later. In the meantime we note how Dodson points to OT narratives which would have been meaningful to the same kind of audience.[34] He instances Jacob's dream at Bethel followed by his building of a sanctuary there (Gen 28:10–22) and similarly with Isaac at Beer-sheeba (Gen 26:23–25). He also refers to Solomon's incubation dream experience at Gibeon (1 Kgs 3:1–15) and the story of the boy Samuel (1 Sam 3). Although specific incubation features are missing in the latter account, Dodson still sees fit to comment that for a Greco-Roman reader, "the cultic setting for the dream oracle would be familiar and perhaps suggestive of an incubation experience."[35] These passages were written before the Hellenistic era with its massive intermingling of Jewish and classical cultures. There is no suggestion from Dodson that the Septuagint deviates in these passages from the Masoretic Text which might account for a Greco-Roman audience understanding them. It would appear anachronistic to suggest that the authors of these OT passages wrote with such an audience in mind. The reason for their understanding was simply shared practices and conventions. The same may hold for Matthew's writing. Although it was intelligible to Greeks and Romans, it is still possible that he did not write with them in mind. However, in the end the difficulty we are faced with is that we do not actually know what audience Matthew intended to read his work. He does not explicitly state his intention.

Dodson has provided a wealth of background material concerning the reporting of dreams in the Greco-Roman world. This does help us appreciate how an audience in this context would understand Matthew's writing. Many of the dream narratives which he examined will also be examined in this monograph: Herodotus's *Histories*; Josephus's *Jewish War*; Acts of the Apostles; Plutarch's *Parallel Lives*; Suetonius's *Lives of the Caesars*; Chariton's *Chaereas and Callirhoe*; and Longus's *Daphnis and Chloe*. Significantly

---

33. See Oppenheim, "Interpretation of Dreams," 179–373.
34. See Dodson, *Reading Dreams*, 58–59.
35. Dodson, *Reading Dreams*, 59.

Dodson does not engage in serious analysis of OT dream narratives. We may wonder if he had concentrated on OT texts alone, whether he would have concluded that Matthew wrote for a Jewish audience and if he had tackled OT and Greco-Roman texts together, whether his conclusion would have been more ambiguous. It is a flaw in his methodology to have paid scant attention to OT texts. It is my intention to include OT dream narratives as well as some from contemporary Jewish texts.

## New Approach

I shall engage in a new methodology, which integrates memory theory and rhetoric. My concern will be with the ways in which the dreams were remembered and transmitted, analyzing Matthew's text in search of "memory patterns," devices used in oral and semi-literate societies with the aim of helping people remember a poem or a narrative. Many of these techniques use sound (e.g., alliteration, assonance, and rhythm), but some engage with the structure of the material; occasionally an image might be applied to aid memory. Thereafter I shall analyze dream reports from a variety of other ancient sources to reveal the memory patterns which underlie them. Subsequently I shall compare the results, focusing attention on the few devices which are culturally specific and elsewhere noting the frequency with which devices are used as authors typically express themselves.

The outcome will be to identify the cultural background within which the Matthean dream narratives emerge. It will demonstrate the overlap of Jewish and Hellenistic cultures, but at the same time it will produce some evidence which suggests that Matthew had a preference for OT styles of expression. A superficial reading of the First Gospel would already suggest that a Jewish background is prominent because of Matthew's frequent quotations from OT and other Jewish content. This monograph will lend some limited support to that view, but at the same time place the First Gospel firmly in its multicultural context.

The way in which I shall go about the task is first to note the context in which Matthew and the recipients of his gospel functioned. It was a society with low levels of literacy. Most people were dependent on the words that they heard spoken or read to them and their own memory of these. Our next chapter will therefore explore the topic of orality. Thereafter we shall consider memory, taking account of what the ancients had to say about it, but focusing on how it is understood today by psychologists and sociologists. There will then follow a chapter on methodology. The method used in the analysis of dream narratives is new and will provide a novel interpretive approach to this section of Matthew and indeed other dream texts from antiquity. Next we shall explore what is known about ancient dreams. Chapters will follow on Matthew with a detailed analysis of his dream narratives, and then a comparison of his text with dream narratives in other literature. Finally there will be a conclusion. However, we must first turn our attention to orality and rhetoric.

# 2

# Orality

## Limited Literacy

IT IS ALL TOO easy for us to assume that the Christians of the first century used texts in the same way as we do today, that most of them could read and write and that the gospel writers would have free access to OT texts and other gospels already written. Certainly there were people throughout the Roman Empire who were able to read and write, but they were a small proportion of the population.[1] Others could do one but not the other.[2] The majority could do neither. However, the illiterate were still able to become familiar with a text through hearing it read or performed aloud. For those who could read, books were available in libraries and for purchase from booksellers, but these texts remained relatively few in number.[3] The result was that they found it necessary to memorize a great deal. Memorization was a pillar of the school system and so played its

---

1. It is difficult to gauge levels of literacy today and even more difficult for the ancient world. However, Gamble estimates that not more than 10 percent of the Christians in any given setting would be literate (Gamble, *Books and Readers*, 5). Clearly it would vary from place to place and be dependent on such factors as gender. Harris offers estimates for the Roman Empire, suggesting that in Rome and Italy the level of male literacy would be below 20–30 percent with female literacy below 10 percent and for the Empire as a whole the figure would be below 15 percent (Harris, *Ancient Literacy*, 259, 267). Bar-Ilan reckons that the literacy rate for the Jewish population in Roman Palestine would be about 3 percent (Bar-Ilan, "Illiteracy in the Land of Israel," 46–61). See also Hezser, *Jewish Literacy*, 496–504.

2. Lee and Scott, *Sound Mapping*, 61.

3. Pliny saw fit to comment on the publication of a thousand copies of a book: "*Eundem inexemplaria mille transcriptum per totam Italiam provinciasque dimisit*" (Pliny, *Epistolae* 4.7.2).

part in the process of someone becoming literate. Even scholars would commit much of their own compositions to memory.[4]

Although by the first century CE the world was less oral than it had been in Homeric times, the society in which NT emerged may best be described as semi-literate. However, there did remain a significant "oral residue."[5] There was a considerable overlap between the two types of culture, so much so that Vernon Robbins has described this kind of situation as a rhetorical culture—that is to say, one in which speech is influenced by writing and writing is influenced by speaking.[6]

## Rhetorical Culture

We shall note some examples which illustrate the intermingling of orality and literacy before we present the case for regarding NT society as being "a rhetorical culture." First we take genealogies which are not given in the form of a chart, a family tree or a table of descent, as we might have today. Instead we find a sequence of statements of what someone did, namely begetting. This derives from the oral use of formulae. Each person is usually mentioned twice, as begetter and begotten.[7] Walter Ong suggests that recurrence of subject-predicate-object produces a swing that assists memory.[8]

The converse is also true with writing affecting orality. Quintilian reflects on the value of writing in the preparation of a speech intended ultimately for oral delivery.[9] He suggests that for the sake of eloquence we need to consider the order in which words should be placed, not necessarily following the order in which they first occur to us, as in conversation. For the same reason he expresses displeasure at the use of dictation: "When we write, however great our speed, the fact that the hand cannot follow the rapidity of our thoughts gives us time to think, whereas the presence of the amanuensis hurries us on, as we are afraid to display

---

4. Pliny tells us that he composed in his memory before summoning his secretary to write what he dictated. "*Cogito si quid in manibus, cogito ad verbum . . . componi teneriue potuerunt. Notarium voco et . . . quae formaveram dicto*" (Pliny, *Epistolae* 9.36.2).

5. Ong uses this phrase (Ong, *Orality and Literacy*, 11). It refers to a situation in which a society has adopted writing, but still displays some of the features of a totally oral society, particularly in relation to its verbal expression and thought.

6. Robbins, "Oral, Rhetorical, and Literary Cultures," 75–91.

7. This is true of the genealogy in Matthew 1, but not in Luke 3. Cf. Gen 4:18 and the journey of the Israelites (Num 33:9–37) which follows a similar pattern.

8. Ong, *Orality and Literacy*, 97.

9. Quintilian, *Institutio* 10.3.3–6.

weakness before a witness."[10] Literacy both affected and was affected by the oral culture from which it emerged.

The structure of material was also influenced by orality and writing. A narrative had to be structured in such a way that listeners could follow it, but the techniques which writers used were oral because that was what they knew.[11] The process could go back and forward. A text might be dictated to a scribe; when complete, it would be read aloud, often to a gathered audience.[12] When a person read a text or had it read to him, he could commit it to memory in much the same way as if it had been delivered orally without ever having been written.[13] If later he wanted to refer to it in his own writing, Werner Kelber suggests he is more likely to have drawn on his memory than scan through scrolls looking for the passage,[14] although there is also evidence of readers making notes when reading which they referred to and used later.[15] Martin Jaffee says the same in relation to the Mishnah: "Biblical citation in rabbinic literature . . . testifies to the commission of the text to memory."[16] There is no doubt that there was interplay between the two media.

Although the majority were illiterate, they could not help being aware of writing, with inscriptions abounding everywhere. When people wanted a letter written or a legal matter attended to, they required a scribe. Equally the literate could not avoid orality. New laws had to be communicated through public criers as well as inscriptions.[17] Even for their own sake the literate had to revert to oral methods because not everything could be encoded in writing which was reserved for events and ideas that were meant to survive a long time. Although not of concern to the rich, writing materials were also expensive.[18]

If we single out the Jews, we can consider whether they were more literate than other nationalities, as we may imagine that the importance of

10. Quintilian, *Institutio* 10.3.19.

11. Davis, *Oral Biblical Criticism*, 47.

12. Davis, *Oral Biblical Criticism*, 61.

13. Many people were acquainted with a wide range of literature and could quote freely from Homer, Herodotus, Virgil, and Cicero, using their memory. See Lee and Scott, *Sound Mapping*, 61.

14. Kelber, "*Oral and the Written Gospel*," 177.

15. E.g., 4QTest. See also Albl, *And Scripture Cannot be Broken*, which argues that many early Christian quotations of OT derive from authoritative written testimonia collections developed to support basic Christian beliefs.

16. Jaffee, "Writing and Rabbinic Oral Tradition," 126.

17. Dewey, "Textuality in an Oral Culture," 41.

18. A roll of papyrus cost two or three days' labor. See Lee and Scott, *Sound Mapping*, 18.

Scripture in their religion may have encouraged literacy. In fact the situation in ancient Israel was extremely complex.[19] We should not be misled by the discovery of the Qumran Scrolls which convey an impression of the community which lived there as having thoroughly appropriated reading and writing into its internal life. Although it is true that most Jews were familiar with the Scriptures, it is probably the case that they gained their knowledge through religious story-tellers.[20] While every male adult Jew was invited to serve as Torah reader in the synagogue, Catherine Hezser comments that only a few individuals will have had the necessary reading skills to carry out this duty.[21] On the other hand, it is possible to underestimate levels of literacy and portray Jewish society as being largely oral. Jaffee argues against "a rabbinic tradition of 'pure' orally-transmitted discourse prior to the Mishnah, uncontaminated by the intervention of writing."[22] In the examination of three Mishnaic extracts[23] he finds characteristics of orally composed and transmitted material,[24] framed in their current mishnaic settings by compositional, exegetical or redactional interventions which reveal the work of written composition. Although his time period is essentially from the second to the fourth century, the situation he describes is not likely to have been different in the first century. Oral and literate traits were interwoven in a complex manner.

We think next of the emerging Christian community. Thomas Boomershine argues that Jesus was literate.[25] He says, "While he could know the scriptures from hearing them read, the likelihood is that Jesus had the ability to read the texts themselves."[26] With the disciples probably being illiterate, Jesus engaged in oral discourse, using a style in his parables which demanded reflection and further thought. Boomershine suggests that this was an oral approach suited to an emerging literate culture. He draws a parallel with Socrates who developed styles of argumentation which led to the full

19. Boomershine, "Jesus of Nazareth," 13.
20. Dewey, "Textuality in an Oral Culture," 46.
21. Hezser, "Private and Public Education," 471.
22. Jaffee, "Writing and Rabbinic Oral Tradition," 127.
23. *Tamid* 3:7–9; *'Erub.* 10:10–14; *Pesaḥ.* 2:5–6.
24. Even with what appears to be oral text there can be no guarantee that it originated unscripted and memorized.
25. Boomershine presents evidence for the literacy of Jesus in Boomershine, "Jesus of Nazareth," 21. See especially Luke 4:16–20. Not everyone would agree, as, for example, Keith, *Jesus's Literacy*.
26. Boomershine, "Jesus of Nazareth," 22.

emergence of philosophy and suggests that Jesus's approach in the parables led ultimately to the development of theology.[27]

When we examine particular NT texts, we find an interplay between the oral and written text. We take as an example Matt 12:3–4 which is an abbreviated version of 1 Sam 21:1–6.[28] It is expressed substantially in Jesus's own words and replicates only words which are easily transmitted orally. It contains a significant number of variations from the written text which Robbins suggests "a literary culture would consider to be errors."[29] Even within NT oral communication was affecting the written.

Having established that the Greco-Roman world was one in which orality and literacy were intermingled, we now concentrate on orality. In the process we shall draw on studies related to Homer, Herodotus and Pausanias. However, this is not meant to contradict what has just been said. It is useful to separate orality and literacy from a theoretical perspective to enable us to see more clearly how oral transmission functions. In defending his work on "The Oral and Written Gospel," Kelber happily acknowledges that there is no "Great Divide" between oral tradition and Markan textuality, but sees theoretical advantage in distinguishing oral and literary operations.[30]

## Orality

Orality is a concept which has been extensively examined over the last eighty years by classicists, sociologists and anthropologists as well as NT scholars.[31] The value of orality for NT studies has recently been called into question by Paul Foster,[32] with particular reference to Historical Jesus research, but it has also been defended by Eric Eve.[33] Related to what was said above about the intertwining of orality and literacy, Eve makes the point that the writing of a text did not necessarily separate it from the oral sphere.[34] A

---

27. Boomershine, "Jesus of Nazareth," 28.

28. Robbins provides several examples. See Robbins, "Oral, Rhetorical, and Literary Cultures," 83–85. Where he refers to Mark, we shall use Matthew, as his gospel is the subject of this monograph.

29. Robbins, "Oral, Rhetorical, and Literary Cultures," 85.

30. Kelber, *Oral and the Written Gospel*, 174–76.

31. Among them are classicists Milman Parry, Albert Lord, and Rosalind Thomas; sociologists Ruth Finnegan and Margaret Orbell; anthropologist Steven Feld; and NT scholars Werner Kelber, Joanna Dewey, and Thomas Boomershine.

32. Foster, "Memory, Orality."

33. Eve, "Orality is No Dead-End."

34. Eve, "Orality is No Dead-End," 14.

written narrative could be re-oralized and transmitted orally alongside or independently of the written text.

We open our discussion of orality with the contribution made by Ong, a professor of English literature with a wide interest in cultural and religious development. He examined the profound impact that writing has upon the way human beings think. However, his most significant contribution in this field arguably lies in identifying what he calls the "psychodynamics of orality,"[35] the characteristics which he claims define an oral culture.[36] Ong cast the net widely by considering the implications of orality for pre-literate people generally, regardless of place or time. He outlined nine distinctive features of orality.[37] All nine of Ong's features have been examined by Rodríguez,[38] who maintains that any or all of these may be found in literate communication as well. He comments: "written language can be just as additive, aggregative and traditionalist as oral language."[39] This is something to be borne in mind when we come to examine the case for Matthew using oral sources for the dream narratives.

As orality covers a wide area of study, it would be helpful for us to distinguish the elements that are of greatest relevance for this study. Ruth Finnegan highlights four: oral communication, oral composition, oral transmission and oral performance.[40] The middle two are particularly important for us, especially transmission. However, to understand properly the nature of oral transmission, we need first to explore oral composition.

---

35. Ong, *Orality and Literacy*, 31.

36. This kind of distinction has been criticized. See, e.g., Finnegan, *Oral Poetry*.

37. (i) Expression is additive rather than subordinative. (ii) It is aggregative rather than analytic. This characteristic is closely tied to reliance on formulae to implement memory. (iii) It tends to be redundant or "copious." (iv) It has a tendency to be conservative or traditionalist. By contrast, the text frees the mind of memory work and enables it to turn to fresh speculation. (v) Thought is conceptualized and then expressed with relatively close reference to the human life world. Oral cultures lack the analytic categories which depend on writing. (vi) Expression is agonistically toned. Proverbs and riddles are not only used to store knowledge but also to challenge hearers to combat, to find something more apposite or contradictory. (vii) It is empathetic and participatory rather than objectively distanced. Where writing separates the knower from the known and allows for objectivity, oral learning involves close identification with the known. (viii) It is homeostatic. Oral societies live in a present which keeps itself in equilibrium by ridding itself of memories which no longer have relevance to that present. (ix) It is situational rather than abstract. See Ong, *Orality and Literacy*, 36–56

38. Rodríguez, *Oral Tradition*, 58–60.

39. Rodríguez, *Oral Tradition*, 69.

40. See Finnegan, *Oral Poetry*, 16–24.

## Oral Composition

Matthew does not tell us how he or his sources composed their material. We, therefore, have to look elsewhere and see if we can find parallels which may help. Sometimes a writer does tell us how he went about his composition.[41] In other cases we can look at what happens in oral or semi-literate societies today and then work back by analogy. In studies of orality during the twentieth century three types of composition emerged. These are composition in performance, "premeditated" composition stored in the memory and "premeditated" composition which is written down but performed orally.[42] As we shall see later, there is variation not only according to society, but also according to genre.[43] For many years "composition in performance" dominated the field, particularly through the work of Milman Parry and Albert Lord.[44] This seems less relevant to Matthew or any source he may have had for the dream narratives than "premeditated" composition, whether stored in the memory or written down. However, this topic is worth pursuing because of the emphasis Parry placed on the use of formulae, for we do find formulaic expressions in Matthew's dream narratives. It also has something worthwhile to say about change and stability in the transmission of a story.

Parry studied the Homeric poems, noting the formulaic epithets in which they abound.[45] Athena is frequently described as θεά, γλαυκῶπις Ἀθήνη, "the goddess, bright-eyed Athena."[46] However, there are other recurring phrases such as τὸν δ' ἠμείβετ' ἔπειτα, "then so-and-so answered him." This particular example is coupled with the description of Athena already given[47] and with twenty-eight other characters. Parry set this study of Homeric formulaic expressions alongside analysis of South Slavic Heroic Song.[48] What emerged is that the formulaic expressions are part of a highly developed technique for making hexameters. When the South Slavic poet is composing or recomposing orally, he has little or no time to choose his

---

41. E.g., Pliny, *Epistolae* 9.36.2.

42. It may seem strange to speak of composition as being *premeditated*, but this is the word used in the literature. In particular it is used by Teffeteller, "Orality," 67–86.

43. The variation of genre which will be observed is in different types of song among the Kaluli people of Papua New Guinea.

44. Parry, *Making of Homeric Verse*; Lord, *Singer of Tales*.

45. Parry, *Making of Homeric Verse*, 376–90.

46. E.g., Homer, *Iliad* 1.206.

47. Homer, *Odyssey* 1.44.

48. Matija Murko had seen the similarity between Yugoslavian epic and Homer before Parry. As far back as 1929 he had published *La Poésie populaire épique en Yugoslavie au debut de XXe siècle*.

descriptions; instead he falls back on standard expressions which he knows will fit his meter. As he tells his tale, he is not singing or reciting it word for word from memory; he is making it up afresh as he goes along. So he has to rely upon conventional formulaic expressions in order to maintain the meter. The assumption Parry made was that the Homeric bard(s) composed in the same way, although clearly at some stage the epic must have been written down, for what we now have is textual.

Parry died unexpectedly before his work was complete, but his research was carried forward by Lord, who was one of his students. When Lord analyzed the themes of the South Slavic poetry or singing, he found that there was great fluidity in each performance with no fixed set of words.[49] This makes it difficult to think in terms of "an original" with which other performances may be compared. Indeed Lord suggests that when we know the nature of oral composition we should abandon any attempt to find the original of any traditional song.[50] It is only when we have a written text that it comes close to being fixed.[51] Nevertheless, the oral story can remain essentially the same despite its many forms and the many changes. Typical changes are additions of details and description, shifting of themes from one place to another, variation in the order of appearance of the *dramatis personae*, changes in action. Memory studies have also indicated that details of names, places and time may be forgotten or changed when a person recalls an incident. This led Robert McIver to suggest that memory functions at a good *gist* level of an event.[52]

Although Parry and Lord made a notable contribution to the study of oral literature,[53] oral composition and transmission are more complicated than their findings would suggest. Lord saw the oral and the written as conflicting media since the singer could not be "both an oral and a written poet at any given time."[54] This distinction is too sharp and he later modified it himself. Rosalind Thomas, a classical scholar, draws attention to a point made by Jensen and Kirk, that there are striking examples in the Yugoslavian material of very close, if not verbatim, repetition of a song even after a period of several years.[55] Moreover, the parallels between Yugoslav and

---

49. Lord, *Singer of Tales*, 68–98.

50. Lord was not aware of "premeditated" composition.

51. Even then there can be changes made by copyists. It is only truly fixed when it is printed.

52. McIver refers to the evidence gathered after the foiled robbery in Burnaby which showed the average was about 80 percent accuracy (McIver, *Memory, Jesus*, 12–13).

53. It is assumed here that the expression "oral literature" makes sense. Ong discusses it at some length in Ong, *Orality and Literacy*, 10–15.

54. Lord, *Singer of Tales*, 129.

55. Thomas, *Literacy and Orality*, 38.

Homeric epics merely provide an analogy and do not give us proof. The Parry-Lord theory cannot cover the composition of all oral literature. Indeed some would argue that it does not account sufficiently for the Homeric texts,[56] as it was based exclusively on a single sub-genre of epic, the Moslem epic. We cannot therefore expect it to be applied successfully to every form in every tradition. The fact is that oral traditions do not all work in exactly the same way in every society and time period.

We have already noted that "composition in performance" is by no means always the norm. When we turn to other cultures, we find some where there is "premeditated" creation of material, either in the poet's head or in writing, which is then delivered orally. Finnegan, a social anthropologist, gives the example of Somali poetry where the poets rarely perform their work until they have finished composing in private.[57] They may spend many hours, and even days, composing before they perform. Another case to which Finnegan refers is that of Medieval Gaelic court poets who composed their poems orally in a darkened room.[58] The poem was then recited to the chief by a bard who memorized it and recited it by heart.[59]

It can also vary within a culture, according to genre. Steven Feld, an anthropologist and ethnomusicologist, carried out research among the Kaluli people who number about 1,200 and live in the tropical rain forest of the Great Papuan Plateau in the Southern Highlands province of Papua New Guinea.[60] In particular he looked at the *sa-yalab*, laments uttered to commemorate individuals who had recently died. He found evidence of features from the oral-formulaic theory associated with Parry and Lord. He went on to compare the *sa-yalab* with five other kinds of Kaluli songs. He found some song genres were the opposite of *sa-yalab*. The texts can be fixed in advance, divorced from performance, worked up and memorized. Other genres had some features and lacked others. There is clearly variation within a single culture and it occurs according to genre.

As far as Matthew's dream narratives are concerned, they were either composed by him or possibly transmitted to him through a source. If he did use a source, we have no way of knowing whether it came into his hands in written form. Either way it is still likely to have gone through a period of oral transmission before it reached him. When the narratives were first

56. An example would be Thomas, *Literacy and Orality*, 40–42, who also cites David Shire.

57. Finnegan, *Oral Poetry*, 74.

58. Finnegan, *Oral Poetry*, 83.

59. We saw above how Quintilian valued writing in the preparation of a speech intended ultimately for oral delivery (Quintilian, *Institutio* 10.3.3–6). In book 11 of *Institutio* he deals with the cultivation of artificial memory for the delivery of a speech already written.

60. Feld, "Wept Thoughts," 85–108.

communicated within the Christian community, it seems unlikely that they were delivered completely extemporaneously and more likely that they were thought through in advance. In other words, "premeditated" composition seems to have occurred. Later we shall explore more fully whether Matthew had any sources transmitted to him orally.

## Oral Transmission

If a poem or song is composed orally at the point of performance, its words may "vanish at the moment of their utterance," to borrow an expression from Kelber,[61] for a performance is of a transitory nature. The fact is that we now have the Homeric epics, *The Odyssey* and *The Iliad*, in the form of printed texts. At some stage someone must have written down these compositions. For a poet or his fellow bards to remember a composition, they are likely to use the same formulaic expressions and other similar devices which the poet used in composing it. Lord made the point that a poet does not memorize formulae, but absorbs them gradually in a similar manner to child learning language.[62]

The same would apply to premeditated oral compositions. Annette Teffeteller, a classical scholar, has shown that poetry of the Mesopotamian tradition is also in some sense formulaic.[63] She rejects formula as defined by Parry,[64] but sees repetition and parallelism as playing a similar role in Sumerian and Akkadian poetry.[65] They are characteristic of such poetry and "provide the constitutive structure" of it. We find an example of repetition in the story of Gilgamesh, Enkdu and the Nether World 1–3:

> In those days, in those distant days,
>
> In those nights, in those far-off nights,
>
> In those years, in those distant years.[66]

---

61. Kelber, *Oral and the Written Gospel*, 1.
62. Lord, *Singer of Tales*, 36.
63. Teffeteller, "Orality," 67–86.
64. "A group of words which is regularly employed under the same metrical conditions to express a given essential idea" (Parry, *Making of Homeric Verse*, 272).
65. Teffeteller, "Orality," 68.
66. Teffeteller points out that this is the same opening as the Old Sumerian narrative poem *Ashan and her Seven Sons* with some embellishment (Teffeteller, "Orality," 67). It had:

> In those days, now it was in those days,
> In those nights, now it was in those nights,
> In those years, now it was in those years . . .

There is also evidence of parallelism with incremental progression as seen in the Akkadian Atrahasis I 70–73:

> It was the mid watch of the night,
>
> the house was surrounded, the god did not know;
>
> it was the mid watch of the night,
>
> Ekur was surrounded, Ellil did not know;

Teffeteller maintains that there is evidence to suggest that Mesopotamian poems were not improvised, but "the result of *premeditated* oral composition, that they were transmitted in a relatively fixed form, that transmission was oral even when a written record of the poem was also kept."[67] The means by which such transmission was achieved was through repetition and parallelism.

What emerges from this discussion is that there were devices which a poet could use to assist the process of oral transmission. These devices functioned by helping him and then his audience remember his material. Parry and Lord have highlighted the use of formulaic expressions, while Teffeteller has drawn attention to repetition and parallelism. It is such devices that we shall be looking for in Matthew's dream narratives. Later we shall extend that search to the dream narratives of other literature in our bid to compare Matthew's usage with that of Greco-Roman and Jewish writers.

## Alternative Transmission

We have seen how Lord recognized that there was great fluidity in each performance, with changes occurring in descriptions and details of names, places and times.[68] The alternative of precise transmission has been claimed for the Vedic literature of India. It is suggested that the *Rgveda* which is an extremely long text[69] was passed down orally through exact transmission for millennia.[70] Naturally this has been disputed. It has been pointed out that we have no external written evidence about the exact form and content of the *Rgveda* in 1000 BCE or 500 BCE.[71] We do not know the exact nature of oral transmission in Roman Palestine. By analogy either or both of the methods just described might have applied.

67. Teffeteller, "Orality," 69.
68. Lord, *Singer of Tales*, 68–98.
69. Around 40,000 lines.
70. The date of composition is reckoned to be between 1500 BCE and 100 BCE.
71. For this and other concerns, see Finnegan, *Oral Poetry*, 151–52.

It is, therefore, not surprising to find that the two theories of transmission, fluid and verbatim, have been reflected in NT study. Kelber reflects the Parry-Lord theory, noting the transitory nature of spoken words which "vanish at the moment of their utterance"[72] and arguing that an oral tradition may be subject to a variety of potential changes, such as expansion, abbreviation or simplification.[73] The alternative view was expressed by Birger Gerhardsson.[74] He suggested that Jesus required his disciples to memorize his teaching[75]; they in turn would have passed it on accurately with little forgetfulness or pious imagination. Regrettably, we have no evidence of how Jesus actually taught. In any case, narrative is different from teaching. For the former we may draw a rough guide from oral societies today where fluid transmission is more common. This may suggest that Kelber may not be too far off the mark.

## The Use of Oral Sources

Most examples of composition which we have so far considered involve poetry, whether it be ancient Homeric, Sumerian or Akkadian or modern from Yugoslavia, Somalia or Papua New Guinea. It may be pointed out that Matthew's text is different because it is prose. However, as far as composition is concerned, the distinction between poetry and prose need not be important. Until the mid-fifth-century BCE poetry had dominated discourse for centuries, and had done so in a variety of genres: "narrative and didactic epic, personal and choral lyric, hymns, drinking songs, oracles, and epinician odes in praise of victorious athletes."[76] The techniques which we have been considering were carried forward from poetry into prose. According to George Kennedy, the earliest oratory must have had many of the characteristics evident in oral poetry.[77] The point may also be made that although we describe Matthew's text as prose, much of it is actually quite poetic, especially if we extend the meaning of 'poetry' beyond formal verse to cover any kind of consciously-crafted verbal art which might be used orally.[78]

72. Kelber, *Oral and the Written Gospel*, 1.
73. Kelber, *Oral and the Written Gospel*, 29.
74. Gerhardsson, *Memory and Manuscript*.
75. Gerhardsson likened this to the way in which rabbis of the Tannaic and Amoraic periods taught.
76. Marincola, "Herodotus," 13.
77. Kennedy, *Art of Persuasion in Greece*, 5.
78. See Green, *Matthew*, which argues that Matthew's version of the Beatitudes exhibits a number of the characteristics of Hebrew poetry. Green goes on to show

A more serious charge would be that most of the examples we have considered belong to the realm of carefully crafted and polished literature,[79] whereas any sources which Matthew may have used belong more to storytelling within the community. We find parallels to this in the writing of Herodotus.

Herodotus is quite explicit in expressing how he sees his task and that is to report what others say: "As for myself, my task in the whole history (λόγος) is to write down what everybody says, as I hear it (ἀκοῇ)."[80] He is equally explicit about his use of sources: "This is what I heard (ἤκουον) from the priests in Thebes"[81]; and "those of the barbarians who returned reported, as I am informed (ὡς ἐγὼ πυνθάνομαι)."[82] Often such references take the form of statements like "the Spartans/Athenians/Egyptians say (φασί)." It is rare for other ancient historians to deal with the question of how they gathered information, and when they do, they typically confine it to preliminary statements at the beginning of their works.[83] It is therefore extremely helpful to hear what Herodotus has to say.

However, we need to treat such statements with care. They should not be regarded as source references comparable to what we find in modern historical works which lend support and authority to what is said in the main text.[84] Indeed Herodotus sometimes uses such statements to distance himself from a story or a particular piece of information: "As for myself, I am bound to tell what is told, but I am absolutely not bound to believe it, and let it be understood that this statement applies to every story I report."[85] Despite this qualification, the stories which Herodotus gathers play an important part in his writing.

Although Herodotus sometimes uses his personal eyewitness testimony (ὄψις), and at times refers to his own reasoning (γνώμη), his most important ingredient is oral information (ἀκοή).[86] It is possible that as much as 80 percent of his material came from some kind of orally formulated

---

that a series of texts found at significant points in the First Gospel disclose similar characteristics.

79. A possible exception would be some of the poetry from Papua New Guinea.
80. Herodotus, *Histories* 2.123.1.
81. Herodotus, *Histories* 2.55.1.
82. Herodotus, *Histories* 8.38.
83. Luraghi, "Meta-*historie*," 76. Examples include Thucydides, *History* 1.22; Luke 1:1–4.
84. Luraghi, "Meta-*historie*," 83.
85. Herodotus, *Histories* 7.152.3.
86. Luraghi, "Meta-*historie*," 77.

sources.⁸⁷ Although ἀκοή carries the suggestion of *hearing*, how can we be sure that Herodotus is referring to oral tradition? He does make reference to a written source when he attributes the story of the Pelasgians to Hecataeus.⁸⁸ Some ἀκοή statements are general references to collective informants, while others are quite specific ones implying personal contact with a particular group of people.⁸⁹ Even when Herodotus used written sources, it is possible that he had to rely on *hearsay*, especially when they were written in a language with which he was unfamiliar.⁹⁰ So there are inconsistencies and difficulties about the way Herodotus cites his sources. There is an ongoing scholarly debate among experts on Herodotus concerning the true extent of his travels.⁹¹ We may even be skeptical about some of his claims, especially his early claim to have access to the accounts of Persian chroniclers (λόγιοι) which have their own variations of Greek legends.⁹²

Despite all the problems, Alan Griffiths is confident that most of Herodotus's source-material *was* orally transmitted.⁹³ Griffiths's reason is not the historian's own statements about his sources, nor his use of techniques of transmission, such as formulaic expressions, repetition and parallelism, but "the nature of the stories themselves, which bear all the tell-tale signs of narratives which have passed from mouth to ear to mouth again." Many of the typical features of the early modern European folktale can be paralleled in the story-motifs and the organic structures of Herodotean pericopes. An objection may be raised against Griffiths's position that there is no good reason why writers could not use folklore motifs directly without having to rely on oral sources. This is something which we shall need to bear in mind when we consider the case for Matthew having used oral sources.

We recall how Herodotus distanced himself from some of the stories which he related. We may therefore ask why he continued to report such stories when he did not believe them. Nino Luraghi suggests that these stories reflect the interests of those who utter them.⁹⁴ Local people are the most competent informers about themselves and their land. Luraghi illustrates his point by referring to Herodotus's account of the causes for the madness

---

87. Byrskog, *Story as History*, 95.
88. Herodotus, *Histories* 6.137.1–2.
89. Herodotus, *Histories* 2.91.3–5; 4.14.
90. Byrskog, *Story as History*, 121.
91. Luraghi, "Meta-*historie*," 83.
92. Herodotus, *Histories* 1.1.1. Griffiths, "Stories and Storytelling," 136–37.
93. Griffiths, "Stories and Storytelling," 137.
94. Luraghi, "Meta-*historie*," 84.

and untimely death of King Cleomenes of Sparta.⁹⁵ Most Greeks offered supernatural explanations, whereas the Spartans connected their king's fate to alcoholism brought on by drinking wine, not watered but neat: a break from Spartan temperance.⁹⁶ Luraghi describes this as "an explanation that reinforced the normative value of the Spartan behavioral code."⁹⁷

It may be that Matthew's dream narratives reflect the interests and beliefs of the individual or group who supplied him with those narratives. They reveal Jewish interests, with Jesus portrayed as the new Moses, Emmanuel and more generally the fulfillment of OT scriptures.⁹⁸ They portray God as active in history, controlling human affairs. The vital question will be whether Matthew's memory patterns reflect similar Jewish influence. To find that out, we shall compare Matthew's usage with that of OT, other Jewish and Greco-Roman writers. What will emerge from such comparison is that Matthew does show some affinity to OT.

An objection may be raised against the use of Herodotus since he lived almost five centuries before Matthew. We therefore look at someone whose general approach was similar to that of Herodotus, but who lived closer to Matthew's time. Such a person is Pausanias who flourished around 160 CE.⁹⁹ He was a Greek traveler and geographer who produced his famous *Description of Greece*.¹⁰⁰ Pausanias did use oral sources and is quite explicit about his use of oral tradition: λέγω δὲ οὐκ ἐς συγγραφὴν πρότερον ἥκοντα, πιστὰ δὲ ἄλλως Ἀθηναίων τοῖς πολλοῖς, "what I am about to say has never been written down before, but it is generally believed by the Athenian people."¹⁰¹ Pausanias travelled around Greece for at least twenty years.¹⁰² He was gathering local information, some of which would be found in libraries, but it is highly likely that there would be a rich oral tradition which he would utilize by engaging in conversations with locals.

Pausanias often introduces a piece of information with phrases such as "they say" (λέγουσιν or φασίν or ὁ ἐκείνων—normally the ethnic is used here—λόγος). He uses terms for local people: οἱ ἐπιχώριοι,¹⁰³ ὁ τῶν ἐπιχωρίων

---

95. Herodotus, Histories 6.75.3.

96. Herodotus, *Histories* 6.84.

97. Luraghi, "Meta-historie," 84.

98. We take the view that the fulfillment quotations stem from Matthew rather than any source, but the details in a source may have inspired his choice of quotation.

99. OCCL 223.

100. Ἑλλάδος περιήγησις (also known in Latin as, "*Graecae descriptio*").

101. Pausanias, *Hellados Periegesis* 1.23.2.

102. Pretzler, "Pausanias and Oral Tradition," 239.

103. E.g., Pausanias, *Hellados Periegesis* 7.25–27; 8.28.1

ἐξηγητής[104]; people who could be found close to a site: οἱ προσοικοῦντες,[105] οἱ περὶ τὸ ἱερόν.[106] However, such phrases do not always guarantee that an author is using oral sources, for ancient authors regularly used λέγουσιν as a typical phrase to introduce quotations from books.[107] How then can we distinguish oral sources from literary ones? Some accounts in the *Periegesis* resemble typical quotations from literary sources. Maria Pretzler gives as an example the Arcadian genealogy at the beginning of book 8.[108] However, she goes on to suggest that we may detect traces of oral tradition in stories from the past which have been adapted to serve present local needs. She says, "Traces of (sometimes recent) adaptation that serves the formation and preservation of community identity are a good indication of contemporary oral tradition."[109] She may not always be right, as it is possible for local tradition already to have been incorporated into a literary source prior to the investigations of Pausanias. Nevertheless, the point stands that Pausanias did at times use oral sources, even if we cannot always identify them.

It follows therefore that Pausanias approached his research in a manner that was not significantly different from that of Herodotus. This should not surprise us, given his admiration for Herodotus.[110] What matters from our perspective is that this was happening in a period much closer to Matthew than that of Herodotus. It suggests that writers in a semi-literate society, whatever the century, could, if they wished, use oral sources as well as written. It was perhaps even necessary to use oral sources if a writer was working close to the time when events happened. Pretzler's identification of oral tradition with the preservation of community identity also reinforces Luraghi's suggestion that oral stories reflect the interests of those who narrate them.

When an ancient writer discovered information, in an oral or written source, it was possible for him to record it in notes. The notebooks and biros of antiquity were waxed wooden tablets, known as πίναξ or *pugillares*,[111]

---

104. E.g., Pausanias, *Hellados Periegesis* 1.13.8; 9.3.3

105. Pausanias, *Hellados Periegesis* 5.6.6.

106. Pausanias, *Hellados Periegesis* 8.37.5.

107. See Pretzler, "Pausanias and Oral Tradition," 245n70, where she cites Meyer, *Pausanias*, 37–38.

108. Pretzler, "Pausanias and Oral Tradition," 246. She does think that at least a part of the genealogy is based on original research, as Pausanias claims.

109. Pretzler, "Pausanias and Oral Tradition," 246.

110. Pretzler, "Pausanias and Oral Tradition," 246.

111. Larger tablets for formal records were known as *codex* or *tabula*. There were also a lot of notebooks made of parchment or papyrus. For example, Pliny the elder was said to have about 200 notebooks of material.

and a metal-tipped *stilus* for scratching them. The tablets were usually made of wood, sometimes ivory, and covered with wax, with two or three bound together, occasionally more up to ten.[112] The process of note-taking is mentioned by at least two of Matthew's contemporaries, Josephus and Pliny.[113] The former tells us that throughout the siege of Jerusalem he made careful notes of proceedings in the Roman camp and of events within the city which he learned about from deserters.[114]

We may draw the thought of this section together and apply it to Matthew. He may have used at least one source for the dream narratives which was orally transmitted. He may have incorporated this originally oral source into his gospel in much the same way as Herodotus and Pausanias, although Matthew does not refer to his use of sources as the other two do. We recognize that there are other ways of viewing the material in the early chapters of Matthew. The Moses-Israel typology of the dreams narratives is to be found right across the first four chapters of the gospel and indeed beyond. It is possible to regard all this as Matthean composition. Alternatively, we may have to see more of the first four chapters as belonging to the same source as the dream narratives and we may then wonder what the function of that source would have been. If Matthew did use a source, we have no way of knowing whether it reached him in oral or written form. If it was still oral, he may have committed it to memory using the very techniques recently referred to. Alternatively, he may have recorded it in a notebook, as Josephus and Pliny did, prior to recording it in the form in which we now have it in the gospel.

## The Question of Oral Sources in Matthew

We shall now explore the issue of whether there is evidence to suggest that Matthew used oral sources for his dream narratives. This is a matter which has long occupied the attention of scholars. In the mid-twentieth century Wilfred Knox attempted to unravel Matthew's sources,[115] but there were others, such as Morton Enslin, who put the case for the narratives being

---

112. Lee and Scott, *Sound Mapping*, 17.

113. "*Liber legebatur, adnotabat excerpebatque*" (Pliny, *Epistolae* 3.5.10); "*Ad latus notarius cum libro et pugillaribus*" (Pliny, *Epistolae* 3.5.15); "*Stilus et pugillares*" (Pliny, *Epistolae* 1.6.1); cf. Pliny, *Epistolae* 9.36.6.

114. Josephus, *Contra Apionem* 1.49.

115. See volume 2 of Knox, *Sources of the Synoptic Gospels*; Davis, "Tradition and Redaction," 420–21.

Matthew's own composition.[116] Even an eminent scholar like Brown postulates pre-Matthean sources for the dreams.[117] His argument is complex, but essentially he believes that for 1:20–24 there has been a conflation of an angelic dream tradition with an annunciation tradition, perhaps joined before Matthew used them.[118] What he says is plausible enough. The dream narrative of 1:20–25 is certainly more complex than those of 2:13–14 and 2:19–21. It is possible that there once existed a simpler angelic dream narrative more in line with those of chapter 2. It is then not difficult to imagine a narrative with an annunciation of the Messiah's birth, patterned on OT annunciations of birth. If so, Brown may be right that at some point Matthew or his source combined them. The problem with this kind of argument is its speculative nature. W. D. Davies and Dale Allison see the material evolving, with three stages of development.[119] The first painted the picture of Jesus's nativity with Mosaic color; the second represents the expansion of the Mosaic narrative in the interests of Davidic Christology; and the third marks the transition from the oral to the written sphere—this is the redactional stage. Their fundamental position is that Matt 1:18—2:23 reproduces a pre-Matthean narrative which was probably oral. The difficulty for all who want to consider sources and how they might have been redacted is that we have no extant evidence of such sources. It follows that any discussion about them is highly conjectural. We therefore cannot say with any degree of certainty what form any pre-Matthean sources may have taken.

We need to restrict ourselves to the search for evidence of oral transmission in the narratives. We have already encountered formulaic expressions, repetition and parallelism used in oral transmission. We shall consider these as well as the use of key words as a mnemonic device. Then we shall turn our attention to the use of story-motifs, as suggested by Griffiths. Finally, we shall examine the vocabulary and style of our narrative. Our concern will be to see whether any or all of these can provide us with a case for believing Matthew used oral sources.

---

116. Enslin, "Christian Stories of the Nativity," 317–38.

117. Brown, *Birth of the Messiah*, 154–63.

118. Concerning an angelic dream tradition, see Brown, *Birth of the Messiah*, 109–110; concerning the annunciation of birth, 155–59; and for Brown's argument, see esp. 154–55, 160–62.

119. Davies and Allison, *Matthew*, 1:190–95.

## Formulaic Expressions

We have already noted the emphasis which Parry placed upon formulae. This was picked up by Joanna Dewey in an article concerning the oral nature of Mark's Gospel.[120] There she suggests that Matthew uses some of the techniques of oral composition and the example which she gives is the use of formulaic expressions. She shows how each time Matthew cites an OT quotation he introduces it with the formula πληρωθῇ τὸ ῥηθὲν preceded by ἵνα (Matt 1:22; 2:15; 4:14; 12:17; 21:4) or ὅπως (2:23; 8:17; 13:35) or τότε with the indicative ἐπληρώθη (2:17; 27:9). However, such expressions can also be found in non-oral poetry and consequently do not always signify oral composition. In the *Aeneid*, Virgil regularly uses the expression *pius Aeneas* and he is certainly not an oral poet.[121] Formulaic expressions are also to be found in Anglo-Saxon, Old French and Old German poetry some of which were composed by literate poets.[122] Even within the context of Matthew's infancy narrative we can question whether the formulae associated with the fulfillment of OT prophecies point to oral origins. Elsewhere in the First Gospel we find Matthew using such expressions along with OT quotations which he may have added to the material himself. We therefore cannot argue that the use of these formulaic expressions points to oral composition of the infancy narratives. The firmest conclusion which we can draw is that such usage is consistent with oral composition or transmission, but it certainly does not prove it.

## Repetition

We saw above how Teffeteller drew attention to the use of repetition in Mesopotamian poetry. One of the most curious examples of repetition in Matthew occurs at 2:13. We have just been told at 2:12 that the Magi δι' ἄλλης ὁδοῦ ἀνεχώρησαν εἰς τὴν χώραν αὐτῶν, "departed to their own country by another route." Then at 2:13 the same information and much the same vocabulary is repeated, albeit now in the form of a genitive construction: Ἀναχωρησάντων δὲ αὐτῶν. To a twenty-first-century reader this seems quite unnecessary. The vital question is how an ancient reader would have viewed

---

120. Dewey, "Oral Methods of Structuring Narrative," 32–44.

121. e.g., Virgil, *Aeneid* 1.220. According to Moseley, Virgil applies the epithet *pius* to Aeneas fifteen times in the narrative, has the other characters refer to him as *pius*, *pietate insignis*, or some equivalent expression eight times, and finally has Aeneas speak of himself as *pius* twice (Moseley, "Pius Aeneas," 387).

122. Thomas, *Literacy and Orality in Ancient Greece*, 42.

it. From our perspective the narrative would have read better if Matthew had simply said: Τότε, "Then." Matthew does use this adverb at 2:7 and 2:16. Why not here? It may be argued that the expression is necessary to achieve an *inclusio* with ἀνεχώρησεν at 2:22. However, this would still be achieved with the ἀνεχώρησαν of 2:12 introducing it. The opening of 2:13 does sound like unnecessary repetition. It cannot be denied that such repetition may occur in a written text. But since it appears here to be almost clumsy, it seems on balance to be more like what we would expect in oral communication. Other explanations are possible: this clumsiness may simply be the sign of an inconsistent author or one who wished to create emphasis or to provide the "dream circumstances" which the standard dream structure required. We cannot claim that these examples of repetition prove the oral transmission of these texts, but only that they lend it a little support.

## Parallelism

We now turn our attention to parallelism, also highlighted by Teffeteller.[123] She points out that though Sumerian and Akkadian poetry is oral in origin and formulaic in nature,[124] it does not rely on the use of formula as defined by Parry, but uses instead the devices of repetition and parallelism. This can be seen in the Akkadian *Atrahasis* I 70–73, quoted above.[125] There is certainly extensive use of parallelism in Matthew. We take the example used at 1:20–21:

1:20 μὴ φοβηθῇς παραλαβεῖν Μαρίαν τὴν γυναῖκά σου

1:21 καὶ καλέσεις τὸ ὄνομα αὐτοῦ Ἰησοῦν

1:20 τὸ γὰρ ἐν αὐτῇ γεννηθὲν ἐκ πνεύματός ἐστιν ἁγίου

1:21 αὐτὸς γὰρ σώσει τὸν λαὸν αὐτοῦ ἀπὸ τῶν ἁμαρτιῶν αὐτῶν.

Here we have two commands and two reasons for them. It is true that parallelism is widely used in oral communication. But as Finnegan says, "whether this makes it a distinctive sign of oral performance or oral

---

123. Teffeteller, "Orality," 67–86.

124. Teffeteller is drawing attention to devices used in poetry, as did Parry and Lord, while Matthew is prose. This does not constitute a problem as prose developed out of poetry and uses many of the same devices.

125. It was the mid watch of the night:
the house was surrounded, the god did not know;
it was the mid watch of the night,
Ekur was surrounded, Ellil did not know.

composition is more doubtful. . . . There are, after all, clear literary effects in parallelism which apply to written as well as oral verse."¹²⁶ There is a certain elegance about it. Again we are forced to acknowledge that we have a usage which is consistent with oral transmission, but by itself does not prove it.

## Other Devices

Ulrich Luz has described ἄγγελος κυρίου as a key phrase, treating it as a literary device, which points to God's guidance.¹²⁷ But he also commented that we are "reminded of oral tradition which uses key-word connecting links as a mnemonic device."¹²⁸ Then he continues, "Key words have become in Matthew a literary means, for they are meant to clarify the theme of a section." To put it another way, what we would count as key words can be mnemonic or literary devices and it can be difficult to distinguish the two. As Thomas puts it, "There are no neat and generally applicable criteria for distinguishing oral tradition."¹²⁹ Despite the work of Parry and Lord, Homeric scholars are still divided over the issue of how the *Iliad* and the *Odyssey* were composed, whether orally or written. Janice Anderson also notes the difficulty caused by the overlap of oral and written: "Many of the features used to identify oral narratives such as repeated phrases and episodes; 'flat,' stereotyped characters; and significant foreshadowing are also characteristics of handwritten narratives in the ancient Mediterranean world. . . . What orally composed and handwritten Greek narratives probably had in common in the first century was aural reception."¹³⁰ We therefore need to try a different approach.

## Use of Story-Motifs

Next we recall a point made above when we were thinking about the use Herodotus makes of oral sources. Griffiths expressed confidence that most of Herodotus's source-material was orally transmitted.¹³¹ His reason was "the nature of the stories themselves, which bear all the tell-tale signs of narratives which have passed from mouth to ear to mouth again"; they have the same typical features as early modern European folktale. Matthew's second chapter

126. Finnegan, *Oral Poetry*, 130.
127. Luz, *Matthew 1–7*, 39.
128. Luz, *Matthew 1–7*, 39.
129. Thomas, *Oral Tradition and Written Record*, 6.
130. Anderson, *Matthew's Narrative Web*, 221.
131. Griffiths, "Stories and Storytelling," 137.

narrates how Jesus was threatened with persecution and death and escaped through the intervention of the angel to Joseph. There are many ancient legends of the persecuted and rescued royal child. Indeed Luz in his commentary presents a table which lists with references the stories associated with Moses, Abraham, Revelation 12, Cypselus, Mithridates, Romulus/Remus, Augustus, Nero, Gilgamesh, Saragon I, Cyrus and the Zarathustra legend.[132] There are also dream stories associated with the birth of important individuals. One such story related how Agariste, the mother of Pericles, dreamt that a god came to her, telling how she would give birth to a lion.[133]

It is not being suggested that any of these legends are the source material for Matthew's narratives. Instead the parallels are being highlighted to suggest that his accounts have story-motifs in common with folklore. Just as Griffiths argued that such motifs in Herodotus pointed to oral transmission of his source-material, so we need to consider whether such features in Matthew's dream narratives point to their oral transmission.

However, when we were dealing with Herodotus, we also noted the objection that authors could draw directly on folklore motifs without having to rely on oral sources. Such motifs in the Matthean text, therefore, cannot prove that Matthew was using oral sources. They do, however, raise the question of where Matthew obtained them. Were these story-motifs created by Matthew himself or did he find them somewhere? We note that they support his Moses typology which in turn serves his Christology. It is possible that he was drawing on legends about Moses. This seems highly likely given the legends concerning the dream of Amram, Moses's father, in Josephus[134] and the dream of Miriam, Moses's sister, in Pseudo-Philo.[135] It is possible that Matthew encountered such legends in oral form, but given the difficulty noted above, we cannot be certain about this.

132. Luz, *Matthew 1–7*, 76–77, gives the following references. For Moses: Josephus *Ant.* 2; Ps.-Philo, *Liber Antiquitatum Biblicarum*; Tg. Exod.; Exod. Rab.; Wünsche, *Lehrallen* 1.61–80; Ginzberg, *Legends* 2.245–69. For Abraham: Str-B 1.77–78; Wünsche, *Lehrallen* 1.61–80; Ginzberg, *Legends* 1.186–89. For Cypselus: Herodotus 5.92; Binder, *Aussetzung*, 150–51. For Mithridates: Justinus, *Epitome* 1.37.2. For Romulus/Remus: Livius 1.3–6; Binder, *Aussetzung*, 78–115. For Augustus: Suetonius, *Aug.* 94.3; Dio Cassius, *Historia Romana* 45.1–2. For Nero: Suetonius, *Nero* 36. For Gilgamesh: Aelianus, *De natura animalium* 12.21. For Saragon I: Pritchard, *Ancient Near East*, 85–86. For Cyrus, Herodotus 1.107–122; Justinus, *Epitome* 1.4; Binder, *Aussetzung*, 17–28. For the Zarathustra legend: Zardusht-Nama, 4–5, 8–9; Binder, *Aussetzung*, 193–95; Saintyves, "Massacre," 257–58.

133. Plutarch, *Life of Pericles* 3.2. We may compare Herodotus, *Histories* 1.107.2, where we find recorded dreams concerning the mother of Cyrus which we shall pick up in more detail later.

134. Josephus, *Ant.* 2.210–16.

135. *Liber Antiquitatum Biblicarum* 9.10.

## Vocabulary

We move on to consider the vocabulary of the infancy narratives and whether it is significantly different from the rest of the gospel. W. C. Allen has already looked at the vocabulary and notes[136] how some words and phrases occur only or chiefly in this section: λάθρᾳ (1:19; 2:7); Ἱεροσόλυμα, fem. sing. (2:3; 3:5); παραγίνομαι (2:1: 3:1, 13); πυνθάνομαι (2:4); κατ' ὄναρ (1:20; 2:12, 13, 19, 22; and besides these only 27.19); παραλαμβάνω (8 times and besides these, 17:1; 20:17; 26:37; and elsewhere, Matt 12:45; 18:16; 24:40-41; 27:27); ἀναχωρέω (five times and elsewhere 9:24; 12:15; 14:13; 15:21; 17:5); κατοικέω (twice and elsewhere, 12:25; 23:21); and the genitive (absolute) construction as in Ἀναχωρησάντων δὲ αὐτῶν (1:20; 2:1, 13, 19; and elsewhere only at Matt 9:32; 28:11). Obviously some vocabulary is determined by the nature of the material that is being narrated. However, there is sufficient variation to suggest that Matthew may be using material which has come to him, taking over at least some of its vocabulary. This is a view supported by Gnuse, commenting that a pre-Matthean origin is quite plausible "due to the very different nature of the writing style and vocabulary in the Infancy Narratives."[137] Soares Prabhu makes a similar remark: "Its vocabulary, on closer examination, proves to be less specifically Matthean than usually supposed."[138] On the other hand, all authors use words with varying frequencies. It therefore follows that the occurrence of certain words not commonly used by a particular author does not prove that he was using a source.[139] We find ourselves in the same position as we did with formulaic expressions, parallelism and repetition. The use of different vocabulary may be due to the use of a source, but it certainly does not prove it.

## Style

We now take up the style of the material in Matthew 1-2. In particular what is being proposed is a comparison of the *inclusio* or ring composition in this section of Matthew with its use in literature which the writer composed

---

136. Allen, *Critical and Exegetical Commentary*, lxi.
137. Gnuse, "Dream Genre," 117.
138. Prabhu, *Formula Quotations*, 189.
139. For there to be strong evidence of a source, we would require the incidence of relatively uncommon words in a particular passage to be significantly higher than other passages by the same writer and not attributable to other factors such as subject matter or allusion.

himself as distinct from using oral sources.[140] The reason for examining *inclusio* is the extent of its usage. It is to be found in Homer where a case can be made for oral composition, in Herodotus where he appears to be using oral sources, but also in speeches of Greek orators which look as if they have been substantially contrived by the writer.[141]

But first we need to note the cases of *inclusio* in Matthew's dream narratives. We shall explore them in greater detail later. The first opens with Τοῦ δὲ Ἰησοῦ Χριστοῦ ἡ γένεσις (Matt 1:18) and then closes with Τοῦ δὲ Ἰησοῦ γεννηθέντος (Matt 2:1). The second opens with καὶ χρηματισθέντες κατ' ὄναρ . . . ἀνεχώρησαν εἰς (Matt 2:12). It is then reinforced with Ἀναχωρησάντων δὲ αὐτῶν (Matt 2:13), but these latter words are not actually part of it. It closes with χρηματισθεὶς δὲ κατ' ὄναρ ἀνεχώρησεν εἰς (Matt 2:22). They are both simple and fairly straightforward.

## Greek Speeches

We begin with a comparison which can be quickly set aside, that of the speeches. They are at an extreme end of the spectrum because they use a particularly complicated form of ring composition. Ian Worthington analyses Dianarchus 1 (*Against Demosthenes*)[142] and finds the following pattern of ring composition—A B C D E F E D C B A. Each part of this can then be further subdivided. Ultimately he finds that some elements of the structure subdivide into a quaternary level. Moreover, they use subject matter and theme to achieve ring composition rather than linguistic similarity. This is far more complicated than anything we find in Matthew's Gospel.

## Longus

Next we take some examples from Longus's *Daphnis and Chloe*. As a romantic novel, it offers a narrative which can then be compared to Matthew's. It is

---

140. An alternative approach might have been to use genitive absolutes or genitive constructions. Fuller notes their use in the birth narrative as a cohesive device to link paragraphs, whereas the next two chapters use nominative participles and τότε for the same purpose. She suggests that these two different cohesion styles may reflect different sources. However, it does not follow that the infancy source was orally transmitted. See Fuller, "Genitive Absolute," 164.

141. Worthington suggests that some speeches were revised for "publication" after being orally delivered and that in that process a more elaborate form of ring composition was developed because what we find is so elaborate that it is likely to have been lost on a listening audience. See Worthington, "Greek Oratory," 166.

142. Worthington, "Greek Oratory," 168–69.

also the fictive creation of its author with no use of sources and examples of *inclusio* found within it must therefore be his work. We find one example of *inclusio* in a dream narrative. All his dream narratives will be examined in the chapter on Comparison of Memory Patterns. It occurs at 2.23.1–2.24.1, opening with the phrase: ἐκ τῶν δακρύων καὶ τῆς λύπης, "out of his tears and pain," and closes with: ὑφ᾽ ἡδονῆς καὶ λύπης μεστὸς δακρύων, "full of tears from pleasure and pain." What we have here are two words in common, both times in the genitive, but used in chiasmus. The fact that this example of *inclusio* involves chiastic word order suggests that it has been contrived by the author. It contrasts with Matthew's dream accounts where the narrative flows with less effort to bring special features of style into the *inclusio*.

We shall consider two other examples of *inclusio* in Longus beyond the dream narratives.[143] In book 1 we read of how Lamo found a male child along with a little purple mantle with a golden clasp and a little sword with an ivory hilt, his tokens of identity,

> καὶ εὑρίσκει παιδίον ἄρρεν, μέγα καὶ καλὸν καὶ τῆς κατὰ τὴν ἔκθεσιν τύχης ἐν σπαργάνοις κρείττοσι: χλαμύδιόν τε γὰρ ἦν ἁλουργὲς καὶ πόρπη χρυσῆ καὶ ξιφίδιον ἐλεφαντόκωπον. Τὸ μὲν οὖν πρῶτον ἐβουλεύσατο μόνα τὰ γνωρίσματα βαστάσας ἀμελῆσαι τοῦ βρέφους.[144]

Later we read of how Dryas found a female child with her tokens of identity, a headband threaded with gold, gilded sandals, and anklets of solid gold,

> Θῆλυ ἦν τοῦτο τὸ παιδίον, καὶ παρέκειτο καὶ τούτῳ γνωρίσματα: μίτρα διάχρυσος, ὑποδήματα ἐπίχρυσα, περισκελίδες χρυσαῖ.[145]

Again we have lovely example of a ring composition with chiastic word order. It opens with the mention of the actual tokens, then the word (γνωρίσματα) for them and it closes with the word for the girl's, followed by a mention of the actual tokens. A reference to *gold* is also to be found in chiasmus on opposite sides of γνωρίσματα. Again it is more complicated than what we find in Matthew.

We find another example of *inclusio* coupled with chiasmus at 2.34.1–3.

> Αὕτη ἡ σύριγξ τὸ ὄργανον οὐκ ἦν ὄργανον ἀλλὰ παρθένος καλὴ καὶ τὴν φωνὴν μουσική . . .

---

143. Further examples may be found in Longus, *Daphnis and Chloe* 3.22–23, 29; 4.29.
144. Longus, *Daphnis and Chloe* 1.2.3–1.3.1.
145. Longus, *Daphnis and Chloe* 1.5.3.

καὶ ἡ τότε παρθένος καλὴ νῦν ἐστι σύριγξ μουσική.[146]

This time the relevant words are *fair maiden* and *syrinx* or *pipe*. However, we have something new here, viz. the use of μουσική at the end of the opening sentence and again at the end of the closing sentence, an example of *antistrophe*. This combination of effects once more makes it more complicated than Matthew's infancy narratives.

## Plutarch

Moving away from Longus, we take an example from Plutarch,[147] who does not generally display a rhetorically embellished style apart from his few declamatory pieces,[148] but does make extensive use of ring composition.[149] The section *Eumenes* 6.4–7 opens with the phrase: ἀποκρύψαι τὸν ἀντιστράτηγον, "conceal [from his soldiers] the name of the opposing general," and closes with καὶ μὴ μόνος ἐν αὑτῷ θέμενος ἀποκρύψαι, "and not to keep hidden away in his own breast alone." There is the repeated use of the verb ἀποκρύψαι. However, there is also repetition of thought without the same vocabulary being used. We have first: ἀγνοοῦντας ᾧ μαχοῦνται, "[his soldiers] not knowing with whom they were fighting," and then at the end Eumenes sticks by his resolve and does not tell his officers πρὸς ὃν ἔμελλεν ὁ ἀγὼν ἔσεσθαι, "who it was against whom their struggle was to be." In that second example we have repetition of thought without linguistic similarity and that was a trait noted in carefully worked speeches, but certainly not a feature of the infancy narratives.

## Sermon on the Mount

Next we consider examples from elsewhere in Matthew. In particular we look to the Sermon on the Mount in chapters 5–7,[150] as Matthew is gener-

---

146. Longus, *Daphnis and Chloe* 2.34.1, 3.

147. There is a wealth of material in Plutarch, *Parallel Lives*, but we restrict ourselves here to examples of *inclusio* in the dream narratives. There are two, to be found at Plutarch, *Cimon* 18.2–4; *Eumenes* 6.4–7. In the first case the text is corrupt.

148. Schmitz, "Plutarch and the Second Sophistic," 32.

149. Moles, *Plutarch*, 13.

150. It may be objected that the material in the Sermon is different from what is found in the dream narratives. Here we have an extended speech of Jesus which, it may be said, is subject to the techniques found in other speech-writing. We stick with it for the reason given, that Matthew is generally associated with organizing it in its current form.

ally credited with compiling or organizing this section of teaching, removing it from its situation in Jesus's ministry.[151] Admittedly Luke does contain material which Matthew has in the Sermon, but he has it scattered at various points in the Third Gospel. Charles Talbert adapts work by Lambrecht and presents us with two tables showing the parallels between Matthew and Luke.[152] The sections of Matthew which will concern us below are (i) 5:1; 8:1; (ii) 5:3, 10; (iii) 6:25, 31, 34; and (iv) 7:16, 20. Luke does not have the equivalent of (iv), nor the latter parts of (i) to (iii). It would appear that where Matthew is using Q, he puts his own stamp on it or at least uses it differently from Luke.

The whole sermon is framed by *inclusio*. It is introduced at 5:1 with the words: Ἰδὼν δὲ τοὺς ὄχλους ἀνέβη εἰς τὸ ὄρος, and closes at 8:1 with Καταβάντος δὲ αὐτοῦ ἀπὸ τοῦ ὄρους ἠκολούθησαν αὐτῷ ὄχλοι πολλοί. Both parts involve compounds of the verb βαίνω. Both parts also have reference to the mountain (ὄρος) and to the crowds (ὄχλοι). However, the latter is used in chiasmus, at the beginning of the sentence in 5:1 and at the close in 8:1. Talbert observes several features involved in this chiasmus and notes them in a table,[153] but we may wonder whether listeners and initial readers could be expected to pick this up. We encountered a similar style in Longus and we noted then that it is more complicated than the *inclusio* highlighted in Matthew's dream narratives.

Sections within the sermon also show evidence of *inclusio*. This is reminiscent of the Greek speeches mentioned above, although not quite as complicated. At 5:3 we have: Μακάριοι οἱ πτωχοὶ τῷ πνεύματι, ὅτι αὐτῶν ἐστιν ἡ βασιλεία τῶν οὐρανῶν. Then at 5:10 we read: μακάριοι οἱ δεδιωγμένοι ἕνεκεν δικαιοσύνης, ὅτι αὐτῶν ἐστιν ἡ βασιλεία τῶν οὐρανῶν. The *inclusio* lies in the second half of each beatitude with the wording identical in each case.[154]

---

151. For example, Mark gives Jesus's teaching on fasting in the context of a dispute over why his disciples do not fast (Mark 2:18-20) and in the episode of the discovery of the withered fig tree (Mark 11:20-25). Matthew presents it devoid of such context (Matt 6:16-18). See Dewey, "Oral Methods of Structuring Narrative," 35.

152. See Talbert, *Matthew*, 70-71, who cites Lambrecht, *Sermon on the Mount*, 36-37.

153. Talbert, *Matthew*, 96.

154. It is debatable whether this is proper *inclusio* or an example of *antistrophe*. The phrase *"for theirs is the kingdom of heaven"* does not appear at the end of the intervening beatitudes which makes it less likely to be *antistrophe*. Achtemeier, "Omne verbum sonat," 21, treats it as *inclusio*. He suggests that an audience accustomed to verbal clues would assume that the first beatitude would contain a signal of *inclusio* and would be listening for the repeated phraseology which they duly receive (Matt 5:10b). He suggests that the final beatitude (Matt 5:11-12), now in the second rather than third person, confirms that for the hearer.

There is another example of simple *inclusio* at 7:16, 20 with the phrase, ἀπὸ τῶν καρπῶν αὐτῶν ἐπιγνώσεσθε αὐτούς.[155]

A further case of *inclusio* is to be found in 6:25–34.[156] At 6:25 we have μὴ μεριμνᾶτε τῇ ψυχῇ ὑμῶν τί φάγητε [ἢ τί πίητε,][157] μηδὲ τῷ σώματι ὑμῶν τί ἐνδύσησθε. The reading at 6:31 is μὴ οὖν μεριμνήσητε λέγοντες, Τί φάγωμεν; ἤ, Τί πίωμεν; ἤ, Τί περιβαλώμεθα; Then at 6:34 there is μὴ οὖν μεριμνήσητε εἰς τὴν αὔριον, ἡ γὰρ αὔριον μεριμνήσει ἑαυτῆς. This section is complicated by the triple command *not to be anxious*. Although the wording of 6:31 closely resembles that of 6:25, the section does not appear to end until 6:34. The common link is the second person plural command of the verb μεριμνάω. However, in 6:34 it is aorist, as in 6:31, compared to the present in 6:25. That the second half of the *inclusio* occurs at 6:34 is confirmed by the repetition of the verb in the third person singular future indicative. We believe that here we have *inclusio*, but it is more complicated than in the dream narratives.

The brief analysis of the Sermon on the Mount where Matthew is believed to have had a hand in organizing it into its present form suggests an approach to *inclusio* which has much in common with the stylised writing of Longus and even to an extent the Greek orators. All these stand in marked contrast to the straightforward use of *inclusio* in the dream narratives. Gnuse concurs with the analysis given here, noting "the general economy of the literary style evident in the Infancy Narratives."[158] This stylistic analysis, therefore, favors the view that Matthew is using source material in this section.

What is notable about the style of Matthew's dream narratives is their simplicity. This suggests material which was orally transmitted. It does not amount to proof, as it is possible to have a written narrative whose style is simple. However, simplicity of style would be a requirement for oral transmission. Worthington, whose analysis of Dianarchus 1 (*Against Demosthenes*) we considered above, tells us that speeches were originally delivered orally and then revised in written form.[159] In the revision the writer might

---

155. Talbert, *Matthew*, 94, notes this.

156. Talbert, *Matthew*, 91, simply notes that here we have three paragraphs, each beginning with, "Do not be debilitatingly anxious," and does not comment on the significance of this for *inclusio*.

157. The phrase in brackets is missing from certain manuscripts. The text may have been assimilated to Matt 6:31. Alternatively, a scribe may have dropped it by oversight because of the similarity between φάγητε and πίητε. See Metzger, *Textual Commentary*, 17.

158. Gnuse, "Dream Genre," 113.

159. Worthington, "Greek Oratory," 165.

add material, but might also give the speech a more complicated structure, especially using ring composition. Worthington suggests that some of the complex levels of ring structuring would be lost on a listening audience and so point to revision after oral delivery.[160] Similarly we might say that some of Matthew's use of *inclusio* in the Sermon on the Mount would be lost on an audience. By contrast the use of *inclusio* in the dream narratives is simple and would be appreciated by an audience. That simplicity of style may point to oral transmission, but it could equally well be due to the subject matter under discussion.

## Summing Up

We have faced the question whether the dream narratives underwent a process of oral transmission at some stage before they reached Matthew. Although we have explored various facets of the issue, we simply cannot be sure. The use of formulaic expressions, parallelism, repetition, key words, peculiar vocabulary, story-motifs and simplicity of style are all consistent with an oral origin of the narrative, but none of them singly or combined can prove an oral source.

We noted that the difficulty with features such as formulaic expressions, parallelism and repetition is how they can appear in written material as well as oral. This is essentially the problem which Rafael Rodríguez sees in attempts to identify features of orality in a written text or use such features to postulate residual traces of oral tradition within it.[161] He refers to this as the "morphological approach" to oral tradition[162] and comments: "The features themselves are neither necessarily oral nor necessarily written. They are features of both oral and written narratives."[163] Rodríguez draws attention to an assumption of the morphological approach which lies at the heart of the problem:[164] it assumes that oral and not written psychodynamics produce certain features of narrative and linguistic style, while the only evidence we have exists within written texts. What we would

---

160. Worthington, "Greek Oratory," 166.

161. Rodríguez, *Oral Tradition*, 56–71.

162. Rodríguez, *Oral Tradition*, 56, tells us that morphology refers to form, shape, or structure of a thing. He proceeds to demonstrate the weaknesses of Ong's psychodynamics of orality; Dewey's appeal to hook words, repetition, and *inclusio*; and Dunn and Mournet's reference to variability and stability (Rodríguez, *Oral Tradition*, 58–66).

163. Rodríguez, *Oral Tradition*, 64.

164. Rodríguez, *Oral Tradition*, 70.

need to show is that such features cannot appear in written texts other than as echoes of an oral past.

It seems unlikely that we can demonstrate what Rodríguez requires. David Strauss drew attention to Joseph's last two dreams, suggesting that only one dream was necessary to direct him to Nazareth instead of Bethlehem.[165] That would certainly appear to be more logical. A lack of clear logic is sometimes seen as a characteristic of oral communication.[166] However, illogical thinking can also occur in written communication.[167] This is the point to which we keep returning, features shared by orality and text.

We return to a point made at the beginning of this chapter: the spheres of orality and literacy were intermingled in the first century. As Samuel Byrskog puts it, written texts had no life of their own: they "were mostly 'transitional' in the sense that they presupposed and supplemented oral modes of communication, regularly returning to oral modalities."[168] With material going back and forward between oral recitation/performance and writing, it is hardly surprising that written texts show evidence of orality, but it does not follow that any particular passage necessarily had a purely oral origin.

However, even if we cannot prove that Matthew used oral source(s), it does not follow that the task with which we are concerned in this study becomes pointless. The devices with which we are dealing are memory patterns rather than features which prove oral communication. Rodríguez makes this point in an endnote.[169] Memory patterns and rhetorical devices can still be used to try and establish cultural leanings, for even when a narrative was written, such techniques continued to be used, as we shall see, to aid memory.

Rodríguez himself advocates a contextual approach, positing "the oral expression of tradition as the context within which the written NT texts developed and were written by authors, recited by lectors (and/or oral performers), and received by audiences (and/or readers)."[170] Rodríguez draws upon John Foley in suggesting that the oral context is what allowed the NT writers to convey their meaning and their audience or readers to interpret and respond to their message.[171] It is possible, therefore, to see the Matthean

---

165. Strauss, *Das Leben Jesu*, 168.

166. Ong, *Orality and Literacy*, 49–56.

167. Strauss was not concerned with the oral/written issue, but wanted to suggest that human imagination was at work rather than divine providence.

168. Byrskog, *Story as History*, 127.

169. Rodríguez, *Oral Tradition*, 61n10, says this in relation to chiasm.

170. Rodríguez, *Oral Tradition*, 72.

171. Foley, *Singer of Tales*.

dream narratives as an "oral derived text," to use Foley's phrase,[172] rather than a written text dependent on an oral source. We shall pick up Foley's notion of *register* later, in the chapter on comparison of memory patterns.

In the meantime we note how it remains possible that Matthew derived his dream narratives from an early Christian source which was at one time oral. However, such a hypothesis cannot be proved and is ultimately not necessary to account for the phenomena in Matthew's text. What is more likely is that he drew on Jewish source(s) and particularly legends connected with the birth of Moses. It is possible that they reached Matthew in oral form and that he has retained at least some of their memory patterns, but written accounts, similar to those in Josephus and Pseudo-Philo, cannot be ruled out.

It also seems high likely that Matthew would have redacted any source material that may lie behind the dream narratives. The formula-quotations suggest evidence of this,[173] as do examples of chiasmus which Vincent Pizzuto claims stem from Matthew.[174] Beyond these it is difficult to determine whether the devices we found belong to any source(s) or to Matthew. It would therefore be appropriate to treat Matthew and anyone who may have provided source material as a single group. It is in relation to that group, however small, that we are seeking to clarify literary practice and establish some understanding of cultural identity. Ultimately, this can still be done if Matthew alone was responsible, producing "an oral derived text."

## Rhetorical Devices

We have already noted the use of formulaic expressions, repetition and parallelism in poetry as aids to memory in the process of oral transmission. We have also seen how Dewey drew attention to the presence of formulaic expressions in the text of Matthew. Paul Achtemeier concerns himself with the use of these and similar techniques throughout the NT, arguing that the various writers consciously used such techniques to assist their audience.[175] He points out how written documents were not com-

172. See, for example, Foley, *Singer of Tales*, 60, which defines this phrase as a "text with roots in oral tradition."

173. Brown observes that if the formula citations are removed from Matt 2:12–23, it will be seen that the evangelist has added very little to the pre-Matthean narrative (Brown, *Birth of the Messiah*, 229). This of course is difficult to verify as we do not actually have that narrative. He would be less inclined to make such a statement regarding Matt 1:18–25.

174. Pizzuto, "Structural Elegance," 712–37.

175. Achtemeier, "*Omne verbum sonat*," 3–27.

posed in silence as nowadays, but were dictated to scribes or verbalized as individuals wrote.[176] Likewise reading was vocalized, whether done for a group or by a slave for his master or by an individual for himself.[177] This happened on most occasions.[178] Achtemeier also draws attention to the difficulty involved in reading ancient documents, where many had no spaces between words, no punctuation, no paragraphs, no headings, no visual aids to reading. The result was that organization of meaning was often conveyed by oral indications of structure within the material. Ancient "readers" or listeners would have been attuned to special effects, such as repetition, alliteration and wordplay.

Achtemeier differs from Parry, Lord, Ong and Dewey, all of whom were concerned with what happened in the process of oral composition. An oral poet or narrator would use a variety of techniques to assist himself in composition and his audience in listening to and remembering his composition. Such devices can still be detected in some ancient literature because the writer was using an oral source, as Herodotus and Pausanias did. Achtemeier is dealing with composition which imitates that oral process and consciously inserts devices into material. The effects to which he refers are sometimes described as rhetorical devices rather than oral patterns of memory. The actual effects may be the same. It depends on whether they belong to a period of oral composition and transmission or enter the tradition at the point of writing. It was also believed that such techniques could produce a more ornate style. Theoretically we can distinguish these functions, but in practice it is much more difficult. We often cannot discern a writer's motivation in using devices and sometimes they may serve a dual role, stylistic as well as mnemonic.

---

176. He illustrates with Zechariah writing the name of his son on the tablet. Luke's Greek, ἔγραψεν λέγων, "he wrote, saying," (Luke 1:63) demonstrates that it was the act of *writing* that proved his speech had been restored.

177. His illustration is how Philip ἤκουσεν, "overheard," the Ethiopian eunuch ἀναγινώσκοντος, "reading," from the book of Isaiah in Acts 8:30.

178. Silent reading was not completely unknown. Achtemeier himself gives the example of Ambrose, Bishop of Milan, reading silently in the late fourth century. Slusser, "Reading Silently in Antiquity," 499, gives an example from earlier in the fourth century (about 350 CE), one in which Cyril of Jerusalem instructs young women to read in silence, moving their lips but making no sound. Gilliard, "More Silent Reading in Antiquity," 689-94, refers to earlier examples: Theseus in Euripides's *Hippolytus* (lines 856-74) apparently reading silently a letter from his dead wife; Demosthenes in Aristophanes's *Knights* (lines 116-27) reading a writing-tablet containing an oracle; and a riddle recounted in *Sappho*, the fourth-century Athenian comedy of Antiphanes, which hints at silent reading. Although silent reading was not as rare in the ancient world as some would have us believe, reading aloud was still much more common.

The kind of approach to which Achtemeier refers in which a writer imitates the oral process with the insertion of devices is relevant to our study of Matthew's dream narratives. We have seen how difficult it is to prove that he used had an oral source or sources. While he may have used Jewish material associated with Moses's birth, it is likely that the composition is ultimately his own. It follows that the devices in his narratives stem from his pen, although we cannot rule out a few from any source material. Either way we cannot distinguish them, but they imitate the oral process in ensuring that his text was memorable.

This discussion of Achtemeier's insights is also relevant in another way. The rhetorical devices which he highlights are to be found in the work of all Greek and Roman prose authors from the fifth century BCE onwards. As dream narratives from such writers are also being examined, we need to acknowledge that the devices which they display may have been created by them rather than any source they used and the devices may serve stylistic purposes as well as or instead of mnemonic purposes. Despite that, their usage may still be able to tell us something about a writer's cultural background, for a writer's repertoire would develop in the cultural setting in which he was reared and educated.

# Rhetoric

We have now moved from the sphere of orality into that of rhetoric. We may ask what is meant by the term "rhetoric." James Williams points out that there was no single definition in the classical period, but one factor present in all definitions was the power of language to persuade and influence others.[179] We see the need for this power of persuasion most clearly in public speaking. As Athens became democratized, a citizen required skill in public speaking if he was to participate in politics or deliver a speech in a court of law. To be persuasive, speeches had to be carefully crafted.[180] It was in this context that rhetoric emerged and it coincided with the move in Greek society from orality towards literacy. Rhetoric could be used not only in speeches, but also in literature. It was Aristotle who provided the first detailed theory[181] in *The Art of Rhetoric*.[182] During the Hellenistic period rhetoric was widely studied

---

179. Williams, *Introduction to Classical Rhetoric*, 9.

180. Williams, *Introduction to Classical Rhetoric*, 11–12, 19.

181. Plato wrote only a limited amount on rhetoric, mainly in criticism of the Sophists, but what he did write paved the way for the fuller theoretical work of Aristotle.

182. It consists of three books which deal with matter, audience psychology, and style. At the beginning of Book 3, he says: "It is not sufficient to know what one ought

in schools set up throughout Greek-controlled areas of the Mediterranean. When the Romans encountered Greek culture, they largely adopted it as their own, including the theory and practice of rhetoric.

According to Philo, rhetoric belonged to the middle stage of education, the area he calls μέση παιδεία, between learning to read and write and studying philosophy.[183] Many would argue that rhetoric and philosophy were alternative termini.[184] We learn much about Roman era rhetorical education from Quintilian's *Institutio Oratoria* and from *progymnasmata*, surviving handbooks on the elements of rhetoric. The development of memory is the first thing which Quintilian suggests a pupil must learn when he goes to school.[185] As he reads, he learns about grammar and the music of words, about how to arrange words and clauses for greatest effect and how to choose the appropriate style for the subject matter and audience.[186] Rhetoric proper begins with the student learning the characteristics of historical narrative, reading and practicing them.[187] Boys go on to confirmations or refutations of narratives,[188] and from there to composing praise or denunciation of famous men.[189] Then there are *topoi*, commonplaces, where the student speaks on behalf of a fictional character, and *theses*, in which he debates various questions. Some of the subjects dealt with in Books 3–11 are style, figures of thought and speech, and rhythm. The *progymnasmata* agree with what Quintilian says, describing exercises which a teacher might give his pupil. In the first stage the student paraphrases a story. Gradually he learns to construct more complicated forms of narrative. These may be mythical, fictitious, personal, political or historical.[190] Later he learns the formal components of an oration. Only a small portion of the population would receive a rhetorical education. We have already noted the small

---

to say, but one must also know how to say it" (Aristotle, *Rhetoric* 3.1403b).

183. See Philo, *On Mating* 11. This middle part includes grammar, geometry, astronomy, literature, musical theory and dialectic as well as rhetoric. However, for many this middle stage was the terminal point of their education, as not everyone went on, as Philo did, to philosophy.

184. E.g., Cribiore, *Gymnastics of the Mind*.

185. Quintilian, *Institutio* 1.3.1.

186. Quintilian, *Institutio* 1.4.6–1.7.35.

187. Quintilian, *Institutio* 2.4.2–4.

188. Quintilian, *Institutio* 2.4.18.

189. Quintilian, *Institutio* 2.4.20.

190. According to Quintilian, historical narrative belongs to more advanced exercises. See Quintilian, *Institutio* 2.4.2.

proportion who were literate; it is a tiny fraction of them who would have had any form of rhetorical education.[191]

The study of rhetoric made an impact upon literature as well as oratory, with a keen interest being taken in style. In this period there flourished a particular style which had developed in the eastern Mediterranean, especially at Rhodes. It was known as Asianism and was very ornate and, to an extent, artificial.[192] It was contrasted with Atticism which was a more direct and natural style of speaking, although it involved writing in a dialect which had long ceased to be any one's mother tongue.[193]

As we compare the Matthean dream narratives with those of other literature, we shall be looking at historical, biographical and fictional writings from the Hellenistic and Roman worlds and in that literature we shall encounter rhetorical influence. Matthew Fox and Niall Livingstone comment: "The idea of Hellenistic historiography as highly rhetorical in character is a well-established orthodoxy."[194] John of Sardis hints at how historians could be trained rhetorically as he comments on an exercise concerned with writing narrative: "This progymnasma is useful preparation both for statements in the law courts and for compositions of the historians."[195] Theon speaks in a similar vein when he states: "The one who has expressed a narration and a fable in a fine and varied way will also compose a history well."[196] They both see historical writing as a combination of narratives.

Some historians displayed a more adorned style than others. Very little in Asiatic style survives because it fell out of fashion so quickly. We may note that Polybius preferred a simpler, less adorned style.[197] He stands in contrast to Diodorus Siculus and Dionysius of Halicarnassus, who, although very different, favored a more elaborate style.[198] We find a similar approach to writing in the realm of fiction, for the Greek novel was developing at a time when there was a strong interest in rhetorical theory.[199] Ruth Webb points out that a careful style and a taste for extended speeches by characters is to

---

191. See Morgan, *Literate Education*, 190–239; "Rhetoric and Education," 303–319.
192. Rose, *Handbook of Greek Literature*, 362.
193. Rose, *Handbook of Greek Literature*, 396–97.
194. Fox and Livingstone, "Rhetoric and Historiography," 542–61.
195. Notes to *Progymnasmata* of Aphthonius, attributed to John of Sardis (Spengel, *Rhetores Graeci*, 2:30). See Kennedy, *Progymnasmata*, 191.
196. Aelius Theon, *Exercises* (Spengel, *Rhetores Graeci*, 2:60). See Kennedy, *Progymnasmata*, 4.
197. Fox and Livingstone, "Rhetoric and Historiography," 554.
198. Fox and Livingstone, "Rhetoric and Historiography," 551.
199. This is sometimes referred to as the period of the "Second Sophistic."

be found in the writing of "the big three" novelists—Achilles Tatius, Longus, and Heliodorus.[200] It is less evident in the work of Chariton.

What emerges from this is that techniques originally designed to serve mnemonic purposes were now used for stylistic reasons, although they could of course have a dual role. We have just noted how some writers preferred a simpler style, while others favored a more adorned one. This needs to be borne in mind as we examine the dream narratives of Greco-Roman authors in search of memory devices. Inevitably some will provide more evidence than others. This is not so much a cultural trait as a personal one. Nevertheless, when they do use them, they may display something of their cultural background. Moreover, when taken together, the evidence from all these writers may show a tendency to use particular devices more than others and consequently reveal something about their culture.

## Conclusion

In this chapter various aspects of orality and rhetoric have been explored, since oral and scribal techniques influenced each other in the world of the first century. We noted various techniques of oral composition and transmission, such as formulae, repetition and parallelism, which continued to be used even when society became more literate, for there remained a "residual orality."[201] With only a small proportion of the population in the Roman Empire able to read and write, people still required aids to memory. Oral transmission continued because copies of books were limited in number due to the cost of papyrus and the time required to reproduce them.[202] Memorization itself continued because readers wanted to be able to reproduce what they read and have it influence their own thought.[203] To assist oral and literary communication the classical world had developed the art of rhetoric. Many writers would deliberately incorporate memory patterns into their work in

---

200. Webb, "Rhetoric and the Novel," 526–41.

201. Ong uses the expression "primary orality" to refer to thought and its verbal expression within cultures "totally untouched by any knowledge of writing or print" (Ong, *Orality and Literacy*, 11). He goes on to use the expression "residual orality" for situations where there has been exposure to writing.

202. There were also situations where teaching was memorized to keep it safe and secret. This was the case with Pythagoreans and the Druids.

203. "In antiquity information was stored primarily in memory. . . . People in the ancient world knew whatever they knew of Homer, Plato, and Aristotle 'by heart'" (Lee and Scott, *Sound Mapping*, 61, 78). Quintilian draws an analogy between trained memory and a beehive full of honey gathered from a variety of flowers (Quintilian, *Institutio* 1.10.7).

much the same way as someone composing orally. They were conscious that their work would be read aloud and the audience or readership would require guidance in following its structure and remembering its content.[204] At other times their aim was to achieve a more polished style of writing. Since memory played such a key role in the transmission of material in first-century society, we shall examine it in our next chapter.

---

204. Kennedy mentions public performances of their works by Herodotus, Virgil, and Asinius Paulus (Kennedy, *Classical Rhetoric*, 111). Pliny tells us that his uncle had a book read even when in the company of friends at a meal, when he was being rubbed down and dried after his bath, or when he travelled. "*Super hanc (sc. cenam) liber legebatur. . . . Nam dum destringitur tergiturque, audiebat aliquid. . . . In itinere . . . ad latus notarius cum libro*" (Pliny, *Epistolae* 3.5.11, 14, 15).

# 3

# Memory

## Introduction

IN THIS STUDY WE are concerned with devices which are used for mnemonic purposes rather than stylistic. They are used for the oral transmission of narratives and other forms of literature in an oral or semi-literate society. In this context they are sometimes referred to as memory patterns. In this chapter we seek to understand the wider context of memory in which they function. We begin with how the ancients themselves understood memory, moving on to some of the insights of psychologists in regard to individual memory, but concentrating more on the contribution of sociologists concerning social memory. We pause over memory distortion, ways in which memories are reshaped in the process of remembering. As well as those noted by others, I suggest the concept of *translation* distortion where a memory was originally narrated in a different language. We then resume our discussion of collective memory with Assmann's writing on cultural memory. We note how Dunn applies social memory theory to the Quest for the Historical Jesus, contrasting this with Bauckham's approach based on the reliability of individual memory. We then relate our study to their approach, noting that they concentrate on memory content, while we pursue some memory processes. We consider the historical veracity of the infancy narratives, recognizing that cultural memory is still applicable even if they are fiction. We finish by considering briefly how narratives may have been transmitted within early Christian communities.

## Ancient Understanding of Memory

We begin with the way the ancients themselves understood memory and we find that for Plato and Aristotle their theories of remembering are tied up with their epistemologies. First we note how Plato invites us to imagine that the mind contains a block of wax. When we seek to remember something we have seen, heard or conceived in our minds, we hold the wax under the perception or ideas and imprint them on it.[1] The process of remembering is similar to the making of a seal on wax with a signet ring. Although Plato recognizes that we have the capacity to preserve in our memories what we have experienced through the senses, he suggests that there is no understanding involved in sense memory and consequently he does not consider that to be knowledge.[2] He is more concerned with concepts knowable without the senses and recovered from a memory latent in the soul. In the *Meno* he propounds his doctrine that knowledge is recollection. The process of recollecting is awakened by skilful questioning through which a person is reminded of knowledge latently stored in his mind, knowledge which was acquired through the immortal soul's existence here and in the other world.[3] In the *Phaedo* Plato deals more fully with the true objects of knowledge which he calls "forms" or "ideas." They are independent of this world and unchanging, but the concrete things of this sensory world participate in them and embody images of them. Mathematical and moral concepts derive from latent memory, whereas historical knowledge does not.[4]

Aristotle shares with Plato the likening of memory to wax being imprinted by a signet ring.[5] However, he is also very different, particularly in his belief that knowledge comes through the senses. This has a bearing on his approach to memory, for he sees memory as a collection of images or mental pictures causally derived from a past act of perception. Although memory is connected with perception, it is different from it in that perception belongs to the present and memory to the past, with memory recognizing the lapse of time.[6] Whether the impression gained through the senses lasts in memory or is erased depends on the age and temperament of the person concerned. In addition to memory, Aristotle speaks about reminiscence or recollection which is a more intellectual activity, as it was for Plato. Recollection begins

---

1. Plato, *Theaetetus*, 191 C–D.
2. Coleman, *Ancient and Medieval Memories*, 9.
3. Plato, *Meno*, 81 C–D.
4. Coleman, *Ancient and Medieval Memories*, 8–9.
5. Aristotle, *De Memoria et Reminiscentia*, 1:450a 32.
6. Aristotle, *De Memoria et Reminiscentia*, 1:449b 24.

with thinking rather than perceiving, consists of a process of reasoning and involves a succession of associated ideas.[7] It is concerned with the recovery of knowledge held or sensation experienced in the past. It involves a deliberate effort by a person to find a way among the contents of memory.[8] Aristotle describes it as a search, but it is one which is self-motivated and does not depend on anyone else.[9] This distinguishes it from learning which does depend on someone else.[10] Although recollection may result in remembering, the two differ in that memory requires sense images, while recollection involves the association of ideas.[11]

When we turn to Roman writers, we find that they also use the wax metaphor, comparing the stamping of memory images on places imagined in the mind with writing on a wax tablet.[12] However, they make no serious effort to define what memory is or explain how it operates. They approach it from the rhetorical tradition and concern themselves with practical techniques to improve memory for the purposes of delivering a long speech with precision. This is sometimes referred to as *artificial memory*. Its origin is generally attributed to a Greek, Simonides of Keos (c. 556–468 BCE). He was chanting a lyric poem at a banquet when the roof fell in. Although the host and all his guests were killed, Simonides survived because he happened to be outside at the moment of the accident. The relatives of the dead were unable to recognize them because they were so badly mangled. Simonides was able to indicate who they were because he remembered the places at which they had been sitting at the table. This experience gave him the principles of the art of memory, particularly the importance of orderly arrangement. Although Aristotle does not mention Simonides, he provides the first full description of the system of places invented by him.[13] In the interval it had been developed by the Sophists, before Aristotle refined it.[14] Thereafter no extended discussion of mnemotechnics has survived until the Romans in the first century BCE. In the intervening period memory became a formal division of rhetoric.

---

7. *De Memoria et Reminiscentia*, 2:451a 18f.
8. Yates, *Art of Memory*, 33–34.
9. *De Memoria et Reminiscentia*, 2:451b 6–18.
10. This is different from Plato, who does see recollection as learning.
11. Coleman, *Ancient and Medieval Memories*, 23.
12. The change from the seal imprint made on wax by a ring to the waxed writing tablet is no doubt connected with the contemporary use of waxed tablets for writing.
13. *De Memoria et Reminiscentia*, 452a12–425a25.
14. Small, *Wax Tablets of the Mind*, 94.

Roman teachers of rhetoric developed the use of orderly arrangement. In *De Oratore* Cicero briefly describes the mnemonic of places and images (*loci* and *imagines*).[15] Two other writers who refer to this are the anonymous author of *Ad C. Herennium libri IV* and Quintilian in his *Institutio Oratoria*.[16] The first step was to imprint on the memory a series of places. Often, but by no means always, an architectural system was used. The practitioner is urged to take a spacious building with a variety of rooms and include statues and other ornaments with which they are decorated and memorize all this. Then he should put in imagination the images of what he wishes to remember on the places in the building already memorized. When he is delivering his speech, he can then move in imagination through his memory building, drawing from the memorized places the images he has placed on them. This system ensures that points are remembered in the right order because the order is fixed by the sequence of places in the building. An alternative to a building might be a journey. The same set of places can be used repeatedly for remembering different material. Once the images which have been placed on them fade, the places remain in the memory and can be used again for a different set of images. The author of *Ad Herennium* advises that the places should be of moderate size, not too brightly lit nor too dark and should be set at moderate intervals.[17] It is striking how much emphasis is placed on the visual as an aid to memory. Evidence from neuropsychological testing supports the linkage between visual and mental imagery.[18]

With regard to images, there are two kinds, one for "things" (*res*), the other for "words" (*verba*). The first makes images to remind the speaker of an argument, a notion or a "thing," whereas the second requires him to find images as reminders of every single word. Cicero makes it clear that "things" are the subject matter of the speech, where "words" are the language in which it is expressed.[19] Clearly some images are more conducive to stimulating memory than others. For this reason the author of *Ad Herennium* urges his students to set up active images (*imagines agentes*). He recommends figures—and he seems to mean human figures—exceptionally beautiful or ugly, strikingly dressed or dramatically engaged in some activity.[20]

15. Cicero, *De Oratore* 2:lxxxvi, 351–54.

16. See especially book 3 of anonymous, *Ad Herennium*, and book 11 of Quintilian, *Institutio*.

17. Anonymous, *Ad Herennium* 3.16.29–3.19.32.

18. Small, *Wax Tablets of the Mind*, 106–7.

19. Cicero, *De Inventione* 1:7, 9.

20. Anonymous, *Ad Herennium* 3.12.

We may well regard the *imagines agentes* as a cumbersome system for mnemonic purposes. With such a view Quintilian seems to agree, for there is a "double task imposed upon our memory," as we seek to remember not only the things, but places for the things.[21] Quintilian also noted that the system did not cover certain kinds of words like conjunctions. He did not use the system of loci and mental imagery himself, but instead he advocated hard and intensive learning by heart.[22] Although Quintilian's attitude to artificial memory is different from that of the author of *Ad Herennium* and of Cicero, the use of places, especially buildings, and images has played a significant role in the practice of memory down through the centuries, switching from oratory to ethics and preaching in medieval times. It is worth noting that it is an art for those who are already highly literate.[23] What lies at the heart of it is a sense of order in which material is presented.

## Individual Memory

Over the last century there have been extensive studies on memory carried out by psychologists and sociologists. They distinguish different types of remembering.[24] There is *habitual* memory used, for example, in the process of walking and there is *procedural* memory used in driving a car. We have *episodic* memory in which we remember an experience by partly reliving it in our imagination and we have *semantic* memory in which we remember facts which we have learned in various ways. There is also *verbal* memory in which we recall simply the words which were spoken or written, but in an oral tradition some words may carry *metonymic referentiality*, meaning that they convey additional meaning to the author and readers familiar with the tradition.[25] We can distinguish *individual* memory which remains within our own cognitive processes from *collective* memory which in some way involves other people. In this study we are largely concerned with *collective semantic* memories, with some attention paid to the verbal symbols in which they are expressed. We are dealing with the memory Joseph's dreams and subsequent actions and that is clearly different from the recall of motor

---

21. Quintilian, *Institutio* 11:2, 23–26.
22. Quintilian, *Institutio* 11:2, 32–33.
23. Small, *Wax Tablets of the Mind*, 100.
24. Eve, *Behind the Gospels*, 88.
25. Foley discusses this, using the example of 'swift-footed Achilles.' He suggests that with this kind of allusion one aspect of Achilles's character represents the whole. See Foley, *Singer of Tales*, 2–7.

skills, such as riding a bike.[26] We are involved in the study of narratives and sometimes the precise words in which they are expressed, but first we look at perceptual or episodic memory and trace it through various processes noting how it becomes encoded and stored in verbal symbols.

Psychologists have shown that the whole process of remembering is extremely complex. However, Aristotle rightly identified that it begins with sense impressions or perception. A person witnesses an event or undergoes an experience, but even this initial perception is complicated. Two people standing at different places with respect to a certain action may see and hear different things.[27] Interpretation is required as the mind analyses what is seen or experienced in relation to various thought categories which in turn were formed by previous experiences as well as being molded by social interaction.[28] Perception may also be affected by anticipation or other pre-existing thoughts. Familiar categories, for example, can shape what the individual is likely to perceive.[29] But once the perception has occurred, the thought categories will potentially be slightly altered in the light of it. In the Matthean narratives the perception is what Joseph saw, if anything, and, more especially, what he heard in the dreams.

After perception comes the real process of remembering. Psychologists see three stages in this process: encoding, storage and retrieval.[30] Encoding involves transforming the sensory input into a form which is able to be processed by the memory system. We do not usually try to encapsulate a photographic panorama. Instead, as adults, we often translate our experience,

---

26. Smith et al., *Atkinson and Hilgard's Introduction*, 269.

27. Redman, "How Accurate Are Eyewitnesses?," 185.

28. For example, when we read, we project an interpretation onto each word. Rawlinson carried out research at Nottingham University on the significance of letter position in word recognition (Rawlinson, "Reibadailty," 55). It showed that randomizing letters in the middle of words had little or no effect on the ability of skilled readers to understand the text. His 1976 PhD thesis has remained unpublished, but he has written about it in New Scientist.

29. Smith et al., *Atkinson and Hilgard's Introduction*, 223, refers to an experiment in which a lecture was interrupted by a workman who spoke with a German accent. Although the individual who played the part of the workman had blond hair and dark brown eyes, a substantial proportion of the students reported confidently that they had seen his *blue* eyes—the color falsely inferred from his Nordic appearance and German accent. This is an example of a schema-based error, something which we shall explore more fully in section 5 where we deal with memory distortions.

30. Smith et al., *Atkinson and Hilgard's Introduction*, 268. For the application of the three stage process to working memory, see Smith et al., *Atkinson and Hilgard's Introduction*, 273–77, and to long-term memory, 281–84.

particularly sequences of events,[31] into verbal symbols.[32] These are then stored or transferred into memory. Finally, the memorized information is located and used when required. However, we should note that what we retrieve is not the experience itself, but the verbal symbols from which we try to reconstruct the experience. Recent studies suggest that these different stages of memory are mediated by different structures in the brain.[33] During encoding most of the activated brain areas are in the left hemisphere, whereas during retrieval most of the activated brain regions are in the right hemisphere.[34] If we are to regard Joseph's dreams as historical, the retrieval occurs when he narrates his experience to an individual or group, prompted perhaps by questions or the direction of conversation.

Just as the initial act of perception required interpretation, so also the final act of recalling involves further interpretation, as it is related to present circumstances. The memory of an event serves some need in the present. It may be prompted by something in the environment, such as a sight, smell or taste.[35] Equally well it may be prompted by a person's social setting, such as a conversation or question from others.[36]

It will be seen that there is a high degree of subjectivity in the perception and interpretation which memory involves. However, social context also plays its part in regulating memory. The perception and the memory of an event are related to thought categories which are socially constructed and are expressed in language which is also a social construct.[37] The use of memory patterns with which we are concerned is another example of a social construct. When they are used in transmitting a story orally, they have to be shared by the storyteller and audience alike.

---

31. Sequences of events can be expressed as verbal narratives, but this is not possible with the memory of tunes or other memories which contain strong sensory imagery.

32. Miller, *Psychology*, 186.

33. Smith et al., *Atkinson and Hilgard's Introduction*, 268.

34. This clear-cut biological bias emerged from brain-scanning studies involving positron emission tomography (PET) or functional magnetic resonance imaging (fMRI) in which measures of brain activity were recorded while participants were engaged in tasks.

35. Miller refers to Marcel Proust, the French novelist, and how in *Remembrance of Things Past* he relates that he tasted small cakes called '*petites madeleines*' and as a result revived a system of memories long since abandoned (Miller, *Psychology*, 180).

36. Erll, "Cultural Memory Studies," 5.

37. Miller says, "New experience is categorized in terms of familiar concepts shared by the culture and symbolized by the language" (Miller, *Psychology*, 190).

## Social Memory

The social dimension of memory is something which the ancient writers did not recognize or write about. However, through the work of twentieth-century sociologists there has emerged the concept of "social memory" or "collective memory."[38] There is a certain ambiguity about what these terms actually mean, for different writers use them in different ways. Eve helpfully suggests six possible meanings.[39] As far as this study is concerned, the dreams of Joseph would be the *content* of the collective memory of any group which related them and may have passed them on to Matthew, while the narrative in which they were expressed, would be part of the *process* by which the dreams were remembered and the memory patterns embodied in them would be the shared *frameworks*.

It is now widely, but not universally,[40] recognized that memory can be held by social groups as well as individuals. Strictly speaking, social groups do not remember; it is only individuals who can do so, for remembering is a cognitive process which takes place inside each person's brain.[41] However, the concept of "remembering" is applied metaphorically to social groups. Barry Schwartz suggests that a good analogy to social memory is public opinion, since opinions, like memories, can only be held by individuals. However, when individuals are questioned and the resulting opinions are aggregated, these opinions take on a new significance.[42]

Even where memory is individual, it is formed within the context of a social group. Such groups could be a family, a community, a generation, an organization such as a political party or a church, even an entire nation. A memory can be shared by a whole group in the following kind of way. Five or six adult siblings may meet from time to time and reminisce on the events of their childhood. One member of the group starts to tell a story. Before he has gone far, a brother may take over and relate the next sequence

---

38. To be strictly accurate, "social memory" refers to individual memories which are informed by group ideologies and "collective memory" those shared by a group. Because of the overlap they have tended to become synonymous.

39. Eve suggests (1) the *processes* by which a group recalls and interprets the past; (2) the *purposes* for which the past is recalled; (3) the ways in which beliefs about and interpretations of the past undergo *change* within a group; (4) the *content* of beliefs about the past that members of the group hold in common; (5) the way the past is *evaluated* and so helps to shape a common sense of identity; and (6) the shared *frameworks* that members of a group use to talk about the past (Eve, *Writing the Gospels*, 107).

40. E.g., Gedi and Elam call the concept into question. See Gedi and Elam, "Collective Memory," 30.

41. Erll, "Cultural Memory Studies," 4–5.

42. Schwartz, "Where There's Smoke," 9.

of events. Then a sister plays her part and narrates what happened thereafter. By the end of the story each of them has played a part in telling it. Their memory is shared. Perhaps one of them does not remember a particular event the first time it is related. After three or four meetings where it is discussed, he feels able to join in the narration. If questioned, he may now claim to remember what happened. His memory has been reinforced, or simply created, by the group. There are also other expressions of collective memory, such as rituals, ceremonies, monuments as well as written texts of which public records are a good example.

Before discussing in detail the theory associated with this concept, it may be useful to refer briefly to its development. Its relevance to the task of the historian has been seen from the 1980s onwards. But it was first expounded by the French sociologist Maurice Halbwachs in 1925 through a monograph entitled "*Les Cadres sociaux de la mémoire.*"[43] Halbwachs drew attention to the role which the present plays in memory. It is on the basis of present needs that memory is reconstructed. He also pointed out that memory is conceived within social frameworks. It is prompted by social cues and operates within social constraints. His move from individual memory to the social frameworks which constrain it led him to study the interdependence of the two spheres. In 1941 he published *La Topographie de Evangelies en Terre Sainte*,[44] in which he worked out his memory theory in relation to the sacred sites of the Holy Land. He saw the commemorated landscape as an example of collective memory. He claimed that medieval European Christians visited Israel with mental images gained from reading the gospels. They superimposed these on the physical landscape and built churches to commemorate events from Jesus's life. He concluded that these sites had value for tracing collective memory but were of no use to historians concerned with the historical events. The result was that Halbwachs himself did not see the value of his work for the historian's task. For him history was an objective science possible only once collective memory had been laid aside. It was Pierre Nora, another Frenchman, who brought history and memory back together. Along with others he published *Les Lieux de Mémoire* in 1984.[45] They mapped France's past onto its present geography, architecture and festivals. This was the first real application of social memory to national history. Nora placed memory at the heart of historical study.

---

43. Halbwachs, *On Collective Memory*.

44. This is available in English in Part 2 of Halbwachs, *On Collective Memory*, 193–235.

45. Nora, *Realms of Memory*.

The concept of social memory has drawn the attention of some NT scholars.[46] They have argued that the memory of the social group is stronger than that of the individual, as they invite us to picture small Christian gatherings discussing aspects of Jesus's life and ministry and from our perspective we might add Jesus's infancy. They vary in the extent to which they believe that social memory preserves a tradition. James Dunn is optimistic about the continuity of the Jesus tradition. He repeatedly emphasizes its stability, especially in relation to the core of a story.[47] However, Dunn offers surprisingly little discussion on the workings of memory, instead focusing attention on the workings of oral tradition. His research student Anthony Le Donne is also confident about the way in which an individual's memory is held in check by the combined memories of the social group to which he belongs. As Le Donne has it, "If a particular individual memory is not rendered plausible in social dialogue, it will be corrected and in some cases rejected. Therefore, as an individual memory becomes a collective memory through this dialogue, it is corrected and completed by established collective memories. Social groups, therefore, stabilize individual memories by providing parameters for their formation."[48] Le Donne may be overconfident about the reliability of a memory which has been stabilized by a group. It is possible for a memory to be handed down in a relatively stable, but nonetheless distorted form, the reshaping having occurred at an early stage.[49] There might also be changes due to shifts in social context. We see evidence of this in the way in which later evangelists reworked the tradition to meet new situations and the challenges which they presented.

At almost the opposite extreme from Dunn and Le Donne we have the "constructivist" or "presentist" approach which sees collective memory as a reconstruction whose primary task is to serve the interests of the group which holds it. In its most extreme form the notion of the past can be seen as a complete fabrication designed to serve present needs. Of the scholars listed in the footnote the one who comes closest to this view is

---

46. E.g., Dunn, *Jesus Remembered*; *New Perspective on Jesus*; Eve, *Behind the Gospels*; Eve, *Writing the Gospels*; Keith, *Jesus's Literacy*; Kirk, "Social and Cultural Memory"; Le Donne, *Historiographical Jesus*, esp. 41–64; *Historical Jesus*, 29–32; Rodríguez, *Structuring Early Christian Memory*; Schröter, "Jesus and the Canon"; Thatcher, "Why John Wrote a Gospel."

47. E.g., Dunn, *Jesus Remembered*, 209.

48. Le Donne, *Historiographical Jesus*, 48.

49. Eve argues in this way against Dunn, drawing on material from his chapter 5 where anecdotal evidence from Bailey compared with an account from Rena Hogg's biography suggests reshaping quite early. See Eve, *Behind the Gospels*, 112.

Jens Schröter.[50] He argues that from the outset the primitive Jesus tradition was "a free and living" one. He sees the purpose of attributing material to Jesus as an attempt to give authority to Church teaching rather than to record historical reminiscences. Where for Dunn the impact Jesus made on his contemporaries is remembered, for Schröter it is the construct of the second generation of Christians which is remembered as they try to meet their current needs. Whereas Dunn and Le Donne see stability in the tradition, Schröter is more inclined towards variability. Other scholars situate themselves in between.

Alan Kirk, Tom Thatcher and Rafael Rodríguez have much in common in rejecting a thoroughly constructivist notion of social memory and favoring instead a model in which the past is seen as continuing to exert influence on the present, with the present offering frameworks for viewing the past.[51] Rodríguez appeals to Schwartz for the notion that the social memory of the past contains a stable core, around which other elements are changed to meet current needs. Rodríguez suggests that one form a stable core may take is in persistent historical reputation. For him Jesus's reputation largely serves the same role as Jesus's impact upon his contemporaries does for Dunn. Although Rodríguez emphasizes the stability and continuity of the Jesus tradition, he is more ready than Dunn to acknowledge its malleability. In particular Rodríguez sees that memory may distort the past, not through deliberately falsifying it, but through interpreting it in the light of present needs.

Thatcher explores the notion of interpretation in relation to the Fourth Gospel. He suggests that as time passed, there developed a need to adjust the community's understanding of Jesus to meet current needs. For John, memory was not essentially concerned with retrieving facts from the past, but with reaching a proper understanding of the past. The role of the Holy Spirit was to lead the disciples to a correct understanding. Thatcher's view is that John subscribed to what he calls a "charismatic" view of memory. By that he means a view in which the Spirit guaranteed the way Jesus was remembered in the community. Thatcher in effect combines his theory of charismatic memory with a notion of collective memory in which the past matters with a role of supporting a particular dogmatic position in the present. He sees shared memory as stable not at the level of fixed content, but at the level of shared meanings.

---

50. Schröter, "Jesus and the Canon," 104–146.

51. Kirk, "Social and Cultural Memory," 1–42; Thatcher, "Why John Wrote a Gospel," 25–42; Rodríguez, *Structuring Early Christian Memory*.

What Thatcher has done is to highlight the role of interpretation in memory. However, to interpret the past we employ shared frameworks and language which themselves stem from the past. This suggests that the past actually remains immanent in the present. This can be used to argue against a "constructivist" approach and in favor of a "continuity" approach. The past is not completely an invention of the present. Nevertheless, those who favor some form of continuity model have to recognize that collective memory is "an interpretation of the past from the perspective of the present."[52] It follows that collective memory is really a complex interaction of past and present. The result is that there is some continuity or stability in memory, but there is also variation. It is at this point social memory theory and some of the theories of oral tradition converge. Kelber, for example, argues "Variability and stability, conservatism and creativity, evanescence and unpredictability all mark the pattern of oral transmission."[53] To sum up, memory cannot survive completely stable and undistorted. We now proceed to consider some of the forms which distortion may take.

## Memory Distortion

"Distortion" is a technical term to describe the shaping and reshaping which occurs with each act of remembering. In the course of time memories may become vague or colored or emphasized. It may apply to both individual memory and collective memory. The simplest act of distortion occurs when we choose to remember something and forget other things. For the avoidance of doubt, it should be said that this form of distortion is not meant to imply any deliberate influence upon memory,[54] such as carried out by Holocaust revisionists who deny that there was ever a plan to exterminate the Jews or that such a plan was ever set in place. Rather this form of distortion is an inevitable part of remembering.

Michael Schudson lists four types of distortion which occur.[55] There is distanciation with which time recedes and memory is reshaped, losing detail

---

52. Eve, *Writing the Gospels*, 111.
53. Kelber, *Oral and the Written Gospel*, 33.
54. Le Donne does not like the expression "memory distortion" for this very reason and suggests in its place "memory refraction" (Le Donne, *Historiographical Jesus*, 52; *Historical Jesus*, 108). He draws his imagery from a telescope and the bending of light in its lenses. The result is that an object not visible to the naked eye appears larger and so becomes visible. We do not see the object as it really is but a "distorted" version through the refracted light. This is a useful image to understand memory distortion, but the term distortion is more widely used in the literature.
55. Schudson, "Dynamics of Distortion," 348–59.

and emotional intensity, allowing people to gain historical perspective regarding events which were hard to grasp when they happened. Then there is instrumentalization, where the past is used in the service of present interests, perhaps to understand the world as it is today. Next we have narrativization where a version of the past is encapsulated into some sort of cultural form for the sake of passing it on, generally taking the form of a story and following the conventions of narrative. The fourth is conventionalization in which the past becomes knowable. Schudson suggests that adults remember, from their own lives, not what they experienced but what they learn they are conventionally supposed to have experienced. He likens this to a traveler who remembers the road signs better than the landscape he has passed through. The point is that the past which comes to be known is one which has been formed in some way according to a social convention rather than the one experienced without being specifically constructed.

At this stage we note a particular kind of "conventionalization" in the form of schema-based errors. To understand such errors, we need to say a little about *schemata*, a topic which we shall explore in greater detail in the Methodology chapter. In the meantime we note that schemata are frameworks which we employ to make sense of our experiences and to help us when we later wish to recall them. A particular type of schemata is known as a *script*. It refers to the sequence of actions with which an event typically takes place. A common example of this is the routine followed when we dine in a restaurant. However, if an event occurs which does not conform to our customary schemata, we may reshape it to fit better the schema we expect. This may be illustrated by an experiment conducted in the early 1930s by Frederick Bartlett.[56] He asked his Edwardian English participants to read the Native American story entitled "War of the Ghosts" and to remember it numerous times at extended intervals. Most significant among Bartlett's findings was that where the story's components did not match the listener's own schemata, these components were dropped from the recollection or radically altered into other more familiar forms.[57]

Although schema theories are generally regarded as successful, progress has been made since Bartlett's day. One flaw in his approach was that his instructions to participants were rather vague. According to Baddeley, when Gauld and Stephenson (1967) gave clear instructions emphasizing the need for accurate recall, almost half the errors were eliminated.[58] It

---

56. Bartlett, *Remembering*, 199–214.

57. The version of the story delivered by each participant reflected his or her culture, in this case Edwardian English. One example was that some participants remembered the "canoes" as "boats."

58. Baddeley, *Memory*, 139.

turned out that many of the distortions which Bartlett had observed were caused by deliberate guessing rather than real memory problems. Brewer and Treyens (1981) suggested that Bartlett's schema theory is not properly applicable to everyday life, since it involved intentional learning with participants reading a text and knowing they would later be assessed, while ordinarily much of what we remember is acquired incidentally.[59] Nevertheless, the experiment which they conducted did show clear evidence of schemas causing memory errors.[60] Research carried out on brain-damaged patients has shown the importance of the prefrontal cortex for script memory.[61] Those who had impairment of this area of the brain had difficulty with tasks requiring script organization. It remains true that some memory distortions are schema based.

One particular form of schema-based error is narrativization distortion which we shall now consider in some detail. We begin with the experience which then passes and what we are left with is the memory or the impact made by the experience. This impact may take more than one form. There may be an emotional side such as fear or encouragement, but there is also an ability to relate the experience to oneself or others. It is appropriate to distinguish these two forms of impact. Psychologist David Pillemer argues that verbal and narrative memory appears to be a different system from memory of emotional and sensory information.[62] This helps to explain why children cannot remember things before age of three: they do not have the vocabulary for narrative memory retention, which helps put things together so they can be remembered. The ability to articulate a memory is closely tied up with the storage of that memory or at least the retrieval of it. For when we remember an experience, we are not simply retrieving a copy of that experience. Instead we recreate or reconstruct our experience by giving it a narrative structure, often in the form of a story. Such stories follow stereotyped patterns familiar both to the narrator and the audience.

Schudson points out that narrativization not only seeks to report the past but also to simplify it and make it interesting. He gives as an example the film "Sound of Music."[63] Although this exemplifies narrativization, it is a more sophisticated form than the story telling for conversation which

---

59. Baddeley, *Memory*, 186.

60. Participants were given time in a graduate student's office which contained schema-consistent objects and schema-inconsistent objects and had some schema-consistent objects missing. Later they recalled confidently schema-consistent objects not present in the room.

61. Baddeley, *Memory*, 183–84.

62. Pillemer, *Momentous Events*, 99–135.

63. Schudson, "Dynamics of Distortion," 357.

children need to learn.[64] Pillemer deals with how children learn to construct and share personal memories.[65] Drawing on research carried out by developmental psychologists, he stresses the important role adults have in guiding this process for children. As they learn to speak, they begin to develop a narrative about their lives. Adults teach them rules about how to remember important details and share these with others. So children learn that an account of the past must choose a point to begin; their story must have a beginning, middle and end; and a fictional story may be introduced with the words, "Once upon a time." Without learning the conventions prevalent in their society children may be unable to express their memories or communicate them successfully to others.

An event may be remembered because it shares something in common with other plots,[66] characters and settings, already known. In the case of dreams, there was a particular convention commonly used throughout the ANE to relate message dreams, which we shall note in the chapter on dreams. Here we simply note that the narration of Joseph's dreams follows that convention. The reconstruction of an experience in its narrative form is what is recalled in future acts of remembering. Neuroscientist Steven Rose comments on what happens in the brain during recall: "Indeed there is good evidence that the act of recall, retrieval, evokes a further biochemical cascade, analogous to, though not identical with, that occurring during initial learning. The act of recall remakes a memory, so that the next time one remembers it one is not remembering the initial event but the remade memory of the last time it was invoked."[67]

We may apply this theory to Matthew 1–2 only if we are prepared to believe the dreams actually occurred.[68] The dreams would then be Joseph's

---

64. Since a film narrates an event for the purposes of public entertainment, it is likely to engage in greater distortion than simple story-telling. Schudson recognizes this himself, for he comments that the "Sound of Music" left the image of the Austrians as noble folk resisting the Nazis, when in fact they may have been willing victims of Nazism.

65. Pillemer, *Momentous Events*, 99–135.

66. Fentress and Wickham draw attention to the function of a plot as a mnemotechnique, saying: "A plot functions as a complex of memory image, and learning a repertoire of plots is equivalent to learning a large-scale mnemotechnique that permits the ordering, retention, and subsequent transmission of a vast amount of information" (Fentress and Wickham, *Social Memory*, 72).

67. Rose, *Future of the Brain*, 161–62, cited by McIver, *Memory*, 68.

68. The present writer does not think so, but France does, saying, "This remarkable concentration (sc. on Joseph), compared with the complete silence on Joseph elsewhere, may indicate that Matthew's infancy material (except for 2:1–12 . . .) derives from special traditions originating with Joseph" (France, *Matthew*, 76).

experience and they could then be distinguished from the narrative in which they are now cast. Moreover, the stories in which Joseph's dreams are presented also incorporate other events such as his taking Mary as his wife, escaping with his family to Egypt and later returning. To this have been added OT fulfillment quotations. The amount of narrativization distortion could then be regarded as considerable.

Le Donne adds a fifth category to Schudson's four—articulation.[69] This can be done in many ways, through ritual, such as a religious observance, or through art, but it is most frequently conveyed through language, verbal or written. This is arguably the most important of Halbwachs's "social frameworks." But it is also a form of distortion, for in the process of communication, we engage in interpretation.

Eve suggests source-attribution error as another form of distortion.[70] We may forget where we learned something or wrongly attribute to a person what someone else said. We may be confused about whether we actually did something or simply thought about doing it. We may imagine that we saw an event which we were only told about.

I wish to suggest yet another form of distortion and that is *"translation distortion."* The dream narratives may have been expressed by Joseph or Matthew's source in Hebrew or, more likely, Aramaic and also preserved in that language before someone, Matthew or another, translated them into the Greek in which we now have them. This could also apply to the narrative of events in Jesus's life as well as his teaching. However, it has to be assumed that these circulated in Aramaic, or even Hebrew, before they ever appeared in Greek in the gospels.[71] Translation inevitably involves interpretation and

---

69. Le Donne, *Historiographical Jesus*, 52.

70. Eve, *Behind the Gospels*, 91; Eve, *Writing the Gospels*, 89.

71. Most current scholarly opinion would hold that Jesus taught in Aramaic. This is a view which can be traced as far back as 1929 and the work of G. Dalman, who stated that, though Jesus may have known Hebrew, and probably spoke Greek, he certainly taught in Aramaic (Dalman, *Jesus-Jeshua*). This is referred to by Porter, whose own view is that it is virtually certain that Jesus used Greek at various times in his itinerant ministry, including to teach (Porter, "Did Jesus Ever Teach In Greek?," 199–235). In that case, no translation would be necessary. Porter also refers to Matthew Black who, pursues a different line of thinking (Black, *Aramaic Approach*). Black admits the "translation" is not literal but literary; in other words, it is doubtful if it can be justly described as translation at all in some cases. If the Evangelists wrote things up in their own style, even where they appear to record Jesus's words, the distortion is all the greater. These issues do not apply to the same extent to the narrative of events, such as Joseph's dreams. However, if translation distortion did occur, we still have to assume that the narratives were first expressed in Aramaic or, less likely, Hebrew. This is certainly possible, given the conclusion reached in this study, that they emerged from a Jewish Christian background, strongly influenced by OT. We cannot know for certain the original form

sometimes a second language does not have a precise word to render the word in the first language. Irrespective of whether the dream narratives had to be rendered into Greek from Aramaic or Hebrew, they are presented to us in a language which is no longer spoken and consequently our understanding of it is limited. This constitutes a problem for Matthew's use of φαίνω (Matt 1:20; 2:13, 19). Does it mean that the angel was seen or that there was a presence without a visual dimension? We shall return to this question in the Matthew chapter, but note here that *translation* distortion is a real problem.

The most relevant forms of distortion for this present study are narrativization, articulation and translation, but instrumentalization is also likely to be involved when we think of the infancy narratives as serving a theological purpose.

## Assmann and Cultural Memory

We leave behind the topic of memory distortion and take up again the development of social memory theory. Jan Assmann has built on Halbwachs's concept of collective memory (*la mémoire collective*) by arguing that as well as social and individual aspects memory also has a cultural dimension.[72] In developing his theory Assmann draws a distinction between cultural memory (*kulturelle Gedächtnis*) and what he calls communicative memory (*kommunikativen Gedächtnis*). The latter is a function of our everyday social and expressive capacities such as conversation, gesture and habit. It is essentially the social aspect of individual memory identified by Halbwachs. It is the kind of memory that binds three or four generations together. Asssmann draws upon Nietzsche's theorizing on the bonding function of memory. In particular Nietzsche had developed the concept of "will's memory." This is based on the resolve to continue to will over and over again what you once willed. It shows that people need memory in order to be able to form social bonds. Assmann comments, "The task of this memory, above all, is to transmit a collective identity. Society inscribes itself in this memory with all its norms and values and creates in the individual the authority that Freud called the superego and that has traditionally been called 'conscience.'"[73]

---

of these narratives and the fact is that we now have them in Greek. However, Pizzuto sees the Aramaic הן underlying the Greek ἰδού (Pizzuto, "Structural Elegance," 724n32). This word is used six times in Matthew 1-2 and sixty-two times throughout the First Gospel. A recent contribution to the debate is made by Gleaves, *Did Jesus Speak Greek?*

72. Assmann, *Religion and Cultural Memory*, esp. 1-30; "Collective Memory," 125-33.

73. Assmann, *Religion and Cultural Memory*, 7.

Against this background Assmann introduces the concept of cultural memory as a special case of communicative memory which has a different temporal structure.[74] It is transmitted through many generations, not simply three or four, reaching far back into the past. It may be suggested that this is not relevant to Matthew's Gospel as he wrote within two or three generations from the time of Jesus. However, his accounts, especially but not exclusively in the infancy narratives, carry echoes of earlier traditions, such as Moses and the decrees of Pharaoh. Moreover, if Matthew was writing with the intention of ensuring that people continued to remember these events, then they would become religious tradition for future generations.

The key to understanding what is distinctive about cultural memory is the concept of tradition. While collective memory (*Kollektivgedächtnis*) refers to shared memories whose task is to transmit a collective identity, cultural memory (*kulturelle Gedächtnis*) is a step beyond this because it refers to shared memories which become part of a tradition. This stands in marked contrast to Halbwachs's thinking which distinguished living memory (*mémoire vécue*) from tradition. Cultural memory encompasses everything that belongs to cultural traditions. The full range includes rituals, festivals, oral stories, writing and canonical texts. All these require to be studied with sensitivity to the way in which they shape and are shaped by cultural memory. But by carefully analyzing them we are able to grasp the structures and dynamics of cultural memory.

For Assmann the concept of tradition takes on added significance. Tradition typically refers to the conscious handing down of a heritage. It leaves no place for the unconscious. Assmann is critical of the idea of a collective or cultural unconscious, but he does want to find room for an expanded concept of tradition "that includes unconscious aspects of transmission and transfer across the generations."[75]

Assmann illustrates his theory with a variety of examples drawn from the cultural memory of ancient Egypt on which he is an expert, the Hebrew Bible and other sources. He shows how Deuteronomy can be read as a text in "making memory" in Nietzsche's sense: "What the children of Israel must not forget is, on the one hand, the law, and, on the other, the story of the exodus from Egypt that has been lived through and that thereby acquires the status of a normative past."[76] He then shows that Deuteronomy lists no fewer

---

74. Assmann says this in the light of a comment by Aleida Assmann that tradition can be treated as a special case of communication with information not exchanged reciprocally but transmitted vertically through generations (Assmann, *Religion and Cultural Memory*, 8).

75. Assmann, *Religion and Cultural Memory*, 26.

76. Assmann, *Religion and Cultural Memory*, 17.

than seven different procedures of culturally formed memory: learning by heart; education and conversational remembering; making visible through body-marking; storing up and publication; festivals of collective remembering; oral transmission; and canonization of the text of the covenant.[77] What we see is that cultural memory is based on communication through media. The most basic form of this is oral speech or conversation, which is what we claim lies behind Matthew's dream narratives. A more sophisticated form of communication is writing a text which is what Matthew has given us. Astrid Erll points out that this has the potential to broaden the temporal and spatial range of remembrance.[78]

Of particular significance in Assmann's theory is how integral cultural memory is to religion. He presents numerous biblical quotations (e.g., Deut 4:9; 31:19–21) which reiterate the need to pass along cultural memories from generation to generation. These memories give a group or a people its identity. So Assmann has grasped the close connection that exists between cultural memory and identity, just as John Locke saw that individual memory and identity are closely linked.[79] When people remember something shared by their community, they are identifying themselves with that community. As the intention here is to analyze the patterns of memory evidenced in ancient dream narratives,[80] it is hoped that something can be said about the identity of any people who may have shared with Matthew in the transmission of the narratives of Joseph's dreams. Assmann has shown that cultural memory is integral to religious identity.

## Social Memory and the Quest for the Historical Jesus

Social memory theory has been applied by Dunn to the Quest for the Historical Jesus. He focuses his attention on oral tradition and the faith of Jesus's first followers. He maintains that Jesus made an impact on those who became his first disciples; that that original impact continued to be expressed, as memories of it were transmitted orally to a variety of audiences; that we today can gain a clear indication of the impression Jesus made on his first disciples by looking at the characteristic features of the

---

77. Assmann, *Religion and Cultural Memory*, 18–19.
78. Erll, "Cultural Memory Studies," 389.
79. Locke, *Essay Concerning Human Understanding* 2.27.
80. This will be done in the chapter entitled "Comparison of Memory Patterns."

Jesus tradition.[81] So what we get back to is Jesus Remembered.[82] We shall never be able to reach back to Jesus himself. The only realistic goal we can have is Jesus remembered.[83]

Dunn is optimistic about how accurate our impression of Jesus may be because of the reliability he attaches to the oral tradition. This reliability is based in part on oral tradition as foundational and formative of group identity.[84] He suggests that the structure, identifying elements, and key words were established, and "corporate memory" was ready to protest if an oral performance varied too much.[85]

Dunn overestimates the reliability of the oral tradition. It seems reasonable to suppose that there would be a certain amount of creativity during the period of oral tradition. Dunn does recognize that there probably were several traditions or versions of the tradition *from the first*. However, this is something which he admits he finds "uncomfortable."[86]

The approach taken in this study is similar to that of Dunn insofar as we both use social memory theory and both lay emphasis on oral transmission. However, our goals are entirely different. Whereas Dunn was concerned to reach back to the impact which Jesus made on his disciples, their perceptions which underpin and underlie the gospel narrative, we are concerned with the techniques built into the narrative to assist its retention in memory.

## Individual Memory and the Quest for the Historical Jesus

Where Dunn concentrated on social memory, there are some NT scholars who have concentrated on individual memory. One example is Richard Bauckham in *Jesus and the Eyewitnesses*. He maintains that the gospel writers would have looked for eyewitnesses rather than recording community traditions. He argues that such eyewitnesses were important in antiquity because they remained accessible sources and authoritative guarantors of their own testimony through the period between the life of Jesus and the writing of the gospels.[87] A major part of Bauckham's argument rests on his

81. This is essentially Dunn's thesis in Dunn, *New Perspective on Jesus*.

82. This is in fact the title of Dunn's major work on the subject: *Jesus Remembered*. Its full title is *Christianity in the Making: Jesus Remembered*.

83. Dunn, *Jesus Remembered*, 327–38.

84. Dunn, *New Perspective on Jesus*, 44.

85. Dunn, *New Perspective on Jesus*, 55.

86. Dunn, *New Perspective on Jesus*, 51.

87. Bauckham, *Jesus and the Eyewitness*, 241.

conviction that the few names that occur in the gospel narratives must be regarded as genuine names of real people who were involved personally in the events reported (e.g., Bartimaeus, Zacchaeus, Cleopas).[88] He uses Tal Ilan's *Lexicon of Jewish Names in Late Antiquity* (2002–2011) to show that in most cases the persons mentioned in the gospel stories bear common Jewish names. Bauckham is here engaged in new and worthwhile research. However, it does not necessarily prove that eyewitnesses lie behind the gospel narratives. Certain names could have been preserved accurately in collective memories transmitted orally.[89]

Moreover, the passage of time undoubtedly affects memory. Details and sometimes whole events may vanish from the memories even of eyewitnesses. Yet while individual memory fades or changes over a period of time, interestingly group memory appears to be more stable.[90] This lends support to Dunn and those who draw on social memory theory. However, this needs to be qualified by noting Assmann's point that such memory is unlikely to survive beyond a few generations unless an effort is made to fix it in some way, such as writing or ritual, and the likelihood is that it will change due to different social circumstances. Bauckham does acknowledge certain aspects of social memory theory,[91] but he still lays his emphasis on individual memory.[92]

Again we have a scholar whose concern is different from ours. Bauckham's attention is focused on the content of memory, whereas our interest lies in some of the processes of memory. However, we have had another

---

88. Bauckham, *Jesus and the Eyewitness*, 39–92.

89. Schröter takes a different view, arguing that the gospel writers simply gave their narratives a "realistic effect" by choosing names which were common in the Jewish context of ancient Palestine where the narrated events took place, in the same way as the authors of good novels or fictional stories (Schröter, "Gospels as Eyewitness Testimony?," 202).

90. Redman, "How Accurate Are Eyewitnesses?," 186, makes this point, citing Weldon and Bellinger, "Collective Memory," 1160–75; Weldon, "Remembering as a Social Process," 67–120.

91. Bauckham, *Jesus and the Eyewitness*, 290–318, deals with Collective Memory theory under the heading "Anonymous Tradition or Eyewitness Testimony?" He distinguishes three features: (a) the social dimension of individual recollection—the language, for example, in which a memory is expressed is a social construct; (b) the shared recollections of a group; and (c) collective memory. He readily embraces the first two aspects, but uses the term "collective memory" to refer to the traditions of a group about events which are recollected personally by any individual member of the group. See Bauckham, *Jesus and the Eyewitness*, 313–14.

92. Bauckham says, "The recollections of individuals may help to form collective memory, but they are not the same as collective memory" (Bauckham, *Jesus and the Eyewitness*, 315).

reason for touching on recent studies in the Quest for the Historical Jesus. The dream narratives belong to the wider context of the infancy narratives. Although Jesus's infancy is far removed from his ministry and passion, it is still part of his life. We now consider the historicity of the infancy narratives and what bearing it has on the present study if it turns out that they are narrative fiction.

## Infancy Narratives

The infancy narratives are not treated in detail by Dunn or Bauckham, although they do make reference to them. Bauckham tells us that he deliberately omitted them from his discussion because he regarded them as a special case,[93] a view shared by the majority of gospel scholars. He suggests that the chronology makes it difficult to relate them to eyewitness testimony in the same way that he postulates for the majority of the other gospel traditions. He confesses that he does not have a firm view on their origins.

Dunn begins his treatment of Jesus's life with his baptism. He prefaces this with a section titled "Why not 'beginning from Bethlehem'?" He lists several reasons for rejecting the synoptic birth narratives as his starting point. His first rationale relates to his proposed historical method that seeks to trace the earliest disciples' memories of Jesus. There is no evidence that the magi became disciples and transmitted to others memories of the events surrounding Jesus's birth. We might want to treat Joseph as the source for the episodes involving him, particularly the dreams. However, he is not mentioned by name in the gospel after 2:19 and does not appear again in Matthew's lengthy narrative. Dunn's second objection is that the birth narratives have been contrived to bring out various significant allusions and theological emphases, not least by Matthew himself. The theory is that the birth narratives are a form of Midrash that wove together OT narrative motifs to create a "theological tale" that has no real basis in history. He questions the veracity of the slaughter of the innocents.[94] While it is not out of character for Herod, it is unlikely to have escaped the notice of Josephus. He suggests that the whole Egyptian episode, including Joseph and Mary's return to settle in Nazareth, does seem somewhat contrived. He takes the view that the birth narratives did not develop until the period after Easter since at their heart

---

93. Bauckham, "In Response to my Respondents," 232.

94. Dunn suggests that memories of the destruction of Sepphoris (or the surrounding villages) in consequence of the uprising which followed the death of Herod in 4 BCE were the contributing factor to the Matthean episode.

lies the affirmation that Jesus is both son of David and Son of God.[95] This suggests that these narratives are not historically reliable.

The matter may be approached from a different angle. The appearance of the angel of the Lord in Joseph's dreams exemplifies a type known as a message dream.[96] Clearly this is very different from our own dreams which tend to be episodic, generally consisting of a sequence of events or experiences. Moreover, we have difficulty in remembering our dreams, even immediately after we wake. In relation to the message dreams of antiquity a classical scholar by the name of William Harris proposed six tests which may indicate lack of authenticity in their descriptions.[97] Some of these apply to the infancy narratives.[98] The accounts claim to describe Joseph's dreams, not Matthew's own experience. They serve the narrator's purposes. The first, for example, makes Joseph reverse his plan to divorce Mary quietly and instead take her as his wife. Moreover the dreams predict events which subsequently occur—the birth of Mary's son who will save his people from their sins and Herod's attempt to slaughter the child. These features[99] suggest that the dreams may have been invented[100] by Matthew or any source he may have used.[101] This is not surprising given the tendency in the ancient world to invent dreams for propaganda as well as literary purposes, as, for example, to enhance a ruler's prestige.

---

95. Dunn, *Jesus Remembered*, 347.

96. Oppenheim, "Mantic Dreams," 341–50, distinguished between message dreams and symbolic dreams.

97. Harris says a dream may be suspect "if (i) it claims to describe someone else's dream, not the writer's own experience; (ii) it in any way serves the narrator's conscious or unconscious purposes; (iii) it makes a fully coherent story; (iv) it lacks dream-like qualities, such as 'bizarreness' or weakened self-control; (v) it in any way predicts an event which subsequently occurred; and (vi) it was dreamt 'on demand'" (Harris, *Dreams and Experience*, 105–6).

98. Three of Harris's tests are especially relevant here: (i), (ii), and (v).

99. There is also none of the bizarreness, illogicality or lack of self control which typify our dreams. However, given that different kinds of dreams occur in different cultures, this particular argument need not apply.

100. The present writer holds that Joseph's dreams did not actually occur, for the reasons given. It is not being suggested that this type of dream could not happen. Indeed Harris takes the view that at least some of the message dreams reported from antiquity may have occurred.

101. Some of the early Christian community may have been reflecting on Moses typology and similar dreams attributed to Moses's father Amram (see Josephus, *Ant.* 2.212–17) and his sister Miriam (see Pseudo-Philo, *Liber Antiquitatum Biblicarum* 9.10).

## Cultural Memory and the Infancy Narratives

However, this conclusion poses a problem for the research being proposed here. If the infancy narratives are not historically reliable, how can we apply cultural memory theory to them? They are, however, presented in the form of history. Brown makes a useful distinction between historical fact and verisimilitude.[102] The former would be events which are widely acknowledged to have happened, the latter events for which there are serious reasons for thinking that they did not occur,[103] but which nonetheless can be related to features of other events of the same era.[104] It is the latter we have here. The threat to the life of the infant Jesus and the massacre of the children of Bethlehem are at least consistent with what we know of Herod's character from other sources, such as Josephus.

But the issue may be pursued. Can we have a memory of an event which did not happen? Clearly we can retain in our memories information which is factually inaccurate. A witness to an accident may claim that he saw a red car hit a lamppost when it was in fact green. We would call that a false memory and we can distinguish it from the correct memory of a story which is fictitious. We may think of a person accurately relating a story about some of the exploits of the Olympian gods. Southwood Smith reports an incident from the late eighteenth century which displays false memory.[105] In fact it combines the correct memory of a real event with false episodic memory with sailors accurately remembering minute details of an incident, but falsely remembering their own involvement in it. In 1797, the crew of the frigate *Hermione* mutinied and killed the cruel captain Hugh Pigot. An Admiralty official later reported, "In my own experience I have known, on separate occasions, more than six sailors who voluntarily confessed to having struck the first blow at Captain Pigot. These men detailed all the horrid circumstances of the mutiny with extreme minuteness and perfect accuracy; nevertheless, not one of them had ever been in the ship, nor had so much as seen Captain Pigot in their lives. They had obtained, by tradition, from their messmates the particulars of the story. When long on a foreign station, hungering and thirsting for home, their minds became enfeebled; at length they actually believed themselves guilty of the crime over

---

102. Brown, *Birth of the Messiah*, 227.

103. The examples which Brown uses are the flight to Egypt and the massacre at Bethlehem.

104. Brown says, "If one can trace the basic story to another origin, there are good clues as to why it has been cast in its present form" (Brown, *Birth of the Messiah*, 227). He goes on to point out that the latter years of Herod's life were filled with horrors.

105. Smith, "Lectures on Forensic Medicine."

which they had so long brooded, and submitted, with a gloomy pleasure to being sent to England in irons for judgment. At the Admiralty we were always able to detect and establish their innocence, in defiance of their own solemn asseverations."[106]

But what are we to make of an event which an individual reports as a memory but which he has knowingly invented? His account is coming from the realm of imagination rather than memory. Just as Assmann used the concept of cultural memory, so we can have a concept of cultural imagination. The term has appeared from time to time in a wide variety of work and has been used in different ways in different fields of study. It has been used recently by Juliette Harrison in a PhD thesis for the University of Birmingham.[107] She uses the term as an extension of cultural memory into the realm of the imagination and of imaginative literature. She says, "Just as certain memories of events or people survive in the cultural memory and form part of a tradition, certain stories, characters and concepts become increasingly important within the cultural imagination and become equally entrenched in a tradition."[108] She suggests that while historical literature deals mainly with cultural memory in a bid to preserve the memory of the past, imaginative literature is more concerned with reflecting the ideas of the present.

If we apply this kind of thinking to Matthew's infancy narratives, where does it lead us? Some of the material, such as the slaughter of the innocents, may undoubtedly be described as historical record. It describes an allegedly public event, irrespective of whether we regard it as authentic.[109] It is at least "historical verisimilitude," to repeat Brown's phrase. An analysis in terms of cultural memory may then be appropriate.

The descriptions of dreams are different because they narrate the private experience of an individual. Moreover, as we have already seen, there is good reason to suspect that they have been invented or developed by Matthew or any source. However, in antiquity people were familiar with stories of dreams associated with the birth of significant individuals. Herodotus records that before the birth of Cyrus his grandfather Astyages had two dreams, in the first of which he dreamed that his daughter Mandane, Cyrus's mother, made water in such enormous quantities that it filled his city and swamped the whole of Asia and in the second of which he saw a vine grow from her private parts and

---

106. Smith, "Lectures on Forensic Medicine."
107. Harrison, *Cultural Memory and Imagination*.
108. Harrison, *Cultural Memory and Imagination*, 13.
109. Arguments can be put forward for and against the slaughter of the innocents. It is consistent with Herod's character. On the other hand, there is no record of it beyond Matthew's Gospel.

spread over Asia.[110] Dreams connected to the births of important people were also know among the Jews. Josephus records that before the birth of Moses his father Amram experienced a dream.[111] Similarly, Pseudo-Philo notes how Miriam, Moses's sister, dreamed about him before he was born.[112] Matthew or his source may, therefore, be drawing upon ideas and stories already current in the cultural imagination.

From a theoretical perspective Harrison is right to distinguish cultural imagination from cultural memory. However, in practice the two would often merge. Once the stories of Joseph's dreams began to circulate within the Christian community, they would become part of the tradition. Although they lacked an event to be remembered, they had historical semblance and would be transmitted like other events associated with Jesus's life. They would become part of the cultural memory of the recorded events.[113] It follows that cultural memory theory is still relevant to Matthew's infancy narratives and an analysis in terms of memory patterns is still appropriate.

## Transmission of Memories

We now switch our attention to the issue of how memories were transmitted in the period between Jesus's ministry and the writing of the gospels. The process was largely oral in nature, certainly in the early stages, but we cannot rule out the possibility that someone created written narratives prior to the compilation of the gospels.[114] Earlier we saw the reliability which Dunn attached to the oral tradition. For his understanding of the process at work he drew upon the writing of Kenneth Bailey. In a couple of articles published in the 1990s Bailey outlined a model of how he believed the Jesus tradition was transmitted.[115] He based it upon community storytelling practices which he observed while he was working for over 37 years in the Middle East. He claims to have witnessed three models of oral transmission: *informal uncontrolled, formal controlled* and *informal controlled*. The word *"informal"*

---

110. Herodotus, *Histories* 1.107.2. We noted earlier the dream of Agariste, the mother of Pericles, recorded in Plutarch, *Life of Pericles* 3.2.

111. Josephus, *Ant.* 2.212-17.

112. Pseudo-Philo, *Liber Antiquitatum Biblicarum* 9.10.

113. Harrison makes a similar point. See Harrison, *Cultural Memory and Imagination*, 16-17.

114. Foster refers to theories of a pre-Markan passion narrative and a pre-Gospel literary form for the material in Mark 2:1-3:6 (Foster, "Memory, Orality," 206).

115. Bailey, "Informal Controlled Oral Tradition," 34-51; "Middle Eastern Oral Tradition," 363-67.

describes the social setting for the transmission process. He comments: "It is informal in the sense that there is no identifiable teacher nor student and no structure within which material is passed from one person to another."[116] A *formal* setting is the opposite because it does have an identifiable teacher or student or block of material. The word *"controlled"* refers to the regulation of traditions either on the part of individuals or the community. An *uncontrolled* situation is one where there is no such regulation. This would apply with tradition which is not considered wise or important for community identity. The model which Bailey proposes for the transmission of the Jesus material is *informal controlled* oral tradition. This is adopted by Dunn who sees it as the best way to address the various phenomena inherent in the Synoptic tradition.[117] Bauckham also takes account of Bailey's model, but argues that the transmission of the Jesus traditions was *formal* and *controlled*.[118] So both Bauckham and Dunn see some kind of control being exercised over the transmission process, but whereas Dunn sees it happening through the community correcting an individual's recollections, Bauckham sees it coming specifically from eyewitnesses to the original events.

How is Bailey's thesis to be evaluated? He bases his theory on a number of anecdotes rather than any kind of methodical study. He tells us that he heard the stories in *hafalat samar*, which he claims means "parties of preservation," linking the Arabic *samar* with the Hebrew verb שמר, meaning "preserve."[119] However, Weeden maintains on the basis of consultation with Arabic experts that *samar* means "entertainment" or "conversation."[120] Eve rightly points out that not all Bailey's examples can be immediately related to *hafalat samar*.[121] One instance of this is the method which the congregation employed to memorize Bailey's sermon which happened in a church service. Significantly Weeden argues that the purpose of the informal controlled oral tradition illustrated by Bailey's anecdotes is not the preservation of "factually accurate historical information," but the preservation of "the essential core of a story, considered indispensable to a community's self-identity."[122] With this in mind we can say that Bailey's theory of informal controlled oral tradition is useful for our goal, for we are not concerned with the content, as such,

---

116. Bailey, "Informal Controlled Oral Tradition," 35.

117. Bailey's model is explored by Dunn, *Jesus Remembered*, 205–9, 212, 224, 238, 239.

118. Bauckham, *Jesus and the Eyewitness*, 257–58.

119. Bailey, "Informal Controlled Oral Tradition," 36; "Middle Eastern Oral Tradition," 364.

120. Weeden, "Kenneth Bailey's *Theory of Oral Tradition*," 38–42.

121. Eve, *Behind the Gospels*, 80–81.

122. Weeden, "Kenneth Bailey's *Theory of Oral Tradition*," 33–34n29.

of the memories related in Matthew 1–2, but with the identity of those who passed them on, as we explore that identity through some of the processes of oral transmission. The question remains whether the performances which Bailey witnessed in Christian communities in twentieth-century Egypt or Lebanon reflect the experience of people in first-century pre-Islamic Palestine. We cannot be certain, but Bailey himself suggests that the Middle East which he knows is likely to be closer to the social context of the early Christians than the modern West and that the way of life in some parts of the Middle East seems to have changed little with the passing of the centuries, an assumption frequently made by NT scholars. It is therefore possible to use Bailey's anecdotes to illustrate what social memory theorists tell us. Whether or not members of a community intervened in the narration of a story, the memory patterns built into the narrative would exercise some control over its outline, but not the details which could vary, with names or places being changed or descriptions added.

## Summing Up

We are now in a position to sum up the line of thought in this chapter. We have seen that memory is a highly complicated process, beginning, as Aristotle saw, with sense impressions or perception. Both perception and the actual act of remembering involve interpretation, which can be subjective. However, it is also accepted that individual memories can be stabilized to an extent by social groups. Memory is conceived within social frameworks, such as thought categories, language and the memory patterns with which we are concerned in our present study. It is also held in some kind of check by the combined memories of the group. Nevertheless, distortion can occur and in the case of the infancy stories narrativization, articulation and even instrumentalization are likely to be at work. I suggested *translation* as another form of distortion, as the dreams may originally have been narrated in Hebrew or Aramaic, but are now in Greek which is also a foreign language to those studying the text today. We saw how Assmann distinguishes communicative memory which is transmitted through three or four generations from cultural memory which is transmitted through many more, the former referring to shared memories whose task is to transmit a collective identity, while the latter refers to shared memories which become part of a tradition. We saw how Dunn applies social memory theory as well as oral tradition to the Quest for the Historical Jesus, while Bauckham works with the reliability of individual memories, but the work of both is concerned with the content of memory in contrast to this study which focuses on the processes of memory in mnemonic aids. However, we did explore the historicity of the infancy narratives, concluding that they are fiction, but at the same time open to the application of cultural memory theory. Finally, we noted how Bailey's model of oral transmission in twentieth-century Arab communities provides a possible analogy to understand how transmission may have worked among the early Christian communities. We suggested that some of the control exercised over narratives would come from the memory patterns with which we are concerned. In the next chapter we shall outline the methodology which is being used for this study.

# 4

# Methodology

## Introduction

THIS CHAPTER IS CONCERNED with the methodology employed in this current study. We are engaged in a search for patterns of memory embedded in the dream narratives of Matthew's Gospel and when we turn to other literature, Jewish, Greek and Roman, we shall be seeking similar patterns, but only in their dream narratives, so that we are comparing like with like. We will include some vision narratives, where they are presented in a similar way to dream narratives apart from the fact that a dream occurs in sleep, whereas a vision is a waking experience.[1] We acknowledge that there are other visions which are substantially different because of their length and complexity. Once these patterns have been found, Matthew's set will be compared with the other sets with a view to establishing Matthew's cultural setting.

In the second chapter we have already noted ways in which memories could be transmitted orally, using formulaic expressions, repetition and parallelism, but we also observed how these techniques could be applied to writing to achieve a more elegant style. In the last chapter we considered memory theory, noting the social context in which memory is learned, expressed, preserved and held in check. In this chapter we outline the methodology which will be used to achieve our goal.

We begin by noting what the ancients themselves had to say about memory patterns and rhetorical devices. We move on from there to try and establish a definition to cover those devices most commonly used to aid memory. We look at ways in which these memory devices may

---

1. Balaam's experience (Num 22:9–13, 20–21); Elijah's *Wecktraümen* (1 Kgs 19:5–7); five visions in Acts (Acts 9:3–9, 10–17; 10:3–8, 9–16; 22:17–21); and Balaam's experience (Num 22:31–35) as recounted in Philo, *De Vita Mosis* 1.273–74.

be recognized and potential problems may be resolved. Finally we consider the difficulty which arises for this study from the cultural overlap of memory patterns and resolve it by looking out for the few patterns which may be culturally specific and by taking account of the frequency with which each device is used author by author in a bid to work out how they typically express themselves.

## Ancient Comment on Memory Devices

Ancient writers were well aware of the devices which were used mnemonically and stylistically. We find comments by the anonymous author of *ad Herennium*, Cicero in *De Oratore*, and Quintilian in *Institutio Oratoria*.[2] We choose to quote Cicero because his writing on these devices is considerably briefer than that of the others. He achieves this brevity through dispensing with definitions and examples. What Cicero has to say is this:

> Of words themselves, as of arms, there is a sort of threatening and attack for use, and also a management for grace. For the reiteration of words has sometimes a peculiar force, and sometimes elegance; as well as the variation or deflexion of a word from its common signification; and the frequent repetition of the same word in the beginning, and recurrence to it at the end, of a period; forcible emphasis on the same words; conjunction; adjunction; progression, a sort of distinction as to some word often used; the recall of a word; the use of words, also, which end similarly, or have similar cadences, or which balance one another, or which correspond to one another. There is also a certain gradation, a conversion, an elegant exaggeration of the sense of words; there is antithesis, asyndeton, declination reprehension, exclamation, diminution; the use of the same word in different cases; the referring of what is derived from many particulars to each particular singly; reasoning subservient to your proposition, and reasoning suited to the order of distribution; concession; and again another kind of doubt; the introduction of something unexpected; enumeration; another correction; division; continuation; interruption; imagery; answering your own questions; immutation; disjunction; order; relation; digression; and circumscription. These are the figures, and others like

---

2. See Anonymous, *ad Herennium* 4.13–34; Cicero, *De Oratore* 3.206–8; Quintilian, *Institutio* 9.1–3.

these, or there may even be more, which adorn language by peculiarities in thought or structure of style.³

On a first reading this appears to be all about style. Cicero speaks about "a management of grace" and figures "which adorn language." Other writers are similar, with the author of *ad Herennium* referring to the figures as *exornationes*.⁴ This term suggests something to do with adornment rather than memory.⁵ However, if Cicero and others wanted to be persuasive, as Aristotle suggested, that would entail a desire that the Senate or whatever audience should remember their speech.⁶ In that case devices for style and memory become entwined. Admittedly Cicero does deal with memory in *De Oratore*, but here his concern is what we would call "artificial memory" and how a speaker might manage to memorize his speech and recite it from memory.⁷ Our concern is how to enable the audience to remember it.

Cicero knew that his readers were already familiar with rhetorical devices. Education in antiquity encouraged young men to read Homer in order to embody it.⁸ Through such reading they would be taught formulaic expressions and other mnemonic devices used by the poet, if they had not already become acquainted with them when they learned language and discourse. The use of such devices would become second nature to them. When it came to their use for stylistic purposes, the students would already be well familiar with many of them. Cicero would be inclined to agree. In the short section which follows the piece quoted above, Crassus who is the voice of Cicero in the dialogue responds in such terms to Cotta who comments on the lack of definitions and examples:

> "These remarks, Crassus," said Cotta, "I perceive that you have poured forth to us without any definitions or examples, because you imagined us acquainted with them." "I did not, indeed," said Crassus, "suppose that any of the things which I previously

---

3. Cicero, *De Oratore* 3.206–8. Watson states that he based his translation on that of George Barnes published in 1762. Watson's own translation is available in book form, for which see the bibliography. It is also available online through the website of Pomona College in California.

4. The writer means "figures of speech." Later Roman writers of rhetoric used the word *figura* as a translation of the Greek σχῆμα, but this had not yet come into use.

5. L & S 690, suggest the basic meaning is "adorning, decorating, embellishing."

6. Admittedly this would be likely to involve short-term memory, as a speaker on most occasions would wish his audience to follow his argument rather than remember his speech long after he had finished.

7. See Cicero, *De Oratore* 2.350–60.

8. For the reading of Homer, see Cribiore, *Gymnastics of the Mind*, 194–97, 204–5; Morgan, *Literate Education*.

mentioned were new to you, but acted merely in obedience to the inclinations of the whole company."[9]

It would be wrong to suggest that all the devices which Cicero mentions serve a mnemonic purpose. Indeed some might have the opposite effect. For example, *division* might lead the speaker into details of an argument and it is precisely details which a listener might find difficult to remember. Likewise *interruption* and *digression* may distract the listener from the flow of an argument. Our difficulty is that there is little hard evidence which allows us to distinguish those devices which assist memory from those which do not. The ancients themselves did not specify how they were using the various techniques. We therefore have to use our own judgment. If a particular technique appears to us to hinder memory, as with the examples just given, then it seems reasonable to assume that its function is not mnemonic. We may ask why a writer would choose a more complicated technique when simpler ones are available, unless his goal is primarily stylistic.

It may also be that a writer has a stylistic goal in mind when he uses a device excessively. For example, Diodorus Siculus says of Gorgias: "He was the first to use extravagant figures of speech marked by deliberate art."[10] Gorgias did not invent such figures, but they are characteristic of his style.[11] Although most ancient critics did not view these devices favorably, orators did use them more sparingly and in less extreme forms.[12] The discernment of stylistic intent may only be possible with a few writers such as Gorgias. The same is true of literature written in the Asiatic style which flourished in the period of the Roman Empire, having developed in the eastern Mediterranean, especially at Rhodes. However, very little in this style survives because it fell out of fashion so quickly.[13] The writer of *ad Herennium* advises against excessive use of devices: "To ensure this virtue (i.e., artistic composition) we shall avoid the frequent collision of vowels, which makes the style harsh and gaping . . . we shall also avoid the excessive recurrence of the same letter . . . and again we shall avoid the excessive repetition of the same word . . . again we shall not use a continuous series of words with like case

---

9. Cicero, *De Oratore* 3.208. See footnote 3.

10. See Diodorus Siculus, *Bibliotheca Historica* 12.53–54. Gorgias lived from c. 485 BCE to c. 380 BCE.

11. Kennedy says, "Gorgias simply borrowed a number of techniques of poetry and developed to an extreme the natural Greek habit of antithesis" (Kennedy, *Art of Persuasion in Greece*, 64).

12. Kennedy, *Art of Persuasion in Greece*, 66.

13. Rose, *Handbook of Greek Literature*, 362–64.

endings."[14] Aelius Theon, the author of a collection of preliminary exercises (*progymnasmata*) for the training of orators in the first century CE, advises avoidance of metrical and rhythmical style.[15]

We may therefore regard rhetorical devices as serving a stylistic purpose, where they appear to hinder memory or where they are used excessively. With regard to the rhetorical devices listed by Cicero, some may have come from an era of oral communication and originally functioned as memory patterns, although they could be used later for style, while others may have come from a more rhetorical era. However, what they all have in common is oral performance.

Our interest does not lie primarily in style, but in their mnemonic function, although we concede that even style may impact memory. A writer may have found such devices already embedded in his source material, intended to aid the process of transmission, as it was passed down to him. Equally well he may have inserted them into his material to assist his readership or audience remember what he has written. This is what we understand properly as "memory patterns."

## Definition of Memory Patterns

We have already encountered formulaic expressions, repetition, parallelism and some examples of *inclusio*. We now consider other techniques used in oral transmission to help preserve the outline of a narrative, variously referred to as memory patterns, aids or devices. Ong refers to the way in which people compose and recall in an oral society:

> How could you ever call back to mind what you had so laboriously worked out? The answer is: Think memorable thoughts . . . you have to do your thinking in mnemonic patterns, shaped for ready oral recurrence.
>
> Your thoughts must come into being in heavily rhythmic, balanced patterns, in repetitions or antitheses, in alliterations and assonances, in epithetic and other formulary expressions, in standard thematic settings . . . in proverbs . . . or in other mnemonic form.[16]

---

14. Anonymous, *Ad Herennium* 4.17.
15. Theon, *Progymnasmata* 71. See Kennedy, *Progymnasmata*, 14.
16. Ong, *Orality and Literacy*, 34.

To support this assertion Ong draws on the work of other writers.[17] In his quotation Ong lists many of the standard memory patterns, recognized by modern writers. Achtemeier lists others used in the semi-literate world of NT: *inclusio*, anaphora, parallelism, and wordplay.[18] We may also add acrostic and typology, as their presence is recognized in the OT.[19]

At this stage a definition of memory pattern is called for. Ong does not offer us one and so we need to look elsewhere. We shall proceed by drawing upon the work of ancient authors and where their writings prove inadequate, we shall draw upon modern authors, gradually expanding until we find an adequate definition.

We noted above how ancient writers refer to various devices without distinguishing their mnemonic and stylistic functions. The unknown author of *Rhetorica ad Herennium* works with his own distinction: he divides the devices into figures of diction and figures of thought and defines each in turn: "It is a figure of diction if the adornment is comprised in the fine polish of the language itself. A figure of thought derives a certain distinction from the idea, not from the words."[20] He speaks of adornment and distinction, showing that his concern is largely the embellishment of style, where our interest in these figures lies in their memory function, which he does not mention explicitly.

We find the same problem in a modern definition of these devices. Kennedy distinguishes a figure of speech from a figure of thought.[21] He says of the former that it "results from manipulation of sound or arrangement of words in the context." He describes a figure of thought as "an unexpected change in syntax or an arrangement of the ideas, as opposed to the words, within a sentence, which calls attention to itself."

---

17. Ong cites Jousse, *Le Parlant*, who "has shown the intimate linkage between rhythmic oral patterns, the breathing process, gesture, and the bilateral symmetry of the human body in ancient Aramaic and Hellenic targums, and thus also in ancient Hebrew" (Jousse quoted in Ong, *Orality and Literacy*, 34). Likewise he draws upon Havelock (Havelock, *Preface to Plato*, 97–98, 294–301) to assert that "among the ancient Greeks, Hesiod, who was intermediate between oral Homeric Greece and fully developed Greek literacy, delivered quasi-philosophic material in the formulaic verse forms." He even uses the fiction writer Chinua Achebe's *No Longer at Ease*, which draws directly on Ibo oral tradition in West Africa, to "provide abundant instances of thought patterns of orally educated characters who move in these oral, mnemonically tooled grooves" (Achebe quoted in Ong, *Orality and Literacy*, 35).

18. Achtemeier, "*Omne verbum sonat*," 3–27.

19. An example of acrostic is to be found in Psalm 25. Allison speaks of Joshua and other OT characters as being portrayed as a "new Moses" (Allison, *New Moses*, 23–91).

20. Anonymous, *Ad Herennium* 4.13.18.

21. Kennedy, *New Testament Interpretation*, 27.

Although Kennedy is concerned about these features as "persuasive tools" in rhetorical style,[22] he does draw attention to sound and the arrangement of words and ideas. Two of these features were in fact highlighted by Quintilian. He tells us first that *figures of speech* fall into two main classes: "One is defined as the form of language, while the other is mainly to be sought in *the arrangement of words*."[23] Later he refers to a third class which "*attracts the ear of the audience* and excites their attention by some resemblance, equality or contrast of words."[24]

First we note the attention focused on sound by both Kennedy and Quintilian. Although sound may have a euphonic role in appealing to an audience, it may also aid memory. If we recall what Ong said about memory patterns, we may note how many of the items on his list involve sound, such as alliteration, assonance and even rhythm. Clearly any definition will need to take account of sound.

Next we take account of what Kennedy and Quintilian say about the arrangement of words and more especially ideas. Again such arrangements may serve stylistic goals. However, we may set this alongside what the ancient writers had to say about artificial memory. We saw in the Memory chapter how the Roman writers discussed a technique which allowed an orator to improve his memory and deliver a long speech with precision. It involved imprinting on the memory a series of places, drawn from a journey or an architectural system, then attaching to these places the images of what he wished to remember. As he delivered his speech, the practitioner could move in imagination through his memory building or road, picking up from the memorized places the images of the points he wished to speak about. What lies at the heart of this theory is a sense of order in which material is presented. The narration of any event or the exposition of thoughts requires orderly arrangement so that they may be easily remembered by the speaker and easily absorbed by the listeners. It would appear that the writers on artificial memory have taken something which already happened and developed it to extraordinary lengths.

We recall how Ong points to the use of pattern, shaped for ease of memorization and ease of future oral expression. Writers on memory often speak about *schemata*, pre-existent patterns or frameworks which enable us to make sense of events, store them in memory, recall them and communicate them to others.[25] There are different types of *schemata*, particularly

---

22. Kennedy, *New Testament Interpretation*, 25.
23. Quintilian, *Institutio* 9.3.2.
24. Quintilian, *Institutio* 9.3.66.
25. Eve, *Behind the Gospels*, 89–90; Eve, *Writing the Gospels*, 87–89.

*frames* and *scripts*. The former is a type of *schema* which stores information about objects and their properties.[26] However, it is the latter which is particularly relevant here. A *script* refers to the sequence of actions with which an event typically takes place. The example which we used in the Memory chapter was the routine followed when we dine in a restaurant.[27] David Rubin suggests that part of the usefulness of *scripts* is due to the fact that the stereotyped sequence of actions involved is a causal chain.[28] The logical necessity of each action in the chain makes it easy to recall and is important for the structure of stories.

When we look at ancient dream narratives, we find that many of them share elements in common. There is a pattern used to relate the dreams, a pattern shared by the writer and his readers or listeners. We shall explore that more fully in the next chapter in which we focus on dreams. In the meantime we note how Harris has suggested that many people find it difficult to describe their dreams and so the epiphany dream pattern provided a simplifying or structuring formula whereby a dreamer was enabled to get his confused recollections into orderly shape.[29] However, once the memory of the dream had been communicated, the structure was such that the listener would be able to recall it and, if he wanted, relate it to others. This means that the structure functioned as an aid to memory. With sound and arrangement in mind, we may begin to define memory patterns as follows: *memory patterns are devices intended to help people remember a narrative through the use of sound and also in the structure of the material.*

We now consider whether a mental image may also be used as a memory pattern. According to James Fentress and Chris Wikham, visual imagery is one aspect of narrative memory.[30] As an example of this they point to the visual images which were used by the medieval church in its teaching. We have already seen how the ancient writers used the image of a

---

26. This is how Baddeley et al. define a *frame* and they illustrate it with a building (Baddeley et al., *Memory*, 182). They tell us that this is a knowledge structure containing fixed structural information such as that it has floors and walls and also containing slots for useful information such as the materials from which the building is constructed.

27. This can give rise to schema-related errors when an event takes place with certain actions differing from the normal sequence. This may happen, for example, if we dine in a restaurant in a foreign country. Schema-based errors have already been discussed in the Memory chapter.

28. Rubin, *Memory in Oral Traditions*, 27–28.

29. Harris, *Dreams and Experience*, 62. Halbwachs saw dreams as the main exception to treating all memory as collective memory, because dream memories do not draw upon the social frameworks in the same way as memories of other experiences. However, the use of the *script* to which Harris refers is a socially-shared model.

30. Fentress and Wickham, *Social Memory*, 50.

building or road to assist memory artificially. Cicero also refers to imagery in the list quoted above.[31] We now consider the possible use of an earlier person or event as an image for the person or event under discussion. This is essentially what is involved in typology. Dale Allison speaks of typology as "extended assimilation."[32] A person or event is likened to a previous one by allusion, analogy or simile.[33]

When typology appears in Matthew's text, it may be regarded as a theological feature, which adds to our understanding of Jesus. However, a case can be made for its use with a memory function. We may use an example to explore this. Take Yoseph Trumpeldor, a twentieth-century person who was likened to heroic characters from history and legend.[34] He was a one-armed military hero who was immortalized in accounts of the battle at Tel Hai in the history of Israel in 1920. At a time when Israel's outlook was bleak, Trumpeldor successfully led a small band of soldiers to defend a group of settlements in northern Galilee against siege. Although it was a small victory, Trumpeldor was linked in speeches, poems and songs to famous Jewish heroes of antiquity such as Bar Kokhba. This had the effect of preserving the memory of Trumpeldor as a hero in the consciousness of Israelis in the 1920s. His memory was linked to the more established collective memory of Israel's heroes. That is to say it was reinforced by the typological appeal to Bar Kokhba.[35]

In the absence of theory on typology from the ancients, we rely on the contribution of modern theorists. The sociologist Barry Schwartz treats typology as a mnemonic strategy.[36] Drawing upon one of the concepts which Goffman identified as central to the formation and transmission of collective memory,[37] Schwartz takes "keying" and treats it as an aspect of typology.[38] Keying associates a present person or event with a past counter-

---

31. Cicero, *De Oratore* 3.207: *imago*.

32. Allison, *New Moses*, 13.

33. In the NT it usually involves looking back to OT characters and events, which are treated as *types*, prefiguring NT characters and events, which are then referred to as *antitypes*. However, it can also link forward from Jesus to Peter and Paul in Acts.

34. Le Donne, *Historiographical Jesus*, 56-59, cites this example, taken from Zerubavel, "Historical, the Legendary," 105-125.

35. Le Donne rightly points out that the typological appeal to Bar Kokhba also reinforced an old heroic memory into Israel's contemporary consciousness (Le Donne, *Historiographical Jesus*, 58). Thus the memories of both figures were reinforced.

36. Schwartz, "Where There's Smoke," 7-37.

37. Schwartz cites Goffman, *Frame Analysis*, 40-82. Goffman's other concept is "framing."

38. Schwartz, "Where There's Smoke," 15-16.

part. Although the process is complex and amounts to more than analogy, it essentially involves looking to the past to explain the present. Schwartz suggests that keying defines social memory's function as (1) a model *of* society, (2) a model *for* society, and (3) a *frame* within which people find meaning for their experience. He says, "In these senses social memory is preserved by and for the functions it performs."[39] James Pula applies the theory of Schwartz to a particular case, speaking of "historical symbolism," where we refer to typology.[40] The case he uses is that of Kościuszko, a Pole who was involved in the American Revolution and later in a vain attempt to bring liberty to his fellow countrymen in Poland. Pula shows how his memory has provided meaning to Polish Americans interpreting their own experience within the framework of American history, but at the same time the memory has been redefined to fit the particular needs of a given generation or social exigency. Pula comments that "symbols are an important form of individual and collective memory."[41]

It therefore seems reasonable to treat typology as a memory pattern in addition to its analogical or theological value. Consequently, we redefine memory patterns to take account of it: *memory patterns are devices intended to help people remember a narrative through the use of sound or an image or the structure of the material.*

The question may be raised whether the devices covered in this definition all contribute to the preservation of memory in the same kind of way. In fact they do not. Devices involving sound, such as repetition, *inclusio* or alliteration, may be employed deliberately to achieve a mnemonic goal. On the other hand, the use of an image or structure involves the application of *schemata*, in particular *keying* and a *script*. These are pre-existent conceptual frameworks which assist us in interpreting the past and in remembering it. We may employ them unconsciously and their memory role functions in a narrower sense. They are, however, all worthy of investigation in relation to cultural background.

## Discussion of Memory Patterns

We looked in some detail at formulaic expressions when we were exploring the Parry/Lord theory in the Orality chapter. We now need to take account of other memory patterns which will feature in this study, using discussion from the ancients where possible. However, the ancient rhetorical writers generally

---

39. Schwartz, "Where There's Smoke," 16.
40. Pula, "Tadeusz Kościuszko," 159–82.
41. Pula, "Tadeusz Kościuszko," 163.

list the devices, offering a definition of each and providing examples, with only limited discussion of them. Where they fall short, we shall revert to modern writers. We shall consider repetition, key words, *inclusio*, parallelism, antithesis and some of the devices which are related to sound. These are the most commonly recognized memory patterns.[42] In our discussion we shall seek to identify potential problems which may arise when we come to search for them in texts and ways to resolve such difficulties.

## Repetition

We take first repetition, one of the most common memory patterns. Quintilian says that repetition which he calls *addition*[43] may be used for emphasis or to excite pity or disparagement.[44] Wilfred Watson comments that it enables an audience to hear again something which they may have missed.[45] While these comments are true, it may also assist them to remember material or recognize the structure of what is being said, for it may take various forms. Repetition can be achieved through sound as in alliteration and assonance. Or it may be achieved through the use of a pattern as in anaphora, epistrophe[46] or *inclusio*. It may be accomplished semantically as in parallelism. We may also have pure repetition involving single words in which case they may be considered as potential key words or it may extend to longer phrases or whole sentences. When we are dealing with verbal repetition, we have a problem in knowing how to handle it if it is not precise. Here Anderson comments: "We may ignore minor variations such as the addition or subtraction of words and change of tense, number, gender or case which do not seriously jeopardize the identification of phrases as verbal repetition."[47] We may agree with Anderson that grammatical changes are acceptable. For example, we may have a command followed by its execution, using almost identical language, but the mood changes from imperative to indicative. Such a change does not detract from the repetition. However, with addition or subtraction of words we need to be more

---

42. See Ong, *Orality and Literacy*, 34; Achtemeier, "*Omne verbum sonat*," 17–18, 21–25.

43. The language which the ancients use for *repetition* is a little confusing. They use *repetitio* for anaphora, while Quintilian uses *adjectio* for repetition of the same word and Cicero uses *adjunctio* in the same way.

44. Quintilian, *Institutio* 9.3.28.

45. Watson, *Classical Hebrew Poetry*, 178.

46. It is also known as epiphora and occasionally as antistrophe.

47. Anderson, *Matthew's Narrative Web*, 23.

wary. While a few words added or subtracted are not likely to interfere with the repetition, the more words changed, the more difficult it becomes for a listener to recognize it as repetition.

## Key Words

When a single word is repeated which has some significance for memory, it will be referred to as a *key word*. Although this expression can be used in a variety of contexts,[48] it will be used here specifically to refer to potential memory patterns. Single words are often repeated in narrative or poetry, but how do we know that such repetition is intended to aid the memorization of a narrative? The repeated word may be integral to the subject matter of the story or express some action which recurs throughout the episode or be central to our understanding of a particular incident. For a word to be described as key, it has to play a critical role in a narrative or section of narrative. When we encounter repeated single words or short phrases, we need to ask what their role is in the narrative. We can only accept as key those which highlight the subject matter or an important theme. Luz suggests that Matthew hints at his themes by repeating key words.[49] He goes on to note that oral tradition uses key word connecting links as a mnemonic device, but suggests that Matthew uses them as a literary device to clarify a theme. Luz's dichotomy may not be as clear cut in oral transmission. Key words may highlight a theme and in so doing assist a listener in remembering it.

One problem which may occur in spotting key words is when they occur in a block of material which is repeated. If certain words only occur in repeated blocks, we should be less inclined to treat them as key. They are already being used as part of another memory pattern, viz. that of lengthy repetition. For them to count as key they would also need to appear at other times in material which is not otherwise repeated. There is a similar problem with potential key words appearing within a formula. The two devices are different. A formula is a standard expression which is used almost automatically in certain circumstances.[50] Such would be the

---

48. In linguistics the term is used to refer to a word which occurs in a text more often than we would expect to occur by chance alone. When someone uses a search engine on the internet, the term refers to what they type to indicate what they are looking for, "plumbers" for example.

49. Luz, *Matthew 1–7*, 39.

50. This is intended as a working definition rather than a precise one. Compare the definition offered by Parry: "A group of words which is regularly employed under the same metrical conditions to express a given essential idea" (Parry, *Making of Homeric Verse*, 272). Teffeteller argues to change Parry's definition to take account of the use

expression used to describe the appearance of an *oneiros* figure in a dream. A key word is applied more widely to highlight some particular aspect of a narrative. To be treated as key we would need to find it occurring at least on occasion beyond the formula.

It should be acknowledged that assessing repeated single words involves an element of subjectivity. Watson recognizes this difficulty and comments: "this is a question of judgment, not a statistical computation."[51] Consequently, each time we encounter repetition of a single word, we need to ask what its function is in the narrative, whether it is being repeated by chance or simply as part of the vocabulary of the narrative or whether it is included deliberately to highlight a theme or some other aspect of the narrative.

## Inclusio

Next we consider the structuring of material, particularly where a block of material is marked out, by using a similar word or phrase at the beginning and end. This creates a section of narrative, bearing resemblance in some respects to a paragraph in written literature. In biblical studies this structuring is known as *inclusio*, but classicists refer to it as ring composition. It may also be called "the envelope figure"[52] or "incomplete chiasmus," only the extremes corresponding (schematically: A . . . A).[53] Sometimes recognition of it seems straightforward, particularly where there are similar sounding phrases at both ends. For example, in Herodotus, *Histories*, the dream opens with ὄψιν ἐν τῷ ὕπνῳ τοιήνδε ἰδόντα αὐτὸν and closes with ἰδόντα δὲ τὴν ὄψιν ταύτην λέγειν αὐτόν.[54] However, it is a little more complicated where the unit is enclosed by only one word at the beginning and end. Artemidorus, *Oneirocritica*, opens with Ἔδοξέ τις γυνὴ ἐν τῇ σελήνῃ and closes with διὰ τὴν σελήνην.[55] There is a single word at each end, viz. σελήνη. The difficulty increases where identical words are not used, but they do have similar

---

of repetition and parallelism in Sumerian and Akkadian poetry (Teffeteller, "Orality," 67–86).

51. Watson advises us that the most frequent words are not necessarily the most significant (Watson, *Classical Hebrew Poetry*, 287). Then lower on the same page he seems to contradict this by commenting that when a word recurs with insistent frequency, it is very probably a keyword.

52. Watson uses this term for phrases repeated at the beginning and end of a stanza or poem (Watson, *Classical Hebrew Poetry*, 282–83). He tells us that the term was coined by the man who first recognized it, Moulton, *Literary Study of the Bible*.

53. Watson, *Classical Hebrew Poetry*, 283.

54. Herodotus, *Histories* 2.139.

55. Artemidorus, *Oneirocritica* 5.12.

roots. Josephus's *Ant.* 2.214 has τοῖς οὐχ ὁμοφύλοις, while 2.216 has παρὰ τοῖς ἀλλοφύλοις.[56] Davies and Allison warn that the process of indentifying *inclusios* in Matthew is "inevitably a somewhat subjective endeavor."[57] Similarly, Luz warns against treating every repeated word as an intended case of *inclusio*, but helpfully he goes on in a footnote to suggest that we should only speak of one "where a clearly discernible textual unit is stressed at the beginning and at the end by like formulations or contents."[58] If we have a unit marked by similar sounding expressions at either end, but containing material which clearly belongs beyond the second expression, we should not regard that unit as an example of *inclusio*.

## Parallelism

We move on to parallelism, which uses components in a sentence to produce parallel structures. Davies and Allison twice refer to it as a Semitic feature.[59] Indeed it is to be found in OT, particularly in poetry (e.g., Ps 46:7; 121:5). However, examples are also to be found in Greco-Roman literature.[60] Indeed O'Connor has observed that "parallelism" is a universal feature of language, there being no single piece of extended discourse in any language that does not illustrate some feature of it.[61] Nevertheless, since Davies and Allison have highlighted it as a Semitic characteristic, it is important to explore OT usage to see if it has any distinctive features and if it does, to discover if any are present in Matthew's narrative, as this may help to establish whether Matthew's cultural background leans more towards OT and Jewish thought.

First we make some general observations. Although parallelism may be regarded as a distinctive feature of OT poetry, it should not be equated with poetry. Francis Landy notes that Berlin, like Kugel, recognizes a continuum between poetry and prose.[62] We should observe that for two clauses to be parallel, they do not have to be precisely the same length. Kugel refers to off-and-on equivalence of length in parallel clauses (whether measured by stresses

---

56. Cf. Herodotus, *Histories* 2.139 τέλος δὲ τῆς ἀπαλλαγῆς and ἑκὼν ἀπαλλάσσετο.
57. Davies and Allison, *Matthew*, 1:92.
58. Luz, *Matthew 1–7*, 40.
59. Davies and Allison, *Matthew*, 1:85, 94.
60. See Diogenes Laertius, *Lives of Eminent Philosophers* 1.117: Heracles's instructions come in two parts, first to Pherecydes with προστάξαι δὲ αὐτῷ . . . τοῦτο, and then to the kings with τοῖς βασιλεῦσι κελεῦσαι Φερεκύδη πείθεσθαι.
61. Kugel, "Feeling of Déjà Lu," 74, citing O'Connor, *Hebrew Verse Structure*, 88–89.
62. Landy, "Recent Developments," 168, citing Berlin, *Dynamics of Biblical Parallelism*, 5.

or the number of syllables or the like).⁶³ There are in fact different types of parallelism, such as grammatical, lexical, semantic, phonological.⁶⁴

Two of the most common types of parallelism are syntactical and semantic. A biblical verse, often quoted in discussions of parallelism, illustrates both: "Adah and Zillah, hear my voice; you wives of Lamech, hearken to what I say" (Gen 4:23). Each component or phrase in the second half means much the same as each component in the first half. There is also perfect syntactical parallelism, as the word order in each of the half lines exactly mirrors the other, with each corresponding term in the same syntactic position. We also find syntactical parallelism in Greco-Roman writing. We take as an example the dream of the Methymnean general, Bryaxis in Longus's *Daphnis and Chloe*.⁶⁵ We find parallelism where Pan rebukes Bryaxis. We have Πολέμου μὲν τὴν ἀγροικίαν ἐνεπλήσατε τὴν ἐμοὶ φίλην, "you have filled the countryside I love with war," followed by ἀγέλας δὲ βοῶν καὶ αἰγῶν καὶ ποιμνίων ἀπηλάσατε τὰς ἐμοὶ μελομένας, "you have driven off herds of cows, goats, and sheep about which I care."⁶⁶ The last three words in each section are particularly striking. Clearly syntactical parallelism cannot be the distinguishing mark of the OT.⁶⁷

Robert Alter lays his stress on meaning, suggesting that semantic parallelism is the peculiar mark of OT poetry. Although there is sometimes a relatively static synonymity between two lines, he suggests that one can often see "a dynamic of meaning emerging from one verse to the next."⁶⁸ An example is to be found in Psalm 88:11-12: "Will your kindness be told in the grave, / your faithfulness in perdition? // Will your wonder be known in the darkness, / your bounty in the land of oblivion?" One set of matched terms remains stable, being a complementary series of linked concepts: kindness, faithfulness, wonder, bounty. The other set of matched terms carries forward "a progressive imaginative realization of death."⁶⁹

63. Kugel, "Feeling of Déjà Lu," 73.
64. Landy, "Recent Developments," 168.
65. Longus, *Daphnis and Chloe* 2.26.5-2.28.1.
66. Longus, *Daphnis and Chloe* 2.27.1.
67. We find further examples of syntactical parallelism in Artemidorus, *Oneirocritica* 5.37, where we have ᾧ λόγῳ . . . τούτῳ τῷ λόγῳ, and in 47, where we read ὁ γὰρ παῖς πατρὸς κόσμος, ὥσπερ ὁ πώγων προσώπου, "for a son embellishes a father, just as a beard embellishes a face."
68. Alter, *Art of Biblical Poetry*, 14.
69. Alter continues: "from the familiar and localized "grave" to *'avadon*, "perdition," a poetic synonym that is quasi-mythic and grimly explicit about the fate of extinction the grave holds; then, to another everyday word, "darkness," which is, however, a sensory realization of the experience of death, and then to a second poetic term for the underworld, "the land of oblivion," which summarizes and generalizes the series,

Alter receives support from Kugel, who argued against the description of some verse halves (A and B) as "synonymous," but maintained that they had the sense of "A, and what's more, B," where B should be seen as A's completion.[70] Alter himself tells us that with semantic parallelism "the characteristic movement of meaning is one of heightening or intensification . . . of focusing, specification, concretization, even what could be called dramatization."[71] Among the examples which Alter provides—e.g., Prov 3:10; Isa 17:1; 48:20–21; 49:23—Jer 7:34 illustrates how a geographical term is followed by a second smaller spatial entity: "I shall put an end in the cities of Judah and in the streets of Jerusalem." When we look at examples of parallelism in the various pieces of literature across the cultural divide, it will be important to distinguish between the syntactical and semantic versions. If semantic parallelism is indeed a distinctive feature of OT poetry, then we may expect to find examples in the OT, but not in Greco-Roman writing. Subsequently, it will be important to see whether or not Matthew also shows evidence of semantic parallelism.

We regard semantic parallelism as a memory pattern, because parallelism itself is a mnemonic aid and the semantic variety is a sub-division of that. However, it is possible to see semantic parallelism as an indication of poetic style. Then if Matthew uses it, he may be influenced by OT examples and deliberately trying to write in a biblical register. We shall return to the issue of register in the Comparison chapter when we set Matthew's writing alongside that of other writers.

## Typology

As we have considered various memory patterns, we have digressed into the issue of whether there is a distinctively Semitic use of parallelism. We continue to digress in a similar vein as we investigate whether typology may be regarded as an OT memory pattern. Allison shows how several OT characters are portrayed as a "new Moses"—Joshua, Gideon, Samuel, Josiah, Ezekiel, Jeremiah, Ezra, etc.[72] However, he begins his discussion of Jewish

---

giving emphatic closure to the idea that death is a realm where human beings are utterly forgotten and extinct, and where there can be no question of God's greatness being recalled" (Alter, *Art of Biblical Poetry*, 14).

70. Kugel, "Feeling of Déjà Lu," 67. Indeed Kugel maintains in this article that Alter has drawn his thinking from his (Kugel's) work, *Idea of Biblical Poetry*, published four years before Alter's was first published.

71. Alter, *Art of Biblical Poetry*, 20.

72. Allison, *New Moses*, 11–95.

figures by referring to two passages which suggest that Alexander the Great sought to emulate Achilles.[73] The fact is that this type of comparison is to be found in all literature.[74] It is, therefore, not in itself a distinctive OT memory pattern, but it does become such if OT figures, rather than Greco-Roman ones, are used as types.

## Antithesis

Just as we have noted semantic parallelism as potentially an OT memory device, we now note something which is distinctively Greek. It concerns the way in which the Greek language expresses antithesis. The use of antithesis itself is widespread with examples to be found even in the Hebrew Bible (e.g., Prov 19:16; Eccl 10:2). What we are about to note is a particular way in which the Greek language expresses antithesis. This is the μέν ... δέ ... construction, something unique to the Greek language. We are not suggesting that this construction is a memory patterns in its own right, but rather that it is a subsection of antithesis, a syntactic feature which Greek writers might employ to set one thing against another. Moreover, we need to be wary when we encounter it, as not all examples are antithesis. The μέν ... part often has no translation in English. The δέ ... part can be translated as *and* or *but*.[75] Even where it means *but*, it is not as strong as the particle ἀλλά. However, there are times when the construction can be rendered into English as "*on the one hand.* ... *on the other hand.*" Or we find οἱ μέν ... οἱ δέ ... which gives a contrast between the action of *some* and *others*. Greek writers regularly use this construction to express antithesis. Josephus has a certain fondness of it. We take as an example the contrast he draws between Jacob's judgment of Joseph's dream concerning the sun, moon and stars and the reaction of Joseph's brothers: Καὶ ὁ μὲν Ἰάκωβος τοιαύτην οὐκ ἀσυνέτως ἐποιήσατο τῆς ὄψεως τὴν κρίσιν, τοὺς δ' ἀδελφοὺς τοῦ Ἰωσήπου σφόδρα ἐλύπησε τὰ προειρημένα.[76]

---

73. Arrian, *Anabasis* 1.12; 7.14.

74. We still use it, referring, for example, to an up and coming scientist as "another Einstein."

75. E.g., we read: τῷ μὲν Ἰωσήπῳ τούτων οὐδὲν ὡς οὐ γνώριμον αὐτοῖς τὸ ὄναρ ὃν διεσάφησαν, ἀρὰς δ' ἐποιήσαντο μηδὲν εἰς τέλος αὐτῷ παρελθεῖν ὧν ὑπενόουν, "they gave no interpretation of it to Joseph, as if the dream were not by them understood: but they prayed that no part of what they suspected to be its meaning might come to pass" (Josephus, *Ant.* 2.12).

76. Josephus, *Ant.* 2.17.

We may consider antithesis more generally. Sometimes in the *Progymnasmata* antithesis is used as an objection in an argument.[77] However, the Roman rhetoricians refer to it as the kind of device we have been discussing. Quintilian tells us that antithesis may be achieved by single words or phrases or complete clauses: "*Antithesis*, which Roman writers call either *contrapositum* or *contentio*, may be effected in more than one way. Single words may be contrasted with single . . . or the contrast may be between pairs of words . . . or sentence may be contrasted with sentence."[78] The author of *Ad Herennium* lists it as both a figure of diction[79] and a figure of thought.[80] In each case it involves setting opposites against each other. As an example of it in speech, he gives: *Inimicis te placabilem, amicis inexorabilem praebes*.[81] For thought his example is: *Vos vestris fortunis diffiditis, iste solus suis eo magis confidit*.[82] He then explains the difference: "the first consists in a rapid opposition of words; in the other opposing thoughts ought to meet in a comparison."[83] The ancient rhetoricians differed widely, some regarding antithesis as a figure of diction, others as a figure of thought, and still others as belonging to both categories.[84] In this study we recognize the distinction and accept that both types of antithesis exist. We may have a sentence consisting of two clauses, contrasted and separated by the conjunction "but." That would be a figure of diction. Another time we may have a thought or action expressed and then later in the narrative the opposite thought or action. That would be a figure of thought. We therefore need to be alert for both types of antithesis as we examine various texts.

---

77. We have *thesis* (the premise or argument), *antithesis* (objection) and *lysis* (solution). Aphthonius the Sophist, *Progymnasmata*, uses this example: *thesis*—marriage is to be praised; *antithesis*—marriage is a cause of misfortunes; *lysis*—you seem to be attacking fortune, not marriage. See Kennedy, *Progymnasmata*, 121–23.

78. Quintilian, *Institutio* 9.3.81.

79. Anonymous, *Ad Herennium* 4.15.

80. Anonymous, *Ad Herennium* 4.58.

81. He does not give a source for this quotation. Presumably it is a proverb. It translates: "To enemies you show yourself conciliatory, to friends inexorable."

82. Again there is no source. The translation is: "While you despair of your fortunes, this knave alone grows all the more confident in his own."

83. Anonymous, *Ad Herennium* 4.58.

84. Cousin provides tables for *Des Figures de Pensée* and *Des Figures de Mots* (Cousin, *Études sur Quintilien*, 472–73, 510–13). The former table includes Cornificius, Cicero's *De Oratore*, and Quintilian. The latter includes Aristotle, Theophrastus, Rutilius, Cornificius, Cicero's *De Oratore* and *Orator*, and Quintilian.

## Sound Memory Patterns and Translation

Some memory patterns, such as assonance and alliteration are related to sound. This means that ultimately they are related to the language in which the memory is expressed. Dream narratives may originally have been expressed and preserved in one language before being recorded in another. The patterns in which they were preserved in the original language may well be different from those in which it is expressed in the second language. Assonance or alliteration may appear in a different place in the translation or disappear altogether. We need to be aware of this when we are dealing with the OT text, which was largely written in Hebrew with a little in Aramaic and later translated into Greek as well as other languages, and also with Pseudo-Philo which is believed to have been originally written in Hebrew, then translated into Greek before being rendered in Latin which is the earliest form in which we now have it.[85] This means that while ideally we should read a text in its original language, it is not possible with Pseudo-Philo. With Matthew we have no way of knowing whether the dreams narratives first circulated in Aramaic, as we have no earlier text than the current Greek one.

## Cultural Question

We aim to discover whether Matthew's dream narratives employed memory patterns and if so, which particular examples. Once the memory patterns in the dream narratives have been identified, they will be compared with those in other dream literature, Greco-Roman as well as Jewish. The aim is to find out whether such comparison can reveal the cultural origin of Matthew's narratives, whether the memory patterns he displays have more in common with those of Jewish literature or Hellenistic writing.

Others have used rhetorical criticism to explore the cultural nature of NT texts. Robbins, for example, considers whether our NT texts view Jewish culture as a dominant culture or as a subculture in a dominant Hellenistic-Roman culture.[86] He does not answer that question, but, drawing upon the work of Mack, he offers suggestions as to how it can be investigated, using the categories of dominant culture, subculture, contraculture and counterculture.[87] The method being pursued here is different. We

---

85. Jacobson, *Commentary*, 215–24.

86. Robbins, "Rhetoric and Culture," 443–63.

87. Robbins cites Mack, *Myth of Innocence*. Robbins and Mack see parallels between the Jesus movement on the one hand and the rhetoric of Jewish, Hellenistic-Roman and Cynic texts. Mack assumes that the existence of rhetorical parallels means that a

seek to establish whether Matthew or his source's usage correspond more closely to Jewish or Hellenistic usage, by working with patterns which the memory uses to store narratives.

## Problem Caused by Cultural Overlap

As we seek to identify the cultural background of Matthew's dream narratives, we encounter a problem, for most memory patterns are not culturally specific, being shared by Jewish, Greek and Roman writers alike. We may consider some examples, beginning with alliteration which was used by both Greeks and Romans,[88] but also evident in Hebrew poetry.[89] Assonance is common in classical literature,[90] but again there are also examples in the Hebrew Bible.[91] Anaphora was extensively used in rhetoric,[92] common among Greek[93] as well as Roman orators,[94] while even existing in verse.[95] It is the

---

relationship exists between the culture of Jesus's followers and that of the literature providing the parallel. However, there may be other ways of explaining the parallels. For example, certain kinds of imagery may be common to rural communities, irrespective of their cultural background.

88. It did not tend to be common in Greek poetry, but was more a feature in Latin saturnian verse and was adopted from there by later Roman poets, including Ennius and Virgil. Examples from Ennius (c. 239-169 BCE) include *fraxinu' frangitur atque abies consternitur alta.* and *pinus proceras pervortunt.* Virgil (70-19 BCE) gives us *magno cum murmure montis* (Virgil, *Aeneid* 1.55).

89. Psalm 122:6-7 provides a good example with the repetition of the ש sound. Other examples include עפר ואפר (Gen 18:27) and כי-בשמחה תצאו ובשלום תובלון (Isa 55:12).

90. It is to be found in the work of the Greek dramatists of the fifth century BCE. Examples nearer the time of Matthew include these. Cicero (106-43 BCE), attempting verse, has *O fortunatam natam me consule Romam!* (Cicero, *De Consulatu Suo*), while Virgil gives us *amissos longo socios sermone requirunt* (Virgil, *Aeneid* 1.217). Farris cites as an example ταπεινούς, πεινῶντας (Luke 1:52-53). See Farris, *Hymns of Luke's Infancy Narratives,* 46.

91. E.g., Genesis 2:25-3.1: ויהיו שניהם ערומים . . . והנחש היה ערום—although *arummim,* "naked," is a different root from *arum,* "crafty," they sound the same in Hebrew. Other examples include Genesis 49:17; Exodus 14:14; Deuteronomy 3:2.

92. We noted above that the anonymous writer of *Rhetorica ad Herennium* (usually dated in the 90s BCE) gave anaphora as an example of a figure of diction (Anonymous, *Ad Herennium* 4.13.18).

93. Demosthenes (383-322 BCE), *On the Crown* 48; Lysias (c. 445-380 BCE), *Against Eratosthenes* 21.

94. Cicero, *In Verrem* 2:2, 10.

95. "*Saevus ubiAecidae telo iacet Hector, ubi ingens Sarpedon, ubi tot Simois . . . volvit!*" (Virgil, *Aeneid* 1.99-100).

easiest type of Hebrew writing form to identify.[96] Formulaic expressions are renowned in the work of Homer (c. 800 BCE),[97] but they are also to be found in Virgil,[98] while in the prophets of the Hebrew Bible we commonly find the formulaic expression, "Thus says the Lord." *Inclusio* is to be found in the Hebrew Bible, with some particularly noteworthy instances in the book of Jeremiah.[99] Ring composition, to use its classical name, is a common feature of Greek oratory.[100] We have already noted that parallelism is commonly used in Hebrew poetry, but it is not unknown in classical writing, as in the work of Longus.[101] Antithesis is found in both classical and biblical literature.[102] The use of acrostic is popular in OT poetry.[103] We saw above how typology is widely used in literature and common speech.[104]

Table 1: Memory Patterns by Culture

| Memory Pattern | Hebrew | Greek |
| --- | --- | --- |
| Acrostic | Yes | No |
| Alliteration | Yes | Yes |
| Anaphora | Yes | Yes |
| Antithesis | Yes | Yes |
| Antithesis μέν ... δέ ... | No | Yes |

96. The phrase ויהי "and it came to pass" is found sixty-two times in the Book of Genesis to begin sentences.

97. A common line is ἦμος δ' ἠριγένεια φάνη ῥοδοδάκτυλος Ἠώς, which is used twenty one times in all (e.g., Homer, *Odyssey* 2.1).

98. The phrase *pius Aeneas* occurs twenty times throughout the *Aeneid* (e.g., Virgil, *Aeneid* 1.220).

99. A rather far-flung example can be found in its first section, Jer 1–24, which are enveloped both by a similar question in the first and last episode (Jer 1:11; 24:3), and by similar imagery—that of almond rods and baskets of figs.

100. See, for example, Aeschines, *Against Ctesiphon*.

101. Longus, *Daphnis and Chloe* 2.10.1; 2.26.5–2.28.1; 4.34.1–3.

102. An example in Classical literature is Cicero, *Pro Cluentio* 2.5. From OT we have Proverbs 10:2. Matthew 5:17–48 is sometimes called "Matthew's Antitheses" because he has Jesus quote six well-known prescriptions of the Mosaic Law and then demand that his followers do more than the Law requires.

103. Psalm 119, the longest psalm, devotes eight verses to each letter of the Hebrew alphabet.

104. Examples include the OT likening Joshua to Moses and in the Greek world Alexander the Great emulating Achilles.

| Memory Pattern | Hebrew | Greek |
| --- | --- | --- |
| Assonance | Yes | Yes |
| Formulaic Expressions | Yes | Yes |
| Inclusio | Yes | Yes |
| Key Word | Yes | Yes |
| Parallelism—Semantic | Yes | No |
| Parallelism—Syntactical | Yes | Yes |
| Repetition | Yes | Yes |
| Typology | Yes | Yes |
| Typology using OT figures | Yes | No |

The problem which emerges is that most memory patterns are not unique to any particular culture. However, this need not be an insuperable problem. If we pick up a novel written in English, we may wonder whether the author is American or British. It need not be immediately obvious. However, we may consider the kind of language which he uses and note whether he speaks, for example, of vacations or holidays, pants or trousers. Even if he does refer to holidays, we need to consider if he is using it in the more restricted sense of a religious festival.[105] Lord likened the way a Yugoslav bard used formulae to the way we speak our native language: "He learns them by hearing them in other singers' songs, and by habitual usage they become part of his singing as well."[106] The use of memory patterns is comparable to the use of language and is likely to throw up local peculiarities. How do we establish what these peculiarities are?

First we look for devices which are culturally specific. One example may be the OT use of acrostic. Antithesis and parallelism may also prove useful. Although antithesis does occur in biblical writing, we saw above how the Greek language has the unique μέν . . . δέ . . . construction which is sometimes used to express it. We have also already noted the various forms which parallelism may take, particularly syntactical and semantic, with the latter being especially a feature of OT writing. Although most memory patterns are not culturally specific, we need to investigate whether Matthew

---

105. The analogy may collapse if pushed too far. It may be suggested, for instance, that the author is channeling a British or American voice and that what is in the text does not actually reflect the author's own cultural background.

106. Lord, *Singer of Tales*, 36.

shows evidence of the acrostic, semantic parallelism and the μέν . . . δέ . . . construction, for they may provide indicators whether he or his sources remember material in the same way as Jewish or Hellenistic writers.

However, with other types of memory pattern we will need to consider frequency of usage. A variety of examples will emerge which may be enumerated. However, we need to proceed with caution. Raw numbers may not tell us very much. If we examine only three dream narratives in Polybius, but forty six in Artemidorus, we shall inevitably have more examples of antithesis or *inclusio* in Artemidorus. Therefore what we aim to find are those features which Polybius typically displays or those which Artemidorus typically displays. Even within a single culture there will be variation from one author to the next depending on the particular style of each writer. Our aim should be to see if particular memory patterns predominate in one particular culture, recognizing that someone like Josephus is both Jewish and Hellenistic. Our search ought to be focused on the most relevant memory patterns which are those present in Matthew's text. If those used by Matthew are more common in the literature of one particular culture than another, that along with the few which are culturally specific may help to establish his or his sources' cultural leanings.

## Conclusion

We recall Lord's comparison between a bard's use of formulae and the way we speak our native language. The learning and acquisition of other patterns of memory would no doubt be similar, although teachers of rhetoric adopted a more formal approach. In a multi-cultural society, one in which Judaism, whatever its location, was affected by Hellenism, individuals would encounter a mixture of people and absorb a mixture of memory patterns. However, when it comes to Matthew's dream narratives, it is hoped to establish which cultural background had a stronger influence on him by looking out, where possible, for those features which were distinctive to one particular culture and, more especially, by taking into account the typical usage in Jewish and Greco-Roman writing compared to that in Matthew.

# 5

# Dreams

## Introduction

THE DREAMS IN MATTHEW'S Gospel are significantly different from anything we experience today. Only three of the Matthean dreams are narrated in detail, but they each involve an appearance of an angel of the Lord who issues Joseph with commands.[1] In contrast we tend to describe our dreams as sequences of events or experiences. Harris puts it this way: "there may be a principal actor (often the dreamer him/herself), and there may be a lesson to be learned, but what we describe is an episode,"[2] though often brief. In our dreams the sense which matters most is the visual. The other senses seldom do much. Even hearing plays less of a part than in waking life. Yet in Joseph's dreams what matters most is his hearing of the angel's messages. Even the language in which we speak about dreams is different. The ancients spoke about dreams in such a way as to suggest that the dreamer passively received a vision. Dodds says,[3] "The Greeks never spoke as we do of *having* a dream, but always of *seeing* a dream—ὄναρ ἰδεῖν, ἐνύπνιον ἰδεῖν." In Joseph's dreams the angel of the Lord appears to him—the passive use of the verb φαίνω. In our understanding of dreams we are very much under the influence of Freud[4] and his successors.[5] We regard them as unreal, subjective phenomena. By

---

1. He is told not to be afraid to take Mary his wife (Matt 1:20) and still in the same dream he is told in the following verse to name the child which she has conceived Jesus; he is told to take the child and his mother and flee to Egypt (Matt 2:13); and he is told to take the child and his mother and go to the land of Israel (Matt 2:20).

2. Harris, *Dreams and Experience*, 46.

3. Dodds, *Greeks and the Irrational*, 105.

4. Freud published his monograph, *Interpretation of Dreams*, in 1900.

5. Walsh attempts to synthesize the psychological work of Carl Jung with a theological clarification of God's revelation through dream experience (Walsh, "Dream of

contrast people in the ancient world believed they had received actual visits from gods or their representatives. Nowadays psychologists treat dreams as clues to a person's past or present.[6] In ancient times they were regarded as guides to the future. We find this in OT, with Daniel, for example, offering interpretations for dreams of pagan kings which refer to the future of their empires or world history. A notable feature of our dreams is an element of bizarreness.[7] The only element there which might apply to Joseph's dreams is the suspension of the laws of biology in Mary's virginal conception. However, since this is explained as the work of the Holy Spirit, even this does not compare to our own experience of laws being suspended in dreams.

## Classification of Dreams

Not only are ancient dreams different from ours, they also vary among themselves, for there are different types. It would therefore be helpful at the outset if we could categorize ancient dreams. Others have already attempted this, most notably Oppenheim.[8] He was by no means the first to classify dreams, several others, ancient and modern, already having attempted it.[9] Oppenheim suggests two types of dream reports, "message" and "symbolic."[10] In the

---

Joseph," 20–27).

6. Freud taught that dreams are prompted by residues of the previous day's experiences (*Tagesreste*) and function to preserve sleep by representing as fulfilled wishes which would otherwise waken the individual.

7. Harris has suggested six forms this might take: (a) discontinuities; (b) improbably combinations (essentially the suspension of the laws of physics and biology); (c) improbable identities (*Mischbildung*)—places and people can have more than one identity—the sun may be the moon; (d) psychological improbability (inappropriate speech and action); (e) absurdity; and (f) sheer oddness of subject matter. See Harris, *Dreams and Experience*, 18.

8. Oppenheim, "Mantic Dreams," 341–50.

9. Homer was perhaps the first, distinguishing dreams which come through the "Gate of Ivory" from those which emerge from the "Gate of Horn" (Homer, *Odyssey* 19.562–67). Philo proposed three types (Philo, *De Somniis* 1:1–2; 2:1–3). In 1939 A. Wikenhauser suggested a system of eight types to classify Greek dreams (Gnuse, *Dreams and Dream Reports*, 103). In 1953 E. Ehrlich sought to classify dreams in the Hebrew Bible in four categories (Flannery-Dailey, *Dreamers, Scribes, and Priests*, 38–39). Others who have attempted the task more recently include Hanson, "Dreams and Visions," 1408; Gnuse, *Dreams and Dream Reports*, 104; Harris, *Dreams and Experience*, 49.

10. In actual fact Oppenheim also has a third type of dream which he refers to as "psychological status dream." It reflects the dreams of common people which were not thought worthy of recording. They are only known to us through references in lists of omens in the dream books. They can be ignored here because our concern is with

former the dreamer was nearly always a man, typically a king, hero, or priest, who in a moment of crisis would receive a visit, usually from a single individual: a deity or his substitute, even a ghost, might appear to him. He recognizes that the visitor is authoritative and consequently likely to be telling the truth or worthy of obedience. The visitor conveys a message, an admonition or pronouncement, the meaning of which is clear to the dreamer or eventually becomes clear. The symbolic type differs from this because its message is not couched in immediately intelligible terms. It may consist of a sequence of more or less rational activities but the relation between these is often irrational. Normally, the services of a dream interpreter are required to decode the underlying message. Such an interpreter is not a diviner, but a wise man whose genius or god enables him to reach the core. Oppenheim attributes this classification to Artemidorus,[11] who differentiated dreams in which the relationship between the signifier and the signified is obvious (*theorematic dreams*) from those which require interpretation (*allegorical dreams*).[12] Artemidorus actually divided dreams into five categories[13] and in that respect his approach differs from that of Oppenheim.

There is a weakness in Oppenheim's classification as not every dream account fits neatly into one of the two categories and there is considerable overlap between them.[14] Some symbolic dreams require no interpreter, while some message dreams do. Moreover, every dream related communicates a message, whether it is formulated in intelligible language or veiled in enigmatic images. Inevitably when we use as few categories as two, there are bound to be exceptions. This could be avoided if we go for a greater number, as Wikenhauser does when he suggests eight to classify Greek dreams. It depends on how important categorization is for the particular work in hand. For the purposes of the present study Oppenheim's classification is adequate. It provides a helpful way of referring to the dream narratives which will be analyzed, using a distinction with which most scholars are familiar and which some still use.[15] The more complicated categories offered by other writers do not actually help to clarify the issues involved in the Matthean dream reports.

---

dream narratives.

11. There is reason to believe that Artemidorus himself may have borrowed this typology from the Stoics. See Meier, "Dream in Ancient Greece," 306, citing *Stoicorum Veterum Fragmenta* 3:605.

12. Artemidorus, *Oneirocritica* 1.2.

13. Enigmatic dream (ὄνειρος), prophetic vision (ὅραμα), oracular dream (χρηματισμός), nightmare (ἐνύπνιον), and apparition (φάντασμα). See Artemidorus, *Oneirocritica* 1.2.

14. This has been observed by Noegel, "Review of Flannery-Dailey's *Dreamers*."

15. E.g., Flannery-Dailey, *Dreamers, Scribes, and Priests*.

In any case classification has no direct bearing on the memory patterns themselves which lie at the heart of this study.

When we apply Oppenheim's classification to Matthew's dream narratives, we find that they fall into the category of "message" dreams, for Joseph is visited by the angel of the Lord who delivers a message to him in intelligible words. We may consider whether there are any features of symbolic dreams in the Matthean texts. In particular we may look for interpretation. Chrysostom thought there was some at 1:21, with the angel acting in the role of *angelus interpres*: "The Angel interprets it (i.e., *the name Jesus*), suggesting good hope, and by this induces him (i.e., *Joseph*) to believe what was spoken."[16] An unknown preacher of the patristic period disagreed, attributing the interpretation to Matthew, despite the fact that he has placed the words on the angel's lips: "The evangelist here interprets the meaning of Jesus in the Hebrew language, saying, 'He shall save his people from their sins.'"[17] While there is undoubtedly interpretation of the name *Jesus*, this occurs within a clause introduced by the conjunction γάρ. Such a clause occurs after each of the commands issued in the dreams—at 1:20; 2:13, 20, as well as here. A command followed by a reason is part of the structure given to the angel's speech in each of the dreams.

Another example of interpretation occurs at 1:22–23. Whether or not it is offered by the angel depends on the further question of whether this verse is part of the angel's speech or a narrative aside made by the evangelist. Juan Maldonato regards it as a comment made by the narrator. He says: "*Now all this* . . . S. Augustin, Theophylact, and Euthymius think these the words of the angel; but they are, beyond doubt, those of the Evangelist, who wished to prove his faith by the testimony of the Prophet."[18] John Gill is of the same opinion.[19] Most recent commentators tend to agree. Brown says: "Occurring where it does, the citation in 1:22–23 is intrusive in the flow of the narrative."[20] Donald Hagner makes a similar comment.[21] However, Davies and Allison acknowledge that it is difficult to decide, drawing attention to the parallel in 26:56 and the quotation in 2:5–6.[22] Alfred Plummer sees this as "the Evangelist's own reflexion on the Angelic message to Joseph." He suggests that Matthew was so convinced of the correctness of the view as to

---

16. Cited by Thomas Aquinas, *Catena Aurea*, concerning Matt 1:21.
17. PG 56:634, cited in ACC 18 as "Incomplete Work on Matthew, Homily 1."
18. Maldonato, *Commentary on the Holy Gospels*, 40–41, commenting on Matt 1:22.
19. Gill, *Exposition of the Bible*, commenting on Matt 1:22.
20. Brown, *Birth of the Messiah*, 144.
21. Hagner, *Matthew 1–13*, 20.
22. Davies and Allison, *Matthew*, 1:211.

the fulfillment of prophecy that he did not hesitate to give it the highest sanction by making it part of what the angel said in the dream.[23] Krister Stendahl agrees: "While the formula quotation must be a contribution by Matthew, it here is meant to be within the message of the angel."[24]

This takes us into the issue of what belongs to sources and what is Matthean redaction. Most scholars regard the formulaic quotations as redactional.[25] If we accept this, there would be no interpretation in the dream as narrated by any source. However, in the text as we now have it, there is interpretation which Matthew appears to have placed within the message of the angel and so within the dream. In that case the interpretation would not be occurring after Joseph has awakened. Moreover, although the formulaic quotation at 1:23 may be construed as interpretation, it is really adding information or authority to the angel's statement at 1:22 which was already intelligible. With "symbolic" dreams, the dreamer usually wakens puzzled by what he has seen or heard and then seeks out an interpreter to help him make sense of it. We may, therefore, continue to regard Joseph's dreams as being of the "message" rather than the "symbolic" type. These labels are helpful when we come to set Matthew's dreams against those of other authors so that we are aware of when we are comparing like with like or with something a little different.

## Pattern of Dream Reports

Oppenheim made a second and arguably more significant contribution to the study of ancient dreams. In the last chapter we discussed *schemata*, pre-existent patterns or frameworks which we use in speaking about events. A particular type of *schema* which refers to the sequence of actions with which an event typically takes place is known as a *script*.[26] When we look at ancient dreams, we discover that many of them are narrated according to a *script*, a pattern shared by the writer and his readers or listeners. Oppenheim outlined this formal pattern which extends across the ancient Near East and the Mediterranean:[27]

---

23. Plummer, *Exegetical Commentary*, 8–9.
24. Stendahl, *Peake's Commentary on the Bible*, 771.
25. E.g., Davies and Allison, *Matthew*, 1:96; Allison, *New Moses*, 165.
26. The example which we have already noted is the routine followed when we dine in a restaurant.
27. Oppenheim, "Interpretation of Dreams," 179–373.

I. Description of the dream setting: who experienced it; when; where; and under what circumstances.

II. Actual report of the dream content.

III. Description of the end of the dream: the reaction of the dreaming person or the actual fulfillment of the prediction or promise made.

He says that accounts of the message dream type "are found in literary texts from the Sumerian and Egyptian royal stelae to the Gospel of Matthew, from the Iliad to Ptolemaic Egypt, and throughout the literary products of the Western civilizations as far as the classical tradition exercised its sway."[28] Nevertheless, there are variations within different cultures. Oppenheim contrasts the passive attitude of the dreamer who is said to "see" a dream with the more active attitude of God in OT where it is said that he "came to such and such a person in a dream."[29]

The criticism can be leveled against Oppenheim that this three-fold structure is very simple and consequently does not serve any useful purpose.[30] Gnuse has suggested that the correspondence between dreams simply stems more from their being divine theophanies in which human beings receive a message.[31] Oppenheim himself recognized from the outset that there was a problem, stemming from the fact that none of the dream reports contain all the stylistic features which constitute the "pattern."[32] Careful analysis was therefore required "to establish the borderline between its typical and its individual traits." If too many individual traits are taken into account, the pattern becomes more complex. Gnuse himself took account of OT traits and came up with a pattern more complicated than Oppenheim's.[33] It is based on eight OT dream narratives[34] and takes the following form:

1. Theophany
2. Recipient
3. Dream Reference
4. Time of Dream

28. Oppenheim, "Mantic Dreams," 347.

29. Oppenheim, "Interpretation of Dreams," 188b. He goes on to draw a further contrast with Greek epics where there is often a description of the appearing deity.

30. Gnuse, "Dream Genre," 97–120, esp. 100.

31. Gnuse, "Dream Genre," 100.

32. Oppenheim, "Interpretation of Dreams," 186b.

33. Gnuse, "Dream Genre," 101.

34. Gen 20:3–8; 28:12–16; 31:1–13, 24; 46:2–4; Num 22:8–13, 20–21; 1 Kgs 3:5–15.

5. Auditory Message Dream Address Formula
6. Message
   a. Introductory Formula (particle hinneh)
   b. Divine Self-Identification
   c. Message Proper: Assurance, Promise, Warnings, or Commands to Recipient
   d. Dialogue
7. Fulfillment

It should be noted that not all the narratives selected by Gnuse fit his own pattern. Genesis 31:24 lacks 6 a, b, d, and 7. That can be a weakness in any pattern. More importantly, it is possible to reduce Gnuse's pattern so that it fits Oppenheim's format. Gnuse's sections 1–4 fit Oppenheim's I; Gnuse's 5 and 6 a–d correspond to Oppenheim's II; and Gnuse's 7 is the same as Oppenheim's III.

Something similar could be said concerning the work of Hanson, who outlines a pattern for Greco-Roman dreams.[35] It would appear then that there is a basic pattern for the reporting of message dreams which spans various cultures, but at the same time allows for local traits. This is confirmed by the way in which scholars on different sides of debate want to claim correspondence between Matthew and their position. Gnuse, as we saw in the first chapter, finds a pattern in common between the Matthean dreams and the patriarchal dreams in Genesis, whereas Dodson detects a correspondence with those of classical literature.[36] If there is a pattern shared between the Elohist dream passages of Genesis and Matthew and if there is one shared between Greco-Roman dream reporting and Matthew, then it seems likely there is a pattern which embraces many features of dream reports in both Genesis and Greco-Roman literature. Certain scholars provide evidence from a variety of sources to support a widely used pattern.[37]

I conclude that there is a pattern in ancient dream reporting. Although the outline provided by Oppenheim is basic, it does embrace the most

---

35. Hanson, "Dreams and Visions," 1405–13.
36. Dodson, *Reading Dreams*.
37. Husser comments regarding Egyptian royal message dreams, written on stelae: "Throughout eighteen centuries the literary forms of the genre changed little" (Husser, *Dreams and Dream Narratives*, 61). Flannery-Dailey has shown that the dream texts of Hellenistic Judaism adhere uniformly to the forms of earlier dream texts, both Jewish and non-Jewish (Flannery-Dailey, *Dreamers, Scribes, and Priests*, 200).

common features. It is therefore adopted here. We now use it for a comparison with the structure of Matthew's dream accounts.

A preliminary examination of Matthew's text reveals the following, though we shall return to it later when we consider repetition as a memory pattern. Each dream opens with an introductory clause in the form of a genitive absolute. So at 1:20, we have: ταῦτα δὲ αὐτοῦ ἐνθυμηθέντος, at 2:13, Ἀναχωρησάντων δὲ αὐτῶν, and at 2:19, Τελευτήσαντος δὲ τοῦ Ἡρῴδου.[38] Then we have the demonstrative particle ἰδού, "behold."[39] Next comes a statement of the angel's appearance to Joseph in a dream: 1:20 ἄγγελος κυρίου κατ' ὄναρ ἐφάνη αὐτῷ; and 2:13, 19 ἄγγελος κυρίου φαίνεται κατ' ὄναρ τῷ Ἰωσήφ. There is slight variation in phraseology,[40] but for present purposes we can overlook it.

In all three cases there follows the participle λέγων, *saying*. Then come the angel's speeches, all three of which have a command, the first introducing it with Joseph's name, the latter two with the participle, ἐγερθείς, "having risen." Indeed ἐγερθεὶς παράλαβε carries the sense of ἐγερθήτι καὶ παράλαβε,

---

38. There are other examples of genitive absolute (Matt 1:18; 2:1). However, there is difficulty with Matt 1:20 where we might have expected the participle ἐνθυμηθέντος to be in the dative, agreeing with αὐτῷ later in the sentence, both referring to Joseph. Although Matt 2:1, 13, 19, are straightforward, there is a similar problem with 1:18. Fuller suggests that we should stop referring to genitive absolutes and refer instead to genitive constructions as they are not grammatically deficient constructions, but a regular feature of Hellenistic Greek used to signal important prior background information and to provide cohesion. See Fuller, "Genitive Absolute."

39. Strictly this is the imperative of the aorist middle of the verb ὁράω. It is used as a demonstrative particle much more frequently in LXX and NT than in classical Greek.

40. The most notable difference is that Matt 1:20 has the aorist ἐφάνη, while 2:13, 19, both have the present φαίνεται. Many treat the latter as an historic present. However, Olsen has argued that the present and aorist forms are not tenses, since they may be used with a range of temporal reference, and goes on to suggest that they indicate grammatical aspect: in the case of the present it is imperfective and with the aorist it is perfective (Olsen, *Koine Greek Verb*). The former represents something that was ongoing rather than completed. However, since the dream is followed by immediate action (ὁ δὲ ἐγερθεὶς παρέλαβεν . . . νυκτός), it seems likely that the angelic appearance came to an end quickly with Joseph rising during the night and that φαίνεται has much the same force as ἐφάνη, with the angelic appearance fading and Joseph taking action. Anderson treats 2:13 as an historic present (Anderson, *Matthew's Narrative Web*, 155). She sees particular significance in its use here: "contemporaneity of the implied reader with Joseph and the angel is achieved with the use of the historical present." This is not necessary at 1:20 as the reader already has the information being imparted to Joseph about Mary's conception. Davies and Allison offer a variation of this understanding, asking: "Does the present tense, φαίνεται (cf. 2:19 but contrast 1:20, which has the aorist), imply simultaneity, that is, does it make the angelic appearance concurrent with the magi's departure?" (Davies and Allison, *Matthew*, 1:259). We can only guess, but whether we go with Anderson or Davies and Allison, it is best to treat φαίνεται as an historic present.

"rise and take."⁴¹ Then a reason for the command is offered in a clause introduced by the conjunction γάρ, "for." With each command issued the angel offers an explanation.⁴²

The first dream has two commands (1:20, 21), each with its own reason. After the dreams, it is reported in all three cases that Joseph arose, ἐγερθείς. Although a single word, ἐγερθείς may function as part of a concluding formula.⁴³ The first example adds the phrase ἀπὸ τοῦ ὕπνου, "from sleep," and goes on to specify Joseph's obedience to the angel. Then all three echo the words of the command. What emerges from this is that Matthew conforms to Oppenheim's pattern with the three dreams which are narrated in full, while the other two are simply dream references.

The pattern discerned by Oppenheim offers a partial explanation of why Joseph's dreams are narrated the way they are. The rest of the explanation will be found in the memory patterns which are embedded in the text. Oppenheim failed to take account of the oral transmission, however long or short, which occurred before the message dreams were recorded. It will be our task to explore the techniques of such transmission both in Matthew and other dream texts.

---

41. Alford, commenting on Matt 2:13, 15, says that ἐγερθείς involves an imperative sense rather than a temporal one (Alford, *Greek Testament Critical Exegetical Commentary*). This construction is a Semitism. Ἐγερθείς + the imperative παράλαβε follows the Hebrew construction קום + imperative. This idiom is usually rendered by the LXX as ἀναστὰς + imperative.

42. *Command*: "Do not fear to take Mary your wife" (1:20).
*Explanation*: "That which is conceived in her is of the Holy Spirit" (1:20).
*Command*: "You shall call his name Jesus" (1:21).
*Explanation*: "He will save his people from their sins" (1:21).
*Command*: "Rise, take the child and his mother, and flee to Egypt, and remain there till I tell you" (2:13).
*Explanation*: "Herod is about to search for the child, to destroy him" (2:13).
*Command*: "Rise, take the child and his mother, and go to the land of Israel" (2:20).
*Explanation*: "Those who sought the child's life are dead" (2:20).

43. Many dream narratives conclude in a formulaic manner with a reference to the dreamer *rising*. Example are where Abimelech rises in the morning (Gen 20:8) and where Archelaus awakens, περιεγρόμενος (Josephus, *Ant.* 17.345). This formulaic ending is also to be found in Greco-Roman dreams, as in where Agamemnon wakes from sleep (ἔγρετο δ' ἐξ ὕπνου) and sits upright (ἕζετο δ' ὀρθωθείς) (Homer, *Iliad* 2.41–42).

## Ancient Dreams

We are fortunate that there is accessible to us an abundance of narratives describing ancient dreams. From Mesopotamia and Egypt we have Dream Books which record ordinary dreams, and although they lack personal detail, they indicate typical experiences of members of their respective societies.[44] As the dreams were thought to contain messages presaging future events in the dreamer's life, the books functioned as practitioners' manuals to guide professionals in their interpretation. They also listed rituals to be used in averting harmful effects from bad dreams. From Mesopotamia there have also survived literary texts, most notably the *Epic of Gilgamesh*.[45] With these we move from real-life experience to literary fiction. Dreams are also to be found in Assyrian and Babylonian royal inscriptions.[46] Egypt too provides us with the records of royal dreams written on stelae.[47] For eighteen centuries the literary form of these dreams changed little. When we turn to the Hittites, examples are much rarer.[48] Husser attributes the exceptions which do exist to Mesopotamian influence stemming from the Hurrians.[49] If we take next the Hebrew Bible, we find dreams occurring in narrative texts, particularly those associated with the hypothetical Elohist tradition of the Pentateuch.[50] There are also dreams in the book of Daniel which require the skills of an interpreter. Depictions of dreams in the Greek and Roman world are vast. They are to be found in epic, short poems, drama, comedy, histories, philosophy, and scientific and medical writings, as well as archaeological and epigraphic remains. We also have the dream books of Artremidorus Daldianus.[51] In the Jewish Hellenistic world there are over

---

44. See Husser, *Dreams and Dream Narratives*, for Mesopotamian dreams (27–51, esp. 38–46) and for Egyptian dreams (59–71, esp. 61–65).

45. What we find in the *Epic of Gilgamesh* are usually symbolic dreams, although there is an allusion to a message dream at 11.186–87. It may be recalled that Oppenheim classified dreams in two categories, symbolic and message.

46. The royal inscriptions include: Sumerian examples (from the end of the third millennium BCE); Akkadian examples from the reign of Assurbanipal (seventh century BCE) and Nabonidus (sixth century BCE). See Flannery-Dailey, *Dreamers, Scribes and Priests*, 18n3.

47. There are Egyptian inscriptions from Thutmose IV (fifteenth century BCE), Pharaoh Merneptah (thirteenth century BCE), and Tanutamon (seventh century BCE). See Oppenheim, "Interpretation of Dreams," 186–87.

48. There is a Hittite text of King Hattushili (twelfth century BCE).

49. Husser, *Dreams and Dream Narratives*, 52.

50. Gnuse, "Dream Genre," 100.

51. He was called *Daldianus* from his mother's native city, Daldis in Lycia. He was also known as Artemidorus of Ephesus. Towards the end of the second century CE he

100 dreamers appearing in the apocrypha, pseudepigraha, Qumran scrolls and the writings of Josephus. With regard to NT apart from Matthew, we have Paul's vision of the man of Macedon in Acts 16:9[52]; the angel of the Lord seen by Cornelius in Acts 10:1–8; Peter's vision in Acts 10:9–10[53]; the encouragement Paul received from the Lord in Acts 18:9; and also in Acts 23:11; 27:23. Gnuse suggests that the experiences of Paul and Ananias in Acts 9:3–17 might be dream-like.[54]

## Comparison with Matthew's Dreams

We need to consider where the Matthean dreams fit into such a wide spectrum. At this stage certain cultural features begin to emerge even before we come to Matthew's use of memory patterns and our comparison with their use in other literature.

## Comparison with Other Message Dreams

We begin with the *message* category. We classified Matthew's dreams above as belonging to this category. We may now go on to compare them with other message dreams. Widespread throughout ANE is the record of message dreams which come only to members of royal families. Instances of this are to be found in Assyrian and Babylonian royal inscriptions,[55] texts of Hittite sovereigns of the New Empire[56] and stelae recording dreams of

---

produced a five-volume work on dreams entitled *Oneirocritica*.

52. It was indicated in the introduction to the Methodology chapter that we would include in our comparison some visions where they closely resemble dreams; others are more complex, such as those involving otherworldly journeys as in 1 Enoch, referred to below.

53. For our purposes dreams and visions may be treated alike. They constitute a similar phenomenon, dreams generally being thought to occur in sleep and visions when the person is awake. More importantly, the literary form of dreams and waking visions are practically indistinguishable.

54. Gnuse, *Dreams and Dream Reports*, 100.

55. In the Sumerian inscription upon the *Vulture Stela* there is related a dream of King Eanatum I (c. 2454–2425 BCE) in which the god Ningirsu reassured him concerning the outcome of a war. See Husser, *Dreams and Dream Narratives*, 38. From the numerous royal neo-Babylonian inscriptions we have a dream in which Nabonidus (555–539 BCE) is visited by the divinities Marduk and Sin to request the rebuilding of a temple at Harran. See Oppenheim, "Interpretation of Dreams," 250.

56. We have the god Gurwashu addressing Queen Puduhepa, wife of Hattušili III in a dream, when the king's health was ailing. See Husser, *Dreams and Dream Narratives*, 55–56.

the Pharaohs.[57] To these we can add the royal character of the dreams in the Homeric corpus[58] and Ugaritic literature.[59] When we turn to Joseph, we note that he was the legal father of Jesus and in the table of descent given in Matt 1:1–17 Jesus is traced back through Joseph to King David and ultimately to Abraham. This must mean that Joseph too is of David's royal line. This may be reinforced by the message dreams coming to him in 1:18–2:23. In OT message dreams come to individuals such as Jacob or Laban who would not be regarded as royal figures. Although we may see individuals like Abraham and Jacob as being significant in the history of Israel and we refer to them as the *Patriarchs*, they were certainly not kings. However, OT authors do accord them special status. The patriarchs receive their covenantal blessing via message dreams in Genesis 15:12–21; 26:24; 28:10–22. Flannery-Dailey comments, "The similarity of the dreams suggests the ancient New Eastern motif of dream repetition to underscore the veracity of the promises, emphasizing even further the patriarchs' special status in comparison to other characters in the sacred history."[60] Although Joseph is merely a carpenter,[61] it may be that he is being accorded special status in a similar way to the patriarchs. Although it was Herod and not Joseph who was King of Judaea, the table of descent makes it clear that he was of royal lineage. It may, therefore, not be going too far to read kingship into the fact that Joseph received message dreams. From a theological perspective this emphasizes that Jesus is descended from the royal line of David. From a cultural perspective it suggests that Matthew's practice is in keeping with custom throughout the ANE.

---

57. We have a visitation of the goddess Satet in a dream to Sesostris I (1962–1928 BCE), recounted on an inscription at the Temple of Satet in Elephantine. We also have a visitation of Harmakhis-Khepri-Re-Atum in a dream to Thutmosis IV (1425–1417 BCE), recorded on the *Stela of the Sphinx* at Giza. See Husser, *Dreams and Dream Narratives*, 61–62.

58. In Homer, *Iliad*, we have the dreams of Agamemnon (2.1–41), Rhesus (10.494–97), Achilles (23.58–107), and Priam (24.677–95). In Homer, *Odyssey*, we have the dreams of Penelope (4.794–841; 20.87–90), and Nausicaa (6.15–50). We may also note Odysseus's imaginary dream (14.482–98), two apparitions of Athene by night (15.1–56; 20.30–55), and Penelope's single symbolic dream (19.535–81). These are, for the most part, message dreams.

59. Husser, *Dreams and Dream Narratives*, 76, refers to Keret being visited by El in the *Keret Epic* (KTU 1.14 i.26–43).

60. Flannery-Dailey, *Dreamers, Scribes, and Priests*, 47.

61. Matthew tells us that people asked concerning Jesus, "Is this not the carpenter's son?" (Matt 13:55).

## Comparison of the Use of Oppenheim's Pattern

We now move on to consider Matthew's use of the *script* for dream reporting in the light of other dream texts. Although the pattern discerned by Oppenheim is widely shared across the Near East and Mediterranean worlds, there are variations in details. As we observe these variations, we may be able to detect cultural differences. It is not a question of whether other cultures use the pattern, but how they use it.

Flannery-Dailey points out that unlike the practice of non-Israelite dreams, the Hebrew God's physical appearance is never described.[62] Husser refers to the "impressive descriptions of the apparition of gods" in dreams of the Mesopotamian tradition.[63] We may therefore ask where Matthew stands in relation to this cultural variation. In his dreams we are simply told that the angel of the Lord *appeared*. Matthew uses the passive of the verb φαίνω at 1:20; 2:13, 19. The vital question is whether this means that there was a physical epiphany or a divine presence manifested without any visual aspect. In Classical Greek the passive of the verb φαίνω tends to mean "to be *seen*."[64] The likelihood is that Matthew's usage is influenced by the Semitic or Septuagintal style which he demonstrates throughout the gospel and in the infancy section in particular.[65] There is a similar ambiguity in the Hebrew verb when OT says that YHWH appeared (נראה). Husser suggests that with verbs such as בוא (come), נצב or התיצב (stand beside), and נראה (appear), their recurrent use "seems to describe not so much a visual perception as the sensation of a presence, or a sense of the nearness of the divinity. An oneiric theophany, in the Old Testament, is a *theophany without vision* of God."[66] No description of the angel is given in Matthew and in this respect he is close to the practice of the Hebrew Bible. He is also close to the practice in Hittite dreams.[67] What about Greek dreams? When they have the dream-figure come under the guise of a particular person known to the dreamer, he

---

62. Flannery-Dailey, *Dreamers, Scribes, and Priests*, 46.

63. Husser, *Dreams and Dream Narratives*, 124.

64. An exception to this would be the way in which Plato uses φαίνεται in some of his dialogues (Plato, *Protagoras* 324d, 332e; *Republica* 333c, 383a), where the conclusion to an argument *appears* to be such and such without anything being physically visible.

65. E.g., we have the construction καλεῖν + τὸ ὄνομα αὐτοῦ + proper name (Matt 1:21, 23, 25). This is a Septuagintism for קרא + שם + proper name. OT examples are Genesis 16:11; 25:26.

66. Husser, *Dreams and Dream Narratives*, 124.

67. Husser says of Hittite dreams, "There is not a single description of a divinity who appears in a dream, the latter being essentially auditory" (Husser, *Dreams and Dream Narratives*, 56).

is usually described. So in *Iliad* 2:20 the *oneiros* figure appears to Agamemnon resembling Nestor, son of Neleus. It could of course be argued that the god as such is not being described, simply his emissary. However, the angel of the Lord is God's emissary in Matthew. Unlike Nestor, he is not described. But we also have the divinity Athene taking the form of Diomedes, son of Tydeus, when she visits King Rhesus.[68] Matthew also stands in contrast to Jewish Hellenistic texts. While they do not depict God materially, they do describe angelic messengers in a variety of ways.[69] They also have angels appearing in the waking reality of the dreamer as well as inside the dream (e.g., 4 Ezra 5:15; Dan 9:21). To sum up, Matthew stands more closely to the OT practice of not describing YHWH, although we recognize that he is dealing with an angel and not God himself, and at a distance from Mesopotamian or Greek accounts with their descriptions of apparitions of gods.

## Comparison with Other Features of Ancient Dreams

We have compared Matthew's dreams with those of other texts in the light of Oppenheim's classification and pattern of dream reporting. We continue with our comparison, looking out for some of the other features to be found in the realms of dream literature.

We may note the following characteristics. Some dreams from ANE and the classical world come from the realm of the dead.[70] Some of the visions in Jewish Apocalyptic literature and beyond involve otherworldly journeys.[71] In Classical and Hellenistic dreaming healing was common.[72] Healing in turn raises the issue of dream incubation, for therapeutic incubation would be performed with a view to achieving healing. The practice of

---

68. Homer, *Iliad* 10.496-97; cf. *Iliad* 23.62-101; 24.682-89; *Odyssey* 4.795-841; 6.19-49.

69. Flannery-Dailey, *Dreamers, Scribes, and Priests*, 201.

70. Homer, for example, has the land of dreams situated near Hades (Homer, *Odyssey* 24.12). However, there is no evidence of dreams coming from the realm of the dead in Herodotus.

71. The Book of the Watchers (1 Enoch 1-36), for example, relates Enoch's heavenly commissioning and his journeys to the west, the east and the four corners of the earth. Although such journeys were known in ANE and Greek literature, they became more developed in Jewish Apocalyptic work and in Cicero's *Somnium Scipionis*.

72. Dream cults, such as those associated with the worship of Asklepios at Trikka, Epidauros, Pergamon, and Kos, were sites of healing and/or oracles. See Flannery-Dailey, *Dreamers, Scribes, and Priests*, 100.

incubation was widespread.[73] An individual, be he king, priest, prophet or ordinary citizen, would spend the night in a sanctuary or in a natural holy site in the hope of receiving from a god a visit or a message in a dream.[74] There would be ritual preparation in the form of fasting, purification, and/or sacrifices.[75] The actual sleeping may have take place at the feet of the god's statue.[76] There might also be rituals performed on wakening. There is little evidence for this practice in ancient Israel.[77]

We now set the Matthean narratives against this background. There is no suggestion that Joseph's dreams come from the realm of the dead. In three dreams the angel of the Lord appears, presumably at God's behest. In the other two the Magi and Joseph are warned (χρηματισθέντες) in a dream. The passive use of the verb suggests that the warning was given by God, as the passive is often used in Hebrew and biblical Greek to express the action of God. In this respect Matthew is closer to Jewish writers and some of the classical who believed that dreams came from God rather than the realm of the dead. Nor does Matthew involve Joseph in any otherworldly journeys. Although Matthew lacks these, there may still be an apocalyptic strand in his narrative through the appearance of an angel within a dream. Dreams involving angels were common in apocalyptic books, such as Daniel and 1 Enoch. This apocalyptic element in Matthew is appropriate since he is dealing with the birth of the Messiah, an eschatological figure associated with the ushering in of the New Age.

---

73. Incubation was practiced at the temple sites of Asklepios, over 400 of which existed throughout the Hellenistic world and Roman Empire. Archaeology has uncovered *Asklepieia* in Palestine at Dor and Shuni. Incubation is also attested in ANE sources, but it is rare compared with Greek and later near eastern sources. See Flannery-Dailey, *Dreamers, Scribes, and Priests*, 34, 100.

74. Examples of incubated dreams include the dreams of the Sumerain King Gudea, the Hittite King Murshili, the Akkadian King Narâm-Sia, and the Assyrian priest of Ishtar. See Oppenheim, "Interpretation of Dreams," 188–89, 191, 205, 224.

75. Incubants at Epidauros underwent ritual bathing as well as offering sacrifice, but fasting was not a requirement there, as it was at many other dream oracles. See Flannery-Dailey, *Dreamers, Scribes, and Priests*, 100. Examples of prayer and mourning in dream incubation are the dreams of Assurbanipal and Sethos. See Oppenheim, "Interpretation of Dreams," 249n10, 252n22.

76. Oppenheim speculates that the form of "message" dreams in which an individual sees a god stems from such an environment (Oppenheim, "Interpretation of Dreams," 190; "Mantic Dreams," 348).

77. The OT texts cited as evidence are hotly debated (Gen 15; 28:10-17; 46:1-4; 1 Sam 3; 1 Kgs 3:4-15; Isa 65:4; Ps 3:6; 4:6; 17:5; 63). Husser, *Dreams and Dream Narratives*, 91, refers to Ehrlich, *Der Traum im Alten Testament*, claiming that only Solomon's dream at Gibeon (1 Kgs 3) is indisputable.

Matthew has no hints of healing involved in the dreams. Nor is there any reference to rituals preceding them. Consequently it is tempting to reject any suggestion of incubation. However, the question may be raised as to what lies behind the use of the word χρηματισθέντες at 2:12 and χρηματισθείς at 2:22. In the seventeenth century Cornelius à Lapide suggested that the Magi had sought divine guidance. He based this on the Vulgate version: *et responso accepto in somnis* ("and having received an answer in sleep") and commented: "the word *answer* implies, that the Magi in a doubtful matter, in the first place asked light of God, and received an answer from Him."[78] In the nineteenth century Johann Lange did the same with χρηματισθείς at 2:22 and had Joseph applying to the Lord for guidance. It is true that χρηματισμός can signify an oracular answer and an answer implies a preceding question. However, it is not clear that Matthew's use of χρηματίζω here necessarily implies the seeking of guidance. It is possible to see God taking the initiative with the dream, as he does with the Joseph dreams which are narrated more fully. Furthermore, the use of a verb in the passive may simply signify action on the part of God. It is reading too much into the use of χρηματίζω to suggest traces of incubation here.

## Comparison with Jewish Dreams

We may explore another cultural issue, one which initially links Matthew's infancy narratives to Hellenistic Judaism. Since Joseph's dreams provide divine protection for Jesus, Flannery-Dailey sees them in the context of warning dreams in Hellenistic Judaism.[79] In these texts dreams come to the patriarchs and others, and their function is to enact divine protection for the patriarchs and their future descendants.[80]

There are two Jewish dreams in particular which have parallels with those recorded by Matthew. These are the dream which Josephus attributes to Amram, Moses's father[81] and the one which Pseudo-Philo attributes to Miriam, Moses's sister.[82] Before we consider them, we observe the parallel drawn in Matthew's text between the infant Jesus and the story of Moses,

---

78. À Lapide, *Great Biblical Commentary*, commenting on Matt 2:12.

79. Flannery-Dailey, *Dreamers, Scribes, and Priests*, 165.

80. Flannery-Dailey gives as examples Abram in 1QGen.Apoc; Abimelech, Laban, and Pharaoh in Josephus, *Ant.* 1.208-9, 313-14; 2.75-86; and Isaac in Testament of Abraham 7.

81. Josephus, *Ant.* 2.210-216.

82. Pseudo-Philo, *Liber Antiquitatum Biblicarum* 9.10.

both in his infancy and his later life. This has been noted by Brown[83] among others and explored in considerable detail by Allison.[84] At 2:20 we read τεθνήκασιν γὰρ οἱ ζητοῦντες τὴν ψυχὴν τοῦ παιδίου, "for those who sought the child's life are dead." The use of the plural here stands out and looks odd, as only Herod has died (see verse 19). It could be taken as a reference to the chief priests and scribes of the people who cooperated with Herod. It seems more likely that it is an echo of a plural in the story of Moses. Exodus 4:19 in the Septuagint reads τεθνήκασι γὰρ πάντες οἱ ζητοῦντές σου τὴν ψυχήν, "for all who sought your life are dead." As an adult, Moses fled from Egypt to the land of Midian after he killed an Egyptian and the Pharaoh sought his life. He only returned to Egypt when the persecuting king had died. This seems to be echoed in Matthew's account of the holy family's return from Egypt.[85] There are also parallels in the life of the infant Moses. Exodus 1–2 records how a new Pharaoh came to the throne of Egypt, fearing that the people of Israel would multiply and pose a threat to his own people. He gave orders for every son born to the Hebrews to be cast into the Nile. Moses's mother hid him and he was rescued by Pharaoh's daughter. In effect he was providentially saved. Similarly, King Herod gave orders (Matt 2:16-18) to do away with the male children of Bethlehem who were two years or under. Jesus was providentially saved (2:13-14) through the action of Joseph in obedience to the angel's message.

We now set this alongside the dreams which the extra-biblical tradition developed concerning the infant Moses. We take first the dream narrated by Josephus. Amram was anxious for the future of his people and concerned about his wife's pregnancy, given Pharaoh's decree. Then "*God stood by him in his sleep, and exhorted him not to despair.*" This links in with Joseph's concern over Mary's pregnancy, albeit not yet threatened by harm from Herod, and the appearance of the angel of the Lord in a dream to reassure him (Matt 1:18-21). God went on to prophesy future greatness for Amram's son: "*he shall deliver the Hebrew nation from the distress they are under from the Egyptians.*" Likewise Joseph was told that Jesus shall *save his people from their sins* (1:21). Similarly in the dream which Pseudo-Philo narrates an angel appeared to Miriam and foretold the greatness of the child to be born to her parents. In particular he prophesied: "*through him . . . I shall save my people.*"

83. Brown, *Birth of the Messiah*, 113-14.

84. For discussion on the Infancy Narratives, see Allison, *New Moses*, 140-65.

85. The parallel is not exact. Moses returns *to* Egypt, while Joseph and company return *from* Egypt. Moses took his family, whereas it was Joseph, not Jesus, who performed that task.

It would exceed the evidence to suggest that the first Matthean dream is modeled on either of these dreams. However, there are sufficient parallels to suggest that Matthew or those close to him may have been moving among Jews who narrated similar stories concerning the infant Moses. Indeed it is possible that if Matthew was dependent on any source for his dream narratives, he may have drawn directly upon Jewish traditions about Moses rather than Christian traditions about the infant Jesus.

As we embarked on this subsection, we noted that the warning nature of the dreams in Matthew points to a Jewish background. However, we have gone on to see a typological parallel with Moses which points in a similar direction. We shall now pursue the typological issue in greater detail.

## Typology

We have seen Jesus portrayed as the new Moses. Such a portrayal is evident or hinted at elsewhere in the First Gospel[86] in the crossing of water (Matt 3:13-17; Exod 14:10-31), the wilderness temptation (Matt 4:1-11; Exod 16:1-17:7), the mountain of lawgiving (Matt 5-7; Exod 19:1-23:33), reciprocal knowledge of God (Matt 11:25-30; Exod 33:1-23), the transfiguration (Matt 17:1-9; Exod 34:29-35), and the commissioning of a successor (Matt 28:16-20; Deut 31:7-9; Josh 1:1-9). In some of these experiences it is also possible to see Jesus's experience related to that of Israel.[87]

Within the dream narratives we may see Jesus portrayed as the new Israel in the quotation at 2:15 of Hosea 11:1, "out of Egypt I called my son." However, Allison sees the quotation of the Hosea text as a clear instance of Moses typology.[88] There is no doubt that Moses is portrayed in OT as the leader of the exodus. However, the "son" to whom Hosea is referring is Israel. Allison himself recognizes that 2:15 can be seen as making Jesus the new Israel and not the new Moses.[89] He responds by suggesting that Matthew construed Jesus's status as the new Israel and his identity as another Moses as "correlative conceptions." He points out that in ancient thought "a king represented, could indeed be said to be, his people." Nevertheless, we cannot be certain about what was in Matthew's mind. It is possible that

---

86. Allison lists the examples given (Allison, *New Moses*, 268). France sees different typology at work later in the gospel (France, *Matthew*, 40-41). He regards Jesus's wilderness testing as corresponding to the wilderness testing of Israel in Deuteronomy and he notes that Jesus was to undergo an experience parallel to that of Jonah (Matt 12:40).

87. France, *Matthew*, 97.

88. Allison, *New Moses*, 140.

89. Allison, *New Moses*, 142.

the Moses typology inspired Matthew's use of the Hosea text and subsequent Israel typology.

Matthew goes on to develop the portrayal of Jesus as the new Israel independently. Jeffrey Gibbs suggests that Jesus "recapitulates or summarizes and repeats the history of the nation of Israel."[90] Gibbs expands upon this in relation to relation to Israel's escape from bondage in Egypt. However, it may also be applied to the Babylonian exile. At 2:18 Matthew quotes Jer 31:15. This is not applied directly to Jesus, but to the slaughter of the children of Bethlehem. However, since Jesus is associated with the event insofar as it was precisely that from which he was escaping, the quotation does relate to him. Jeremiah is referring to the return of people from exile.[91] Jesus, therefore, recapitulates the Exodus and the return from Exile, the two major events in the history of his nation. Whether we think of Jesus as the new Moses or the new Israel, such discussion is largely along theological lines. Typology is being used to help establish the identity of the infant Jesus.

However, it was argued in the methodology chapter that typology can also be used as a memory pattern. The question is whether that applies in Matthew's dream narratives. With the new Moses type, there are many parallels between the story of the infant Jesus and Moses, both in infancy and later life. Although there are also differences, these are outweighed by the instances of similarity. Moreover, we do not require two identical accounts for typology to function mnemonically. In the case of Trumpeldor, considered in the methodology chapter, his band of soldiers was small and his victory less significant than that of Bar Kokhba or other heroes of Jewish antiquity. Nevertheless, the typological analogy was sufficiently strong to preserve his memory as a hero in the Israeli consciousness of the 1920s. Similarly, it can be argued that the analogy with Moses reinforces the memory of events surrounding the infant Jesus, with details of the story reinterpreted or even changed. The question has to be raised whether the Moses typology was consciously chosen as a mnemonic device or more for its interpretive value. The latter seems more likely as the first Christians sought ways to expound the significance of Jesus. However, in the Methodology chapter when we included typology as a memory pattern, we noted that it involved the use of a *schema*, particularly *keying*. It was said then that this framework served as a way of interpreting the past, but at the same time carried a memory function in a narrow sense. While Matthew's prime concern is likely to have been expounding the significance of Jesus, the

---

90. Gibbs, *Concordia Commentary*, 142.

91. Nicholson, *Jeremiah 26–52*, 66. The poem (Jer 31:15–22) originally foretold the return of the people of northern Israel who had been exiled in 722 BCE.

parallels between his infancy and that of Moses would have had the effect of reinforcing the former with readers.

We shall see in the chapter on comparison of memory patterns how typology is unique to Matthew as far as dream narratives are concerned. However, given that he uses Moses and Israel as types, we can detect Jewish influence.

## Summary

Since we have digressed a little in our discussion of typology from the main thrust of this section where we have been comparing Matthew's dreams with other ancient dreams, we now summarize our line of thought. When we apply Oppenheim's classification, we see that Matthew's narratives fall into the category of message dreams, despite having an element of interpretation at 1:21, 22–23. We noted how in ANE sources message dreams are described as coming to royal personages and behind our text may lie a reminder that Joseph was of David's royal line. An analysis of the Matthean text suggests that his dreams fit Oppenheim's pattern of reporting. Variations of detail reveal points of cultural significance. Unlike the dream messengers of ANE and Homeric texts, but like God in OT dreams, the angel of the Lord is not described. Comparisons with other ancient dream texts suggest that Joseph's dreams differ from some in ANE and classical world insofar as they do not come from the realm of the dead and do not involve healing or incubation. Parallels with the enactment of divine providence for the patriarchs also emerged, pointing to a Jewish background. Finally, in the typological use of Moses and Israel we observe further Jewish influence.

In these comparisons we have looked at two devices which contribute to the preservation of memory, the structure or *script* of dream reports and typology or *keying*. These are pre-existent conceptual frameworks which help us to remember the past. We tend to use them unconsciously. Although they do preserve memory, they function in a different way from memory patterns such as repetition or alliteration which are used deliberately. It is these latter patterns which form the main thrust of this study. In our next chapter we shall look for evidence of them in Matthew's text.

# 6

# Matthew

## Introduction

IN THIS CHAPTER WE shall look at issues relating to the Gospel of Matthew as a whole, but concentrating in particular on the dream narratives. We begin by considering to which genre the gospel belongs, when and where it was written, who its author was, and how much rhetorical education he received. We move on to a sound analysis of Matthew's text, before we explore the memory patterns present in Matthew's text, the subject with which this study is primarily concerned.

## Genre of Gospel

What kind of literature is the first book in the NT? The following options have been considered: midrash, lectionary, catechetical manual, missionary propaganda and polemic against the rabbis, but none is a perfect fit.[1] Since Richard Burridge first published his monograph, *What Are the Gospels?*, in 1992,[2] there has been a wide acceptance that Matthew's Gospel belongs to the genre of ancient biography, βίος. There are different expectations between modern and ancient biographies, with the latter able to omit some aspects of a subject's life. It is therefore not a problem that Matthew does not cover Jesus's childhood. An ancient biography might begin with a person's birth or arrival on the public scene and end with his death, and in between narrate stories, anecdotes, speeches, and sayings, all related to him. Examples involving philosophers and "thinkers" tend to be "more anecdotal" and "arranged

---

1. Hagner, *Matthew 1–13*, lvii–lix.
2. The second edition was published in 2004. Burridge, "About People," 113–46, summarizes his case.

around collections of material displaying their ideas and teachings."[3] They also tend to focus disproportionately on the subject's death.[4]

Luz argues against this classification: "Matthew does not tell the typical story of an exemplary human being but the unique story of God with the human Jesus."[5] He suggests that Matthew took his cue from Mark,[6] who opens his account of Jesus's life with a reference to "gospel,"[7] which would make it a distinct category in its own right. It is possible to resolve the difficulty by seeing the gospels as incorporating elements of several literary genres.[8] Robert Kinney suggests, "while it is likely that Matthew wrote in the tradition of Greco-Roman biography, his work deviated from the form and was also received as a Gospel."[9] Eve notes the affinity that the gospels have with the Jewish Scriptures and consequently proposes "the hybrid genre of *biblically oriented bioi*."[10] What emerges from such discussion is that although the gospels do not fit precisely the *bios* genre, they do display some of its traits.

There is a subgenre of biography known as encomiastic because it embraces the encomium element which students of rhetoric were encouraged to practice as they wrote about the virtues and greatness of individuals. Insofar as the First Gospel praises Jesus and promotes his reputation, it may be treated as an example of encomiastic biography.[11] In that case the dream narratives have an important role to play, for dreams were sometimes recommended by the rhetoricians for developing the birth topos.[12]

## Date and Location

Neither date nor location has strong relevance to our argument. We therefore note in passing the most likely timescale and place. Dating is established on the basis of internal and external evidence. Although internal

3. Burridge, "About People," 122.
4. Burridge, "About People," 122.
5. Luz, *Matthew 1–7*, 45.
6. Luz, *Matthew 1–7*, 46.
7. Ἀρχὴ τοῦ εὐαγγελίου Ἰησοῦ Χριστοῦ [υἱοῦ θεοῦ].
8. Davies and Allison say "not one of these categories taken in isolation does justice to the totality of the gospel. . . . The text is an omnibus of genres" (*Matthew*, 1:3).
9. Kinney, *Dimensions*, 75.
10. Eve, *Writing the Gospels*, 23–24.
11. Talbert, *Matthew*, 6.
12. Hermogenes, *Progym.* 7.22–24 [15]: "You will mention also any marvelous occurrences at birth, for example, from dreams (ὀνειράτων) or signs or things like that." See Kennedy, *Progymnasmata*, 82.

data cannot offer precision, a plausible *terminus a quo* seems to be around 70 CE.[13] External material suggests a *terminus ad quem* of around 100 CE.[14] As to the place of writing, early Church tradition suggests Jerusalem or elsewhere in Palestine,[15] but many modern scholars favor Syrian Antioch.[16] Other suggestions include Edessa, Jerusalem, Caesarea Maritima, Phoenicia—maybe a town like Tyre or Sidon, Alexandria, Damascus, Pella or one of the other cities of the Decapolis, one of the cities of Galilee—such as Sepphoris or Tiberius.[17] We simply have to accept that the evidence for any location remains inconclusive.

This may seem disappointing if it is suggested that the place of writing has some relevance for Matthew's cultural background. It used to be thought that if Matthew belonged to Antioch or indeed any of the locations beyond Palestine, he would automatically be exposed to Hellenism, whereas if he lived in Jerusalem or elsewhere in Palestine, the major influence upon him would be normative Judaism. Such thinking is flawed in two respects. First, diversity within Judaism has been revealed through study of the Qumran scrolls and it now makes sense to speak of Judaisms in the plural.[18] More significantly, the influence of Hellenism embraced Palestine as well as the Diaspora. Hengel argues in *Judaism and Hellenism* that the spread of Hellenism was massive from the time of Alexander's conquests in 330s BCE onwards and that both the geography and chronology of Judaism

---

13. There appears to be a reference to the destruction of Jerusalem at Matt 22:7. For discussion of this, see Luz, *Matthew 1–7*, 92; Gibbs, *Concordia Commentary*, 65; Gundry, *Matthew*, 599. For discussion of evidence for a break between the church and the synagogue, see Hagner, *Matthew 1–13*, lxxiii; Davies and Allison, *Matthew*, 1:137; Harrington, *Gospel of Matthew*, 16. For other internal evidence, see France, *Matthew*, 29; Gundry, *Matthew*, 604; Hagner, *Matthew 1–13*; Davies and Allison, *Matthew*, 1:132–33.

14. Eusebius, *Historia Ecclesiastica* 3.39, has preserved a quotation from Papias, written around 100 or earlier, which may refer to our Gospel of Matthew. For other citations or allusions, see Davies and Allison, *Matthew*, 1:129–30; Luz, *Matthew 1–7*, 93; Harrington, *Gospel of Matthew*, 8.

15. Gibbs, *Concordia Commentary*, 67.

16. Arguments in its favor are these. "Syria" (Matt 4:24) replaces "Tyre and Sidon" (Mark 3:8; Luke 6:17), suggesting the possibility that Matthew wrote somewhere in Syria. We are told that the coin known as a stater is equivalent to two double drachmae (Matt 17:24–27), which was only the case in Damascus and Antioch in Syria. The First Gospel assigns a major role to Peter, especially at 16:17–19, and we know that he had status in Syrian Antioch (Gal 2:11–14). The Didache and Letters of Ignatius, bishop of Antioch, exhibit knowledge of Matthew's Gospel. Ναζωραῖος (Matt 2:23) was a Syrian designation for Christians. Scholars who favor Syria or Syrian Antioch are Schweizer, *Good News according to Matthew*, 16–17; Gundry, *Matthew*, 609; Davies and Allison, *Matthew*, 1:143–47; Hagner, *Matthew 1–13*, lxxv; Luz, *Matthew 1–7*, 90–92.

17. Most scholars who offer these suggestions simply present a list and do not argue for any of them, e.g., Talbert, *Matthew*, 4. However, Davies and Allison do present a case for some of them (*Matthew*, 1:139–43, 146).

18. Kinney, *Dimensions*, 20–21.

in Palestine cannot be separated from the influence of Hellenistic culture.¹⁹ Wherever Matthew and his associates lived, they were exposed to Hellenism. We see evidence of this in that he wrote in the common dialect of Greek (Κοινὴ Ἑλληνική) and that the literary genre to which his work most closely conforms is βίος. However, Judaism and Hellenism were not completely syncretised. Jews adhered to the religion of their ancestors in ancient Israel, albeit expressed in a variety of belief systems. They were held together by focusing on the Scriptures, Moses, and the Sabbath.²⁰

## Authorship

There is a prima facie case for saying that the First Gospel was written by the disciple Matthew of Capernaum. The earliest evidence for Matthean authorship is Papias who tells how "Matthew made an ordered arrangement of the oracles in the Hebrew (or: Aramaic) language [Ἑβραΐδι διαλέκτῳ], and each one translated (or: interpreted) [ἡρμήνευσεν] it as he was able."²¹ There are difficulties with this: our First Gospel is written in Greek; there is no extant Semitic version; and what we have is not likely to be the work of a translator.²² However, the major problem for Matthean authorship is to explain why someone who had accompanied Jesus would allow the arrangement of his material to be determined by the Second Gospel when elsewhere our author shows himself capable of redacting Markan verses and adding new material?²³ Luz sees this difficulty as insurmountable.²⁴

If Matthew the disciple did not write the First Gospel, what are we able to work out concerning its author? A significant number of scholars regard him as a Jewish Christian,²⁵ while a few see him as Gentile.²⁶ Lin-

---

19. Hengel, *Judaism and Hellenism*.

20. Kinney, *Dimensions*, 28.

21. Eusebius, *Historia Ecclesiastica* 3.39.

22. There are those who try to counter these difficulties and maintain Matthean authorship: Gundry, *Matthew*, 619–20; Gibbs, *Concordia Commentary*, 61.

23. The priority of Mark is being assumed, but not argued for here. For this position, see Kümmel, *Introduction to the New Testament*, 33–60. The matter continues to be debated with recent work (MacEwen, *Matthean Posteriority*; Garrow, "Streeter's 'Other' Synoptic Solution," 207–226) supporting the Matthean Posteriority Hypothesis, suggesting that Matthew used Luke as well as Mark and other sources. On the other hand, Watson, *Gospel Writing*, supports the Farrer Hypothesis that Luke used Matthew and Mark.

24. Luz, *Matthew 1–7*, 94. Others, like Gundry, *Matthew*, 621, and Hagner, *Matthew 1–13*, lxxvi, recognize the problem, but think it can be resolved.

25. E.g., Davies and Allison, *Matthew*, 33; Hagner, *Matthew 1–13*, lxxvii; Harrington, *Gospel of Matthew*, 8; Schweizer, *Good News according to Matthew*, 17.

26. Davies and Allison, *Matthew*, 1:10–11, list several from K. W. Clark, in 1947, to

guistic evidence has been called into play, although first language does not equate to ethnicity. Attention has been drawn to the finished Greek of the First Gospel,[27] which does not suggest a man whose first language was Aramaic or Hebrew. Davies and Allison counter this by stating that it is not the same standard of Greek as that of Josephus.[28] It is also possible for bilingual people to write their second language with precision. There has been some discussion as to whether Matthew's language betrays ignorance of Jewish matters.[29] On the one hand, the author avoids words like Βοανηργές[30] and Ταλιθα κουμ[31] found in Mark, and it is suggested that the reason is that he has a poorer understanding of Aramaic. However, it is possible that he wants to improve Mark's Greek. In the section where he omits Ταλιθα κουμ, he has abbreviated the whole pericope and so his omission is not surprising. On the other hand, there are Semitisms which are unique in the First Gospel.[32] For example, at 1:21 we have a Hebrew wordplay: καλέσεις τὸ ὄνομα αὐτοῦ Ἰησοῦν, αὐτὸς γὰρ σώσει τὸν λαὸν αὐτοῦ ἀπὸ τῶν ἁμαρτιῶν αὐτῶν. "Jesus" (Ἰησοῦς) is the Greek for the Hebrew "Joshua" (יהושע). By popular etymology this was related to the Hebrew verb "to save" (ישע) and to the Hebrew noun "salvation" (ישועה). The evangelist does not clarify this as he does with "Immanuel" at 1:23. The questions which arise are these: did the Semitisms occur in our author's source? If so, he still chose to retain them where he cut out those in Mark referred to above. Many of the Semitisms occur in LXX: was this a conscious or unconscious imitation? Did our author derive his Semitisms from LXX without any underlying knowledge of Hebrew or Aramaic? The problem is that we have no way of knowing the answers.[33]

It seems likely that the First Gospel should be attributed to a Jewish Christian in a later generation than Matthew the disciple. In the absence of any other name we shall follow convention and call him Matthew.

---

M. J. Cook, in 1983.

27. France, *Matthew*, 32; Luz, *Matthew 1-7*, 94.
28. Davies and Allison, *Matthew*, 1:25.
29. Davies and Allison, *Matthew*, 1:17-25.
30. Mark 3:17; cf. Matt 10:2.
31. Mark 5:22-43 corresponds to Matt 9:18-26.
32. Davies and Allison, *Matthew*, 1:80-85.
33. For further evidence and discussion of Jewish authorship, see Davies and Allison, *Matthew*, 1:7-58; France, *Matthew*, 75; Harrington, *Gospel of Matthew*, 8-9.

## Matthew's Education

If Matthew wrote reasonably good Greek and made use of Semitisms, we may wonder how much rhetorical education, if any, he had received. First we ask whether his location would make such education possible. We indicated above that Matthew is often associated with Antioch. This was the largest city in Roman Syria and the third-largest in the Empire. As such, it would have had teachers of rhetoric.[34] However, even if he was reared away from any major city, he may still have had some tuition in rhetoric. Teresa Morgan suggests that while only the major cities of the Empire had specialized teachers, in towns and villages one or two teachers may have covered whatever was learned locally,[35] but what they would be teaching would be preliminary studies and not advanced level rhetoric. Even if Matthew was brought up in Palestine, it would still have been possible for him to be rhetorically educated. Kennedy points out that Palestine and Syria were not rhetorical backwaters and to support his point he refers to Theodorus, one of the most famous rhetoricians of the first century BCE, who was a native of Gadara.[36] From all this we may infer that wherever Matthew lived, it is possible that he may have had a certain basic amount of rhetorical education. However, we need to bear in mind that few people actually attained a full rhetorical education. We saw in the Orality chapter how only a small proportion of the population were literate. It is a tiny fraction of them who would have received a rhetorical education. In an article in *The Oxford Handbook of Jewish Daily Life in Roman Palestine*, Hezser says, "Few students will have advanced to this level [sc. secondary, grammar school level], however, and even fewer would have proceeded to third-level education, the study at a law school, with a philosopher, or rhetorical training."[37]

We may ask what evidence of Matthew's rhetorical education exists in the text. We take the Sermon on the Mount as an example. Kennedy sees its structure as conforming entirely to Greco-Roman oratorical categories.[38] The *exordium*[39] consists of Matt 5:3–16, while the *narratio*[40] is formed by

---

34. Libanius taught rhetoric in Antioch, although he belonged to the fourth century.
35. Morgan, "Rhetoric and Education," 309.
36. Kennedy, *New Testament Interpretation*, 9.
37. Hezser, "Private and Public Education," 468, cites Rawson, *Intellectual Life*, 90; Marrou, *Histoire de l'Éducation*, 419. See also Morgan, *Literate Education*, 57.
38. Kennedy, *New Testament Interpretation*, 39–72.
39. Introduction to an oration.
40. The main proposition or statement of facts.

5:17–20. Then we would expect *partitio*,[41] *confirmatio*,[42] and *refutatio*,[43] but the *partitio* is missing.[44] The *confirmatio* is made up of 5:21—7:20, while elements of *refutatio* are to be found at 5:17; 6:31. The *peroratio*[45] comes at 7:21–27. Although Kennedy's analysis is possible, it is by no means compelling. Other scholars analyze the Sermon in different ways, often according to themes or subject matter.[46]

Kinney draws attention to several literary features or rhetorical figures used in the Sermon.[47] He refers to Socrates's use of rhetorical questions to drive someone to *aporia*, a feeling of doubt or frustration, and he suggests that Jesus uses rhetorical questions at 5:13, 46–47, albeit "in monological form." He finds *hyperbole* at 5:29–30; a *parable* at 7:24–27; *anaphora*[48] in 5:3–12, 21–48; 6:1–18; and *synecdoche*[49] at 6:11. The difficulty here is that these figures, with the possible exception of *aporia*, can be found in the Hebrew Bible. This is something which Kinney himself recognizes.[50] While he would not want to argue that their appearance there is a matter of Hellenistic influence, he considers it probable that Matthew would be influenced by Greco-Roman rhetorical ornamentation. We cannot simply assume this, given Matthew's use of OT elsewhere. We conclude that the case for Matthew drawing upon Greco-Roman literary features is not proven.

None of this proves that Matthew actually received a rhetorical education. It would have been possible for him to have had some kind of rhetorical awareness without any formal training.[51] If we were to assume that Matthew received his education in a Jewish context, what form would that have taken? In a later era Jewish higher education involved study with a rabbi who would teach orally and whose opinions would be memorized. Although attention was focused on the Torah, Hezser comments: "this did

41. A summary used to close the introduction.
42. The main body of the discourse.
43. Counterarguments to anticipated points of contention.
44. This need not be regarded as serious, since Quintilian, *Institutio* 4.5, recommends that *partitio* be blended with the *propositio* and it may be said that we have this in Matt 5:17–20.
45. Conclusion to the discourse. Kennedy uses the term *epilogue*.
46. E.g., Talbert, *Matthew*, 75–96.
47. Kinney, *Dimensions*, 210–14.
48. Repetition of a sequence of words at the beginning or end of adjacent clauses.
49. Use of a term for a part of something to refer to the whole.
50. Kinney, *Dimensions*, 211.
51. Kennedy says that the evangelists would have been hard put to escape an awareness of rhetoric as practiced in the culture around them (Kennedy, *New Testament Interpretation*, 10).

not prevent rabbis from employing Greco-Roman rhetorical forms."[52] What is not clear is whether such rabbinic teaching was taking place in the first century. It is equally possible that Matthew may have learned some of his rhetorical techniques from the OT. The importance of speech is evident in the OT and readers would learn its techniques by imitation.[53]

## Relation of Matthew 1-2 to the Rest of the Gospel

This study is focused upon the dream narratives of the First Gospel. It is important to remember that they belong to the wider context of Matthew's birth and infancy narratives. These in turn are integrated into the gospel as a whole. Whatever sources Matthew may have had here, he used them as he used his other sources, such as Mark and Q, to achieve his goals. We therefore need to consider the role which our narratives play in the complete gospel. Some scholars see 1:1—2:23 functioning as a preamble or prologue to the gospel.[54] Others see 1:1—4:16 as forming the introduction to Matthew's book.[55] Others again offer no literary structure.[56] Given the diversity of opinion, it would appear that there is no obvious structure.

Of greater significance than the structure of the gospel is its content. Ten times the evangelist cites the OT to the effect that some event in Jesus's life happened "in order that what was spoken by the prophet might be fulfilled." Four of these citations occur in the infancy narratives (Matt 1:22-23; 2:14-15, 16-18, 23). Their presence is intended to indicate that the fulfillment of OT scriptures has begun with the birth of Jesus. At 1:23 Matthew quotes Isa 7:14—"and his name shall be called Immanuel"—with the added statement that this name means "God with us." This is picked up at 28.20 where the risen Jesus promises the eleven disciples, "I am with you always." The infancy narratives engage in typology presenting Jesus as "the New Moses."[57] This typology is developed elsewhere in the gospel.[58]

52. Hezser, "Private and Public Education," 474.

53. Kennedy, *New Testament Interpretation*, 11.

54. Davies and Allison, *Matthew*, 1:59, citing the view of B. W. Bacon; Talbert, *Matthew*, 8.

55. Schweizer, *Good News according to Matthew*, 21; France, *Matthew*, 63; Gibbs, *Concordia Commentary*, 40-43.

56. Hagner, *Matthew 1-13*, liii. Gundry suggests, "It is doubtful that the first evangelist thought in terms of one (i.e., *a structure*), for his favorite points keep reappearing" (Gundry, *Matthew*, 10).

57. It is most clearly seen in Jesus's flight to and return from Egypt, with Matt 2:19 drawing upon the LXX text of Exod 4:19-20.

58. E.g., the temptation story (Matt 4:1-11) and the teaching on the mount (Matt

Many of the major Christological titles of the First Gospel are introduced in the infancy narratives. Jesus is identified as "Christ" (1:1, 16), "Son of David" (1:1), "Immanuel" (1:23), "King of the Jews" (2:2), and "Son of God" (2:15).[59] These titles are used and enhanced later in the gospel.[60]

Jesus's passion is also foreshadowed in the infancy narratives. Features of chapter 2 reappear in chapters 26 and 27: we have the gathering of the Jewish leaders (2:4 referring to the chief priests and scribes and 26:57 referring to the high priest, scribes and elders with 27:1 referring to the chief priests and elders), the use of the title, "King of the Jews" (2:2; 27:11, 29), and the desire of the ruling authority to get rid of Jesus (2:13, 16; 27:1, 20). Furthermore, the mission to the Gentiles which Jesus commanded after his resurrection (28:19) is anticipated by the visit of the Gentile Magi (2:1). What emerges is that Matthew has integrated any infancy source(s) into his work and there is overall unity in his work. It is of course possible to argue that this unity is due to Matthean composition of the infancy section.

## The Function of the Dream Narratives

When we consider the function of the dreams in Matthew's account of Jesus's nativity, we see that they serve both a literary and a theological purpose. With the former, all five dream narratives work to move the plot along. We commence with the two dreams for which the content is not reported in any detail (2:12, 22). The first of these contributes to having the Magi return to their own country by another route, thus avoiding Herod who intended to harm the child. The second causes Joseph to take his family to Galilee in order to avoid coming under the jurisdiction of Archelaus. These two dreams clearly prompt direct action in the plot. They provide the tool by which God directs human affairs. The same is true of the other three dreams where the content is spelt out (1:20-21; 2:13, 19-20). The first makes Joseph reverse his plan to divorce Mary quietly and instead take her as his wife. The next serves to make Joseph escape to Egypt with Mary and the child because he has been warned of Herod's evil intent. The final one leads Joseph to take Mary and the child

---

5:1-2). For a closer examination of the New Moses theme in the rest of the gospel, see Allison, *New Moses*, 165-270.

59. At Matt 2:15 we have the quotation of Hosea 11:1 where the "Son of God" title is merely hinted at. It becomes more explicit at 3:17; 4:1-11.

60. For "Christ," see 2:4; 11:2; 16:16, 20; 23:10; 26:63, 68; 27:17, 22.
For "Son of David," see 9:27; 12:23; 15:22; 20:30-31; 21:9, 15; 22:42-45.
For "Emmanuel," see 28:20.
For "King of the Jews," see 27:11, 29, 37, and "King of Israel" at 27:42.
For "Son of God," see 4:3, 6; 8:29; 14:33; 21:37; 26:63; 27:43, 54.

to Israel because he has now been informed that it is safe to return. Three of the five dreams prompt action that fulfils prophecy (1:23; 2:15, 23). All five dreams serve a function in the narrative by moving the plot along.[61]

The dreams also serve a theological purpose. Insofar as they purport to describe historical events, the dreams portray God as being in control of human affairs, especially those relating to the infancy of Jesus.[62] In particular they provide a means by which God can intervene in the world. Through them he directs the actions of Joseph and the Magi. By issuing commands which are then obeyed he changes their proposed course of action. In this way the infant Jesus is saved from slaughter. So the dreams demonstrate divine providence and guidance, with God taking the initiative through his angel. This is true of most message dreams, biblical, ANE and classical. It is the divinity himself who takes the initiative to visit the sleeper or send a messenger in order to speak directly to him. Sometimes a dialogue is involved (e.g., Gen 20:3-7; 1 Kgs 3:4-15).[63] However, Joseph does not utter a single word to the angel. Instead the angel issues commands and for each offers an explanation (1:20, 21; 2:13, 20). With Joseph entirely passive within each dream, emphasis is placed on God's initiative. He has a plan and he is acting to ensure its fulfillment. The quotations from Scripture are intended to show that the action taken accords with God's will as revealed in OT. It is important to see God's action in this section, since Matthew is dealing with God's intervention in history, as the child is born who is called Immanuel, *God with us.*

## Sound Analysis

Most of those who first received Matthew's text would hear it read to them and even a solitary reader is likely to have read aloud. Therefore the sound of the text would matter. Margaret Lee and Bernard Scott have highlighted the importance of sound for NT studies.[64] They call upon us to pay attention to how words sound in the Greek text of the NT. Words, as we know them, are not as important as syllables, for in these basic units sounds are phonetically inscribed.[65] Patterns of repetition encode a text with sound markers in the form of syllables, which give it structure. Themes are established through associated sounds. Lee and Scott assume that the writers

---

61. Anderson makes a similar point (Anderson, *Matthew's Narrative Web*, 157).
62. See Edwards, *Matthew's Story*, 14.
63. Dialogues are particularly common in Homeric dreams.
64. Lee and Scott, *Sound Mapping*.
65. People in oral societies did not have the same understanding of what a *word* is, as we have.

of the NT intend to make the text memorizable. Since the audience would be using memory, the content would be more easily memorized when it has fairly short rhythmical phrases which repeated certain sounds. These sound memories would live on after a text was read or heard. Rubin would support this claim, for he argues that we are sensitive to patterns of sound and other surface features and use them, where we can, to recall.[66] He says, "The repetition of a sound is an aid to memory. When a sound repeats, the first occurrence of the sound limits the choices for the second occurrence and provides a strong cue for it."[67] When Rubin wrote in 1995, he found limited support from psychologists, but more recent research is favorable.[68] Psychologists speak of phonological as well as visual aid codes and argue that memory has two distinct stores, the first of which holds information in an acoustic code and the second in a visual or spatial code.[69]

One of the difficulties of Lee and Scott's approach is that we have only limited knowledge of how Greek was pronounced in the first century.[70] Indeed there may have been variation from place to place. Kennedy suggests that evidence from inscriptions and papyri indicate that long and short syllables are often not accurately and systematically differentiated in the pronunciation of Koine Greek.[71] It may still be possible to use Lee and Scott's principles if we apply consistently whatever form of pronunciation we adopt and bear in mind Kennedy's point about long and short syllables.

A more serious problem lies in the subjectivity involved in this approach. Lee and Scott admit themselves that recognizing sound patterns as a means for detecting a text's structure involves intuition: "Perception of sound patterns is an intuitive process based on multiple auditory signals. Repetition's grouping function, the basis of structuring power, depends upon the intuition of similarity and proximity."[72] The subjectivity is best seen in an example. As it happens, they offer a sound analysis of Matt 1:18—2:23 which is the section being considered here.[73] As we proceed to critique their analysis, the various sections of the text will emerge, but I shall propose different divisions from Lee and Scott.

66. Rubin, *Memory in Oral Traditions*, 70-89.
67. Rubin, *Memory in Oral Traditions*, 75.
68. Smith et al., *Atkinson and Hilgard's Introduction*, 269.
69. Some recent brain-scanning studies indicate that the two stores are mediated by different brain structures. See Smith et al., *Atkinson and Hilgard's Introduction*, 275.
70. Gignac, *Grammar of the Greek Papyri*.
71. Kennedy, *New Testament Interpretation*, 30.
72. Lee and Scott, *Sound Mapping*, 156.
73. Lee and Scott, *Sound Mapping*, analyze the Greek text on 323, but offer the equivalent analysis in English in an appendix on 346-47.

They divide the narrative into five distinct scenes: Joseph's dream (1:18-25); Herod hears of the Magi's visit to Jerusalem (2:1-6); the Magi's journey (2:7-15); Herod's slaughter of the infants (2:16-18); and Joseph's dream (2:19-23). Each scene begins with a temporal marker and ends with a quotation from scripture which interprets the episode. Despite the importance which they attach to sound, their analysis does not involve any Greek sounds. It could have been made simply on the basis of the English text. The only reference to Greek is when they say that the temporal marker is usually a genitive absolute construction, as in 1:18; 2:1, 19, but can be the adverb τότε, as in 2:7, 16.

Essentially they have allowed the quotations to determine where they think each scene finishes and the next one starts. It could be said in their defense that the reader would hear similarity of sound as each quotation is introduced: πληρωθῇ τὸ ῥηθὲν ὑπὸ κυρίου διὰ τοῦ προφήτου λέγοντος preceded by ἵνα at 1:22 and 2:15 and ὅπως at 2:23 with ὑπὸ κυρίου dropped and the plural διὰ τῶν προφητῶν used. There is then the variation of τότε with the indicative ἐπληρώθη at 2:17 with ὑπὸ κυρίου again dropped and the prophet named as Ἰερεμίας. However, they do not highlight this in their analysis, simply giving the actual quotations. In any case the quotation at 2:6 is introduced differently: οὕτως γὰρ γέγραπται διὰ τοῦ προφήτου. It is only the last three words which are shared with previous statements. It is actually questionable whether the second scene closes with the quotation at 2:6. Since it is a response to Herod's question in 2:5 rather than a fulfillment quotation, it allows for the narrative to continue with the Magi's journey to Bethlehem.

It is also questionable whether the OT quotation at 1:23 closes the first scene. It could be part of the angel's message, offering an interpretation, or alternatively a narrative aside. But either way, the scene continues with Joseph's reaction to the angel's message in obeying the instructions given. Lee and Scott do give the scene as running from verse 18 to 25, but focus on the quotation at verse 23 and assert that it closes the episode.

An alternative analysis to that of Lee and Scott is offered here as follows. We begin with the genealogy in the first chapter. Its beginning and end are clearly marked out in the form of an *inclusio* which readers would pick up through the similarity of sound from Βίβλος γενέσεως Ἰησοῦ Χριστοῦ at 1:1 to Τοῦ δὲ Ἰησοῦ Χριστοῦ ἡ γένεσις at 1:18.

There then follows the first of the dream narratives. Again there is *inclusio* opening with Τοῦ δὲ Ἰησοῦ Χριστοῦ ἡ γένεσις at 1:18 and closing with Τοῦ δὲ Ἰησοῦ γεννηθέντος at 2:1. We suggest that the conventional structure of dream narratives also matters here. We have already observed how Oppenheim discerned a pattern in ANE dream narratives in three parts, opening with a description of the dream setting, followed by the actual report of the dream content, and closing with a description of the end of the dream. Matthew's readers would already be familiar with this pattern and would grasp it as his narrative was read. Although this structure does not in itself involve repeated sound, the readership would hear it. With Matthew relating three dreams in detail there is repetition of some of the language from the first to the other two.

We can explore the first in a little more detail. Its opening section consists of only two verses (i.e., 1:18–19). This is what Lee and Scott would call a "period." The basic unit from which to work is called a "colon." It represents what a reader could say in a single breath. They tell us that sound mapping moves up and down the hierarchy of discourse to analyze syllables and periods.[74] A new period opens at 1:20: ταῦτα δὲ αὐτοῦ ἐνθυμηθέντος with ταῦτα briefly recapitulating the content of verses 18 and 19. Here we have an introductory clause in the form of a genitive construction which is part of the highly stylized pattern which is followed in each of the angelic dreams.[75] Then comes ἰδού which in both meaning and sound encourages the listener to sit up and take note. Thereafter we have ἄγγελος κυρίου κατ' ὄναρ ἐφάνη αὐτῷ λέγων which is echoed at 2:13, 19, the start of the other two dream sequences which are narrated in full. Next we have a command and then a reason for the command, following the particle γάρ ("for"). Finally we are told how Joseph arose and fulfilled the command. Matthew has deviated a little from the usual dream pattern by providing the reader/listener with information in advance (1:18–19).

The next section opens at 2:1 with a genitive construction summing up Jesus's birth very rapidly. It closes at verse 12, where we have a dream summed up in the phrase καὶ χρηματισθέντες κατ' ὄναρ μὴ ἀνακάμψαι πρὸς Ἡρῴδην. This is followed by the pattern of obedience to the dream, here carried out by the Magi. This is substantially different from Lee and Scott's analysis, where they divide this section into 2:1–6 and 2:7–15. However, the sounds expressed at 2:12, 13 make it clear that a transition is taking place from one scene to another. At 2:12 we have δι' ἄλλης ὁδοῦ ἀνεχώρησαν εἰς τὴν χώραν αὐτῶν. Then 2:13 has Ἀναχωρησάντων δὲ αὐτῶν. The αὐτῶν in 2:13 picks up the αὐτῶν at the end of 2:12. Also because it is in the (plural) genitive form, it allows for the change of form in the verb ἀναχωρέω. In 2:12 it is third person plural aorist indicative, where in 2:13 it is masculine plural aorist participle in the genitive. Moreover, the χωρ sound in χώραν echoes the similar sound in ἀνεχώρησαν and prepares for its recurrence in

---

74. Lee and Scott, *Sound Mapping*, 157.

75. In an earlier footnote we saw how Fuller, "Genitive Absolute," suggested we should speak of "genitive construction" rather than the conventional "genitive absolute."

ἀναχωρησάντων. It would have been possible for Matthew to use γῆν instead of χώραν, as indeed he does at 2:20-21.

The final section runs from 2:12 or 2:13 to 2:23 with the phrase χρηματισθεὶς δὲ κατ' ὄναρ ἀνεχώρησεν at 2:22, which of course echoes similar phraseology at 2:12, giving us another case of *inclusio* and indicating that the section is coming to a close. This final section may be divided into three subsections. We have the flight to Egypt in 2:13-15; the slaying of the infants in 2:16-18; and the return from Egypt in 2:19-23. The first and last of these involve angelic dreams in accordance with the pattern outlined above. While 2:13, 19, echo 1:20, there is a minor difference in that they have the present tense φαίνεται where 1:20 has the aorist ἐφάνη. The phrase ὁ δὲ ἐγερθείς coupled with παρέλαβεν at 2:14 and 2:21 echoes the use of these words, albeit separated, at 1:24. The third section also has a condensed dream with χρηματισθεὶς δὲ κατ' ὄναρ. All the echoes help the listener recall previous dreams.

My analysis results in a different division of the text. The first section which is largely the genealogy runs from 1:1 to 1:18. This is followed by Joseph's dream with its prophecy of Jesus birth, running from 1:18 to 2:1. Thereafter we have the visit of the Magi from 2:1 to 2:12. Finally we have the flight to Egypt and return from 2:12 to 2:23.[76] It will be noted that the sections have overlapping verses at 1:18; 2:1, 12. This overlapping is due to his use of *inclusio*. The only section not involving *inclusio* or indeed any sound pattern is 2:1-12. It emerges from the meaning of the text, the arrival of the Magi to their departure. This structure has no particular significance for this study, but the use of *inclusio* in creating it certainly does. It is to this usage and other memory patterns that we now turn.

## Memory Patterns

In the methodology chapter, "memory patterns" were defined as *devices intended to help people remember a narrative through the use of sound or an image or the structure of the material*. Examples of such patterns include repetition, alliteration, assonance, anaphora, rhythm, proverb, antithesis, formulaic expressions, *inclusio*, parallelism, acrostic, and typology. We now search for such patterns in the dream narratives which are found in Matt 1:18—2:1 and 2:12-23. Although we will take account of some devices elsewhere in Matthew, only those from the dream narratives will

---

76. The unspecified prophetic quotation at 2:23 may not have been part of the original narrative.

count for our comparison with dream narratives from other literature, as we seek to compare like with like.

## Inclusio

We begin with *inclusio* because it has already emerged in the section on sound. We detected the following examples: 1:1 and 1:18; 1:18 and 2:1; 2:12 and 2:22. Here we examine examples of *inclusio* which other writers claim to have found in the dream narratives.

Pizzuto found *inclusio* between 1:18 and 1:25.[77] Each verse uses the name *Jesus* and refers to his birth, γένεσις at 18 and ἔτεκεν (aorist of τίκτω) at 25. However, Jesus's name is also used at 1:21 which in addition involves the verb τέξεται (future of τίκτω). This binds verse 25 more closely to 21 than 18. On the basis of language a case can be made for 1:21 and 1:25 creating *inclusio*. However, it is a less complete unit than Pizzuto's original suggestion. We may still hesitate to accept his example of *inclusio*, since the words relating to birth in 18 and 25 sound so different and the name *Jesus* is significantly separated from the verb ἔτεκεν. This may be overcome if we extend the unit in question to include the first four words of 2:1: Τοῦ δὲ Ἰησοῦ γεννηθέντος, where Ἰησοῦ is genitive as in 1:18 and more significantly next to γεννηθέντος which sounds similar to γένεσις.[78] I therefore adhere to the *inclusio* suggested above, involving 1:18 and 2:1a.

Another possible example was suggested by Anderson.[79] She suggests that *inclusio* exists at 2:15a and 2:19a, the phrase ἕως τῆς τελευτῆς Ἡρῴδου opening it and Τελευτήσαντος δὲ τοῦ Ἡρῴδου closing it. In the first phrase we have a noun and in the second the verb, but the sounds and meanings are reasonably similar. Presumably Anderson means the enclosed episode to consist of the slaying of the infants. However, there would also be included the quotation of Hosea 11:1 applied to Jesus and it is by no means clear that this is part of the episode. I would suggest that not every repeated word should be treated as an intended *inclusio*, but only those which mark a clearly discernible unit. Again I adhere to my original analysis, claiming the

---

77. Pizzuto, "Structural Elegance of Matthew 1–2," 712-37.

78. The similarity would be slightly greater if we were to read γέννησις (*birth*) rather than γένεσις (*genealogy, generation, creation, birth*) at 1:18. Indeed there is some manuscript evidence for γέννησις. However, there is good support in early manuscripts for γένεσις and it seems likely, as Metzger argues, that copyists would substitute γέννησις to correspond more closely with the verb γεννάω, especially since it had been used so frequently in the preceding genealogy (Metzger, *Textual Commentary*, 8). Ultimately it is not important, as γένεσις and γέννησις are so similar phonetically.

79. Anderson, *Matthew's Narrative Web*, 155.

*inclusio* at 2:12–13 and 2:22 is more convincing, both on the basis of sound patterns and as a discernible unit.

When we come to compare Matthew's usage with that of other writers, we shall discover that *inclusio* is widely used by writers from diverse cultural backgrounds, but particularly popular with OT and Josephus.

## Repetition

Even in a superficial reading of Matthew's infancy narratives one is struck by the amount of repetition. The phrase κατ' ὄναρ is used five times in these short sections. Similar repetition is to be found throughout the gospel as a whole.[80] Sometimes there are double stories, as in the feeding of crowds (Matt 14:13–21; 15:32–38)[81]; or repeated sayings, as in passion predictions (Matt 16:21; 20:17–19)[82]; or gestures associated with healing (Matt 8:3; 12:49; 14:31).[83]

Repetition can take various forms: verbal, sound, structure. Sometimes it is straightforward, such as at 1:24–25, where Joseph awakens and obeys the command of the angel in words which echo it. There are eleven words in common with 1:20–21.

> 1:20–21 ταῦτα δὲ αὐτοῦ ἐνθυμηθέντος ἰδοὺ ἄγγελος κυρίου κατ' ὄναρ ἐφάνη αὐτῷ λέγων, Ἰωσὴφ υἱὸς Δαυίδ, μὴ φοβηθῇς παραλαβεῖν Μαρίαν τὴν γυναῖκά σου, τὸ γὰρ ἐν αὐτῇ γεννηθὲν ἐκ πνεύματός ἐστιν ἁγίου· τέξεται δὲ υἱὸν καὶ καλέσεις τὸ ὄνομα αὐτοῦ Ἰησοῦν, αὐτὸς γὰρ σώσει τὸν λαὸν αὐτοῦ ἀπὸ τῶν ἁμαρτιῶν αὐτῶν.

> 1:24–25 ἐγερθεὶς δὲ ὁ Ἰωσὴφ ἀπὸ τοῦ ὕπνου ἐποίησεν ὡς προσέταξεν αὐτῷ ὁ ἄγγελος κυρίου καὶ παρέλαβεν τὴν γυναῖκα αὐτοῦ· καὶ οὐκ ἐγίνωσκεν αὐτὴν ἕως οὗ ἔτεκεν υἱόν· καὶ ἐκάλεσεν τὸ ὄνομα αὐτοῦ Ἰησοῦν

Joseph's fulfillment of the command in the second dream at 2:14 is even more striking with almost verbatim repetition and again eleven words shared.[84]

---

80. Anderson helpfully supplies two appendices which list the repetitions in Matthew (Anderson, *Matthew's Narrative Web*, 226–42).

81. Involving fifty-six words.

82. Involving ten words.

83. (καὶ) ἐκτείνας τὴν χεῖρα.

84. The numbering of the dreams can be confusing. If we consider only those dreams which are narrated in full, there are three (Matt 1:20–25; 2:13–15, 19–21). If we

2:13 Ἀναχωρησάντων δὲ αὐτῶν ἰδοὺ ἄγγελος κυρίου φαίνεται κατ' ὄναρ τῷ Ἰωσὴφ λέγων, Ἐγερθεὶς παράλαβε τὸ παιδίον καὶ τὴν μητέρα αὐτοῦ καὶ φεῦγε εἰς Αἴγυπτον, καὶ ἴσθι ἐκεῖ ἕως ἂν εἴπω σοι· μέλλει γὰρ Ἡρῴδης ζητεῖν τὸ παιδίον τοῦ ἀπολέσαι αὐτό.

2:14 ὁ δὲ ἐγερθεὶς παρέλαβεν τὸ παιδίον καὶ τὴν μητέρα αὐτοῦ νυκτὸς καὶ ἀνεχώρησεν εἰς Αἴγυπτον,

The same is true of the third dream and the obedience expressed at 2:21 which has twelve shared words.

2:20 λέγων, Ἐγερθεὶς παράλαβε τὸ παιδίον καὶ τὴν μητέρα αὐτοῦ καὶ πορεύου εἰς γῆν Ἰσραήλ, τεθνήκασιν γὰρ οἱ ζητοῦντες τὴν ψυχὴν τοῦ παιδίου.

2:21 ὁ δὲ ἐγερθεὶς παρέλαβεν τὸ παιδίον καὶ τὴν μητέρα αὐτοῦ καὶ εἰσῆλθεν εἰς γῆν Ἰσραήλ.

While such repetition may reflect a memory pattern, it may also be used here deliberately to emphasize the complete obedience of Joseph.

When we compare the second and third dreams, we find nineteen words in common, particularly in the introductions and in the wording of the angel's messages.

2:13 Ἀναχωρησάντων δὲ αὐτῶν ἰδοὺ ἄγγελος κυρίου φαίνεται κατ' ὄναρ τῷ Ἰωσὴφ λέγων, Ἐγερθεὶς παράλαβε τὸ παιδίον καὶ τὴν μητέρα αὐτοῦ καὶ φεῦγε εἰς Αἴγυπτον, καὶ ἴσθι ἐκεῖ ἕως ἂν εἴπω σοι· μέλλει γὰρ Ἡρῴδης ζητεῖν τὸ παιδίον τοῦ ἀπολέσαι αὐτό.

2:19-20 Τελευτήσαντος δὲ τοῦ Ἡρῴδου ἰδοὺ ἄγγελος κυρίου φαίνεται κατ' ὄναρ τῷ Ἰωσὴφ ἐν Αἰγύπτῳ λέγων, Ἐγερθεὶς παράλαβε τὸ παιδίον καὶ τὴν μητέρα αὐτοῦ καὶ πορεύου εἰς γῆν Ἰσραήλ, τεθνήκασιν γὰρ οἱ ζητοῦντες τὴν ψυχὴν τοῦ παιδίου.

It may also serve an additional function of marking the fulfillment of the promise made by the angel to Joseph regarding his return from Egypt. For this repetition to be treated as a memory pattern used in oral transmission, we have to assume that the two dreams belonged together in the same source. This does seem likely, as they are both part of the same story, the departure to Egypt and the subsequent return.

It may also be said that there is repetition with ζητεῖν τὸ παιδίον at 2:13 and οἱ ζητοῦντες [τὴν ψυχὴν] τοῦ παιδίου at 2:20. I have chosen not to count it, as it is significantly separated from the rest of the repetition.

---

include the dreams references (Matt 2:12, 22), there are five. Here the references are to the full dream narratives.

We may consider whether nineteen words is too long for repetition to function as an aid to memory. As we saw in the chapter on orality, when Lord analyzed the themes of the south Slavic poetry or singing, he found that there was no fixed set of words.[85] There was great fluidity in each performance. However, the situation here is different from what Lord had in mind because the passages are so close together. Moreover, verbatim repetition is not unknown even in an oral context. Teffeteller points out that Mesopotamian poems were composed differently from the Parry-Lord South Slavic model.[86] They were the result of "premeditated" oral composition and were transmitted in a relatively fixed form. Even within the Parry-Lord model we have set pieces which the Homeric poet seems to have known by heart, for example the lengthy descriptions of preparing of a meal,[87] and they can run verbatim to some forty words. Matthew is well within that range. It is therefore possible to have nineteen words repeated verbatim even in an oral context.

We shall encounter notable repetition among both Jewish and Greek writers in the next chapter, but those whose usage most closely resembles Matthew's are OT and Herodotus.

## Formulaic Expressions

We now focus on formulaic expressions which are a form of repetition. Formula-quotations occur ten times in Matthew's Gospel.[88] In five cases the prophet is named and in one (2:5-6) the fulfillment element is not expressed. The wording can vary slightly: πληρωθῇ τὸ ῥηθὲν preceded by ἵνα (1:22; 2:15) or ὅπως (2:23) or τότε with the indicative ἐπληρώθη (2:17). They occur beyond the dreams themselves, but in the surrounding narrative.[89] We noted above that most scholars see the formulaic quotations as being redactional. This raises the suggestion that a tendency to use formulaic expression is a feature of Matthew's style. If so, we need to be open to the possibility that any other formulaic expression may stem from Matthew's pen rather than source material.

A second example, this time from within the dreams, would be: ἰδοὺ ἄγγελος κυρίου κατ' ὄναρ ἐφάνη αὐτῷ λέγων (1:20) or with the present

---

85. Lord, *Singer of Tales*, 68-98.

86. Teffeteller, "Orality," 69.

87. We find such a scene in Homer, *Odyssey* 1.136-43. Stanford tells that the passage is repeated four times later in the *Odyssey* (Stanford, *Commentary*, 221).

88. See Matt 1:22-23; 2:5-6, 15, 17-18, 23; 4:14-16; 8:17; 12:17-21; 21:4-5; 27:9-10.

89. This holds true if we regard 1:22 as a narrative aside. However, if it is taken as interpretation offered by the angel, then it is included within the dream.

φαίνεται κατ' ὄναρ τῷ Ἰωσήφ (2:13, 19). There is also χρηματισθέντες (2:12) or χρηματισθεὶς κατ' ὄναρ (2:22). The second example needs to be qualified to some extent, for this expression also belongs to the form of dream reporting. The standard way in which message dreams were presented throughout the ANE involved a reference to the dream, the messenger and his appearing or coming. It might be argued that it is so much part of the form of the dream that it should be ignored as a formulaic expression to aid memory. However, a case can be put for it serving a dual purpose. Matthew is entirely consistent in the way in which he uses this phrase, only varying the verb tense and position of κατ' ὄναρ. We shall see when we look at memory patterns in other authors that he is very different from Josephus who has no consistent phraseology to introduce dreams, even when he is narrating the same dream for a second time.[90] The fact that the wording is used so consistently suggests that it is being used both as a formulaic expression and as part of the form of dream reporting.[91] A third example is ἐγερθείς which is part of a terminating formula. At 1:24 it is combined with ἀπὸ τοῦ ὕπνου, "from sleep."

## Key Words

Other repetition is achieved through key words. Luz gives as an example the phrase ἄγγελος κυρίου which occurs four times in 1:18–2:23, seeing it as pointing to God's guidance.[92] There are two problems here. The first concerns whether we may treat this as a key phrase given the fact that we have already taken account of it in the preceding paragraph as an element in the formulaic expression ἰδοὺ ἄγγελος κυρίου φαίνεται κατ' ὄναρ. In the methodology chapter it was suggested that a word or phrase could perform such a double function if it also appeared outside the formulaic expression. That happens in this instance at verse 24 where we are told that Joseph ἐποίησεν ὡς προσέταξεν αὐτῷ ὁ ἄγγελος κυρίου. The second problem is whether the phrase is used to highlight a theme. Luz suggests that it points to God's guidance. That may be true within the formulaic expressions, but it is more questionable at verse 24 where the theme is Joseph's obedience, albeit a response to God's guidance through the angel. As the whole content of verses 24 and 25 is concerned with Joseph's obedience, the theme of divine guidance slips into the background. It is therefore to be rejected as a key phrase.

90. See his accounts of the Glaphyra dream in Josephus, *War* 2.114-16; *Ant.* 17.349-53.

91. We shall find later that consistent use of phraseology in introducing dreams is something which Matthew shares with Artemidorus.

92. Luz, *Matthew 1-7*, 39.

Another potential example is the verb παραλαμβάνω, used six times in the infancy section (1:20, 24; 2:13, 14, 20, 21), always in the aorist, with 1:20 being infinitive, 2:13, 20, imperative, and the rest indicative. Is there significance in the fact that the word recurs six times in a relatively short section? It is possible that it is simply part of the vocabulary used to narrate the story, the word used to expressed the action commanded of Joseph and executed by him, "taking" once in marriage and twice on a journey. However, it is also possible that it functions to highlight that command-obedience theme. In each pair of uses, the first expresses a command the second relates obedience. It may be that Joseph is being portrayed as "the obedient disciple." Attention is drawn to this in the phrase: ἐποίησεν ὡς προσέταξεν αὐτῷ ὁ ἄγγελος κυρίου. With some hesitation παραλαμβάνω is proposed as a key word.

Later our research will show that almost all writers use key words and consequently we need to regard it as a memory pattern which extends beyond the cultural divide.

## Parallelism

Arguably the most significant memory pattern is the use of parallelism. This can be achieved in a variety of ways, through components which are grammatically the same or similar in construction, meaning, sound or meter. The first dream has parallels at 1:20, 21 because they both contain commands:

1:20 μὴ φοβηθῇς παραλαβεῖν Μαρίαν τὴν γυναῖκά σου

1:21 καὶ καλέσεις τὸ ὄνομα αὐτοῦ Ἰησοῦν.

However, they are structured rather differently. The first involves a negative,[93] while the second does not. The first has an imperative, while the second uses a second person future. The first involves a dependent infinitive, while the second does not. It has to be acknowledged that these differences are not insignificant. However, it is not necessary for them to be structured exactly the same. Kugel refers to off-and-on equivalence of length in parallel clauses (whether that is measured by the number of words or syllables or stresses).[94] We see such variation in OT examples.[95]

As in the other Matthean dreams, each command is followed by a reason.

93. Negated imperatives are rare in Classical and Hellenistic Greek where other verbal forms tend to be preferred.

94. Kugel, "Feeling of Déjà Lu," 73.

95. "Their tongue is a sharpened arrow, they speak deceit" (Jer 9:7). See also Prov 3:10; 19:5; Isa 17:1; 48:20–21; 49:23.

1:20 τὸ γὰρ ἐν αὐτῇ γεννηθὲν ἐκ πνεύματός ἐστιν ἁγίου

1:21 αὐτὸς γὰρ σώσει τὸν λαὸν αὐτοῦ ἀπὸ τῶν ἁμαρτιῶν αὐτῶν.

The second command at 1:21 is preceded by a piece of information or prophecy: τέξεται δὲ υἱόν. This, coupled with the command, finds a parallel in the scripture quotation at 1:23.

1:21 τέξεται δὲ υἱὸν καὶ καλέσεις τὸ ὄνομα αὐτοῦ Ἰησοῦν

1:23 καὶ τέξεται υἱόν, καὶ καλέσουσιν τὸ ὄνομα αὐτοῦ Ἐμμανουήλ

Even if 1:23 is regarded as a narrative aside,[96] the parallelism in the narrative of this section remains strong.

We have further parallelism in some of Joseph's actions:

1:24 ἐποίησεν ὡς προσέταξεν αὐτῷ ὁ ἄγγελος κυρίου

1:25 καὶ οὐκ ἐγίνωσκεν αὐτὴν ἕως οὗ ἔτεκεν υἱόν.

Although the number of words or syntactical *lemmata* is not the same, the grammatical structure (the use of an indicative verb in a past tense followed by a subordinate clause) is similar. Both involve superfluous phrases. The section of 1:24 quoted is not required as Joseph's total obedience is later expressed in his taking his wife and in his calling the child's name Jesus. However, as we shall shortly see, Matthew may be engaging in a form of semantic parallelism. The words from 1:25 are also superfluous in the sense that they portray Joseph as carrying out action which was not actually commanded by the angel. However, the subordinate clause allows Matthew to express fulfillment of the prophecy made by the angel at 1:21: τέξεται δὲ υἱόν.

There is also a parallel between some of the words spoken by the angel and some of the information provided by Matthew prior to introducing the dream:

1:18 εὑρέθη ἐν γαστρὶ ἔχουσα ἐκ πνεύματος ἁγίου

1:20 τὸ γὰρ ἐν αὐτῇ γεννηθὲν ἐκ πνεύματός ἐστιν ἁγίου.

There are other less significant and shorter parallels. The ἐν γαστρὶ ἔχουσα of 1:18 is found in the form of a future tense at 1:23 in ἐν γαστρὶ ἕξει. The word γεννηθέν at 1:20 echoes γένεσις[97] in the phrase Τοῦ δὲ Ἰησοῦ Χριστοῦ ἡ γένεσις οὕτως ἦν at 1:18.

---

96. It was discussed above whether 1:23 is a narrative aside or part of the dream, the latter view being favored.

97. The echo would be slightly stronger if we were to read γέννησις rather than

We noted in the methodology chapter different types of parallelism with Alter and Kugel laying stress on semantic parallelism as the peculiar mark of OT poetry.[98] Much of the parallelism in Matthew is syntactical. However, one of the examples above is semantic. At 1:24 we have an instance of what Alter calls "*specification*,"[99] for each of the three new statements specify what it meant to say that *Joseph did what the angel of the Lord commanded*. The first and third statements fulfill particular commands which the angel is recorded as having given. The second introduces new material. This would mean that Matthew displays semantic parallelism, the characteristic of OT poetry. However, we need to acknowledge that an alternative explanation is possible. Davies and Allison see 1:24-25 as employing an "OT sentence form" and they illustrate their point with Exodus 7:10 where Moses and Aaron do "as the Lord has commanded."[100] On the other hand, this example also involves specification, for the verse goes on to say that Aaron threw down his rod before Pharaoh and his servants. Another scholar detects parallelism here. Gundry tells us that Matthew's love of parallelism leads him to conform the phraseology of the end of 1:25 to the wording of verse 21ab,[101] but this does not involve semantic parallelism or specification. We adhere to the view that in 1:24-25 we have an example of semantic parallelism in the form of specification, regarding it as similar to Alter's example of Isa 48:20.[102] Just as the phrase "they did not thirst in the wastelands" explains the preceding phrase "God has redeemed his servant Jacob," so Joseph's actions in taking Mary as his wife, not having relations with her and naming the child Jesus specify how he fulfilled the angel's command. It is potentially important for when we compare the memory patterns of Matthew's dream narratives with those of other literature. It could be a significant indicator of a possible Semitic background. However, we need to balance this by noting that we have only the one example in Matthew and alternative explanations of his phraseology have been offered by others. We shall see that Greco-Roman writers display syntactical parallelism, but not semantic.

---

γένεσις.

98. Alter, *Art of Biblical Poetry*, 6-7; Kugel, "Feeling of Déjà Lu," 67.

99. We noted in the Methodology chapter how Alter saw semantic parallelism involving a movement of meaning which could be heightening or intensification, specification, concretization, or dramatization (Alter, *Art of Biblical Poetry*, 20).

100. Davies and Allison, *Matthew*, 1:218.

101. Gundry, *Matthew*, 25.

102. Alter, *Art of Biblical Poetry*, 21.

## Chiastic Structures

Pizzuto has detected chiastic structures in 1:18-23; 2:1-12, 13-23, each with prophetic citations as their central components.[103] He suggests Matthew uses this arrangement of material to convey his conviction that the God who acted throughout the history of Israel is the very God who is now acting in the life of Christ. In the first section the chiasmus takes the form A B C D E F E D C B A; in the second A B C D C B A; but in the third A i-v B A i-v. One of the difficulties is that different writers see different structures[104] and we have no way of knowing what Matthew himself intended. The first two vignettes are more plausible than the third, which has three prophetic citations, where the first two have only one each. It is questionable whether the middle citation in the third, the quotation of Jer 31:15 at 2:18, plays the pivotal role which Pizzuto claims for it. Although it lies in the centre of his vignette, it is only indirectly connected to Jesus and has no messianic undertones. Moreover, the form of chiasmus in the third vignette is different from that in the first two. Pizzuto uses Bengel's terminology and describes it as a "direct chiasm" (chiasmus directus) rather than "inverted parallelism" (chiasmus inversus).[105] He uses this to explain why there are two dream sequences in 2:19-23 rather than just one: "The second dream sequence becomes structurally necessary in order to balance chiastically the prophetic reference to Egypt in v. 15b. Matthew has not edited his material carelessly here, but with great precision."[106] If Pizzuto is right, then it would appear that Matthew has sacrificed the flow of his narrative and economy of words simply to achieve a certain structure. Pizzuto's approach to 2:19-23 raises the suspicion that he may be reading more into the narrative than Matthew intended, especially when he reverts to direct chiasm instead of inverted. We therefore reject Pizzuto's third example, regarding the first two as more plausible, but still not certain. We shall also come upon chiasmus in six Jewish writings and eight Hellenistic works.

---

103. Pizzuto, "Structural Elegance of Matthew 1-2," 712-37.

104. Talbert, *Matthew*, 33, follows Kingsbury in seeing for 1:18-25 a structure of A (direct address to the reader—1:18a) B (narration of the story—1:18b-21) A' (direct address to the reader—1:22-23) B' (narration of the story—1:24-25). Talbert notes that each section of the narration ends with the name Jesus at 1:21a, 25.

105. Pizzuto cites Bengel, *Gnomon Novi Testamenti*, 2:758-60.

106. Pizzuto, "Structural Elegance of Matthew 1-2," 727.

## Foreign Words

A foreign expression is not a memory pattern as such, but it can sometimes be memorable. It makes an impact because it stands out from the surrounding text, but for it to be retained in memory it needs to be relatively brief, expressed in a language to which readers or listeners have access or have a translation offered. We have one example in the dream narratives at 1:23, with others later in the crucifixion narrative with the place named as *Golgotha* at 27:33 and the quotation in Hebrew of Psalm 22:1 at 27:46.[107] At 1:23 Matthew quotes Isa 7:14 and gives the Hebrew name עמנו אל transliterated into Greek as Ἐμμανουήλ with a translation supplied, "God with us." We shall later come across a Latin writer who twice gives Greek quotations.

## Summary

We now draw together our findings from the investigation into the memory patterns displayed in the Matthean dream narratives. Through the use of sound patterns we established three cases of *inclusio*, but one was prior to the dream narratives. We looked at four cases of verbal repetition, with verbatim phrasing extending from eleven or twelve words to nineteen. We investigated three formulaic expressions, regarding those associated with the appearance of the angel and the rising of Joseph as serving the dual purposes of aiding memory and belonging to the form of dream reporting. We gave thought to two possible key words, dismissing ἄγγελος κυρίου because at 1:24 it ceased to highlight God's guidance, but tentatively suggesting παραλαμβάνω as a candidate. We found several cases of parallelism, most of them syntactical, but at 1:24 we had "*specification*," which takes us into the realm of semantic parallelism, the characteristic of OT poetry. We accepted two of Pizzuto's suggestions of chiasmus and noted the use of the foreign name *Immanuel*.

Table 2: Matthew

|  | Matthew |
|---|---|
| Dreams | 5 |
| Acrostic | 0 |

---

107. Mark 15:34 gives the quotation in its Aramaic form.

|  | Matthew |
|---|---|
| Alliteration | 0 |
| Anaphora | 0 |
| Antithesis | 0 |
| Association | 0 |
| Assonance | 0 |
| Chiasmus | 2 |
| Formulaic Expressions | 3 |
| Inclusio | 2 |
| Key Word | 1 |
| Metre | 0 |
| Numerical Aids | 0 |
| Onomatopoeia | 0 |
| Parallelism | 5 |
| Pun | 0 |
| Repeated Blocks | 4 |
| Typology | 2 |

We are now in a position to explain why the narration of Joseph's dreams appears as it does. It is due partly to the formal pattern of dream reporting discerned by Oppenheim in ancient literature and partly to the memory patterns built into the narrative to assist in its oral transmission.

## Conclusion

In the course of this chapter we have seen how the genre of gospel most closely resembles that of encomiastic biography, a literary form found in the Greco-Roman world. However, we have also noted Matthew's use of Semitisms. We have a particularly good example at 1:21 where Joseph is told καλέσεις τὸ ὄνομα αὐτοῦ Ἰησοῦν. This involves a biblical expression[108] and

---

108. The Septuagintal form of קרא + שם + proper name.

a Hebrew wordplay.[109] The overall picture, therefore, remains complicated and shows multi-cultural facets.

We are seeking an answer the question of Matthew's cultural background through his use of memory patterns. Those which we found in Matthew are verbal repetition, formulaic expressions, a possible key word, a foreign word, examples of chiasmus and several cases of parallelism. One of these is particularly significant, viz. parallelism. Although most of the parallelism was syntactical, we found one example of semantic at 1:24, which shares affinity with OT practice. Also worthy of note was the lack of antithesis, a popular Greek device. These two factors suggest that the Jewish or OT influence was somewhat stronger than the Greek.

However, it is not sufficient merely to highlight the memory patterns present in Matthew. We now need to compare these with what is to be found in the dream reporting of other ancient texts, Jewish and Greco-Roman. That is what we propose to do in the next chapter.

---

109. Ἰησοῦς/יהושע linked to ישע.

# 7

# Comparison of Memory Patterns

## Introduction

IN THE METHODOLOGY CHAPTER we noted patterns of memory found in ancient literature to help keep the audience or readers on track and to assist them in memorizing a story. These include acrostic, alliteration, anaphora, antithesis, assonance, formulaic expressions, *inclusio*, key word, parallelism, proverbs, repetition and typology. We are not including structure at this stage because we have already discussed it in the chapter on dreams. There is a *script* for dream reporting that was widely used across the ANE and Mediterranean, but it left scope for cultural variations, which we duly noted.

Here we are concerned with the other devices listed above. They are to be found in some literature because the writer was using an oral source in which their presence was intended to aid transmission. In other literature the writer has made use of them with a view to assisting his readership in remembering his material. Yet again a writer may insert them primarily for stylistic reasons. Theoretically we can distinguish these functions, but in practice it is much more difficult. We often cannot discern a writer's motivation in using them and sometimes they may serve a dual role, stylistic as well as mnemonic. Consequently, we cannot say whether the phenomena found in Matthew are mnemonic aids or stylistic traits, but they are formulaic expressions, *inclusio*, key word, parallelism, repetition, typology and chiasmus.

This chapter compares these devices with those found in over 250 examples of dream narratives from other ancient writers. The purpose of this comparison is to try and establish whether Matthew and any person or persons who transmitted Joseph's dreams to him, lay closer to Jewish or Hellenistic literary practice. The use of such devices stems from a person's upbringing or education. Lord suggested that when an oral poet performs, he uses formulaic expressions—and we may assume other such devices—in much the same way as we use language and they were acquired in a similar manner.[1] Rhetorical devices were also taught to school children in ancient Greece and Rome with a view to turning them into effective writers and speakers. That is just as much culturally based as memories transmitted orally within a particular community.

What emerges from this discussion is an apparent weakness in the methodology being used in the present study. We cannot rely on memory patterns alone to discern cultural identity. We need to explore stylistic traits more generally, some of which will indeed be mnemonic, but others will be stylistic, rhetorical or even habitual. Moreover, since we were unable to prove that Matthew was using an orally transmitted source, we need to be open to the possibility that he composed the dream narratives himself. If so, he may have been employing a particular register. John Foley quotes Hymes as defining registers as "major speech styles associated with recurrent types of situations."[2] As an illustration, we may contrast the register appropriate to a speech delivered at a political rally with the register appropriate to a speech delivered by a lawyer in a court of law as he sums up his defense of his client. Registers involve the use of special language such as formulaic phraseology, thematic structure or story pattern, style, changed word order, peculiar vocabulary.[3] Foley points out that the Homeric poems often use archaic expressions no longer used as idioms for everyday communication.[4] However, for a register to convey meaning effectively it depends on both the compositional fluency of the performer and the receptive fluency of the audience.[5] We need to be open to the possibility that Matthew is employing a specific kind of register.

The results of the analysis carried in this chapter will show that Matthew lacks the verbal antithesis that is to be found in many Greek writers. He shares *inclusio*, syntactical parallelism and repetition with a wide range of authors. We suggest that he has one example of semantic parallelism which is a distinctive feature of OT. His use of lengthy repetition comes closest to the practice of Herodotus and OT. It will be argued that on balance he has closer affinity to OT than to Hellenistic works. It may therefore

---

1. Lord, *Singer of Tales*, 36.
2. Foley, *Singer of Tales*, 15, refers to Hymes, "Ways of Speaking," 440.
3. Foley, *Singer of Tales*, 52–53.
4. Foley, *Singer of Tales*, 83.
5. Foley, *Singer of Tales*, 53.

be that Matthew is using a biblical register, something that we need to consider as we progress.

## Choice of Literature

To ensure that we were comparing like with like, the choice of dream narratives to be examined was restricted to prose, relatively brief passages,[6] and the time era between 200 BCE and 200 CE.[7] Although much of the Old Testament predates our time scale, it was included because of its frequent use in Matthew's text and the possible influence it may have had on his approach. It was examined both in the Hebrew text and the Septuagint, as Matthew appears to show familiarity with both.[8] Some Jewish literature was also selected beyond OT and Apocrypha. With regard to Hellenistic writing, an initial selection was made in line with those texts examined by Dodson, as this study is to some extent a reaction against Dodson's work.[9] Although the work of Herodotus belongs to the fifth century BCE, it was included because Dodson covered it and also Herodotus is quite explicit about his use of oral sources. The range of literature was extended beyond Dodson's selection to give a more comprehensive analysis. The *Oneirocritica* of Artemidorus was especially included because it is the first extant Greek work on the subject of dreams. Examples were drawn from different types of literature: biography,[10] history,[11] and fiction.[12]

---

6. This led to the exclusion of lengthy visions narrated in apocalyptic literature such as 1 Enoch.

7. This time range was chosen largely for convenience but also to be relatively close to the period in which Matthew wrote.

8. His use of Isa 7:14 (Matt 1:23) is close to LXX, while his use of Hosea 11:1 (Matt 2:15) corresponds to the Hebrew, but not LXX.

9. Dodson, *Reading Dreams*.

10. This is the category which most closely resembles the gospels.

11. Although history is different from biography, they are relatively similar in their approach. In any case Matthew reports what is ostensibly presented as an historical event when he relates the massacre of the children of Bethlehem.

12. In some respects fiction is an artificial category, as some narratives, such as the dreams of Xerxes (Herodotus, *Histories* 7.12–14, 19), although in the guise of historical narrative, may be fictitious.

## The Septuagint in Relation to Hebrew OT

We begin with the Septuagint, as it clearly belongs to a culture in which Judaism and Hellenism were intermingled. Here a total of twenty-three dream narratives were examined, eleven of them auditory message type and thirteen symbolic.[13] However, we need to recognize that we do not simply have an author or even a group of writers narrating dreams in their own words. It is a translation in which we might expect those producing it to follow reasonably closely the original text in front of them. We need to recognize that there are occasions on which LXX does differ from MT. These variations may be explained by the translators' use of a different Hebrew text from what we possess and by their tendency at times to make alterations to suit their own theological presuppositions. The question for us is whether they preserve memory patterns embedded in the Hebrew text, drop some or add devices of their own. We therefore need to examine LXX dream narratives alongside the equivalent passages in the Hebrew text. At this stage we are not concerned to relate LXX to Matthew, but simply to the Hebrew text.

We take as an example Gen 15:12–21 because it illustrates *translation* distortion which we discussed in the Memory chapter.[14] It does so in the way in which it introduces sound mnemonics in the form of assonance and alliteration, whilst faithfully preserving the *inclusio*, parallelism and repetition of the Hebrew text. What we have here is Abram's dream of the covenant, which consists of an auditory message dream and a symbolic dream. There is *inclusio* with verse 12 using the phrase περὶ δὲ ἡλίου δυσμάς and verse 17 ἐπεὶ δὲ ἐγίνετο ὁ ἥλιος πρὸς δυσμαῖς. It has to be acknowledged that verse 17 does not bring Abram's experience to a close. However, there is an end to the first phase of it, namely God's message to Abram. In what follows there is a visual element as well as a further message from God. There is assonance in verse 13 with

---

13. Abraham (Gen 15:12–21), containing both a message and a symbolic dream; Abimelech (Gen 20:1–8); Isaac (Gen 26:24); Jacob and the Ladder to Heaven (Gen 28:10–22); Jacob and the Goats (Gen 31:10–13); Laban (Gen 31:24); Joseph and the Sheaves (Gen 37:5–7); Joseph and Sun, Moon, and Stars (Gen 37:7–9); Pharaoh's Cupbearer (Gen 40:9–13); Pharaoh's Baker (Gen 40:16–19); Pharaoh and the Seven Sleek and Fat Cows (Gen 41:1–4, 14–45); Pharaoh and the Ears of Grain (Gen 41:5–8, 14–45); Jacob at Beersheba (Gen 46:1–8); Balaam's Experience (Num 22:9–13); Balaam again (Num 22:20–21); Midianite predicting Gideon's victory (Judg 7:13–14); Samuel's Call (1 Sam 3:2–15); Solomon (1 Kgs 3:3–15); Elijah's *Wecktraümen* (1 Kings 19:5–7); Nebuchadnezzar and the Great Statue (Dan 2:31–35, 36–45); Nebuchadnezzar and the Tree felled by the Watcher (Dan 4:5–15, 16–24, 25–34); Daniel and the Animals (Dan 7:1–8); Daniel and the Throne Room (Dan 7:9–14); Interpretation of these dreams (Dan 7:15–27); Daniel and the Ram and Goat (Dan 8:1–14, 15–26).

14. We suggested "translation" distortion as an additional form to those cited by Schudson, "Dynamics of Distortion," 348–59.

the phrase καὶ δουλώσουσιν αὐτοὺς καὶ κακώσουσιν αὐτοὺς καὶ ταπεινώσουσιν αὐτούς[15] and something close to assonance at verse 16 with ἀναπεπλήρωνται αἱ ἁμαρτίαι τῶν Ἀμορραίων. There is parallelism in God's promise at verses 14 and 15 with ἐξελεύσονται ὧδε μετὰ ἀποσκευῆς πολλῆς followed by σὺ δὲ ἀπελεύσῃ πρὸς τοὺς πατέρας σου μετ' εἰρήνης. There is plenty of repetition. We have ἐπέπεσεν and ἐπιπίπτει both in verse 12. We have γινώσκων γνώσῃ in verse 13 and the phrase might be treated as alliteration as well. We also have δουλώσουσιν ("enslave") in verse 13 followed by δουλεύσωσιν ("serve as slave") in verse 14. There is also τὸ σπέρμα σου in verse 13 followed by the same phrase in the dative in verse 18. And the word ποταμοῦ with the definite article appears three times in quick succession in verse 18.

In the Hebrew text there is a similar *inclusio* with ויהי השמש לבוא at verse 12 and at verse 17 ויהי השמש באה. We also find parallelism at verses 14 and 15 with ואתה תבוא אל-אבתיך בשלום followed by ואחרי-כן יצאו ברכש גדול. It is perhaps less clear in the Hebrew text because, unlike the Greek, different verbs are used. However, the description of it as parallelism is valid as the first half describes the future of Abram's descendants and the second half the future of Abram himself. The assonance which the Greek text has at verses 13 and 16 and the alliteration at 13 is missing in the Hebrew. However, the Hebrew does have הנה used at the end of each half of verse 16. Admittedly the sense is different in each case. In the first half it suggests a place, '*hither*,' but in the second half it is more temporal '*yet*.' Nevertheless it is a sign of repetition and hint of assonance. There is further repetition as in the Greek with נפלה and נפלת in verse 12, ידע תדע in verse 13, ועבדום in verse 13 and יעבדו in verse 14, זרעך in verse 13 and לזרעך in verse 18, and הנהר three times in verse 18.

What emerges from this example is that *inclusio*, parallelism and repetition have been preserved from Hebrew into Greek, but alliteration and assonance appear in the Greek which are missing in the Hebrew. These devices, added by the translators, illustrate translation distortion.

What we discovered, once all OT dreams were examined, was that LXX does have devices which are largely the same as those in the Hebrew text; where they differ, it is usually because the two languages differ in sound and therefore cannot use the same alliterations or assonance. In particular Greek has the case-endings of nouns and adjectives and also verb-endings which lend themselves to assonance as illustrated by LXX Gen 15:13 on the previous page, while these are not so readily available in Hebrew. Nevertheless, the translators seem to pick up features such as alliteration and

---

15. Brayford points out that LXX-G uses three verbs instead of only two in MT, "serve" (עבד) and "oppress" (ענה). See Brayford, *Genesis*, 300.

assonance and try to reproduce them at a different point in the text, if they can. So we find in Gen 20:1–8, where the dream of Abimelech is recorded, that the Hebrew text has alliteration with ויגר בגרר in verse 1 and בעלת בעל in 3. There is also assonance with the phrase אבימלך מלך in verse 2. The LXX does have alliteration, but at a different point from the Hebrew. It is present in the opening phrase: καὶ ἐκίνησεν ἐκεῖθεν and later at verse 6 in the phrase: καθ' ὕπνον κἀγὼ ἔγνων ὅτι ἐν καθαρᾷ καρδίᾳ. We find that occasionally LXX does insert devices of its own. We see an example of this too in LXX Gen 20:1–8, in which there is *inclusio* with ἐφοβήθη in verse 2 and ἐφοβήθησαν in verse 8. However, in the Hebrew text there is no *inclusio*, for there is no reference to Abraham's fear in verse 2.[16] This might be an explanation for Abraham's deception offered by the translators, unless they read a different Hebrew text from us. LXX may also omit or change expressions. Susan Brayford suggests at 20:3 where the Hebrew text reports that God came to Abimelech "in a dream of the night," ויבא אלהים אל-אבימלך בחלום הלילה, LXX alters the Hebrew formula, stating that God "entered" him (εἰσῆλθεν) "in sleep" (ἐν ὕπνῳ).[17] However, I would dispute this example, for ἐν ὕπνῳ may mean "in a dream"[18] and εἰσῆλθεν may simply be a strengthened form of ἦλθεν, meaning "visit."[19] However, I do concede that the translators did sometimes make changes, adding their own devices or taking away, but generally these are relatively few.

What we have seen here is *translation* distortion which we argued in the Memory chapter was a form of distortion not usually discussed in relation to the reliability of narratives. However, we acknowledge that for the most part, LXX reflects the memory patterns or rhetorical devices of the Hebrew dream narratives.

---

16. Brayford comments on the fear of Abimelech's servants at verse 8, suggesting that fear is a defining motive behind the recent actions of many men, e.g., Abraham (Gen 20:2) and Lot (Gen 19:30). See Brayford, *Genesis*, 323.

17. Brayford says that here, as elsewhere, LXX-G avoids dream language. Only in narrating the story of Jacob's dream on his way to Haran (Gen 28:12) does LXX-G render MT יחלם as ἐνυπνιάσθη. All other dream language occurs only in the Joseph Narrative (Gen 37–50). See Brayford, *Genesis*, 323.

18. LSJ give examples of this meaning in Euripides, *Iphigenia Taurica* 44; Plato, *Respublica* 476c, and of the plural in Plato, *Respublica* 572b; *Sophista* 266b; *Isocrates* 9.21, and of καθ' ὕπνον, κατὰ τοὺς ὕπνους in Plutarch, *Moralia* 2.717e, 555b.

19. LSJ have εἰ. πρός τινα *enter* his *house, visit* him, Xenophon, *Cyropaedia* 3.3.13; of a doctor, *pay a visit*, Galen, *Galenic Corpus* 18(2).36.

## Old Testament in Relation to Matthew

At this stage we treat the Old Testament as a unit. We recognize that it is in fact a collection of books, written by different authors and belonging to different time periods. However, we can deal with the complete unit as long as we are seeking an answer to the major question raised in this study, whether Matthew and any source(s) are more subject to Jewish or Hellenistic influence. Towards the end of this chapter when we sum up, we will need to consider whether there is any particular OT book or single narrative on which Matthew may have based the dreams. Then the OT results will be divided according to books.

In the 23 OT dreams that were examined, the most common form of memory pattern was repetition. This varied from single words through short phrases to longer expressions and occasionally whole verses or sentences.[20] There were many instances of a single word being repeated, but some were less significant, merely being the subject matter of a passage. I would suggest that there are nine dreams where there are possible examples of key words.[21] There is extensive repetition in several of the dreams.[22] There are examples of *assonance*[23] and *alliteration*.[24] There can also be *onomatopoeia*.[25] There were seven cases of *inclusio*, but only six in each of MT and LXX.[26] *Parallelism* was found in two of the dream narratives, but with five cases altogether.[27] Two examples of *chiasmus* were detected,[28] and two instances of *numerical* aids to memory.[29] We note the use of *formulaic expressions* as well. There is a form of wording to introduce or close a dream,[30] which is

---

20. Genesis 28:10-22 contains both single word and extensive repetition. Genesis 40:9-13 illustrates single word repetition, while 31:10-13 has the extensive variety. Further examples for each category will be given below.

21. Gen 28:10-22; 40:9-13, 16-19; 41:25-31; 1 Kgs 3:5-15; Dan 2:31-35; 4:5-15; 7:9-14; 8:1-14.

22. Gen 28:10-22; 31:10-13; 41:5-8, 17-21, 22-24, 25-31; 46:1-8; Num 22:9-13; 1 Sam 3:2-15; Dan 4:25-34; 7:15-27.

23. Gen 15:12-21; 20:1-8 (Hebrew only); 46:1-8 (Hebrew only); Dan 2:31-35 (LXX only).

24. Gen 20:1-8; 31:10-13 (LXX only); 46:1-8 (LXX only); 1 Sam 3:2-15 (LXX only); 1 Kgs 3:5-15; Dan 2:31-35; 8:1-14.

25. 1 Sam 3:2-15.

26. Gen 15:12-21; 20:1-8 (LXX only); 28:10-22 (Hebrew only); 46:1-8; Dan 2:36-45; 4:5-15; 8:15-26.

27. Gen 15:12-21; 1 Kgs 3:5-15.

28. Gen 37:5-7; 1 Kgs 3:5-15.

29. 1 Sam 3:2-15; Dan 7:1-10.

30. Gen 15:12; 20:3, 8; 26:24; 28:11-12, 18; 31:10, 24; 37:5, 6, 9; 40:9, 16; 41:1, 5;

## COMPARISON OF MEMORY PATTERNS

required by the pattern of dream reporting. However, there may be as few as three real formulaic expressions.[31] There are also formulaic epithets repeated in descriptions.[32] There are three examples of antithesis,[33] the second two of which require comment. The fat and lean cows and later the plump and thin ears of grain are set in contrast, which is in itself memorable,[34] rather than being involved in antithesis in a strict sense. I have treated these two cases as antithesis, partly because of this contrast, but also partly because of their actions, the lean cows devouring the fat, the latter being devoured, and the same with the ears of grain.

There are five devices shared in common between OT and Matthew: formulaic expressions, key words, *inclusio*, parallelism, chiasmus and lengthy repetition. One type of formulaic expression is epithets repeated in descriptions, examples of which we find in Pharaoh's two dreams in Genesis 41. Descriptions of the fat and lean cows and the plump and thin ears of grain are repeated throughout, albeit with some variation. It is noteworthy that some of the epithets are transferred from the cows to the ears: ἐκλεκτοὶ καὶ καλοί, "choice and good"; good fat בריאת, "fat" or "plump"[35]; and λεπτοί, דקות, "thin."[36] Formulaic epithets are not evident in Matthew. The other type of formula is the introductory or closing expression used in dream narratives. These may vary, but as an example of an introductory expression we

---

46:2; Judg 7:13; 1 Kgs 3:5; 19:5, 7, 8; Dan 2:31; 4:5; 7:1; 8:1.

31. a) God came to X in a dream by night (Gen 20:3):
ויבא אלהים אל-אבימלך בחלום הלילה; cf. Gen 31:24 and the variation with "appeared" (1 Kgs 3:5): נראה יהוה אל-שלמה בחלום הלילה.

b) X dreamed a dream (Gen 37:5, 9): ויחלם יוסף חלום.

c) God spoke to X in visions of the night (Gen 46:2)
ויאמר אלהים לישראל במראת הלילה.

32. There is evidence of formulaic epithets in Pharaoh's two dreams recorded in Genesis 41.

33. Gen 20:1-8; 41:1-7.

34. This figure of contrast may be a memory pattern in its own right. We find it exemplified in Matthew in the contrast between the speck and the plank in the eye.

35. We may note how LXX has substituted for בריאת "fat" or "plump" ἐκλεκτοὶ "choice."

36. It is equally noteworthy that the LXX handles repetition of these epithets in a slightly different way from the Hebrew text. E.g., in the dream of the ears the description of the poor ears is repeated in full in LXX: λεπτοὶ καὶ ἀνεμόφθοροι, "thin and blasted with the wind," but in the Hebrew the original phrase דקות ושדופת קדים, "thin and blasted with the east wind," is reduced to דקות, "thin." In bringing back an epithet which has gone missing in the Hebrew text, are the translators consciously bringing back a memory aid which had become lost in the written text or are they consciously composing anew for rhetorical purposes or do they repeat unconsciously not realizing that the Hebrew text has dropped an epithet? We can only guess.

take Gen 31:10 telling how Jacob said he saw in his dream: וארא בחלום, εἶδον τοῖς ὀφθαλμοῖς αὐτὰ ἐν τῷ ὕπνῳ and for a terminating formula we use Gen 20:8 where Abimelech rises in the morning: וישכם אבימלך בבקר, καὶ ὤρθρισεν Ἀβιμελεχ τὸ πρωΐ. It is the second type of formulaic expression which we find displayed in Matthew. However, we need not detect any direct relationship between Matthew and OT here, since the use of such an expression was part of the form of a dream narrative throughout ANE.

It was suggested above that of all the repeated words encountered there may be only nine dream passages where a key word is present. An example of this is the use of τόπος, מקום, *place*, in Jacob's experience in Genesis 28 where Bethel is being treated as a sacred place.[37] Another is ἑπτά שבע, *seven*, in Pharaoh's two dreams in Genesis 41, where in verses 26 and 27 the word *seven* is used no fewer than eight times in relation to both cows and ears and it will become significant in the interpretation. With regard to *inclusio* an example has already been given in the analysis of Genesis 15 with the reference at verses 12 and 17 to the sun going down.

We now take up parallelism which is quite pronounced in Matthew. Reference was made earlier to the example in Genesis 15 with its prediction for Abram's descendants in verse 14 and for himself in 15. At this stage we reflect on the parallelism present in the Solomon narrative at 1 Kings 3:5–15 because it illustrates *specification*, one of the particular forms of Hebrew parallelism. There are several examples of parallelism (1 Kgs 3:6-7, 8, 12, 12–13). We find it between the end of 6 and beginning of 7:

a. ותתן-לו בן ישב על-כסאו, δοῦναι τὸν υἱὸν αὐτοῦ ἐπὶ τοῦ θρόνου αὐτοῦ,

b. אתה המלכת את-עבדך תחת דוד אבי, σὺ ἔδωκας τὸν δοῦλόν σου ἀντὶ Δαυὶδ τοῦ πατρός μου.

The same act of God is described in both parts, where in the first it is what God has given David and in the second part what he has done for Solomon. There is a minor example in verse 8 in the description of the chosen people as being innumerable:

a) עם-רב אשר לא-ימנה (and b) מרב) ולא יספר, but this is not present in LXX. The next case is to be found in verse 12 where both parts carry similar meaning:

a) הנה עשיתי כדבריך, ἰδοὺ πεποίηκα κατὰ τὸ ῥῆμά σου

---

37. We find it twice in verse 11 and once in each of 16, 17, 19. Brayford points out the first instance of τόπῳ at 28:11 is anarthrous, while the Hebrew המקום is not. However, the other examples of τόπος do have the article. See Brayford, *Genesis*, 354.

b) הנה נתתי לך לב חכם ונבון, ἰδοὺ δέδωκά σοι καρδίαν φρονίμην καὶ σοφήν. There is a further instance between b) and c) where instead of הנה or ἰδού c) opens with a negative, what Solomon did not request:

c) וגם אשר לא-שאלת נתתי לך גם-עשר גם-כבוד, καὶ ἃ οὐκ ᾐτήσω, δέδωκά σοι, καὶ πλοῦτον καὶ δόξαν. There is then another example of parallelism between the end of 12 and end of 13:

i) אשר כמוך לא-היה לפניך ואחריך לא-יקום כמוך, ὡς σὺ οὐ γέγονεν ἔμπροσθέν σου καὶ μετὰ σὲ οὐκ ἀναστήσεται ὅμοιός σοι

ii) אשר לא-היה כמוך איש במלכים כל-ימיך, ὡς οὐ γέγονεν ἀνὴρ ὅμοιός σοι ἐν βασιλεῦσι.

In the Methodology chapter, attention was drawn to Alter's analysis of parallelism in OT and how he distinguishes three types: meaning, syntax and rhythm.[38] Many of the examples in the Solomon narrative are syntactical, but there is a particularly interesting case of semantic parallelism in verse 12. It takes the form of what Alter calls *specification*. For the second part, "Behold, I give you a wise and discerning mind," specifies what was said in the first part, "Behold, I now do according to your word." Most of Matthew's examples are syntactical, but he does have a case of *specification* where "Joseph did what the angel of the Lord commanded" is explained by the statements that "he took his wife and he called his name Jesus."

We come now to extensive repetition, of which there were 11 examples, but the greatest is to be found in Daniel 4, especially in LXX, where we find Nebuchadnezzar's dream of the tree felled by the watcher. There are 46 words in common between verses 7–9 and 17–18 in LXX. Similarly, when we compare the section of the dream in verses 10–13 with Daniel's repetition of it at verse 20, we find 50 words in common. However, the Aramaic text is not always as precise as LXX. In all the cases cited there is more verbatim repetition in LXX than there is in the original Hebrew or Aramaic texts. It would appear that we have *translation* distortion occurring here. Some changes we may explain by the way the Semitic languages add prefixes and suffixes to certain words. At other times the translators seem to have put more effort into achieving verbatim repetition, as they pursue their own goals.

There are some particular examples where the OT repetition bears some resemblance to Matthew's usage. We have already noted how in Genesis 41 in the dream about the ears of grain, there is phraseology carried over from the previous dream about the cows. The carrying over of language from one dream to another is a feature of Matthew. Although this is a symbolic dream as opposed to the message dreams in Matthew, the interpretation of Joseph in

---

38. Alter, *Art of Biblical Poetry*, 6–7.

Genesis repeats language from the dream in a way comparable to the repetition of language as Matthew's Joseph obeys the commands given by the angel in the dream. In Numbers 22 we have Balaam's dialogue with God where he echoes information already given to the reader in verses 4 and 5, just as the angel does with Joseph in relation to Mary's conception through the Holy Spirit. There is also a little of God's instructions conveyed in the narrative which follows. We note in 1 Samuel 3 the echoes between Samuel's statement ("Here I am, for you called me") and Eli's response ("I did not call, my son") and between Eli's commands ("Go, lie down . . . if he calls you, you shall say, 'Speak, Lord, for thy servant hears'") and Samuel's action ("So Samuel went and lay down . . . And Samuel said, 'Speak, for thy servant hears'"). This can be related to the angel's command and Joseph's obedience. In the case of Elijah's experience at 1 Kings 19:5–7 there is the superficial connection of *the angel of the Lord*. That apart, we note how Elijah obeys the command given by the angel ("arise and eat"), just as Joseph does and there is a double take with incident repeated, the command and obedience occurring twice, just as the angel reappears to Joseph with fresh commands.

There is no single OT passage whose devices exactly match those of Matthew 1–2. However, the examples cited above are those which have greatest affinity with Matthew. Extensive repetition was the common factor between OT and Matthew in all but Solomon's dream where the common factor was parallelism including a case of specification. These examples were cited to illustrate and highlight memory patterns present in Matthew which also have a significant presence in certain OT passages. As we seek to establish whether Jewish or Hellenistic influence was stronger on Matthew or his source, these passages support a case for OT influence. However, it is not being suggested that Matthew or his source was influenced by any specific OT text, but rather they shared with OT writers a common interest in preserving narratives in memory and used similar memory techniques. This common ground between Matthew and OT writers may suggest that Matthew has absorbed and internalized aspects of OT style and register. This is in line with the possibility which we noted above that Matthew may be deliberately aiming at a biblical register through echoing OT memory patterns.

## The Apocrypha

In the Apocrypha there are only three dreams, two of which occur in the additions to Esther which are found in LXX, but not in the Hebrew text. At the beginning of the book[39] we have Mordecai's dream.[40] It has an example of anaphora, with each of the three sections of the dream opening with the phrase καὶ ἰδοὺ, "and behold," at verses 4, 5, and 7. That apart, there is repetition of single words, nouns and corresponding verbs, and phrases. We do not regard any of these as key words. Next we have a symbolic dream experienced and interpreted by Mordecai.[41] The only memory pattern to be found is the repetition of ποταμός, "river," from the account of the dream to its interpretation. There is little in these two dreams in common with Matthew. The writer would appear to be following a different literary practice from Matthew and indeed OT.

Outside OT altogether there is the dream of Maccabaeus in 2 Maccabees 15:12–16. If we take into account the preceding verse and those that follow, there is evidence of *inclusio*. At verse 11 we have: καθοπλίσας . . . ὡς τὴν ἐν τοῖς ἀγαθοῖς λόγοις παράκλησιν; then at 17 we find: παρακληθέντες δὲ τοῖς Ἰούδα λόγοις πάνυ καλοῖς. There is considerable repetition of particular words and phrases, especially those relating to the people, the holy city, the temple, prayer, and God's gift. Perhaps the most significant is the word ἅγιος which appears altogether three times, at 14, 16, and 17. It may amount to a key word. This passage has in common with Matthew *inclusio*, repetition of short phrases and a possible key word, which are among the most common memory devices.

Table 3: Old Testament

|  | Matthew | OT–Heb | LXX | Apocrypha |
|---|---|---|---|---|
| Dreams | 5 | 23 | 23 | 3 |
| Acrostic | 0 | 0 | 0 | 0 |
| Alliteration | 0 | 4 | 7 | 0 |
| Anaphora | 0 | 0 | 0 | 1 |
| Antithesis | 0 | 3 | 3 | 0 |
| Association | 0 | 0 | 0 | 0 |
| Assonance | 0 | 3 | 2 | 0 |

39. The reference is sometimes given as Esther 11:2–12. Elsewhere 11:2–12:6 is referred to as A 1–17, making the dream reference A 1–11.

40. In LXX he is referred to as Mardochaeus.

41. Esther 10:4–8 or F 1–5.

|  | Matthew | OT–Heb | LXX | Apocrypha |
|---|---|---|---|---|
| Chiasmus | 2 | 2 | 2 | 0 |
| Formulaic Expressions | 3 | Frequent 3 Types | Frequent 3 Types | 0 |
| Inclusio | 2 | 6 | 6 | 1 |
| Key Word | 1 | 9 | 9 | 1 |
| Metre | 0 | 0 | 0 | 0 |
| Numerical Aids | 0 | 2 | 2 | 0 |
| Onomatopoeia | 0 | 1 | 1 | 0 |
| Order | 0 | 0 | 0 | 0 |
| Parallelism | 5 | 5 | 5 | 0 |
| Repeated Blocks | 4 | 11 | 11 | 0 |
| Typology | 2 | 0 | 0 | 0 |

## Other Jewish Writings

In addition to OT and the Apocrypha, we shall look at dream narratives in other Jewish texts. In particular we shall consider the writings of Philo, Josephus, and Pseudo-Philo, the *Testament of Naphtali* and *Genesis Apocryphon*.

## Philo

We move on to Philo, a Hellenistic Jew, who represents an intermingling of Jewish and Hellenistic cultures and significantly wrote a treatise on dreams. That treatise is entitled *Quod A Deo Mittantur Somnia*, abbreviated to *De Somniis*. Two books of this treatise have survived.[42] Book 1 deals with dreams in which the mind is inspired and can foresee the future. Philo uses two examples from the story of Jacob: the heavenly ladder at

---

42. According to Eusebius of Caesarea, there were originally five books (Eusebius, *Historia Ecclesiastica* 2.18). However, on the basis of internal evidence, we can only be sure of three books. We learn in the opening section of what is now book 1 about an earlier book which is now lost. It dealt with dreams in which the dreamer's own thoughts had no part. We then have the two books which are extant, but we know nothing of the other two books to which Eusebius refers.

Bethel[43] and the dream of the goats.[44] Book 2 deals with dreams which contain no direct divine message, but something that is seen by the dreamer which requires explanation involving the art of dream interpretation. The examples here consist of three pairs of dreams: those of Joseph himself as a boy,[45] those of the chief baker[46] and chief butler in prison[47] and those of Pharaoh,[48] the last two pairs being interpreted by Joseph himself.[49] However, when the dreams in *De Somniis* are examined, it emerges that Philo does not express them in his own words. Those in book 1 he lifted straight from his Septuagint translation. This is largely true also of the symbolic dreams in book 2. However, this requires some qualification. In relation to Joseph's dream of the sheaves, he begins by quoting the opening words straight from LXX Gen 37:7: ᾤμην ὑμᾶς δεσμεύειν δράγματα.[50] Then later in his interpretation Philo goes on quote Joseph's words in the form of indirect speech. Where LXX has καὶ ἀνέστη τὸ ἐμὸν δράγμα καὶ ὠρθώθη, Philo has θαρρεῖ λέγειν, ὅτι καὶ ἀνέστη τὸ αὐτοῦ δράγμα καὶ ὠρθώθη.[51] These are almost exactly the same words except that the first person personal possessive ἐμόν has become the third person αὐτοῦ.[52] This kind of change has no bearing on patterns of memory. Since Philo quotes from LXX rather than express the dreams in his own words, it is not possible to examine his use of memory patterns in *De Somniis*.

However, we may look elsewhere in Philo's works for any dream which he records in his own words. In *De Vita Mosis* we find the experience of Balaam[53] which OT gives at Numbers 22:31–35. This is a vision of an angel with no suggestion that Balaam was sleeping.[54] Again it is

---

43. Philo, *De Somniis* 1.2–3.
44. Philo, *De Somniis* 1.189. The biblical references are Gen 28:12–15; 31:11–13.
45. Philo, *De Somniis* 2.6.
46. Philo, *De Somniis* 2.206.
47. Philo, *De Somniis* 2.159.
48. Philo, *De Somniis* 2.216–18.
49. See Gen 37:7, 9; 40:9–11, 16–17; 41:17–24.
50. Philo, *De Somniis* 2.6.
51. Philo, *De Somniis* 2.78.
52. Another example is to be found in Pharaoh's dream of the seven sleek and fat cows. Philo appears to quote directly from LXX, but there are minor variations. Cf. LXX Gen 41:18; Philo, *De Somniis* 2.216. They are the kind of differences we might encounter with different manuscript readings. Alternatively, the variation in Philo's version may be due to his quoting from memory.
53. Philo, *De Vita Mosis* 1.273–274.
54. This means that it is not strictly a dream. We noted at the beginning of the Methodology chapter the distinction that a dream occurs in sleep, while a vision is a

difficult to find features that we have labeled memory patterns. What we do have are repeated words and phrases, but sometimes the repetition of ideas does not involve the same vocabulary. So the experience opens with a statement where the angel is referred to as ἄγγελος, but later as ὄψις, an apparition or vision. There are four references to "turning": ἐτράπετο[55] when he turned to prayer; mention of his duty to return, ὑποστρέφειν δεόν[56]; a question to the angel about whether he should return, ἐπυνθάνετο τῆς φανείσης ὄψεως εἰ ἀνακάμπτοι πάλιν τὴν ἐπ' οἴκου[57]; and the suggestion by the angel that he would turn or direct his organs of speech, τρέποντος. It would appear that some of the repetition is determined by the content of the story being narrated and not because Philo wants to highlight a theme or to assist his readers to remember something. However, it may be that πυνθάνεσθαι is functioning as a key word, highlighting along with other relevant vocabulary (ἄγνοια, συνίημι) Philo's desire as a philosopher to contrast Balaam's ignorance with the understanding of the angel. With Philo exhibiting few devices, the only area which he and Matthew have in common is in the use of key words. It may be that he is less concerned than Matthew to assist his readers to remember his narrative and simply wants to drive home his philosophical point.

## Josephus

We turn now to the work of Josephus, who was a first-century Hellenistic Jewish scholar, historian, and hagiographer. Living in Rome, he represents the intermingling of Jewish and Hellenistic cultures. Indeed this intermingling of cultures may have already begun before he left Judaea, for some claim he had received a first-rate aristocratic education, which gave him a basic facility in Greek language, literature and even thought.[58] His work is of interest to us because he is contemporary with Matthew and more significantly he used sources, just as we suggested but could not prove for Matthew's dream narratives. He had made his own notes during the Jewish War concerning proceedings in the Roman camp outside Jerusalem

---

waking experience, but otherwise they are very similar.

55. Philo, *De Vita Mosis* 1.273.
56. Philo, *De Vita Mosis* 1.274.
57. πυνθάνεσθαι is repeated when the angel ponders why he should ask about a matter so evident.
58. Mason, *Josephus and the New Testament*, 55. As we shall see below, Josephus himself tells us that he employed assistants for the sake of the Greek.

and was kept aware of events within the city by deserters.[59] He was in correspondence with King Agrippa throughout the production of *War*.[60] He had access to the memoires and commentaries of Vespasian and Titus.[61] For the pre-war period he used Nicolas of Damascus, author of a universal history in 144 books.[62]

The literary style of the *Jewish War* has been described as "an excellent specimen of the Atticistic Greek fashionable in the first century."[63] This is in some respects surprising for someone whose native language was Aramaic, although it is possible for a bilingual person to become competent in a second language. However, Josephus offers an explanation himself in his use of assistants for the sake of the Greek: χρησάμενός τισι πρὸς τὴν Ἑλληνίδα φωνὴν συνεργοῖς.[64] The use of such collaborators, admirable though they be, poses a problem for our study. When we encounter devices in the text, we have no way of knowing from whose hand they come.[65] The problem of distinguishing memory patterns derived from oral transmission and rhetorical devices inserted by a writer is also more acute with multiple hands at work.

When we look at those narratives which relate dreams already recorded in the text of the OT, we might have anticipated that the memory patterns would have been the same or reasonably similar. This is particularly so when we bear in mind how Josephus describes his *Antiquities* as a translation from the Hebrew scriptures into Greek: ἐκ τῶν Ἑβραϊκῶν μεθηρμηνευμένην γραμμάτων.[66] He later reinforces this with an assurance of his intention to render the Hebrew books into Greek: μεταφράζειν τὰς Ἑβραίων βίβλους . . . εἰς τὴν Ἑλλάδα γλῶτταν and with a promise of no addition or omission: μήτε προστιθεὶς τοῖς πράγμασιν αὐτὸς ἰδίᾳ μήτ' ἀφαιρῶν ὑπεισχημένος.[67] However, it becomes clear that Josephus's narrative is rather different from the Hebrew

---

59. Josephus, *Contra Apionem* 1.47–49.

60. Josephus, *Vita* 364–367.

61. The commentaries (ὑπομνήματα) are mentioned three times: Josephus, *Vita* 342, 358; *Contra Apionem* 1.53–56.

62. Thackeray says, "For the pre-war period (books 1–2) we can confidently name one writer, frequently mentioned in the *Antiquities*, as having furnished material also for the *Jewish War*—Nicolas of Damascus" (Thackeray, *Jewish War*, xxii).

63. Thackeray, *Jewish War*, xiii.

64. Josephus, *Contra Apionem* 1.50.

65. Occasionally Josephus's own style may be detected in some autobiographical passages. There is less of a problem with *Antiquities*, where books 1–14 and 20 appear to have been written by the author himself, with assistance given for only 15–19. See Thackeray, *Jewish War*, xv.

66. Josephus, *Ant.* 1.5.

67. Josephus, *Ant.* 10.218.

text or even the LXX translation. If we assume that the OT preserves memory patterns from a period of oral transmission, this means that Josephus is not continuing that transmission, but freely narrating stories and inserting rhetorical devices of his own.

We may compare Jacob's dream of the ladder at Bethel recorded at Gen 28:10-22 and Josephus's *Ant.* 1.279-84. The most significant feature of OT is the amount of repetition. A statement made by God in the course of the dream is repeated by Jacob in the Genesis account after he wakens. Although it is still recognizable as God's promise, Jacob makes significant changes to it with an additional reference to food and clothing and an extra condition of his loyalty which is no doubt based on a promise God made earlier at verse 13. There is no such repetition in Josephus. There are also several words and phrases which are repeated throughout the biblical passage. The most notable is *the place*, המקום, ὁ τόπος, which occurs six times—three in verse 28:11 alone—and then in 16, 17, and 19. This must surely be functioning as a key word. However, this is not so in Josephus. He does not use τόπος at all. He uses the word χωρίον for *place*[68] and then only once. It is clearly not a key word for him. So there is no shared device here between OT and Josephus. He is not passing on memory patterns transmitted to him. There appears to be an example of *inclusio* in the Hebrew text. It is formed with מצבה, "pillar," in verses 18 and 22 combined with מצב, "set up," in verse 12. Interestingly enough, there is no similar *inclusio* in LXX. However, Josephus does have *inclusio*, but it is formed in a totally different way from the Hebrew. In the introduction to the dream,[69] Josephus refers to λίθοις, the stones which Jacob had gathered and on which he placed his head for sleep. Then, he tells us of Jacob polishing the stones, λίθους, on which he lay as great blessings were predicted.[70] He also tells us that God called Jacob by name—ὀνομαστί.[71] In *Antiquities*, we find Jacob giving the place the name—ὄνομα—Bethel,[72] and Jacob's name is actually used by God—'Ἰάκωβε.[73] When the dream is complete, Josephus sums up by referring to what God had foretold to Jacob—'Ἰακώβῳ.[74]

It is difficult to conclude that this is anything other a free paraphrase of the biblical story[75] and that Josephus is not reproducing memory patterns

---

68. Josephus, *Ant.* 1.284.
69. Josephus, *Ant.* 1.279.
70. Josephus, *Ant.* 1.284.
71. Josephus, *Ant.* 1.279.
72. Josephus, *Ant.* 1.284.
73. Josephus, *Ant.* 1.280.
74. Josephus, *Ant.* 1.284.
75. Feldman, *Flavius Josephus*, 109-11, draws attention to the changes: whereas

or rhetorical devices as they came down to him. He is freely composing for his own ideological purposes. So he omits the divine self-identification in his account of Jacob's experience at Bethel.[76] Similar reworking of the story is also to found with Solomon's two dreams in Josephus,[77] when compared with the equivalent passages in OT (1 Kgs 3:5–15; 9:1–9).

We find the same free approach to narration in two non-biblical dreams both of which Josephus relates twice.[78] Even details of the dreams are different,[79] but more importantly from our perspective, the so-called memory patterns also vary. Although both versions of the Archelaus dream have alliteration, the examples of it are different in each. *War* has ἄλλων δ' ἄλλως[80] and this is picked up later with ἀλλάσσειν; but *Antiquities* has ἑτέρων ἐφ' ἑτέροις.[81] If these examples of alliteration serve a mnemonic rather than stylistic purpose, they must be intended to help the reader remember rather than be part of the transmission of the narrative to Josephus. The same may be said of the *inclusio* to be found in the *War* version of the Glaphyra dream, but missing the *Antiquities* version. The *War* narrative opens with Ἄξιον δὲ μνήμης ἡγησάμην καὶ τὸ τῆς γυναικὸς αὐτοῦ Γλαφύρας ὄναρ[82] and closes with τοῦτο διηγησαμένη τὸ ὄναρ.[83]

---

Gen 28:12 has angels ascending and descending in Jacob's dream, Josephus states that Jacob *thought* (ἔδοξεν) he saw a ladder; instead of angels he speaks of *phantoms* (ὄψεις) and he has them descending since they would not be ascending from the earth prior to their descent; he has God urge Jacob "to show courage" (θαρρῶν), where Gen 28:18 simply has God's promise to be with Jacob; he omits the information of Gen 28:19 that the former name of Bethel was Luz; and where LXX Gen 28:22 has οἶκος Θεοῦ, "house of God," Josephus puts θεία ἑστία, "divine hearth."

76. Gnuse believes that this had the potential to suggest polytheism to a Hellenistic audience "for God's self-identification would imply the divine need to distinguish one particular deity from all the others" (Gnuse, *Dreams and Dream Reports*, 149).

77. Josephus, *Ant.* 8.22–25, 125–29.

78. The dream of Archelaus is narrated in Josephus, *War* 2.112–13, and again in Josephus, *Ant.* 17.345–48. Likewise the dream of Glaphyra appears in Josephus, *War* 2.114–16, and again in Josephus, *Ant.* 17.349–53.

79. The *Antiquities* version of the Archelaus dream increases the number of ears of corn from nine to ten to reflect the number of years Archelaus actually ruled. Again the *Antiquities* version of the Glaphyra dream is more elaborate than the *War* account, with Glaphyra seeking to embrace Alexander and Alexander's message being expanded. We find similar changes in detail when Josephus retells OT dreams, especially in Joseph's dreams regarding the sheaves and the sun, moon and stars. Josephus has Joseph consult his brothers on the interpretation of the first dream and has Jacob offer the interpretation of the second.

80. Josephus, *War* 2.113.

81. Josephus, *Ant.* 17.346.

82. Josephus, *War* 2.11.

83. Josephus, *War* 2.116. Admittedly ἡγέομαι carries the idea of "*thinking or*

We single out for special attention the dream of Amram,[84] because it is sometimes referred to in discussions of the infancy narratives due to the parallels between them, although it is never actually suggested that Matthew modeled Joseph's dreams on this.[85] Amram was the father of Moses, as Joseph was of Jesus; both had dreams; and a Moses typology is evident in our section of Matthew. The dream is referred to as ὄνειρος.[86] There is an introductory formula: ἐφίσταται κατὰ τοὺς ὕπνους αὐτῷ and a closing one: Ταῦτα τῆς ὄψεως αὐτῷ δηλωσάσης περιεγερθείς.[87] There is some repetition with God assuring Amram that he had their piety in remembrance: τήν τε εὐσέβειαν αὐτῶν ἔλεγε διὰ μνήμης ἔχειν[88] and later in fairly similar words Amram suggesting they would be deemed impious not to remember help given by God in war: κἂν ἀσεβεῖς εἶναι δόξητε καὶ μὴ διὰ μνήμης ἔχοντες.[89] Again we have a reference to Jacob's great prosperity: ἐπί τε μεγέθει τῆς εὐδαιμονίας[90] and this is echoed later by a reference to the greatness of the blessing which was to come upon Moses: ἐπὶ μεγέθει τοσαύτης εὐδαιμονίας.[91] There is expression of the same thought using contrasting words from the same root, one of which has been negated. So at 2.214 we have reference to Jacob becoming famous for his prosperity among an alien people—τοῖς οὐχ ὁμοφύλοις—and at 2.216 Moses is to be remembered even by alien nations—παρὰ τοῖς ἀλλοφύλοις. Reference is made twice to the growth of the Hebrew nation, but the first time in general terms and the second with detailed numbers. So at 2.212 we have τοσοῦτον πλῆθος αὐτοὺς ἐξ ὀλίγων and at 2.214 οὗ μετὰ ἑβδομήκοντα τῶν πάντων εἰς Αἴγυπτον ἀφικομένου ὑπὲρ ἑξήκοντά που μυριάδας ἤδη γεγόνατε. We have two references to all time, but using different expressions, both in 2.216: ὅσον μενεῖ χρόνον τὰ σύμπαντα, "for as long a time as everything remains," and διὰ παντὸς τοῦ χρόνου, "throughout

---

*considering"* and διηγέομαι the idea of *"relating* or *narrating."* However, διηγέομαι is derived from ἡγέομαι. More importantly, the sounds are the same.

84. Josephus, *Ant.* 2.212–217.

85. E.g., Brown, *Birth of the Messiah*, 115.

86. Josephus, *Ant.* 2.217. Gnuse, *Dreams and Dream Reports*, 164, wrongly refers to it as ὄναρ.

87. These formulae bear some resemblance to those used in the dreams of Genesis, although they are not expressed quite as precisely. Gnuse suggests that Josephus may have used the language unconsciously rather employing it deliberately (Gnuse, *Dreams and Dream Reports*, 164).

88. Josephus, *Ant.* 2.212.

89. Josephus, *Ant.* 2.214.

90. Josephus, *Ant.* 2.214.

91. Josephus, *Ant.* 2.217.

all time." It seems likely that these repetitions are due to variation of writing style rather than serving as memory patterns.

If we compare the memory patterns used by Josephus and Matthew, we find they have in common formulae and repetition. However, Matthew uses different formulae and engages in more extensive and more precise repetition. Too much variation in repetition can detract from its value as an aid to memory, but Josephus's concern may be more stylistic than mnemonic. There is not enough in this example to lead us to conclude that they share a common literary approach. However, we need to take account of Josephus's other dreams.

All of Josephus's thirty-three dream narratives were examined,[92] of which the majority were message dreams, as in Matthew, with only twelve being symbolic. The results were as follows. Josephus introduces most dreams with formulaic expressions, and sometimes he also uses formulae to conclude them.[93] However, he has no standard expression which he uses to introduce all dreams, unlike Matthew who does use the same expression throughout, albeit he is narrating significantly fewer dreams.[94] There are seven examples of *inclusio*[95] and some evidence of alliteration in three dreams.[96] There is one suggestion of assonance.[97] Numerical aids to memory occur in the two Glaphyra dreams.[98] There is plenty of repetition. We have, for example, the

92. Josephus, *War* 2.112–113 (Archelaus); 2.114–116 (Glaphyra); *Ant.* 1.208–209 (Abimelech); 1.279–284 (Jacob at Bethel); 1.313–314 (Laban); 1.331–334 (Jacob at Penuel); 2.10–17 (Joseph); 2.63–73 (Butler and Baker); 2.75–86 (Pharaoh); 2.171–76 (Jacob at Beersheba); 2.212–217 (Amram); 5.215–216 (Gideon); 5.218–22 (Midianite); 5.277–278 (Manoch's Wife); 5.348–350 (Samuel at Shiloh); 6.37–40 (Samuel as an adult); 7.92–93 (Nathan); 8.22–25 (Solomon's First); 8.125–129 (Solomon's Second); 10.194–211 (Nebuchadnezzar and the Statue); 10.216–217 (Nebuchadnezzar and the Tree); 10.269–277 (Daniel); 11.326–328 (Jaddus); 11.333–335 (Alexander the Great); 12.112 (Theopompos); 13.332 (Hyrcanus); 17.345–348 (Archelaus); 17.349–353 (Glaphyra); 20.18–19 (Monobazus); *Life* 208–210 (Josephus).

93. The second dream of Archelaus is concluded with a reference to Archelaus awakening, περιεγρόμενος (Josephus, *Ant.* 17.345), and the interpretation is concluded with the formula ὁ μὲν ταύτῃ ἐξηγήσατο τὸν ὄνειρον, "thus did this man expound the dream" (Josephus, *Ant.* 17.348).

94. With the Glaphyra dream narrated twice, each has a slightly different formula: ἔδοξεν ἐπιστάντα τὸν Ἀλέξανδρον αὐτῇ λέγειν in *War* and τοιόνδε ὄναρ θεᾶται· ἐδόκει τὸν Ἀλέξανδρον ἐπιστάντα θεασαμένη . . . φάναι in *Antiquities*.

95. Josephus, *War* 2.112, 113; 2.114, 116; *Ant.* 1.279, 284; 8.22, 25; 8.125, 129; 10.269, 277; 10.269, 272; *Life* 208, 210.

96. We have already noted instances in the two Archelaus dreams (Josephus, *War* 2.113; *Ant.* 17.346). In the second dream of Solomon alliteration may occur up to three times (Josephus, *Ant.* 8.128, 129), and possibly between 8.127–128.

97. Josephus, *Ant.* 20.18.

98. Josephus, *War* 2.114, 116; *Ant.* 17.352.

details of Glaphyra's three marriages given in both dream narratives prior to the reporting of the dream and then repeated within the dream content.[99] As we saw with OT, some repetition may be explained in terms of the subject matter.[100] It can be argued that the dream command μηδὲν ὑβρίζειν in Abimelech's dream and the double use of ἀνύβριστον are deliberate since a moral idea is involved and may even amount to a key word.[101] We have many examples of antithesis,[102] three instances of chiasmus[103] and some cases of extensive repetition. However, this repetition does not always occur where we might expect it. It is missing in the Pharaoh dreams where it is present in the biblical text.[104] Where we do find some is in the Midianite dream,[105] Nebuchadnezzar's dream of the statue[106] and in Daniel's vision[107] because in each of these instances we have the dream or vision given and then the interpretation of it. However, in none of these cases is the repetition verbatim. There is also repetition in the Midianite dream and the Daniel vision where obedience to a command is expressed. In the former it is said that God ordered Gideon to take one of his soldiers—προσλαβόντα ἕνα τῶν στρατιωτῶν—and in the following section Gideon's obedience is expressed—Φρουρὰν τὸν ἑαυτοῦ θεράποντα παραλαβών; Gideon was to advance to the tents of the enemy—πλησίον χωρεῖν ταῖς Μαδιηνιτῶν σκηναῖς—and he did so—πλησιάσας σκηνῇ τινι.[108] In the case of Daniel, *Ant.* 10.269 closes with an instruction to rise, κελεύοντος ἀναστῆναι, and *Ant.* 10.270 opens with that carried out, ἀναστάντι δ' αὐτῷ δειχθῆναι. We see that in neither case is the obedience expressed verbatim.

We may now compare the work of Josephus with that of Matthew. The latter has information given to Joseph prior to his first dream and then

99. Josephus, *War* 2.114–116; *Ant.* 17.349–353.

100. In Samuel's second theophanic experience (Josephus, *Ant.* 6.37–40), where the issue is a request from the Israelites to appoint them a king, regardless of whether or not it is a dream, it is hardly surprising to find βασιλεύς used three times and βασιλεύω used twice. Similarly in Nathan's experience (Josephus, *Ant.* 7.92–93), where the issue is the building of the temple (τὸν ναὸν), it is understandable that we find three phrases referring to it.

101. Josephus, *Ant.* 1.208–209. Feldman, *Flavius Josephus*, 79, points out that Josephus uses ὑβρίζειν, "to do violence," where LXX Gen 20:4 has οὐκ ἥψατο to indicate that Abimelech had not gone near Sarah.

102. Josephus, *Ant.* 2.12, 17, 63, 66, 68, 69–70, 72, 73, 75, 76, 80, 81, 83, 86; 10.195, 199, 200, 204, 207, 208, 210, 217, 269, 270, 272.

103. Josephus, *War* 2.114–116; *Ant.* 1.208–209, 279–284.

104. Josephus, *Ant.* 2.75–86.

105. Josephus, *Ant.* 5.218–222.

106. Josephus, *Ant.* 10.194–211.

107. Josephus, *Ant.* 10.269–277.

108. Josephus, *Ant.* 5.218.

repeated in the dream itself. This is comparable to what we find with the two versions of the Glaphyra dream. Matthew is fairly consistent in his use of the dream formula, while Josephus is not. Both have *inclusio* and also key words. When Matthew repeats phrases, they tend to be longer than those repeated by Josephus. Even where Josephus gives longer repetition, it tends not to be verbatim. Some of Matthew's repetition comes through Joseph obeying the commands issued by the angel. However, we saw that Josephus makes no attempt in the Midianite dream and the vision of Daniel to express the action in language which repeats precisely the command. Josephus makes considerable use of antithesis, but there is no obvious verbal antithesis in Matthew's dream narratives. It would be fair to conclude that Josephus and Matthew use devices differently.

We noted in the introduction to Josephus that he used sources, as we suggest Matthew may have done. Are we able to say whether Josephus reflects the use of memory patterns in his sources? This seems unlikely for three reasons. First, we have noted already the free paraphrase which he offers for OT dreams and the free approach he adopted for the dreams of Archelaus and Glaphyra. Secondly, with the notable exception of the scriptures which he uses in the first half of his *Antiquities*, Josephus has a tendency to play down his authorities and sources, making no allusion to them in the *War* and giving only hints in *Contra Apionem* and *Vita*. Thirdly, devices may have stemmed from the writing style of the assistants Josephus used rather than sources, particularly since they were employed to produce a good style. If this reasoning is correct, we may say that the approach of Josephus is different from what we believe Matthew is doing.

Ultimately, the assistants may have influenced the writing of Josephus more than his sources, as they strove for Atticistic Greek style.[109] Much would depend on the extent to which he gave them freedom of expression, whether they had an entirely free hand or simply tidied up what he dictated. Although Matthew and Josephus share *inclusio*, key words and some repetition, their writing style is different with Matthew favoring more extensive repetition. We note that Josephus has twenty-five instances of antithesis, which is a popular Greek device. However, when we recall that he has seven cases of *inclusio* in thirty-three dreams, while OT has six instances in twenty-three narratives and, as we shall see, this is a higher proportion than in classical writers, we may still see him as displaying Jewish traits, albeit with a different overall literary style from Matthew or OT.

109. Mason, *Flavius Josephus*, 74, points out that in Josephus, *War* 2.112, Josephus uses the old Attic plural στάχυς, in keeping with the Atticizing tendencies of the *War*, whereas in LXX (Gen 41:7; Matt 21:1; Mark 2:23; Luke 6:1), the form is στάχυας which Josephus himself uses in Josephus, *Ant.* 2.83.

## Pseudo-Philo

We move on to other Jewish texts of the same era and take up consideration of *Liber Antiquitatum Biblicarum* by Pseudo-Philo. There is no certainty about the date of this work, belonging to the first or second century CE. The original form of this work is believed to have been written in Hebrew, which was then translated into Greek before being rendered in Latin which is the earliest version now in existence.[110] As the available Latin text is a translation and not the original, it might seem sensible to ignore it, since we cannot be sure that any memory patterns discovered go back to the original and were not created by the translator(s). However, some of the dreams, particularly that of Miriam in 9:10, bear some affinity to those of Matthew and are sometimes referred to in discussions of the infancy narratives.[111] They are therefore worth a look.

There are altogether six dreams in LAB[112] or, more accurately, five when we bear in mind that 8:10 only refers to the dreams of Pharaoh without actually narrating them.[113] We single out for special attention the dream of Miriam already mentioned. This is a brief narrative in which we are told that Miriam had a dream (*vidit somnium*) and told it to her parents. There is repetition in which Miriam obeys the instructions of the visitor, possibly an angel (*vir . . . in veste bissina*, "a man in a linen garment"). However, the obedience (*enarravit parentibus suis mane dicens*, "told her parents in the morning saying") is expressed before we are told of the command (*dic parentibus tuis*, "tell your parents"). There is antithesis between the water into which the baby will be thrown (*in aquam proicietur*) and the water which will be dried up by him (*per eum aqua siccabitur*). There may be *inclusio* with the section opening with *enarravit parentibus suis* and closing with *cum enarrasset Maria somnium suum, non crediderunt ei parentes eius*.

When Pseudo-Philo narrates biblical dreams, he makes considerable changes. So we find him recasting Joshua's covenantal renewal ceremony in what appears to be a message dream which involves a long speech from God on the early history of the Israelites.[114] Or in Samuel's call experience, Pseudo-Philo gives us God's personal reflections before we are told

---

110. Jacobson, *Commentary*, 215–24.

111. E.g., Brown, *Birth of the Messiah*, 114n42.

112. LAB 8:10 (Pharaoh); 9:10 (Miriam); 18:3–9 (Balaam); 23:3–14 (Joshua); 28:4–5 (Eleazar); 53:1–13 (Samuel).

113. The phrase used is: *postea vidit somnium rex Egipti*, "after that the king of Egypt saw a dream."

114. LAB 23:3–14.

about Samuel's prophetic call.[115] He also has *Heli* or Eli at one stage telling Samuel that if the voice calls a third time, it is an angel. This differs from the OT text of 1 Samuel 3 where Eli says that it is the Lord. When Eli does understand that God is calling, he issues different instructions.[116] Over all there is not the same level of repetition as we find in the biblical account. While this may not help us in our comparison with Matthew, other than by providing a contrast, it does tell us something about the way Pseudo-Philo handles his sources. He is willing to change the content and consequently it is not surprising that he is less concerned to preserve repetition as a memory aid. As he pursues different goals from the biblical writers, he puts his own slant on stories.

The phenomena found in Pseudo-Philo may be summed up as follows. We note that four of the dreams show evidence of repetition of single words, some of which may amount to keywords.[117] Two have examples of antithesis,[118] something missing from Matthew. There is one case of *inclusio*,[119] and some repetition associated with obedience.[120] The summing up of Abraham's obedience in 23:3-14 is worthy of note, even though it is not a memory pattern: *Et accepit sicut precepi ei*, "And he took them as I commanded him." That makes it similar to Matt 1:24.[121] However, Samuel's nocturnal experience does not have the repetition we might have expected in line with OT. Pseudo-Philo and Matthew have in common key words, *inclusio* and repetition associated with obedience, but little else. However, as these are features found in many writers, they do not allow us to draw any conclusions in relation to Matthew's cultural leanings.

---

115. LAB 53:1-13.

116. Instead of the simple biblical command, "Speak, Lord, for your servant hears," we have in Pseudo-Philo: *Aure tua dextra intende, sinistra tace*, "With thy right ear attend and with thy left refrain." This is followed by an explanation and then the command is repeated thus: *dicito: Dic quid vis, quoniam audio, tu enim me plasmasti*, "Say thus: Speak what thou wilt, for I hear thee, for thou hast formed me." When the time came, what Samuel said was: *Si possibilis sum, loquere quoniam tu plus de me nosti*, "If I be able, speak, for thou knowest well concerning me."

117. 18:3-9; 23:3-14; 28:4-5; 53:1-13.

118. 9:10; 18:3-9.

119. 9:10.

120. 9:10.

121. ἐποίησεν ὡς προσέταξεν αὐτῷ ὁ ἄγγελος κυρίου.

## Testament of Naphtali

There are two symbolic dreams in the *Testament of Naphtali*[122] which belongs to the *Testaments of the Twelve Patriarchs* and can be dated to the second century BCE.[123] What was found here was repetition of single words or short phrases in the first dream. We see ὁ ἥλιος καὶ ἡ σελήνη used four times,[124] but that is not surprising, given that that is the subject matter of the dream. The word δώδεκα, "twelve," is used three times and may be a key word.[125] There are examples of antithesis in both.[126] There is also repetition involving command and obedience in both. In the first dream Isaac says at 5:2: Προσδραμόντες κρατήσατε ἕκαστος κατὰ δύναμιν καὶ τοῦ πιάσαντος ἔσται ὁ ἥλιος καὶ ἡ σελήνη, "Run forth, seize them, each according to his capacity; to the one who grasps them will the sun and the moon belong." His grandsons' obedience is expressed at 5:3 with: Καὶ ἐδράμομεν πάντες ὁμοῦ καὶ ὁ Λευὶ ἐκράτησε τὸν ἥλιον καὶ ὁ Ἰούδας φθάσας ἐπίασε τὴν σελήνην, "We all ran, but Levi seized the sun and Judah, outstripping the others, grasped the moon." Some of this vocabulary is repeated in later verses. So we find in 5:5 προσδραμόντες and ἐκράτησαν and in 5:6 πιάσαι. In the second dream we have the command at 6:3: Δεῦτε ἀνέλθωμεν εἰς τὸ πλοῖον ἡμῶν, "Get into our boat"; and the obedience at 6:4: Ὡς δὲ εἰσήλθεμεν, "When we boarded it." There the obedience is expressed in the form of a subordinate clause. Although the repetition is largely in the form of obedience to a command, as in Matthew, there is in neither example here the substantial verbatim repetition given by Matthew. Key words are shared by the *Testament of Naphtali* and Matthew, while the level of repetition and antithesis separate them. The result is something of a contrast between the two writers.

## Genesis Apocryphon

When we turn to the Dead Sea Scrolls, we find four dreams in *Genesis Apocryphon* (1QapGen).[127] Strictly speaking there are only three dream

---

122. 5:1-8; 6:1-10.

123. Kee suggests the Maccabean period, but points out that early Christian interpolations probably date from early second century CE (Kee, "Testaments of the Twelve Patriarchs," 777-78).

124. 5:1, 2, 3, 4.

125. It is twice in 5:4 with *date palms* and with *rays* and once in 9 with reference to the *scepters* of Israel.

126. 5:6-7; 6:4-5; three examples in 6:6; and a minor case in 6:7-8.

127. 1QapGen 20:22 (Herqanosh); 13-15 (Arboreal Dream of Noah); 19:14-21 (Abram's First); 21:8-22 (Abram's Second).

narratives because 20:22 is really only a dream reference.[128] We see cases of repeated words in Noah's dream[129] and the first of Abram's. There are two examples of *inclusio* in Abram's second dream.[130] There is reasonably substantial repetition in Noah's dream amounting to six words in the Aramaic text—קצין ונסבין להון מנה חזה הוית[131]—and the expression is used three times in the space of three lines.[132] Abram's second dream has two instances of command and obedience. In the first only three words in Aramaic are repeated. The opening words of the command at 8 were: סלק לך לרמת חזור, "Go up to Ramat-Hazor"; and the obedience is expressed in line 10 thus: וסלקת למחרתי כן לרמת חזור, "So on the following day I went up to Ramat-Hazor." In the second there are only two words in common between command and obedience. At 13–14 God said: קום הלך ואזל וחזי, "Get up, walk around, go and see." Then at 15:12 have: ואזלת אנה אברם למסחר ולמחזה ארעא, "So I, Abram, embarked to hike around and look at the land." The cases of *inclusio* and repetition are the devices which *Genesis Apocryphon* and Matthew share. Although the use of these particular devices knows no cultural boundaries, it is worth recalling that they are both used extensively in OT, including Genesis to which this Qumran document is related.

## Acts of the Apostles

We move on now to the Acts of the Apostles, where we find four message dreams[133] and five visions.[134] The only other vision which we have so far included was that of Balaam but we do so on this occasion to extend our material in Acts and because of their similarity to dreams. Indeed four of the visions resemble message dreams with only one being the symbolic

---

128. All we are told is ארי בחלם חז [ני], "This was because he had seen (me) in a dream."

129. No doubt there was more repetition than we can now see, for in places the text is missing. Machiela, *Dead Sea Genesis Apocryphon*, provides new readings made possible by narrowband infrared photographic technology. Despite that there are still blanks.

130. God's second speech and Column 21 as a whole.

131. "(They) were chopping and taking of it for themselves. I kept watching."

132. Lines 9, 10, and 11.

133. Acts 16:6–10 (Macedonian); 18:9–11 (the Lord to Paul); 23:11 (second of the Lord to Paul); 27:23–26 (Angel of God to Paul).

134. Acts 9:3–9 (Jesus to Saul on Damascus road); 9:10–17 (Ananias); 10:3–8 (Angel of God to Cornelius); 10:9–16 (Peter's vision of clean and unclean animals); 22:17–21 (the Lord to Paul in Jerusalem).

type.¹³⁵ Three of the visions are repeated later in the book.¹³⁶ The results of investigation were as follows: two cases of antithesis¹³⁷; one of onomatopoeia¹³⁸; two of parallelism¹³⁹; one of chiasmus¹⁴⁰; some key words¹⁴¹; and two of *inclusio*.¹⁴²

We explore the parallelism further to see whether our examples may be described as semantic or syntactical. At 23:11 we have ὡς γὰρ διεμαρτύρω τὰ περὶ ἐμοῦ εἰς Ἰερουσαλὴμ followed by οὕτω σε δεῖ καὶ εἰς Ῥώμην μαρτυρῆσαι. We think this is a case of syntactical parallelism. However, it may be argued that it is a semantic case, as both parts share a meaning related to "testifying." The verbs are διαμαρτύρομαι and μαρτυρέω respectively. The former in the middle voice is an intensive form of the latter which is in the active. Although there is a shared meaning, there is no real progression in meaning which Alter told us to look out for where semantic parallelism occurs.¹⁴³ The differences here concern location, a move from Jerusalem to Rome, and time, what has already occurred to what must happen in the future. We find a similar example in chapter 27 between the introduction to the dream in 23 and the message of the angel in 24: παρέστη . . . μοι . . . τοῦ θεοῦ . . . ἄγγελος followed by Καίσαρί σε δεῖ παραστῆναι. Here the verb in both parts is παρίστημι. Again we would treat it as syntactical parallelism.

We now note the repetition in Acts of which there are several examples, but it tends to be less precise than Matthew's usage. There are four dreams or visions where a command is given and obedience follows. We have it with the man from Macedonia in 16:6–10. His invitation is: Διαβὰς εἰς Μακεδονίαν βοήθησον ἡμῖν; and the response is: εὐθέως ἐζητήσαμεν ἐξελθεῖν εἰς Μακεδονίαν. Inevitably the place has to be the same in both, but significantly the verbs are different. Then there is the vision associated with Paul's conversion in 9:3–9. The command ἀνάστηθι in 6 leads to Paul's obedience in 8: ἠγέρθη δὲ Σαῦλος ἀπὸ τῆς γῆς. Again the verb is totally different. It is interesting to note what happens with Ananias's obedience in 9:10–17. The words Ἀναστὰς πορεύθητι, "rise and go," at verse 11 are not repeated. Instead

---

135. Acts 10:9–16.

136. Acts 9:3–9; cf. 22:6–11; 26:12–18. 10:3–8; cf. 10:30–33. 10:9–16; cf. 11:4–11.

137. Antithesis probably exists in the dream at 16:6, 10, but it may simply be a matter of Luke's style. There is a more definite example in the vision at 22:9.

138. Acts 18:9.

139. Acts 23:11; 27:23; cf. 27:24.

140. Acts 9:7.

141. There may be a few key words in Acts 26:12–18, particularly where they coincide with the other accounts of Paul's conversion. There are also four references to οὐρανός, "sky," "heaven," in Acts 11:4–11.

142. Acts 10:11; cf. 10:16. 11:5; cf. 11:10.

143. Alter, *Art of Biblical Poetry*, 14.

at verse 17 we are told Ananias Ἀπῆλθεν, "went away." ζήτησον ἐν οἰκίᾳ in 11 becomes εἰσῆλθεν εἰς τὴν οἰκίαν in 17. Then εἶδεν ἄνδρα ... εἰσελθόντα in 12 gives way to εἰσῆλθεν in 17 which is fair enough since it is the same verb. Next we have ἐπιθέντα αὐτῷ [τὰς] χεῖρας in 12 mirrored with reasonable precision by ἐπιθεὶς ἐπ' αὐτὸν τὰς χεῖρας in 17. There is then significant material in 17, εἶπεν, Σαοὺλ ἀδελφέ, ὁ κύριος ἀπέσταλκέν με, Ἰησοῦς ὁ ὀφθείς σοι ἐν τῇ ὁδῷ ᾗ ἤρχου, which is not preceded by anything in 12. Then back in 12 the words ὅπως ἀναβλέψῃ are repeated in 17 with ὅπως ἀναβλέψῃς. This is then picked up with the fulfillment ἀνέβλεψέν in 18. However, the purpose clause in 17 is further expanded with καὶ πλησθῇς πνεύματος ἁγίου. We move on to the vision of Cornelius in 10:3-8. The instruction πέμψον ἄνδρας εἰς Ἰόππην in 5 is carried out in verses 7 and 8, but using entirely different vocabulary: δύο τῶν οἰκετῶν καὶ στρατιώτην εὐσεβῆ ... ἀπέστειλεν αὐτοὺς εἰς τὴν Ἰόππην. The men are specified in 7; a different verb for *sending* is used in 8; and the definite article is used with the name Joppa in 8. There is no precise repetition with obedience and command. Do we find such repetition elsewhere?

We look for it in Paul's speeches in 22:6-11; 26:12-18 where he relates his conversion experience. Precise repetition is to a considerable extent missing. Let one example suffice. In 26:14 the phrase, σκληρόν σοι πρὸς κέντρα λακτίζειν, appears which was not present in Jesus's dialogue with Paul at 9:4; 22:7. However, some manuscripts of 9:4 do have this additional phrase,[144] but it seems likely that they were introduced by copyists who assimilated the passage to Paul's account of his conversion in 26:14.[145] There is one case of repetition which is more like what we find in Matthew. We find it in the vision of Peter, when he comes to relate it himself at 11:4-11, and we compare that with Luke's narration at 10:9-16. There are instances extending to nine words,[146] five words[147] and seven words.[148]

To sum up, the areas where Matthew and Acts have something in common are in the use of key words, *inclusio*, parallelism and repetition, four of the categories used by Matthew. However, we note that Acts has antithesis which Matthew lacks and we have argued that Acts does not display any semantic parallelism, as Matthew does. The usage in Acts is certainly consistent with that of Matthew and differences may be explained largely in terms of style.

---

144. E 431, vg mss, syr[p, h with *], Petilianus, Jerome, and Augustine. It occurs in 9:5 in it[gig, h, p], vg[mss], Lucifer and Ambrose.

145. See Metzger, *Textual Commentary*, 361-62.

146. Cf. Acts 11:5; 10:11.

147. Cf. Acts 11:7; 10:13.

148. Cf. Acts 11:9; 10:15.

## Summary of Jewish Writings

If we take the Jewish writings just considered, and initially treat them separately from OT, we find that what Matthew has in common with them are formulae, *inclusio*, key words, parallelism and repetition, although they tend not to engage in the same amount of verbatim repetition as Matthew. He lacks the antithesis that we find in Josephus, Pseudo-Philo, the *Testament of Naphtali* and Acts. Formulae, *inclusio*, key words, repetition and antithesis were all found in OT. What we have not come across in the other Jewish writings is a case of semantic parallelism, but that may be due to the limited amount of literature examined. Certainly the lines of text studied in *Genesis Apocryphon* were not extensive with the result that we may not have received a true estimate of its style. What emerges so far is that Matthew is closer to OT usage than other Jewish texts, particularly in his use of extensive repetition and semantic parallelism. We may wonder why this is the case. It may simply be that other Jewish writers are not as keen on these and other memory techniques as OT authors were or their goals were different. We have noted how Josephus and Pseudo-Philo drop such techniques, as they leave out other details of narratives in reporting some OT dreams. Alternatively the explanation may lie with Matthew himself. Repetition may simply be a feature of his style and he uses it out of habit. On the other hand, his usage may be deliberate as he seeks to write in a biblical register. It may be that Matthew or his source has learned the use of OT devices through reading or listening to the OT or perhaps he was even trained as a scribe. What we have still to establish is whether Matthew has greater or less affinity with Hellenistic writing in general.

Table 4: Jewish Literature

|   | Matthew | Josephus | Philo | Pseudo-Philo | Naphtali | Gen. Apoc. | Acts |
|---|---|---|---|---|---|---|---|
| Dreams | 5 | 33 | 1 | 6 | 2 | 4 | 9 |
| Acrostic | 0 | 0 | 0 | 0 | 0 | 0 | 0 |
| Alliteration | 0 | 3 | 0 | 0 | 0 | 0 | 0 |
| Anaphora | 0 | 0 | 0 | 0 | 0 | 0 | 0 |

| | Matthew | Josephus | Philo | Pseudo-Philo | Naphtali | Gen. Apoc. | Acts |
|---|---|---|---|---|---|---|---|
| Antithesis | 0 | 25 | 0 | 2 | 6 | 0 | 3 |
| Association | 0 | 0 | 0 | 0 | 0 | 0 | 0 |
| Assonance | 0 | 1 | 0 | 0 | 0 | 0 | 0 |
| Chiasmus | 2 | 3 | 0 | 0 | 0 | 0 | 1 |
| Formulaic Expressions | 3 | Most | 0 | 0 | 0 | 0 | 0 |
| Inclusio | 2 | 7 | 0 | 1 | 0 | 2 | 2 |
| Key Word | 1 | Yes | Yes | 4 | 1 | 0 | 2 |
| Metre | 0 | 0 | 0 | 0 | 0 | 0 | 0 |
| Numerical Aids | 0 | 2 | 0 | 0 | 0 | 0 | 0 |
| Onomatopoeia | 0 | 0 | 0 | 0 | 0 | 0 | 1 |
| Order | 0 | 0 | 0 | 0 | 0 | 0 | 0 |
| Parallelism | 5 | 0 | 0 | 0 | 0 | 0 | 2 |
| Repeated Blocks | 4 | 5 | Phrases | 0 | 0 | 3 x 6 | 0 |
| Typology | 2 | 0 | 0 | 0 | 0 | 0 | 0 |

## Greek, Hellenistic, and Roman Writers

We leave behind Philo and Josephus, who, although classified here as Jewish, are also widely recognized as Hellenistic, and we move on to writers who are decidedly Greco-Roman or Hellenistic, as we seek to discover whether Matthew has more in common with them or Jewish writers or OT and thereby attempt to establish which culture had more influence on his writing. As we explore the use of memory patterns and rhetorical devices in the dream narratives of each author, we shall attempt, where possible, to relate our findings to their use of such devices in their work as a whole. Drawing then upon the studies of classicists, we shall be restricted by the extent to which they have studied their style and the limited extent to which they have concentrated on figures of speech rather than other stylistic features such as irony or presentation of characters. We may expect to find some affinity between Herodotus and Matthew, because it is claimed that they both use oral sources. However, with the other writers we are more concerned to look for such affinity, if it exists, in relation to a group as a whole.

## Historical writers

We begin with historical writers before proceeding to biographers, writers of fiction and finally, Artemidorus who recorded and interpreted dreams.

## Herodotus

We take up first the *Histories* of Herodotus, who lived from c. 490 BCE to 425 BCE.[149] He belonged to Asia Minor, having been born in Halicarnassus, modern-day Bodrum. Although he wrote approximately 500 years before Matthew in a different cultural context, he was very much involved with oral storytelling. Herodotus uses the term *logos* for his discourse and, as he seeks to record the experience of the entire known world, he makes use of the *logoi* of others and integrates them in various ways into the texture of his own.[150] Egbert Bakker points out that when Herodotus reports accounts given by others he uses indirect speech, using φασί ("they say") + an infinitive. In this respect Herodotus is different from Homer and the epic tradition where we find direct speech.[151]

Herodotus narrates seventeen dreams altogether. Eight of these are message type[152]; seven are symbolic[153]; and two are referred to without any detail.[154] On examination these dreams reveal the following memory patterns: key words,[155] formulaic expressions,[156] *inclusio*,[157] verse and riddle,[158]

---

149. OCCL 146.
150. Bakker, "Syntax of Historie," 92.
151. Bakker, "Syntax of Historie," 101.
152. Herodotus, *Histories* 1.34 (Croesus); 2.139 (Sabacos); 2.141 (Sethos); 3.30 (Cambyses); 5.56 (Hipparchus); 7.12–14 (Xerxes x 2); 7.17–18 (Artabanus).
153. Herodotus, *Histories* 1.107–8 (Astyages x 2); 1.209 (Cyrus); 3.124 (Polycrates's daughter); 6.107 (Hippias); 6.131 (Agariste); 7.19 (Xerxes).
154. Herodotus, *Histories* 3.149 (Otanes); 6.118 (Datis).
155. Herodotus, *Histories* 2.141; 7.12–14.
156. Herodotus, *Histories* 5.56; 7.12.
157. Herodotus, *Histories* 2.139, 141; 7.17.
158. Herodotus, *Histories* 5.56.

parallelism,[159] antithesis[160] and some repetition.[161] We note an interesting example of formulaic expression in Herodotus's work. In the first dream of Xerxes, the dream figure is introduced with the description, ἐδόκεε ὁ Ξέρξης ἄνδρα οἱ ἐπιστάντα μέγαν τε καὶ εὐειδέα εἰπεῖν, "Xerxes thought that a man tall and comely of shape came and stood by him and said."[162] This was exactly the way in which Hipparchus's dream was introduced,[163] with the only changes being the name and verb of speaking. This expression has some semblance of being a formulaic expression. The dream closes with a similar expression with the verb εἰπεῖν now becoming the participle: τὸν μὲν ταῦτα εἰπόντα ἐδόκεε ὁ Ξέρξης ἀποπτάσθαι. Also worthy of note is the fact that the examples of antithesis tend to be found in Herodotus's symbolic dreams rather than message dreams. The instance of parallelism found in the closing expression of Xerxes's second dream is interesting: ὡς καὶ μέγας καὶ πολλὸς ἐγένεο ἐν ὀλίγῳ χρόνῳ, οὕτω καὶ ταπεινὸς ὀπίσω κατὰ τάχος ἔσεαι, "as you became great and powerful in a short time, so in turn you shall become low quickly."[164] Although the balance is structural with ὡς καί followed by οὕτω καί, it is not evenly balanced. Where μέγας καὶ πολλός involves two adjectives, ταπεινός is only one. ἐν ὀλίγῳ χρόνῳ is balanced by κατὰ τάχος, but the former comes after the verb and the latter before it. The apparent difference in verbs is not really significant: ἐγένεο, "you became," and ἔσεαι, "you will be."[165]

We should also note Herodotus's use of *inclusio*, or ring composition as classical scholars tend to call it.[166] Bakker relates Herodotus's use of it to his inclination to digress, marking the end of the digression with it.[167] In the summary given above it was indicated that we find ring composition

---

159. Herodotus, *Histories* 7.14.

160. Herodotus, *Histories* 1.34, 107–108, 209; 3.124; 6.107; 7.19.

161. Herodotus, *Histories* 1.34, 209; 2.141; 3.30, 124; 5.56; 6.107; 7.12–14, 19.

162. Herodotus, *Histories* 7.12. It is sometimes held that Herodotus has modeled this narrative after the dream of Agamemnon in Iliad 2. See Dodson, *Reading Dreams*, 109.

163. Herodotus, *Histories* 5.56.

164. Herodotus, *Histories* 7.14.

165. The real difference here lies in tense, which is required by the sense of the threat: ἐγενόμην is used regularly as the aorist of εἰμί, which does not create an aorist out of its own root.

166. Worthington is a classicist who uses this expression (Worthington, "Greek Oratory," 165–77). He analyzes the use of ring composition in Dianarchus 1 (Worthington, *Against Demosthenes*).

167. Bakker, "Syntax of Historie," 93.

in three of the dreams.[168] In the first two narratives there are two examples each. We look here at the first narrative. The section opens with the phrase, τέλος δὲ τῆς ἀπαλλαγῆς τοῦ Αἰθίοπος, "the final deliverance from the Ethiopian," and closes with ἑκὼν ἀπαλλάσσετο ἐκ τῆς Αἰγύπτου ὁ Σαβακῶς, "Sabacos departed out of Egypt of his own free will." The *inclusio* is formed through the use of the noun ἀπαλλαγή, "deliverance," at the beginning and the related verb ἀπαλλάσσω in the middle, meaning "depart," at the end. There is further *inclusio* in the dream, opening with ὄψιν ἐν τῷ ὕπνῳ τοιήνδε ἰδόντα αὐτόν, "he had seen in his sleep a vision," and closing with ἰδόντα δὲ τὴν ὄψιν ταύτην λέγειν αὐτόν, "having seen this dream." There is chiasmus in this case with ὄψιν coming before ἰδόντα in the first half, but after it in the second half. The use of two examples gives a structure in terms of ring composition of A B B A. The use of *inclusio* is clearly something Herodotus has in common with Matthew.

Overall, repetition is not widely used by Herodotus. There are two cases where it appears to involve back-looping.[169] In the dream of Hippias we have the phrases συνεβάλετο ὧν ἐκ τοῦ ὀνείρου and ἐκ μὲν δὴ τῆς ὄψιος συνεβάλετο.[170] And in the dream of Xerxes we have τὴν οἱ Μάγοι ἔκριναν and κρινάντων δὲ ταῦτα τῶν Μάγων.[171] Even more significantly we have one case of lengthy repetition found in the dream of Cyrus. Early on, the dream is related: ἐδόκεε . . . ὁρᾶν τῶν Ὑστάσπεος παίδων τὸν πρεσβύτατον ἔχοντα ἐπὶ τῶν ὤμων πτέρυγας καὶ τουτέων τῇ μὲν τὴν Ἀσίην τῇ δὲ τὴν Εὐρώπην ἐπισκιάζειν, "it seemed to Cyrus that he saw the eldest of the sons of Hystaspes having wings upon his shoulders, and that with the one of these he overshadowed Asia and with the other Europe."[172] Then, when Cyrus gets hold of Hystaspes, he tells him the dream in his own words: εἶδον τῶν σῶν παίδων τὸν πρεσβύτατον ἔχοντα ἐπὶ τῶν ὤμων πτέρυγας καὶ τουτέων τῇ μὲν τὴν Ἀσίην τῇ δὲ τὴν Εὐρώπην ἐπισκιάζειν, "I saw the eldest of thy sons having wings upon his shoulders, and with the one of these he overshadowed Asia and with the other Europe."[173] There are twenty words in common here. This is comparable to some OT passages and also to Matthew.

When we compare Herodotus's use of memory patterns with Matthew's use, we find that they have in common key words, formulaic expressions, *inclusio*, parallelism and repetition, but Matthew lacks the antithesis

---

168. Herodotus, *Histories* 2.139, 141; 7.17.
169. See Ong, *Orality and Literacy*, 39–40.
170. Herodotus, *Histories* 6.107.
171. Herodotus, *Histories* 7.19.
172. Herodotus, *Histories* 1.209.1.
173. 1.209.4.

found in Herodotus. However, it would be fair to say that Herodotus does not have the same concentration of usage as Matthew. The former has three examples of *inclusio* in fourteen dreams, where the latter has two examples in five dreams. Herodotus displays only one example of parallelism and two repeated blocks, compared to Matthew's five cases of parallelism and four repeated blocks. Nevertheless, Herodotus's repetition of nine words and more especially twenty words compares favorably with Matthew's eleven, fifteen and nineteen. It may be that the explanation for this lengthy repetition does not lie in common cultural characteristics, but in the fact that they may both be using oral sources.

## Polybius

We move on to Polybius who was a Greek of the Hellenistic period, living between c. 200 BCE and c. 118 BCE.[174] His *Histories* describe the rise of the Roman Republic, but their relevance for us lies in three dreams which they record.[175] The first narrative is extremely short.[176] However, it is noteworthy because, although the contents of the dream are given, they appear before the mention of the dream itself. We are told κατὰ τοὺς ὕπνους τὸν Φίλιππον ταῦτ' ὀνειρώττειν, "Philip in his sleep dreamt of these things."[177] The dream narrative is too short to provide patterns of memory. The second is a fictitious dream which Publius Scipio the Elder tells his mother he had experienced twice before he narrates the alleged contents to her. We realize that the dream has been invented because of the words with which the narrative closes: ὧν οὐδὲν ἦν ἐνύπνιον, "it was not a matter of a dream at all." Although it is fictitious, it is later fulfilled as described, but there is little repetition of language carried through from the dream to the fulfillment.[178]

174. OCCL 241.

175. Polybius, *Histories* 5.108.5 (Philip); 10.4.4—10.5.6 (fictional dream invented by Scipio); 10.11.5–8 (Scipio).

176. Polybius, *Histories* 5.108.5.

177. Now these things were previously mentioned as being the recovery of the revolted cities, making war on Scerdilaidas, crossing to Italy and arranging matters in Illyria.

178. The dream at 10.4.6 says ἅμα τἀδελφῷ καθεσταμένος ἀγορανόμος, "he had been elected aedile along with his brother." The fulfillment at 10.5.3 says ἀμφότεροι γεγονότες ἀγορανόμοι, "both having become aediles." Again the dream describes them ἀναβαίνειν ἀπὸ τῆς ἀγορᾶς ὡς ἐπὶ τὴν οἰκίαν, "going from the forum to their house." However, the fulfillment is expressed as παρῆσαν ἐπὶ τὴν οἰκίαν, "they were present at their house." The only phrase which is common between both is ἐπὶ τὴν οἰκίαν. The dream speaks of how their mother ἐκείνην δὲ συναντᾶν αὐτοῖς εἰς τὰς θύρας, "met them at the door." The fulfillment says that she πρὸς τὰς θύρας ἀπήντα, "met them at the door." The meaning is

The same dream has an example of antithesis: τῇ μὲν οὐδ' ἐν νῷ τὸ ῥηθὲν ἦν, ὁ δὲ λαβὼν πρῶτον λαμπρὰν ἐσθῆτα ... παρῆν εἰς τὴν ἀγοράν, "what she had said had entirely gone out of her head, whereas Scipio receiving the white toga appeared in the forum."[179] There are two more cases of antithesis in the third dream.[180] The latter also has a few instances of repeated words or related words being used.[181]

To sum up, there is only limited evidence of memory patterns or rhetorical devices in the dream passages of Polybius. This appears to be consistent with Polybius's usual style. Matthew Fox and Niall Livingstone comment: "He writes in a deliberately simple, unadorned style, and criticizes other historians for their excessively elaborate narrative devices that detract from the serious purpose of history."[182] Brian McGing is even more negative, speaking of "a rather workmanlike, at times even awkward style of Greek."[183] Even in ancient times his work was recognized as heavy going, for Dionysius of Halicarnassus suggested that Polybius's style made it difficult to read his work all the way through.[184] What Polybius does display stands in contrast with Matthew who does not use antithesis and who does have repetition where an event fulfils a dream. As with Polybius, Matthew's style may be described as relatively simple. However, the latter does retain memory patterns used in oral transmission and preserves them to assist his readers remember his narratives. This would appear not to have been a concern of Polybius.

## Dionysius of Halicarnassus

We take now the dreams recorded by Dionysius of Halicarnassus. He was a Greek historian and teacher of rhetoric who lived at Rome for many years

---

the same. Indeed the verb stem is the same, but the prefix varies, as does the preposition used. The dream goes on to say that περιπτύξασαν ἀσπάσασθαι, "she welcomed them with an embrace." The fulfillment states how περιχαρὴς οὖσα καὶ μετὰ παραστάσεως ἠσπάζετο τοὺς νεανίσκους, "she was overjoyed and welcomed the young men with deep emotion." The only word that is common is ἀσπάζομαι, "welcome," but the first usage is aorist infinitive, while the second is aorist third person singular. Essentially there is no repetition where we might have expected it.

179. Polybius, *Histories* 10.5.1.

180. Polybius, *Histories* 10.11.6, 8.

181. We have the verb παρακαλεῖν, "encourage," and later the noun παράκλησις, "encouragement"; the verb ἐπαγγέλλω, "promise," and later the related noun ἐπαγγελία.

182. Fox and Livingstone, "Rhetoric and Historiography," 554.

183. McGing, *Polybius's Histories*, 4.

184. Dionysius of Halicarnassus, *De Compositione Verborum*, 4.110.

from 30 BCE.[185] In his *Antiquitates Romanae*, or at least in what has survived, he records nine dreams altogether.[186] There is a real dearth of devices here. In 7.68.3-6 we find three message dreams all experienced by the same person, a certain Titus Latinius. Here we find a case of *inclusio*[187] and two of antithesis. The first case of antithesis draws a contrast between the first part of the penalty Latinius has had to pay for his contempt of the god's words, viz. the death of his son, and the rest which he will shortly pay: τὴν μὲν ἤδη δέδωκε δίκην τὸν υἱὸν ἀφαιρεθείς, τὰς δ' ὀλίγον ὕστερον δώσει. There is also another instance of antithesis in 3.67.3. Other than odd single words there is little repetition. The only point of contact with Matthew would be the *inclusio*. Otherwise Dionysius is more of a contrast with him, since *Antiquitates Romanae* lacks the kind of devices which we find in the First Gospel. This lack is in many ways surprising, for Dionysius was keen on rhetoric, making the remark at 1.1.3 that the style is the man. His concern may have been to produce a polished narrative, for he does not appear to be doing the same as Matthew and his source in trying to assist the readers or audience to remember the content of the narrative.

## Diodorus Siculus

Next we have the dreams recorded by Diodorus of Sicily. He was a Greek historian who wrote c. 40 BCE.[188] In the extant parts of his universal history *Bibliotheca Historica* there are three dreams.[189] Again we have an author who does not display the kind of devices for which we are searching. This too is surprising, as Diodorus also saw a role for rhetoric in historical writing.[190] He may achieve his stylistic goals in other ways or the sample of his work examined here, three short narratives, may be too small to get the full flavor of his writing. There are, however, two examples of antithesis in the first dream,[191] the first in the dream itself with the second in

---

185. OCCL 103.

186. Dionysius of Halicarnassus, *Ant. Rom.* 1.56.5 (Aeneas); 1.57.4 [2] (first Latinus and later Aeneas); 3.67.3 (Tarquinius); 5.54.2 (Publius and Marcus Tarquinius); 7.68.3-6 [3] (all three Titus Latinius); 20.12.1-2 (Pyrrhus).

187. We have ἐπὶ κλινιδίου, "in a litter," near the beginning and ἐκ τοῦ κλινιδίου, "from the litter," near the end.

188. CGS 179.

189. Diodorus of Sicily, *Biblio.* 13.97.6 (Thrasybulus); 16.33.1 (Onomarchus); 17.103.7 (Alexander).

190. Fox and Livingstone, "Rhetoric and Historiography," 551.

191. Diodorus of Sicily, *Biblio.* 13.97.6.

its interpretation. We use the first as an example: αὐτός [Θρασύβουλος] τε καὶ τῶν ἄλλων στρατηγῶν ἐξ ὑποκρίνεσθαι τραγῳδίαν Εὐριπίδου Φοινίσσας· τῶν δ' ἀντιπάλων ὑποκρινομένων τὰς Ἱκέτιδας, "he [Thrasybulus] and six of the other generals were playing the Phoenician Women of Euripides, while their competitors were performing the Suppliants." There is also some repetition of single words and use of related words in all three. As Matthew does not use antithesis in his dream narratives and has only one key word, there is little common ground between them. However, Diodorus is like Polybius and Dionysius in his shortage of devices, although classicists who make more extensive examination of their style would compare him with the Dionysius rather than Polybius.[192]

## Appian

Appian, who was born in Alexandria at the end of the first century CE, was a Roman historian of Greek origin.[193] His principal surviving work is Ῥωμαϊκά, known in Latin as *Historia Romana*.[194] Altogether Appian refers to nine dreams.[195] Again we detect few devices, but this time the shortage may be partly explained by the brevity of Appian's dream narratives. There is a dream referred to at *Hist. Rom.* 8.1.1, but it is not narrated. There are several dreams which are narrated very briefly.[196] One is so brief that it consists of only three words.[197] That leaves only two dreams where a search is more feasible.[198] Largely what we find in these is repetition of single words[199]

---

192. Fox and Livingstone link Diodorus with Dionysus and also with Arrian as three examples of writers who combine rhetoric and history (Fox and Livingstone, "Rhetoric and Historiography," 551).

193. Brodersen, "Appian," 7.

194. The most important remnants are the five books on the *Civil Wars* (*Bella Civilia*)—books 13–17 of the *Roman History*.

195. Appian, *Bell. Civ.* 1.11.97; 1.12.105; 2.16.115; 4.14.110; *Hist. Rom.* 8.1.1; 8.20.136; 11.9.56; 12.2.9; 12.4.27.

196. Appian, *Hist. Rom.* 12.2.9; 12.4.27; *Bell. civ.* 1.11.97; 1.12.105; 2.16.115; 4.14.110.

197. φοβήσαντος αὐτὸν ἐνυπνίου: The context (Appian, *Hist. Rom.* 12.4.27) is that Mithridates was cutting down a grove dedicated to Latona and *because a dream caused him terror*, he spared the wood.

198. Appian, *Hist. Rom.* 8.20.136; 11.9.56.

199. The mother of Seleucus saw in a dream that whatever ring she found she should give him to carry (Appian, *Hist. Rom.* 11.9.56). Later she found an iron ring with an anchor engraved on it. It is therefore not surprising to find repeated the words: δακτύλιος, "ring" or "seal-ring"; ἄγκυρα, "anchor"; and σφραγίς, "seal" or "seal-ring."

or related words.²⁰⁰ We have one significant repetition amounting to fifteen words.²⁰¹ However, the repetition does not occur in the same narrative. At *Bell. civ.* 4.14.110, Appian refers to this dream experienced by Octavius. Plutarch refers to the same dream²⁰² in almost identical words.²⁰³ This similarity does not amount to a memory pattern. It simply suggests the possibility that they both drew from the same source. The little found in Appian's work does not allow for serious comparison with Matthew.

## Valerius Maximus

We turn to Valerius Maximus who lived in the early-first century CE.²⁰⁴ He was not strictly an historian, but a writer of historical anecdotes and a moralist. As we deal with his work, we switch from Greek writers to a Latin one. This should not constitute a problem, as we have already handled a Latin text with Pseudo-Philo. We have also dealt with Hebrew text in OT and Aramaic in OT and *Genesis Apocryphon*. Our concern is not the language as such, but the memory patterns and rhetorical devices for which the language is used. Examination of dream narratives in different languages suggests that rhetorical devices and memory patterns are widespread and supersede language divisions.

Around 30 or 31 CE Valerius produced an important collection of historical anecdotes for use in the schools of rhetoric, which is known as *Factorum ac dictorum memorabilium libri IX*, "Nine Books of Memorable Deeds and Sayings."²⁰⁵ Book 1, section 7, contains eighteen dream narratives,

---

200. Caesar wrote a memorandum as a result of a dream—ἐς μνήμην ὑπογράψασθαι—and this was later found by Augustus—ἐντυχὼν ἄρα ταῖς ὑπογραφαῖς (Appian, *Hist. Rom.* 8.20.136).

201. αὐτοῦ δι' ἐνύπνιον ἔνδον οὐκ ὄντος, ἀλλὰ φυλαξαμένου τὴν ἡμέραν, ὡς αὐτὸς ἐν τοῖς ὑπομνήμασιν (ἔγραψεν).

202. This is noted by Horace White in the Loeb Classical Library translation of Appian's *Civil Wars*.

203. The only change is that Plutarch has substituted ἱστορεῖ ("relates") for ἔγραψεν ("has written").

204. OCCL 299.

205. It is also known as *De factis dictisque memorabilibus* or *Facta et dicta memorabilia*.

covering twenty-one dreams altogether.[206] Of these, thirteen are of the message type[207] and eight are symbolic.[208]

Valerius is traditionally considered the first of the Silver writers.[209] In his introduction to the Loeb text Shackleton Bailey describes Valerius as "steeped in the art of rhetoric and eager to show off his literary talent."[210] Despite that, he writes in a turgid style. This can be seen in his tendency to outline the dreams in an indirect form. For example, in the first dream instead of using a verb to relate the appearance of Minerva, he uses the noun *species*, "a likeness"; rather than relate the words of the goddess, he presents her message indirectly: *praecepit ut illum. . . . moneret ne propter aduersam ualitudinem proximo proelio non interesset*, "told him to warn him . . . not to let sickness keep him from being present at the forthcoming battle." This form of expression may be attributed to Valerius's desire to differ from the wording of his source.[211]

He also seems to go out of his way to avoid repetition. In the seventh narrative the figure who appeared to Cassius Parmensis is described initially as *hominem ingentis magnitudinis, coloris nigri, squalidum barba et capillo inmisso*, "a man of huge proportions, black in color, with unkempt beard and his hair hanging down." Then when we are told this frightened him, it is shortened to *taetro uisu*, "horrible sight." Thereafter in the question Parmensis asks his servants the description of the figure is abbreviated to *ecquem talis habitus*, "anyone of that appearance," and in their response it is simply *neminem*, "nobody." Finally when he resumed sleep the reappearance of the figure becomes *eadem . . . species*, "the same apparition."[212] With such an attitude to repetition it is hardly surprising that little is to be found when a command is obeyed or a prophecy fulfilled. In this respect he is very different from Matthew. The nearest we get to repetition is in the final narrative. There we first read *in tabernam meritoriam deuertit*, "lodged at an

---

206. The first eight narratives relate the dreams of Romans and the remaining 10 the dreams of foreigners.

207. These are to be found in Valerius Maximus, *Factorum ac dictorum* 1, 3–7, ext. 1–3, 8, 10.

208. See Valerius Maximus, *Factorum ac dictorum* 2, 8, ext. 4–7, 9.

209. Bloomer, *Valerius Maximus*, 230.

210. Bailey, *Valerius Maximus*, 3.

211. Bloomer sees such a tendency in his variation of simple and compound forms from the same stem (Bloomer, *Valerius Maximus*, 232) and his complicated word order (Bloomer, *Valerius Maximus*, 241).

212. Another example, this time from the first dream, is where an illness experienced by Augustus is described first as *graui morbo* and then later as *aduersam ualitudinem*.

inn," followed by *tabernamque, in qua is deuersabatur*, "the inn where his friend was lodging."

However, repetition may take other forms such as *inclusio* or key words. Four narratives appear to have *inclusio*.[213] We illustrate it from the thirteenth narrative with its *frustra discutere temptauit*, "he tried in vain to shake off (two dreams)," near the beginning and *frustratus est . . . inpedire conando*, "he frustrated himself in trying to impede," towards the end. Three have key words,[214] with *filius* and *pater* each appearing three times in the first of these narratives at ext.4.[215] There are also three examples of alliteration[216] and one of assonance.[217]

What Valerius does have in abundance are cases of antithesis, to be found in ten narratives, sometimes with several instances in each.[218] Indeed 1.7.ext.4 has as many as five examples: *maximo prius metu*, "first with extreme fear," contrasted with *deinde etiam dolore*, "then also with sorrow"; *solitus erat [iuuenis] ad bella gerenda mitti*, "the young man used to be sent on campaigns," contrasted with *domi retentus est*, "he was kept at home"; *ad bella gerenda mitti*, "to be sent on campaigns"; contrasted with *ad eum opprimendum mitteretur*, "that he be sent to destroy the animal"; *non dentis*, "not tusk," contrasted with *sed ferri saevitia*, "but cruelty of steel"; and *filius a patre extorsit*, "the son wrung from his father," contrasted with *cui tutela filii a patre mandata erat*, "to whom the father had entrusted his son's guardianship." Not all these examples are antithesis in the strict sense of the term. Some of them simply offer contrast, as with what happened "first" and "then" later. However, since we have not treated contrast as a category in its own right, we have included examples of it under the heading of antithesis.

Valerius also uses chiasmus in two of the narratives.[219] At 1.7, ext.6 we have *inimica Syracusarum libertati capitibusque insontium infesta.*, "hostile to the liberty of Syracuse and the lives of the innocent," hostility being expressed by the adjectives, *inimica* and *infesta*. In addition there is some parallelism in three narratives.[220] We use as an example 1.7.3: *consulibus sacrificio uel expiaturis, si posset auerti, uel, si certum deorum etiam monitu uisum*

---

213. See Valerius Maximus, *Factorum ac dictorum* 1.7, ext. 5, 6, 8, 10.

214. Valerius Maximus, *Factorum ac dictorum* 1.7, ext. 4, 6, 8.

215. A similar example of three is *caelum conscendit, caeli duce* and *caelesti custodia* in Valerius Maximus, *Factorum ac dictorum* 1.7 ext. 6.

216. Valerius Maximus, *Factorum ac dictorum* 1.7.1, 4, ext. 9.

217. Valerius Maximus, *Factorum ac dictorum* 1.7, ext. 7.

218. Valerius Maximus, *Factorum ac dictorum*, 1.7.2, 3, ext. 1–6, 8, 10.

219. Valerius Maximus, *Factorum ac dictorum*, 1.7, ext. 6, 10.

220. Valerius Maximus, *Factorum ac dictorum*, 1.7.3, ext. 1, 6.

*foret, exsecuturis*, "the Consuls made sacrifice, intending either to expiate the prophecy, if it were possible to avoid it, or to carry it out, if a warning from the gods too confirmed the vision." This is an example of syntactical parallelism, although the wording is arranged almost chiastically.

When we set the work of Valerius Maximus alongside the writing of Matthew, there is only a limited amount in common. Matthew has extensive repetition, whereas Valerius seems to go out of his way to avoid it. The most distinctive feature of Valerius is his use of antithesis which Matthew does not have in his dream narratives. They do share examples of *inclusio*, key words and parallelism. In short their usage could suggest that they come from rather different cultural backgrounds. Certainly they do have different approaches to style.

## Tacitus

We move on to Tacitus, a Roman historian, living from 56 or 57 CE till sometime after 117 CE.[221] In his writing about the Roman Empire he offers us five dream narratives, four in his *Annals*[222] and one in his *Histories*.[223] S. P. Oakley draws attention to the way Tacitus's style varies between historical works such as those mentioned and others such as *Dialogus*, how it varies even within historical works and how it developed throughout his writing career, becoming more taut, compressed and solemn in the later *Annals*.[224] Once more we do not find many patterns of memory. This is due at least in part to the brevity of these dream narratives. Tacitus does show an awareness of the sounds which words carry. In the dream at *Annals* 11.4 there seems to be a play on words beginning with 'sp': sp*ecies*, a vision, apparition, appearance in sleep; sp*icea*, consisting of ears of corn; and sp*ica*, an ear (of grain) or a point. It is therefore not surprising to find examples of alliteration[225] and assonance.[226] There is also some repetition,[227] but not significantly lengthy and certainly nothing on the scale of what we find in Matthew. Beyond the dream narratives, Oakley suggests that characteristics of Tacitus's pointed style include parallelism and balance as well as antithesis.[228] However,

---

221. OCCL 279.
222. Tacitus, *Annals* 1.65; 2.14; 11.4; 12.13.
223. Tacitus, *Histories* 4.83.
224. Oakley, "Style and Language," 195.
225. Tacitus, *Annals* 1.65, i.e., *visus est velut vocantem*.
226. Tacitus, *Annals* 1.65; 2.14, e.g., *ducem*que *terruit* dira *quies*.
227. Tacitus, *Annals* 1.65; 11.4; 12.13; *Histories* 4.83.
228. Oakley, "Style and Language," 199. Oakley gives an excellent example of the

limiting ourselves to the sample of dream narratives here examined we have once more a contrast with the First Gospel. Based on this sample alone, we may form the impression that Matthew and his sources belonged to a significantly different literary background from Tacitus.

## Summary of Historical Writers

If we treat all the historical writers together, what we observe is a general lack of the devices which we indicated at the beginning of this chapter we are looking for. Most of them engage in repetition of single words or short phrases; six out of the seven use antithesis; Valerius Maximus and Tacitus are the only ones who, when talking about dreams, use sound mnemonics such as alliteration or assonance; Herodotus, Dionysius and Valerius make a little use of *inclusio*; Herodotus has the greatest variety of memory patterns. He undoubtedly uses repetition and parallelism, but it is arguable that he does not use them to the same extent as Matthew. Ultimately Herodotus is the historical writer who bears closest resemblance to Matthew. This is interesting considering the time difference between them, but may be related to the fact that Herodotus is explicit about his use of oral sources. Other writers, if they used oral material, did not seem inclined to retain its memory patterns. As a group, the historical writers provide little evidence to suggest that Matthew is strongly subject to Hellenistic influence.

Table 5: Classical or Hellenistic Historians

|  | Matthew | Herodotus | Polybius | Dionysius | Diodorus |
|---|---|---|---|---|---|
| Dreams | 5 | 14 | 3 | 9 | 3 |
| Acrostic | 0 | 0 | 0 | 0 | 0 |
| Alliteration | 0 | 0 | 0 | 0 | 0 |
| Anaphora | 0 | 0 | 0 | 0 | 0 |
| Antithesis | 0 | 6 | 5 | 4 | 2 |
| Association | 0 | 0 | 0 | 0 | 0 |
| Assonance | 0 | 0 | 0 | 0 | 0 |
| Chiasmus | 2 | 0 | 0 | 0 | 0 |

---

combined effects of parallelism and antithesis in Tacitus, *Germania* 27.1 (Oakley, "Style and Language," 200–201).

|  | Matthew | Herodotus | Polybius | Dionysius | Diodorus |
|---|---|---|---|---|---|
| Formulaic Expressions | 3 | 1 | 0 | 0 | 0 |
| Inclusio | 2 | 3 | 0 | 1 | 0 |
| Key Word | 1 | 2 | 1 | Odd Words | 3 |
| Metre | 0 | 1 | 0 | 0 | 0 |
| Numerical Aids | 0 | 0 | 0 | 0 | 0 |
| Onomatopoeia | 0 | 0 | 0 | 0 | 0 |
| Order | 0 | 0 | 0 | 0 | 0 |
| Parallelism | 5 | 1 | 0 | 0 | 0 |
| Repeated Blocks | 4 | 2 | 0 | 0 | 0 |
| Typology | 2 | 0 | 0 | 0 | 0 |

|  | Matthew | Valerius Maximus | Tacitus | Appian |
|---|---|---|---|---|
| Dreams | 5 | 21 | 5 | 9 |
| Acrostic | 0 | 0 | 0 | 0 |
| Alliteration | 0 | 3 | 2 | 0 |
| Anaphora | 0 | 0 | 0 | 0 |
| Antithesis | 0 | 20 | 0 | 0 |
| Association | 0 | 0 | 0 | 0 |
| Assonance | 0 | 1 | 1 | 0 |
| Chiasmus | 2 | 2 | 0 | 0 |
| Formulaic Expressions | 3 | 0 | 0 | 0 |
| Inclusio | 2 | 4 | 0 | 0 |
| Key Word | 1 | 3 | 0 | 2 |
| Metre | 0 | 0 | 0 | 0 |
| Numerical Aids | 0 | 0 | 0 | 0 |
| Onomatopoeia | 0 | 0 | 0 | 0 |

|  | Matthew | Valerius Maximus | Tacitus | Appian |
|---|---|---|---|---|
| Order | 0 | 0 | 0 | 0 |
| Parallelism | 5 | 3 | 0 | 0 |
| Repeated Blocks | 4 | 1 | 0 | 0 |
| Typology | 2 | 0 | 0 | 0 |

## Biographical Writers

### Plutarch

We begin with Plutarch who lived from c. 46 CE till after 120 CE.[229] He was a Greek historian, biographer, and essayist, known primarily for his *Parallel Lives* and *Moralia*. We find twenty-one dreams in his *Lives*. Fourteen of these are symbolic,[230] five are message type[231] and two are referred to without any detail.[232] It is difficult to find trace of any devices in five of them.[233] Of these, three are narrated very briefly; in one the content is not given[234]; and in another we simply cannot find any devices.[235] Several do display antithesis, giving fourteen examples in total.[236] There was one case of alliteration.[237]

---

229. OCCL 238.

230. Plutarch, *Themistocles* 26.2-4; *Alexander* 2.2-3 [2]; 18.4; 24.3-5 [3]; *Caesar* 32.6; 68.2-3; *Cimon* 18.2-4; *Pericles* 3.2; *Alcibiades* 39.1-2; *Anthony* 16.3; *Eumenes* 6.4-7.

231. Plutarch, *Themistocles* 30.1-3; *Alexander* 26.3; *Aristides* 11.5; 19.2; *Pericles* 13.8.

232. Plutarch, *Caesar* 63.5-7; *Anthony* 22.2.

233. Plutarch, *Anthony* 16.3; 22.2; *Pericles* 3.2; *Aristides* 11.5; 19.2.

234. This is the dream of a friend of Caesar (Plutarch, *Anthony* 22.2). Plutarch simply tells us that Caesar claims in his memoirs that he withdrew before the battle in consequence of a friend's dream. With no content given, we can only assume it is supposed to have created foreboding.

235. The Dream of the Lydian in Plutarch, *Aristides* 19.2.

236. Plutarch, *Caesar* 63.5-7; 68.2-3; *Alexander* 2.2-3; 18.4; 26.3; *Cimon* 18.2-4; *Alcibiades* 39.1-2; *Eumenes* 6.4-7.

237. Ἀθηνᾶς ἀνέστησεν ἐν ἀκροπόλει found in Plutarch, *Pericles* 13.8.

Three dreams made use of meter[238] and interestingly one of these involves a quotation from Homer.[239] There are two possible examples of *inclusio*.[240]

One case of *inclusio* is a little uncertain. The narrative in the *Life of Cimon* narrative opens with ἐπ' Αἴγυπτον καὶ Κύπρον αὖθις ἐκστρατευσόμενος and closes with τῶν νεῶν ἑξήκοντα μὲν ἀπέστειλεν εἰς Αἴγυπτον. The double reference to Egypt suggests potential *inclusio*. Although repetition of a single word is adequate to establish *inclusio*, Egypt and Cyprus are grouped together in the opening phrase. The case for *inclusio* would, therefore, have been stronger had there also been a closing reference to Cyprus.[241] However, the text is corrupt at this point.[242]

There are several examples where single words are repeated,[243] but there is no extensive repetition. However, the repetition of single words does appear to be a feature of Plutarch's style.[244] There may be an example of parallelism in the *Life of Eumenes*.[245] We have: ἀγνοοῦντας ᾧ μαχοῦνται, "[his soldiers] not knowing with whom they were fighting," followed by ἀποκρύψαι τὸν ἀντιστράτηγον, "he should conceal from them the name of the opposing general." The two phrases are not structured in quite the same way. The first uses a participle where the second uses an infinitive. The meaning is roughly the same, although the second half is slightly more specific. Moreover, the two phrases are not consecutive, as the words προενσεῖσαι τῷ Κρατερῷ intervene.

The dream of Calpurnia is presented in two forms in the *Life of Caesar*,[246] but there is no overlap between them. Instead Plutarch seems to go out of his way to vary the vocabulary. The two versions both refer to *weeping* but they use different words in Greek—κλαίειν and δακρύειν. Calpurnia asked Caesar to postpone the meeting of the senate and later he did so, but again different expressions are used—ἀναβαλέσθαι τὴν σύγκλητον

---

238. Plutarch, *Themistocles* 26.2-4; *Cimon* 18.2-4; *Alexander* 26.3.

239. Plutarch, *Alexander* 26.3 quotes Homer, *Odyssey* iv.354f. νῆσος ἔπειτά τις ἔστι πολυκλύστῳ ἐνὶ πόντῳ, Αἰγύπτου προπάροιθε· Φάρον δέ ἑ κικλήσκουσιν. In this dream the visitant is none other than Homer himself.

240. Plutarch, *Cimon* 18.2-4; *Eumenes* 6.4-7.

241. Perrin suggests that *Cyprus* may originally have been in the text, for he translates, "with the rest he made again for Cyprus" (Perrin, *Plutarch's Lives*, 462).

242. πάλιν ... ἔπλει: Perrin suggests either πάλιν is a corruption (περὶ Παμφυλίαν) or words have fallen out.

243. Plutarch, *Alexander* 2.2-3; 24.3-5; *Caesar* 32.6; *Eumenes* 6.4-7; *Themistocles* 30.1-3.

244. Moles, *Plutarch*, 13-15.

245. Plutarch, *Eumenes* 6.4-7.

246. Plutarch, *Caesar* 63.5-7.

and ἀφεῖναι τὴν σύγκλητον. Earlier reference was made to both Caesar and Calpurnia sleeping and again we have two different words—κοιμώμενος and καθεύδουσαν. Even references to divination are kept different with διὰ μαντικῆς ἄλλης one time and οἱ μάντεις the next.

There is a message dream in the *Life of Themistocles*[247] where obedience is expressed, but the repetition is minimal. The initial appearance of the goddess is described thus: τὴν μητέρα τῶν θεῶν ὄναρ φανεῖσαν. Later we are told of Themistocles's wonder at her appearance: θαυμάσας τὴν ἐπιφάνειαν τῆς θεοῦ. So ἐπιφάνειαν echoes φανεῖσαν. She made her request thus: σε αἰτῶ θεράπαιναν Μνησιπτολέμαν. Then the obedience is expressed: τὴν θυγατέρα Μνησιπτολέμαν ἱέρειαν ἀπέδειξεν. However, the only repetition we have there is the name *Mnesiptolema*. Even her role is changed from *handmaid* to *priestess*. What we do get in this dream is some word play. An ambush was being prepared to slay Themistocles in the village called Lion's Head, Λεοντοκεφάλῳ. The goddess tells him to shun *a head of lions*, ὑστέρει κεφαλῆς λεόντων. Then she gives the reason—that he should not encounter a *lion*, ἵνα μὴ λέοντι περιπέσῃς. There may be a further sound play on the word as we are told that Themistocles forsook the way, τὴν μὲν λεωφόρον ἀφῆκεν.

To sum up the position with Plutarch, his writing is significantly different from that of Matthew. He does not display abundant use of the kind of devices for which we have been searching. Thomas Schmitz comments that Plutarch displays a more rhetorically embellished style in the few declamatory pieces which he wrote than in most of his other work.[248] He points out that the difference in style between the *Lives* and the declamations may be due to the fact that they are a different genre.[249] Often the lack of devices in the *Lives* is due to his dream narratives being extremely brief. Plutarch uses antithesis, meter and alliteration which we do not find in Matthew. In the examples examined he makes very limited use of *inclusio*, although J. L. Moles comments that ring composition is "a device used very extensively by Plutarch."[250] There is limited use of parallelism and extensive repetition which are apparent in the First Gospel. Matthew has a different style from

---

247. Plutarch, *Themistocles* 30.1–3.
248. Schmitz, "Plutarch and the Second Sophistic," 32–42, esp. 32.
249. Schmitz, "Plutarch and the Second Sophistic," 33.
250. Moles, *Plutarch*, 13. Although Moles makes his comment in a work concerned with "the Life of Cicero" in which there are no dream narratives, he is speaking generally of Plutarch's style. He receives support from Verdegen, who points to Plutarch's use of repeated words and images to mark the structure of the narrative (Verdegen, *Plutarch's Life of Alcibiades*, 414).

Plutarch with decidedly more emphasis on memory aids. Whether there are cultural factors at work is less clear.

## Suetonius

Next we take Suetonius who was born c. 70 CE. He became a well known author by the 90s and is not heard of after 122 CE.[251] He was a Roman historian whose most important surviving work is a set of biographies of twelve successive Roman rulers, from Julius Caesar to Domitian, entitled *De Vita Caesarum*. There we find twenty-five dreams. Sixteen of these are symbolic,[252] five are message type[253] and four are referred to without any detail.[254] However, in these narratives there is dearth of devices which fit our criteria, with none at all in ten of them.[255]

We take as an example one of Suetonius's narratives where there are at least some points of interest, that of Domitian at 23.2. The introduction to the dream is of note, as Suetonius relates events leading up to the slaying of Domitian. He tells of how a raven on the Capitol uttered the words: ἔσται πάντα καλῶς "All will be well." The words are memorable because they are Greek within a Latin text. There then follows an interpretation of the event. It is notable because it is given in verse: "*Nuper Tarpeio, quae sedit culmine cornix. "Est bene," non potuit dicere; dixit, "Erit."*" "Late croaked a raven from Tarpeia's height, "All is not yet, but shortly will be, right.""" Meter is a form of memory pattern. As to the dream itself, Domitian saw that *gibbam sibi pone ceruicem auream enatam*, "a golden hump grew out of the back of his neck." Domitian himself interpreted this symbolic dream as a certain sign of happy days for the empire after him. Suetonius himself comments that such an auspicious change took place shortly afterwards through the moderation of succeeding emperors. There is no repetition from the dream in either Domitian's interpretation or in Suetonius's comment.

The results which emerge from examination of all the dreams are these. There are six examples of single word repetition[256] and one of a two-word

---

251. OCCL 277.

252. Suetonius, *Julius* 7.2; 81.3 [3]; *Augustus* 94.4 [2], 5, 8 [2], 9; *Caligula* 57.3; *Nero* 46.1; *Vespasianus* 5.5; 25; *Domitianus* 15.3; 23.2.

253. Suetonius, *Augustus* 91.2; *Tiberius* 74; *Galba* 4.3; 18.2; *Vespasianus* 7.2.

254. Suetonius, *Augustus* 91.1; *Nero* 7.1; *Galba* 9.2; *Otho* 7.2.

255. Suetonius, *Nero* 7.1; 46.1; *Galba* 4.3; 9.2; 18.2; *Julius* 7.2; *Augustus* 94.5, 9; *Domitianus* 15.3; *Tiberius* 74.

256. Suetonius, *Augustus* 91.1, 2; 94.4; *Vespasianus* 5.5.

phrase repeated.[257] There is a hint of alliteration[258] and one of assonance,[259] but as each only involved two words they are dubious. We find four examples of antithesis[260] and a single instance of chiasmus.[261] We have the use of meter in the case cited above and the quotation of Greek in a Latin text which occurs also in one other dream.[262] We saw in the Matthew chapter that quotations from a foreign language can sometimes be memorable, although they are not standard memory patterns. For them to become stored in memory they require to be fairly short, expressed in a language to which listeners and readers have access or be accompanied by a translation. It is a relatively rare feature, appearing only here and in Matthew's text. All in all, Suetonius lacks rhetorical devices. This may be explained by the brief way in which he narrates his dreams, treating them like the other omens and auspices which surrounded the superstitious lives of the emperors. It may also be explained by Suetonius's general style. Catherine Edwards tells us that some scholars see Suetonius as having no style: he simply shifts between styles under the influence of whatever source he is using.[263] She also tells us that some ancient writers admired his style. The collection of biographies of later emperors describes Suetonius's characteristic as being "to love brevity."[264] Either way Suetonius stands in marked contrast to the dream narratives of Matthew where the memory patterns are relatively plentiful. With Suetonius displaying few rhetorical devices, it is again difficult to say much on the cultural issue.

## Philostratus the Athenian

In coming to the work of Philostratus the Athenian, we are reaching the limits of our comparisons, for he lived between c. 170 CE and c. 250 CE.[265] When he settled in Rome, he was referred to as *Atheniensis* because, although he was born in Lemnos, he had studied and taught in Athens.[266] We

---

257. Suetonius, *Augustus* 94.8.
258. Suetonius, *Augustus* 91.1.
259. Suetonius, *Augustus* 94.8.
260. Suetonius, *Augustus* 91.1; *Caligula* 57.3; *Vespasianus* 7.2.
261. Suetonius, *Julius* 81.3.
262. Suetonius, *Otho* 7.2.
263. Edwards, *Lives of the Caesars*, xxv.
264. Firmus, Saturninus, Proculus, and Bonosus 1.1–2.
265. We are concerned not to move too far beyond the NT era.
266. CGS 183.

are concerned here with his work *Vita Apollonii*.[267] There are nine dreams recorded here[268] and they are generally narrated at reasonable length. Two exceptions are those which make only reference to dreams and in so doing show no evidence of memory patterns.[269] There are examples of antithesis in four of the dreams, amounting to nine cases in total.[270] Repetition of single words occurs in six dream narratives[271] and one dream has repetition of two phrases.[272] We are hard pressed to find other rhetorical devices in the work of Philostratus. We may have an example of *inclusio*,[273] although it is open to question. The brief narrative opens with the king sacrificing in the company of the Magi, ἔτυχε μὲν θύων παρόντων αὐτῷ τῶν μάγων, and closes with the king inviting a visitor to join him in sacrifice, κάλει . . . καὶ γὰρ ἂν καὶ ἀπὸ τοῦ καλλίστου ἄρξαιτο ξυνθύσας. The common link is sacrifice. However, it is only one word and, more significantly, the second usage is a compound verb. Although the opening has the company of the Magi and the close the company of the visitor, they are expressed in different terms. So it may not be *inclusio* after all. Furthermore, there does not appear to be extensive use of repetition. Apollonius experienced a symbolic dream in which fish were cast out of the sea onto the land.[274] He conjectured an interpretation himself. Later he met Damis who offered another interpretation. There is only a little repetition from the dream into each of the interpretations. The dream revealed the fish as ἰχθῦς ἐκπεπτωκότες τῆς θαλάττης, "fishes cast up from the sea," and ἐκβεβηκέναι τοῦ ἤθους, "they had gone out of their customary place." Damis speaks of ἡμεῖς ὥσπερ ἰχθύες ἐκπεσόντες τῶν ἠθῶν, "us like fishes thrown out of our haunts." Both have the plural of ἰχθύς.[275] At the first mention of the fish in the dream the verb ἐκπίπτω is used in the perfect participle; the second time it is the verb ἐκβαίνω as perfect infinitive. When Damis uses a verb for the fish, he chooses ἐκπίπτω, but uses the aorist participle. The dream uses ἦθος in the singular and Damis in the plural. Then we note how the dream narrative states that the fish were just like human beings: ὥσπερ τῶν ἀνθρώπων οἱ

---

267. This relates the life of Apollonius of Tyana who was a Pythagorean philosopher and teacher.

268. Philostratus, *Vita Apollonii* 1.5, 9, 10, 23, 29; 4.11, 34; 8.7.5, 12.

269. Philostratus, *Vita Apollonii* 4.11; 8.7.5.

270. Philostratus, *Vita Apollonii* 1.9, 10, 23; 8.12.

271. Philostratus, *Vita Apollonii* 1.5, 9, 10, 23, 29; 4.34.

272. Philostratus, *Vita Apollonii* 4.34.

273. Philostratus, *Vita Apollonii* 1.29.

274. Philostratus, *Vita Apollonii* 1.23.

275. Of minor significance is the fact that Philostratus's narration of the dream has a contracted plural, whereas in Damis's speech it is the slightly extended plural.

ἐν τῇ ξένῃ κλαίοντες, "weeping in a foreign land." Damis suggests that we may πολλὰ ἐλεεινὰ ἐν τῇ ἀλλοδαπῇ εἴπωμεν, "utter many pitiable things in a foreign land." The wording is substantially different with ξένη being replaced by ἀλλοδαπή. However, ἐλεεινὰ on Damis's lips does pick up ἐλεεινοὶ used in the dream to describe the state of the fish. Apollonius's own interpretation moves further away from the wording of the dream. He simply refers to the Eretrians treated at their capture like the fishes (ἰχθύων) seen in the dream. We conclude that there is repetition in this narrative, but it is not of the precise or lengthy variety.

When all this is related to the First Gospel, there is not a great deal in common. Matthew does not use antithesis, whereas there are nine examples in the writing of Philostratus. Matthew uses reasonably lengthy repetition, whereas Philostratus does not. Certainly Philostratus repeats several single words and two short phrases and some of this does compare to Matthew's repetition of the verb παραλαμβάνω. For the most part Philostratus and Matthew display different usage. Although it must be taken into account, this one comparison is not enough to establish cultural difference.

## Summary of Biographers

When we deal with all the biographical writers together, we observe a general lack of memory patterns. This is perhaps surprising, given that the tradition of Greek biography begins with *Evagoras*, an encomium by Isocrates, for he did favor polished and dignified rhetorical prose.[276] All three writers examined here engage in the repetition of single words or short phrases; they all use antithesis; two of them display alliteration or assonance and use of meter; Plutarch has only two examples of *inclusio* and a possible case in Philostratus is likely not one; we have a possible case of parallelism in Plutarch; none of these writers engage in extensive repetition. The general impression we are left with is one of dissimilarity in relation to Matthew. However, the cultural issue cannot be settled by examining biographical writers alone. It can only be done when we consider all the Hellenistic writers together.

---

276. See Fox and Livingstone, "Rhetoric and Historiography," 552–53.

Table 6: Classical or Hellenistic Biographers

|  | Matthew | Plutarch | Suetonius | Philostratus |
|---|---|---|---|---|
| Dreams | 5 | 21 | 25 | 9 |
| Acrostic | 0 | 0 | 0 | 0 |
| Alliteration | 0 | 1 | 1 | 0 |
| Anaphora | 0 | 0 | 0 | 0 |
| Antithesis | 0 | 14 | 4 | 9 |
| Association | 0 | 0 | 0 | 0 |
| Assonance | 0 | 0 | 1 | 0 |
| Chiasmus | 2 | 0 | 1 | 0 |
| Formulaic Expressions | 3 | 0 | 0 | 0 |
| Inclusio | 2 | 2 | 0 | 1 |
| Key Word | 1 | 5 | 8 | 6 |
| Metre | 0 | 3 | 1 | 0 |
| Numerical Aids | 0 | 0 | 0 | 0 |
| Onomatopoeia | 0 | 0 | 0 | 0 |
| Order | 0 | 0 | 0 | 0 |
| Parallelism | 5 | 1 | 0 | 0 |
| Repeated Blocks | 4 | 0 | 0 | 0 |
| Typology | 2 | 0 | 0 | 0 |

# Fiction

We now turn our attention to dreams in Greco-Roman novels. We have reason to anticipate the use of rhetorical devices in the novels. Ruth Webb points out that the burgeoning of the Greek novel coincided with the period of the Second Sophistic which had a strong interest in rhetorical theory, practice and performance.[277] This manifests itself in various ways, but particularly in the language used—the classicizing Attic dialect favored by the Sophists—and in a careful style.[278] We shall examine the dream

277. Webb, "Rhetoric and the Novel," 527.
278. See Webb, "Rhetoric and the Novel," 528. She notes this feature in "the big

narratives of two novelists, Chariton and Longus, the former being less 'sophistic' than the latter.

## Chariton

We begin with Chariton's *Chaereas and Callirhoe*. This is a prose romance, written no later than the second century CE.[279] Here we find nine dreams.[280] We take as an example a dream experienced by Callirhoe. There are several which she undergoes, but we look at the one described in 5.5.5–7, because it is a symbolic dream with an interpretation and as such it offers greater potential for the use of devices and particularly repetition. The dream re-enacts the wedding day of Chaereas and Callirhoe, already past. Afterwards an interpretation was sought from Plangon, Callirhoe's maidservant, who provided a positive, although general, explanation. Although the dream concerned a past event, the meaning of it was prospective, foreshadowing the reunion of Callirhoe and Chaereas. Although this dream scenario is similar to some of those of symbolic dreams in Genesis, it is narrated differently. The dream is not repeated when Callirhoe relates it to Plangon. We simply have τὸ ὄναρ διηγεῖτο, "she related the dream." Even the interpretation itself does not repeat any of the phraseology from the dream. Of the dream we are told: ὄναρ ἔβλεπεν αὐτὴν ἐν Συρακούσαις παρθένον εἰς τὸ τῆς Ἀφροδίτης τέμενος εἰσιοῦσαν . . . καὶ προπεμπομένην αὐτὴν ὑπὸ πατρὸς καὶ μητρὸς εἰς τὴν οἰκίαν τοῦ νυμφίου, "she saw a dream: herself in Syracuse entering Aphrodite's shrine, still a maiden; . . . and herself being escorted by her father and mother to the bridegroom's house." There is a minimal amount of repetition in the instructions which Plangon gave Callirhoe: Ἄπιθι εἰς τὸ βασιλέως δικαστήριον ὡς ἱερὸν Ἀφροδίτης . . . ἀναλάμβανε τὸ κάλλος τὸ νυμφικόν, "go to the king's courthouse as to Aphrodite's temple . . . take up the nuptial beauty." Even the word for temple is different—in the dream it was τέμενος, whereas in the instructions it is ἱερόν. However, τὴν οἰκίαν τοῦ νυμφίου, "the bridegroom's house" is echoed by τὸ κάλλος τὸ νυμφικόν, "the nuptial beauty." There is also syntactical parallelism in the

---

three"—Achilles Tatius, Longus, and Heliodorus.

279. OCD 227.

280. Chariton, *Chaereas and Callirhoe* 1.12.5, 10 (Dreams of Theron and Leonas); 2.1.2 (Dream of Dionysius); 2.3.5 (Dream of Callirhoe); 2.9.1–6 (Dream of Callirhoe); 3.7.4; 4.1.1–3 (Two dreams of Callirhoe); 5.5.5–7 (Dream of Callirhoe); 6.2.2 (Dream of the Babylonian king).

phrase ὥσπερ γὰρ ὄναρ ἔδοξας, οὕτω καὶ ὕπαρ, "just as it seemed to you in the dream, in the same way it will happen while you are awake."

In Chariton's dream narratives there are very few rhetorical devices resembling what we have found elsewhere. This is not entirely surprising, as Webb tells us that Chariton's novel is "generally regarded as less 'sophistic.'"[281] This view is supported by Stefan Tilg, who, in trying to establish a date for Chariton, points to there being few, if any, examples of Atticism.[282] Out of nine dreams there are four where there are no devices at all.[283] Where a symbolic dream is being interpreted, there is a distinct lack of repetition.[284] There are two dreams where a single word is repeated.[285] There are three dreams where we have antithesis, four examples altogether.[286] There is one case of assonance[287] and one of parallelism.[288] Matthew lacks antithesis and assonance, but he does have parallelism in abundance. By and large Chariton differs from Matthew. Here we have two authors with different styles and potentially different cultural leanings.

## Longus

We turn now to Longus's *Daphnis and Chloe*, also a romance, written in the late second or early third century CE.[289] In it we find six dreams.[290] Unlike the work of Chariton, there are here many examples of the rhetorical devices for which we are searching. This is noteworthy because Longus is not dependent on oral sources, as we would claim for Matthew. However,

---

281. Webb, "Rhetoric and the Novel," 529–30.

282. Tilg, *Chariton of Aphrodisias*, 37. He draws upon the work of Papanikolaou, *Chariton-Studien*, who argues for a complete lack of Atticism in Chariton and upon Lara, *Estudios sombre el aticismo*, who suggests 9.5 percent of his vocabulary is genuinely Atticist.

283. Chariton, *Chaereas and Callirhoe* 1.12.5, 10; 4.1.1–3; 6.2.2.

284. Apart from the example just given, the same is true of the dream of Dionysius (Chariton, *Chaereas and Callirhoe* 2.1.2).

285. Chariton, *Chaereas and Callirhoe* 2.1.2; 3.7.4.

286. Chariton, *Chaereas and Callirhoe* 2.3.5; 2.9.1–6; 3.7.4.

287. Chariton, *Chaereas and Callirhoe* 2.9.1–6.

288. Chariton, *Chaereas and Callirhoe* 5.5.5–7.

289. OCCL 91.

290. Longus, *Daphnis and Chloe* 1.7.1–1.8.2 (the dream of Dryas and Lamon); 2.10.1 (the dreams of Daphnis and Chloe); 2.23.1–2.24.1 (the dream of Daphnis); 2.26.5–2.28.1 (the dream of the Methymnean general, Bryaxis); 3.27.1–3.28.1 (the dream of Daphnis); 4.34.1–3 (the dream of Dionysophanes).

it is to be explained by Longus's status as a 'sophistic' writer.²⁹¹ There are three dreams which display antithesis with ten examples altogether,²⁹² and also one case of each of assonance²⁹³ and *inclusio*.²⁹⁴ There is repetition of single words in four of the dreams.²⁹⁵ The dream of Daphnis²⁹⁶ is interesting because it has two examples of an imperative being used and then almost immediately the same verb in an aorist participle.²⁹⁷ There are four dreams where obedience to a command is expressed,²⁹⁸ but, as we have found with other writers, Longus does not go out of his way to have the wording of the obedience match that of the command. The command was κελεῦσαι λοιπὸν ποιμαίνειν τὸν μὲν τὸ αἰπόλιον, τὴν δὲ τὸ ποίμνιον, "for the future he commanded that Daphnis look after the herd of goats, and Chloe to look after the flock of sheep"; whereas the obedience is expressed in these words: ὡς ποιμένας ἐκπέμπουσιν αὐτοὺς ἅμα ταῖς ἀγέλαις, "they sent the children out as shepherds with the flocks."²⁹⁹ The command has the verb ποιμαίνειν, "to be shepherd, to tend a flock," and the related noun ποίμνιον, "flock." The obedience has another related noun ποιμένας, "shepherds, herdsmen." However, this cannot really be counted as repetition. The same happens in two other dreams as well.³⁰⁰ That leaves one dream where the obedience does reflect the wording of the command.³⁰¹ However, even in that case details which are not present in the command are added to the obedience. The command is given in these terms: κελεῦσαι τῷ Διονυσοφάνει πάντας τοὺς ἀρίστους Μυτιληναίων θέμενον συμπότας, ἡνίκα ἂν τὸν ὕστατον πλήσῃ κρατῆρα, τότε δεικνύειν ἑκάστῳ τὰ γνωρίσματα, τὸ δὲ ἐντεῦθεν ᾄδειν τὸν ὑμέναιον, "Eros then told Dionysophanes to ask all the best of the Mytileneans to come to a feast, and when he had filled the last mixing bowl, to show each person the tokens [of Chloe's identity]—and then sing the wedding song." The obedience is expressed like this: κελεύσας λαμπρὰν ἑστίασιν παρασκευασθῆναι . . . πάντας τοὺς ἀρίστους Μυτιληναίων ποιεῖται συμπότας. Ὡς δὲ . . . ἐπέπληστο

---

291. Webb, "Rhetoric and the Novel," 527, tells us that his novel is frequently described as 'sophistic' and in footnote 3 she cites as an example Anderson, *Second Sophistic*, 158.

292. Longus, *Daphnis and Chloe* 1.7.1–1.8.2; 2.23.1–2.24.1; 3.27.1–3.28.1.

293. Longus, *Daphnis and Chloe* 2.23.1–2.24.1.

294. Longus, *Daphnis and Chloe* 2.23.1–2.24.1.

295. Longus, *Daphnis and Chloe* 1.7.1–1.8.2; 2.10.1; 2.23.1–2.24.1; 3.27.1–3.28.1.

296. Longus, *Daphnis and Chloe* 3.27.1–3.28.1.

297. σὺ πρόσελθε καὶ προσελθὼν ἀνελοῦ καὶ ἀνελόμενος δός.

298. Longus, *Daphnis and Chloe* 1.7.1–1.8.2; 2.26.5–2.28.1; 3.27.1–3.28.1; 4.34.1–3.

299. Longus, *Daphnis and Chloe* 1.7.1–1.8.2.

300. Longus, *Daphnis and Chloe* 2.26.5–2.28.1; 3.27.1–3.28.1.

301. Longus, *Daphnis and Chloe* 4.34.1–3.

ὁ κρατὴρ ... εἰσκομίζει τις ἐπὶ σκεύους ἀργυροῦ θεράπων τὰ γνωρίσματα καὶ περιφέρων ἐνδέξια πᾶσιν ἐδείκνυε, "he gave orders for the preparation of a glittering feast ... and invited as his guests all the best of the Mytileneans. When ... the mixing bowl had been filled ... a servant brought in the tokens on a silver tray and carried them round from left to right, showing them to everyone." The obedience is fuller in words than the command with the result that some phrases have been omitted from the quotation given here. However, what is evident is that there is some repetition such as πάντας τοὺς ἀρίστους Μυτιληναίων, συμπότας, τὸν ... πλήσῃ κρατῆρα/ ἐπέπληστο ὁ κρατὴρ, δεικνύειν ἑκάστῳ τὰ γνωρίσματα/ εἰσκομίζει τις ... θεράπων τὰ γνωρίσματα καὶ ... πᾶσιν ἐδείκνυε. Clearly the wording of the obedience repeats the command, but with added detail. We compare this to Matthew's handling of repetition in command and obedience, which generally tends towards greater precision, except for 1:24–25 where he gives us the added detail: καὶ οὐκ ἐγίνωσκεν αὐτὴν ἕως οὗ ἔτεκεν υἱόν.

There are also three different dreams where we find examples of parallelism with eight cases in total.[302] In each case it is syntactical parallelism which is displayed. We take as an example the dream of the Methymnean general, Bryaxis.[303] We find parallelism where Pan rebukes Bryaxis. We have Πολέμου μὲν τὴν ἀγροικίαν ἐνεπλήσατε τὴν ἐμοὶ φίλην, "you have filled the countryside I love with war," followed by ἀγέλας δὲ βοῶν καὶ αἰγῶν καὶ ποιμνίων ἀπηλάσατε τὰς ἐμοὶ μελομένας, "you have driven off herds of cows, goats, and sheep about which I care."[304] The last three words in each section are particularly striking. There is also parallelism with Οὔτ᾽ οὖν Μήθυμναν ὄψεσθε μετὰ τοιούτων λαφύρων πλέοντες, "you will never see Methymna, sailing on with these spoils," followed by οὔτε τήνδε φεύξεσθε τὴν σύριγγα τὴν ὑμᾶς ταράξασαν, "nor will you escape this piping which has troubled you."[305] It should be noted that the participles are different, the first being nominative plural masculine and the second accusative singular feminine. Again we have it in ['Ηγήσομαι δὲ ἐγὼ] καὶ σοὶ τοῦ πλοῦ κἀκείνη τῆς ὁδοῦ.[306]

From the examples given it would appear that Longus makes extensive use of rhetorical devices. Ronald McCail describes the writing of Longus as belonging to the 'sweet' style, one of whose characteristics Hermogenes tells us is figures of speech.[307] Paul Turner describes it as *Euphuistic* style

---

302. Longus, *Daphnis and Chloe* 2.10.1; 2.26.5–2.28.1; 4.34.1–3.
303. Longus, *Daphnis and Chloe* 2.26.5–2.28.1.
304. Longus, *Daphnis and Chloe* 2.27.1.
305. Longus, *Daphnis and Chloe* 2.27.2.
306. Longus, *Daphnis and Chloe* 2.27.3.
307. McCail, *Longus*, xx–xxi. See Hermogenes, *Opera*, 344.

which shows a liking for neatly balanced phrases and striking antitheses.[308] The two οὔτε clauses, cited in the last paragraph, are a good example of the balanced phrases, with 19 and 18 syllables respectively. This is known technically as *parisosis*. McCail comments that parisosis is used in the Preface, but when the narrative begins in book 1, a more sober style predominates, with a return to the balanced style in passages of high emotion.[309] In other words, it is a varied style, something with which Turner would agree.[310]

Dealing solely with the dream narratives and not the novel as a whole, we conclude that Longus differs from Matthew in two respects. Most significantly, Longus makes extensive use of antithesis whereas Matthew does not. Longus also appears to be less interested in repetition than Matthew. Of four dreams which involve command and obedience, Longus uses repetition in only one, where Matthew has it in all three of his. On the other hand, they do share the common feature of parallelism. Indeed of all the authors examined Longus is the one who makes most use of it apart from Matthew.

We have noted the tendency that Longus has to use rhetorical devices. Such usage is something he has in common with OT and Herodotus as well as Matthew. There is something of a paradox here given that Longus is a 'sophistic' writer and the others apparently use oral sources. It may be that Longus is deliberately mimicking the oral approach and using devices for stylistic purposes which originally belonged to oral transmission. What are the implications for Matthew? It is possible to argue that he is also pursuing a stylistic goal in his use of devices, but we are limited in what we know about the extent of his rhetorical education. However, in the Orality chapter we examined the case for believing that Matthew may be using sources orally transmitted and since we could not prove it, we considered it appropriate to describe Matthew's work as an "oral-derived text." It may be that their approach is not significantly different.

## Summary of Fictional Writers

If we compare the work of the two fictional writers considered here, they stand in marked contrast, for Longus displays the rhetorical devices of the kind for which we have been searching far more than Chariton. This is not surprising when we recall that of the two Longus is traditionally considered the more "sophistic." As we go on to consider them both beside the historical and biographical writers, Longus again stands out because he makes considerable use

308. Turner, *Daphne & Chloe*, 8.
309. McCail, *Longus*, xxi.
310. Turner, *Penguin Classics Introduction*, 8.

of these features where to a large extent they are missing in the work of the others. As we have seen, this is something which he shares in common with Matthew, albeit he is not using oral sources. Consequently, he provides us with some scope for comparison in our search for Matthew's cultural leaning.

Table 7: Hellenistic Fiction Writers

|  | Matthew | Chariton | Longus |
|---|---|---|---|
| Dreams | 5 | 9 | 6 |
| Acrostic | 0 | 0 | 0 |
| Alliteration | 0 | 0 | 0 |
| Anaphora | 0 | 0 | 0 |
| Antithesis | 0 | 4 | 10 |
| Association | 0 | 0 | 0 |
| Assonance | 0 | 1 | 1 |
| Chiasmus | 2 | 0 | 1 |
| Formulaic Expressions | 3 | 0 | 0 |
| Inclusio | 2 | 0 | 1 |
| Key Word | 1 | 2 | 4 |
| Metre | 0 | 0 | 0 |
| Numerical Aids | 0 | 0 | 0 |
| Onomatopoeia | 0 | 0 | 0 |
| Order | 0 | 0 | 0 |
| Parallelism | 5 | 1 | 8 |
| Repeated Blocks | 4 | 0 | 1 |
| Typology | 2 | 0 | 0 |

# Artemidorus

Finally, we consider dreams recorded by Artemidorus Daldianus. His work, known as *Oneirocritica*, is the first extant Greek work on the subject of dreams.[311] Artemidorus lived in the second century CE. As this was the peak

---

311. The edition of the Greek text used here was Pack, *Artemidori Daldiani*

of the Second Sophistic,[312] we may expect a display of rhetorical devices. Although there are examples of dreams throughout the five volumes, the final book is a collection of ninety-five dreams which Artemidorus intended his son to use as practice material.[313] He tells us in the introduction to that volume that his aim was to gather dreams which have come true and that he collected as many dreams as he could "at festal assemblies throughout Greece and Asia as well as Italy."[314] Although he does not actually tell us that he interviewed the dreamers at these gatherings, it is not unreasonable to assume that at least some of the dreams which he narrates stem from them. But we also know from the introduction to the first volume of *Oneirocritica* that Artemidorus had made the effort to obtain every book written on the interpretation of dreams and throughout his work he mentions other dream writers.[315] Clearly he may have received some dream accounts from these writers. However, no matter what the sources are for the dreams of Artemidorus, they display his editorial hand, for he says in the introduction to book 5 that what he has recorded are the bare essentials of each dream.[316] This means that although some memory patterns may derive from his source and consequently belong to the process of oral transmission, he may be responsible for some devices himself. We cannot differentiate the two, but both types may still display cultural background.

Artemidorus shows a clear preference for using a specific formula to introduce dreams. Eighty-seven in the final volume begin with the phrase Ἔδοξέ τις, "someone dreamt." Of the eight which do not, the word ἔδοξε appears later in the narrative.[317] It seems likely that this is Artemidorus's own expression, for it is phrased in the third person and even if we allow

---

*Onirocriticon.*

312. White draws attention to this, not to suggest heavy usage of rhetorical devices, but to point to the rhetorical movement's attempts to preserve its ties with philosophy (White, *Interpretation of Dreams*, 4).

313. The first three books were dedicated to Cassius Maximus, believed to be a sophist. However, they seem to be intended for a general readership and give an encyclopedic treatment of dreams. The remaining two were written for the private use of Artemidorus's own son, who was a novice dream interpreter. Book four is particularly concerned with the technique of dream interpretation.

314. Artemidorus, *Oneirocritica* 5.

315. Antiphon of Athens (Artemidorus, *Oneirocritica* 2.14); Aristander of Telmessus in Lycia (1.31; 4.23); Demetrius of Phalerum (2.44); Antipater (4.65); Alexander of Myndus (1.67; 2.9, 66); Phoebus of Antioch (1.2; 2.9; 4.48, 66); Artemon of Miletus (1.2); Panyasis of Halicarnassus (1.2, 64; 2.34); Nicostratus of Ephesus (1.2); Apollonius of Attalia (1.32; 3.28); Apollodorus of Telmessus (1.79); and Geminus of Tyre (2.44).

316. Artemidorus, *Oneirocritica* 5.

317. Artemidorus, *Oneirocritica* 5.9, 48, 55, 72, 78, 79, 92, 94.

for the original speaker using the first person, it is difficult to imagine that they all said the same thing. However, Artemidorus does show variation. In the third dream, although he begins with Ἔδοξέ τις, he later has εἶτα ἐδόκει αὐτῷ and λέγειν ᾤετο, "he dreamt that he said."[318]

Of the ninety-five dreams in book 5, I have selected forty-six to be examined for memory patterns.[319] Most of them have been chosen on the basis of length, since longer narratives have a greater chance of displaying memory patterns or rhetorical devices than shorter ones. In fact the actual dreams are as briefly narrated as they are in Matthew's text, but we consider them along with the interpretations or the narration of subsequent events, just as we also consider the surrounding material in Matthew.

There was plenty of single-word repetition in Artemidorus's work. Often it was the same word used twice, once in the dream and then in the interpretation. We find this with ἀετός, "eagle," and σπλάγχνα, "intestines."[320] However, in the same narrative we have παῖς used five times along with ἄπαις once. Since the subject matter of this narrative is the dream of a childless man who goes on to have a child who becomes illustrious, we may reasonably treat this as a key word. Sometimes there is repetition of a word root, but there is variation of the actual word. We find this with περὶ τῆς ἐγκρίσεως, "about the preliminary examination"; τὸν Ἀσκληπιὸν κριτήν, "Asclepius the judge"; and ὑπὸ τοῦ θεοῦ ἐκκεκρίσθαι, "to have been eliminated by the god."[321] These should not have key word status. However, there are three other cases where we may be reasonably confident that we have a key word. There is ἑπτά, "seven," used of days and letters at 5.26, and of months (twice) and days at 5.30, while βουλόμενος, "willing," is used three times at 5.29, two of these in the negative.

There are seven examples where the repetition extends beyond a single word.[322] It is important to look at this because of the important role which repetition plays in Matthew's text. At *Oneirocritica* 5.51 there is exact repetition involving four words: τὸ βάκτρον αὐτοῦ κατεάχθαι. The narrative where these words occur is significant, because it contains two dreams. In the first the dreamer heard someone say that *his staff was broken*. In the second the dreamer dreamt that *his staff was broken*. In the first the phrase quoted above is preceded by ἀκούειν τινός, whereas the second has nothing beyond ἔδοξε.

---

318. Artemidorus, *Oneirocritica* 5.3.

319. Artemidorus, *Oneirocritica* 5.2, 3, 5, 9, 12, 13, 20, 23, 24, 26–31, 33, 35, 37, 39, 42, 43, 47–49, 51, 56–58, 63–65, 67, 69–71, 74, 75, 78, 79, 82, 84–87, 92, 94.

320. Artemidorus, *Oneirocritica* 5.57.

321. Artemidorus, *Oneirocritica* 5.13.

322. Artemidorus, *Oneirocritica* 5.2, 9, 27, 51, 78, 79, 92.

At 5.92 the repetition extends to five words, but the word order is different: τὴν δεξιὰν αὐτῷ χεῖρα . . . ἐπισεῖσαι and τὴν χεῖρα . . . τὴν δεξιὰν ἐπισείειν αὐτῷ.[323] The opening six words of the narrative at 5.78 are the same as the opening words at 5.79 with slight variation in word order, the repetition no doubt being due to the fact that they share the common theme of a runner about to take part in a competition.[324] So Artemidorus and Matthew share repetition in common, but none of the examples we have just looked at display the same length of repetition as we find in the First Gospel.

Artemidorus makes extensive use of antithesis. There are twenty-four examples spread across thirteen dream narratives.[325] There are three examples at 5.39. We have a contrast drawn between two daughters with ἡ μὲν προτέρα and ἡ δὲ ἑτέρα used twice and Ἀφροδίτη and ἄμπελος, "vine," used once. The dream 5.85 also provides us with three cases. There is a contrast between the shell and the egg: τὸ μὲν λεπύριον . . . τῷ δὲ ᾠῷ. Then we have a contrast between a woman and her baby, the former being in the nominative and the latter in the accusative: αὐτὴ μὲν ἀπέθανε . . . τὸ δὲ βρέφος λαβών. Finally we have a contrast between the outer container and the enclosed past, the participle of the same verb being used, first in the active and then in the passive: τὸ μὲν περιέχον . . . τὸ δὲ περιεχόμενον. In dream 78 six contrasts are drawn.[326]

There are five instances of chiasmus.[327] At 5.47 a father and son who are together for a brief time become separated: συνεγένοντο ἀλλήλοις . . . χωρὶς ἀλλήλων ἐγένοντο. We note how short this examples is. The same sort of brevity is to be found with Artemidorus's use of *inclusio*. Six examples of this emerged in the texts examined.[328] The twelfth dream narrative opens with Ἔδοξέ τις γυνὴ ἐν τῇ σελήνῃ and closes with διὰ τὴν σελήνην. The *inclusio* is achieved through a single word used near the beginning and at the end. Given the brevity of these examples, we may wonder whether an audience would actually hear them as *inclusio*. However, this appears to be the norm in Artemidorus. We may question whether he intended them to function as

---

323. Such changes in syntax need not matter. We find the same in Matthew, changing from ἄγγελος κυρίου κατ᾽ ὄναρ ἐφάνη αὐτῷ to ἄγγελος κυρίου φαίνεται κατ᾽ ὄναρ τῷ Ἰωσὴφ.

324. Δρομεὺς μέλλων ἱερὸν ἀγῶνα ἀγωνίζεσθαι ἔδοξε and Δρομεὺς μέλλων ἀγωνίζεσθαι ἱερὸν ἀγῶνα ἔδοξεν.

325. Artemidorus, *Oneirocritica* 5.2, 23, 30, 39, 42, 64, 65, 71, 74, 78, 85, 92, 94.

326. The spring/the contest; the channels of the spring/ the judge of the contest; the water/ the crown; the earthenware jar/ the man's training; his failure to obtain water/ his failure to obtain the crown; and the man's futile training/ the breaking of the jar.

327. Artemidorus, *Oneirocritica* 5.30, 47 (x2), 58, 64.

328. Artemidorus, *Oneirocritica* 5.12, 28, 39, 63, 75, 85.

memory patterns. Certainly his usage is very different from Matthew's who has several similar sounding words to form an *inclusio*.

Three cases of parallelism emerge.³²⁹ At 5.37, we have ᾧ λόγῳ ... τούτῳ τῷ λόγῳ, giving us an instance of syntactical parallelism. We have another example at 5.47, with ὁ γὰρ παῖς πατρὸς κόσμος, ὥσπερ ὁ πώγων προσώπου, "for a son embellishes a father, just as a beard embellishes a face." No cases of semantic parallelism were found. The use of syntactical parallelism is common in most literature. However, Artemidorus engages in no other type to make him significantly different from other writers.

There is also one example of alliteration and two of assonance. The former is to be found at 5.65, with ἄχρις ἄκρας, while the latter is illustrated with ἡ ἀφαίρεσις τὴν ἀναίρεσιν at 5.84. Playing as they do on sound, these features would play an important part if oral transmission were involved or in listening to the text being read. Likewise quotations in verse and the use of puns can be striking. We have an example of the former in the dream at 5.39 with a quotation from Homer: ἀλλὰ σύ γ' ἱμερόεντα μετέρχεο ἔργα γάμοιο.³³⁰ We have two puns. The example in dream five is only recognizable in Greek, with διακριθέν, "separated," and κριτοῦ, "judge." Artemidorus bases his interpretation on κρίνειν, applied to strainers and colanders in the sense of "separate" and to judges in the sense of "distinguish, decide."³³¹ The example at 5.43 is even more obscure.³³²

When we pull together our analysis of Artemidorus and compare it with Matthew's use of memory patterns, what we find is that the two writers are noticeably different. With regard to longer repetition, Artemidorus has examples in seven narratives which vary from three to six words. This contrasts with the usage in Matthew which is more extensive. One situation where it works the other way round is with antithesis. Artemidorus has it in abundance with twenty-four examples spread over forty-six narratives, where Matthew has none. There are five cases of *inclusio* found in Artemidorus, each involving a single word with article. He has five cases of chiasmus. There is also one example of alliteration and two of assonance, a verse quotation and two puns, none of which we find in Matthew. One area in which the two writers overlap is with parallelism. As we saw in the Methodology chapter, there are different types of parallelism. The examples which Artemidorus and Matthew have in common are syntactical. However, if the

---

329. Artemidorus, *Oneirocritica* 5.37, 47, 64.

330. "Concern yourself only with the lovely secrets of marriage" (Homer, *Iliad* 5.429).

331. See White, *Interpretation of Dreams*, 244n2.

332. There is a play on δαίμων ("destiny") and δαιμονᾶν ("to be under the power of a daemon"). See White, *Interpretation of Dreams*, 245n14.

case put forward in the previous chapter is valid, the First Gospel may also have an instance of semantic parallelism which *Oneirocritica* lacks. When all the features are taken together, the differences are more significant than the similarities with the result that they draw a distinction between the two authors. This is important given that *Oneirocritica* is the first extant Greek work dealing with dreams. It does not lend support to the view that Matthew and his sources have a strong Hellenistic cultural background.

Table 8: Artemidorus

|  | Matthew | Artemidorus |
|---|---|---|
| Dreams | 5 | 46 |
| Acrostic | 0 | 0 |
| Alliteration | 0 | 1 |
| Anaphora | 0 | 0 |
| Antithesis | 0 | 24 |
| Association | 0 | 0 |
| Assonance | 0 | 2 |
| Chiasmus | 2 | 5 |
| Formulaic Expressions | 3 | 0 |
| Inclusio | 2 | 6 |
| Key Word | 1 | 4 |
| Metre | 0 | 1 |
| Numerical Aids | 0 | 0 |
| Onomatopoeia | 0 | 0 |
| Order | 0 | 0 |
| Parallelism | 5 | 3 |
| Pun | 0 | 2 |
| Repeated Blocks | 4 | 7 |
| Typology | 2 | 0 |

## Summing Up

We must now consider the conclusion which is to be drawn from these comparisons. We begin with some general points. The writers examined fall into two categories, those who display an abundance of memory patterns and those who do not. The ones who do have them in good measure are OT (both Hebrew text and Septuagint), Josephus, Herodotus, Longus and to a lesser extent Acts.

Those which have a minimal appearance of rhetorical devices are to be found in many of the Greco-Roman writers.[333] In general terms, this is a surprising result because rhetoric was such an important element in classical education and widely used in its literature. However, with someone like Polybius it was perhaps to be expected, as he was noted for his "unadorned style." With other writers, such as Tacitus and Appian, the dreams are narrated briefly and so might not allow them to use many devices. With Diodorus we restricted ourselves to his dream narratives and in so doing we did not experience the full flavor of his work. The same may be true of Dionysius or it may be that he sought to achieve a polished narrative without using rhetorical devices. Whatever the reason, these writers stand out as different from Matthew who displays them in abundance.

Many Greek writers show evidence of antithesis.[334] There are also four examples in Suetonius and three in OT. We have already noted how the Greek language lends itself to this with its use of the μέν . . . δέ . . . construction.[335] However, this stands in marked contrast to the practice of Matthew who shows no evidence of antithesis in the dream narratives.[336] This perhaps needs to be qualified by saying that, within the infancy narratives, he does contrast the intentions of the Magi and those of Herod in wanting to find the infant Jesus, the former to *worship* him (Matt 2:2) and the latter to *destroy* him (Matt 2:13). That form of antithesis is a figure of thought rather than a figure of speech.[337] Clearly the brevity of the dream narratives is an issue. On the other hand, Matthew might have used antithesis to highlight the fact that Herod sought Jesus's life, but Jesus survived, while Herod himself lost his life.

---

333. E.g., Polybius, Dionysius, Diodorus, Tacitus, and Appian.

334. There are six examples of antithesis in Herodotus, twenty-five in Josephus, three in Acts, two in Diodorus, five in Polybius, four in Dionysius, fourteen in Plutarch, nine in Philostratus, four in Chariton, ten in Longus, and twenty-four in Artemidorus.

335. See the Methodology chapter.

336. There is evidence of the μέν . . . δέ . . . construction elsewhere in the First Gospel, e.g., Matt 3:11; 13:8; 21:35.

337. For this distinction, see the section on antithesis in the Methodology chapter.

When we looked at Matthew's memory patterns, we found formulaic expressions, *inclusio*, key words, parallelism, lengthy repetition and typology. We need to explore how these relate to our findings in the work of other authors. We begin with typology. It is not unique to Matthew because OT writers engage in it.[338] However, it is unique in the sense that we did not find evidence of it in any of the other dream narratives examined. In Matthew's narrative it functions as an analogy of theological significance. In the Methodology chapter I argued that typology can also serve a mnemonic function and suggested that is the case in Matthew's dream narratives. If this is correct, it is a unique memory pattern in the narratives explored here.

The appearance of a dream figure, such as the angel in Matthew,[339] is part of the standard form of dream reporting. However, I argued in the previous chapter that because of the consistent way Matthew expresses the appearance, his phrase also functions as a formulaic expression. Josephus does not show such consistency, for he even has different expressions in narrating the same dream of Glaphyra in *Wars* and *Antiquities*.[340] However, Artemidorus does show consistency in the expression he uses to introduce dreams. In so doing he lends support to the view that the phraseology used to introduce a dream can function as a formulaic expression. Although other writers express the appearance of a dream figure, none do so with the same consistent phraseology as Matthew and Artemidorus.

Matthew shares the use of *inclusio* with OT, Josephus, Herodotus, Acts, Dionysius, Plutarch, Philostratus, Longus, Artemidorus, Pseudo-Philo and Genesis Apocryphon. Despite the wide usage, we cannot go so far as to describe it as a standard feature of dream narratives. It is simply a popular memory pattern. With some writers *inclusio* is achieved by repeating a single word at either end,[341] whereas Matthew has a longer string of words.[342] This strengthens the ability of the readership or audience in grasping the structure of his text and in remembering it. Since *inclusio* is so widely used by writers from diverse cultural backgrounds, that does not in itself help us to

---

338. Allison speaks of Joshua and other OT characters as being portrayed as a "new Moses" (Allison, *New Moses*, 11–95).

339. Angels are only one type of *oneiros* figure and would be restricted to Jewish texts. However, some of the *oneiroi* in Greek literature take the form of winged creatures which fly and to that extent they resemble angels. For example, Euripides, *Phoenissae* 1546, has Oedipus refer to "a *hovering* dream."

340. Josephus, *War* 2.114–16; *Ant.* 17.349–353.

341. E.g., Artemidorus, *Oneirocritica* 5.12, opens with Ἔδοξέ τις γυνὴ ἐν τῇ σελήνῃ and closes with διὰ τὴν σελήνην, this being a single word with the article.

342. See especially Matt 2:13, 22: καὶ χρηματισθέντες κατ' ὄναρ . . . ἀνεχώρησαν εἰς followed by χρηματισθεὶς δὲ κατ' ὄναρ ἀνεχώρησεν εἰς.

establish whether Matthew or any source(s) lean more towards Hellenism or Judaism. However, as was suggested in the Methodology chapter, we need to take account of frequency of usage. When we do that, we find that there are proportionately more examples of *inclusio* in OT and Josephus.[343] This may suggest some Jewish influence in Matthew.

Almost all writers also use key words, the exceptions being Genesis Apocryphon and Tacitus. The reason for not detecting key words in the latter two is probably that the sample of their work examined was in each case small. With key words we have a memory patterns whose popularity extends beyond the cultural divide. Consequently, we are unable to employ this to identify Matthew's background.

Matthew uses parallelism and shares this practice with OT, Acts, Plutarch, Chariton, Longus and Artemidorus. Again it may appear that we have a device which cannot help us establish cultural identity. However, as with *inclusio*, we need to consider frequency of usage.[344] Such comparison would suggest that Matthew has a common bond with Longus and OT and so this time frequency of usage does not resolve the cultural issue. We go on therefore to consider a type of parallelism which is culturally specific. Reference has already been made to the analysis of parallelism in OT texts by Alter and Kugel.[345] We recall how Alter distinguishes three types of parallelism—meaning, syntax and rhythm—with the first being characteristically Hebraic. Matthew displays both semantic and syntactical parallelism. The latter is something he shares with many of the other writers. We take one example, the reasons given for the commands in the first dream. We have τὸ γὰρ ἐν αὐτῇ γεννηθὲν ἐκ πνεύματός ἐστιν ἁγίου (Matt 1:20) and αὐτὸς γὰρ σώσει τὸν λαὸν αὐτοῦ ἀπὸ τῶν ἁμαρτιῶν αὐτῶν (Matt 1:21). We set this alongside an example from Longus, the dream of Dionysophanes,[346] where there is a careful balancing with details of the feast: τῶν ἀπὸ γῆς with τῶν ἀπὸ θαλάττης and καὶ εἴ τι ἐν λίμναις with καὶ εἴ τι ἐν ποταμοῖς. We find similar balancing with ἐκλύσαντα τὸ τοξάριον and ἀποθέμενον τὴν φαρέτραν; also with τότε δεικνύειν ἑκάστῳ τὰ γνωρίσματα and τὸ δὲ ἐντεῦθεν ᾄδειν τὸν ὑμέναιον; and with ἰδών and ἀκούσας. This similarity which Matthew shares with Longus and other writers does not help us with the cultural issue.

---

343. OT has *inclusio* in 8 out of 25 dreams, Josephus in 7 out of 33, Herodotus in 3 out of 14, Acts in 2 out of 9, Dionysius 1 in 9, Plutarch 2 in 21, Philostratus 1 in 9, Longus 1 in 6, Pseudo-Philo 1 in 6, and *Genesis Apocryphon* 2 in 3.

344. Matthew has 5 examples in 5 dreams, Longus 8 in 6, OT 5 in 23, Artemidorus 3 in 46, Acts 2 in 9, Plutarch 1 in 21, and Chariton 1 in 9.

345. See the Methodology chapter and also above in OT section, especially in relation to 1 Kings 3:5–15.

346. Longus, *Daphnis and Chloe* 4.34.1–3.

However, we can take into account his one example which is semantic. At 1:24 we have an instance of what Alter calls "specification," for each of the three new statements specify what it meant to say that "Joseph did what the angel of the Lord commanded." The first and third statements fulfill particular commands which the angel is recorded as having given. The second introduces new material. In his use of semantic parallelism Matthew may be said to share something in common with OT. As it happens, Solomon's dream at 1 Kings 3:5–15 comes closest to Matthew in its use of parallelism. It is extensive with four examples to be found at verses 6–7, 12, 12–13. Verse 12 displays similar "specification" to Matthew's: "Behold, I now do according to your word. Behold, I give you a wise and discerning mind." This must help settle the cultural question. It is a clear case where Matthew has something in common with OT which is not shared by other texts. It suggests OT influence on Matthew or his source. Can we broaden this and speak of Jewish influence? Acts has two examples of parallelism (Acts 23:11; 27:23; cf. 27:24). We argued above that although a case can be made for treating them as semantic examples, it is more likely that they are simply syntactical. It is therefore OT influence which stands out.

Matthew uses repetition, sometimes at notable length, amounting to 11, 15, or even 19 words. There is evidence of substantial repetition in OT, Josephus, Pseudo-Philo, *Testament of Naphtali*, *Genesis Apocryphon*, Herodotus, and Longus. However, some writers do not use repetition in quite the same way as Matthew who favors verbatim usage in reasonably long phrases. Josephus is an example of someone whose cases of repetition are not especially long and do not even come close to being verbatim. Much of Matthew's repetition is achieved through carrying forward phraseology from the expression of a command to the expression of its execution. Not everyone tackles the repetition of command and obedience in the same way as Matthew. We saw above how both the dreams in *Testament of Naphtali* have such repetition,[347] but they each differ from Matthew in that the second expresses the obedience in a subordinate clause and the first does not involve substantial verbatim repetition. We also looked at the two instances of command and obedience in Abram's second dream in *Genesis Apocryphon*.[348] In the first only the opening phrase is repeated, amounting to three words in Aramaic, while in the second there are only two words in common between command and obedience. There is reasonably substantial repetition in Noah's dream,[349] amounting to six words in the Aramaic text

---

347. *Testament of Naphtali* 5:1–8; 6:1–10.
348. *Genesis Apocryphon* 21:8–22.
349. *Genesis Apocryphon* cols. 13–15.

and the expression is used three times in the space of three lines. Although this comes closer to Matthew than the command/obedience phrasing, it is still not extensive. Longus too differs from Matthew. In three out of four dreams[350] the wording of the obedience does not reflect the wording of the command. In the one where it does,[351] there are added to the obedience details which are not present in the command. Miriam's dream in Pseudo-Philo[352] is an interesting example because it has the expression of obedience before the actual command. The summing up of Abraham's obedience in LAB 23:3–14 is similar to Matt 1:24, without involving a memory pattern. However, Samuel's nocturnal experience[353] does not have the repetition we might have expected in line with the OT account. If we lay aside these cases where repetition is handled differently from Matthew, we are essentially left with one example in Herodotus,[354] and eleven in OT.[355] Although we have not considered the Homeric epics because they are far removed both in time and kind from the Matthean narratives, we may note now that Homer shows a certain fondness for extensive repetition.[356] There is also lengthy repetition in the English language in some fairy tales and certain kinds of poetry and song, perhaps partly as a memory aid. This raises the possibility that it may not be cultural background which is at stake, but instead it may be a matter of genre.

When we pull the evidence together, what we find is this. Matthew has areas which he shares with both Hellenistic and Jewish writers and other areas distinguish him from the Hellenistic group. In the first category we saw how Matthew's use of formulaic expressions resembles that of Artemidorus, a Greek writer. *Inclusio* is a memory pattern, popular with both Greek and Jewish writers, and the same is true of key words. Syntactical parallelism is to be found in a wide range of writings which cross the cultural divide. This also holds for repetition. This is in fact in line with what we already know of the intermingling of Judaism and Hellenism, for example, through the work of Hengel.[357] Just as Oppenheim has shown that there is a standard pattern of dream reporting widely used throughout ANE, with minor local

---

350. Longus, *Daphnis and Chloe* 1.7.1–8.2; 2.26.5–28.1; 3.27.1–28.1.
351. Longus, *Daphnis and Chloe* 4.34.1–3.
352. LAB 9.10.
353. LAB 53.1–13.
354. The dream of Cyrus (Herodotus, *Histories* 1.209).
355. See Gen 28:10–22; 31:10–13; 41:5–8, 17–21, 22–24, 25–31; 46:1–8; Num 22:9–13; 1 Sam 3:2–15; Dan 4:25–34; 7:15–27.
356. E.g., he has Zeus give lengthy instructions to Hermes, who later repeats the message to the recipient.
357. Hengel, *Judaism and Hellenism*; Hengel, *'Hellenization' of Judaea*.

variations,[358] we can now claim that there are memory patterns widely used by Greek, Roman and Jewish writers.

We may consider whether there is any other way of interpreting this cultural overlap in the use of memory patterns. It may be suggested that people from diverse cultural backgrounds use the same devices because this is simply the way in which human beings remember narratives in oral and semi-literate societies. To consider this issue we need to look beyond the peoples of the Mediterranean and Near East. Jan Vansina has done considerable work on mnemonic devices worldwide and especially among African peoples.[359] He has shown that material objects,[360] landscapes[361] and melody/rhythm[362] can all be used to preserve traditions. However, verbal mnemonics are not entirely missing. Finnegan draws attention to the use of repetition in dirges, hymns, prayers, proverbs and drum literature.[363] She also highlights the use of parallelism,[364] formulae in stories[365] and alliteration.[366] Noteworthy are some of the verbal mnemonics which she does not list in her index: assonance, antithesis, *inclusio* and key words. From this it would appear that some mnemonic devices are linked to particular cultures. In fact we have already seen evidence of this in the fondness of the Greeks for antithesis and of OT authors for semantic parallelism. We are therefore justified in claiming that the analysis carried out here has validity and that the common devices which Matthew shares with Hellenistic and Jewish writers are attributable to the overlap of the two cultures.

358. Oppenheim, "Interpretation of Dreams," 179-373.

359. See particularly Vansina, *Oral Tradition as History*, 43-47; *Oral Tradition*, 36-39.

360. In Peru a *quipu* is used which consists of a series of knotted cords of different colors and lengths attached to a head dress in the form of a fringe. The colors, knots and lengths are all mnemonic devices. Vansina comments: "the *quipu* could be read just as if they were books" (Vansina, *Oral Tradition*, 37). The Sioux used buffalo skins on which the owner painted figures as an aid for remembering significant winter events. Vansina points out that this comes close to pictographs and ultimately to a form of writing (Vansina, *Oral Tradition as History*, 44).

361. On the Luapula places are associated with well-known local legends which are only recited when passing these locations (Vansina, *Oral Tradition*, 38) and in various regions guardians of royal tombs relate the history of the kings buried there (Vansina, *Oral Tradition*, 39).

362. In different parts of sub-Saharan Africa, where languages are tonal, drum rhythms are used to transmit information (Vansina, *Oral Tradition as History*, 46-47).

363. Finnegan, *Oral Literature in Africa*, 160, 178, 389, 447-48, 469, 474.

364. Finnegan, *Oral Literature in Africa*, 75, 128, 130, 178, 222, 298, 391, 444, 447.

365. Finnegan, *Oral Literature in Africa*, 368-69.

366. Finnegan, *Oral Literature in Africa*, 129.

We now need to consider antithesis and semantic parallelism as we pursue the cultural leanings of Matthew and his source(s). Importantly Matthew does not engage in verbal antithesis as many Greek writers do. Moreover, Matthew shows evidence of semantic parallelism which is characteristic of Hebrew poetry, although it can be found in prose narrative (e.g., 1 Kgs 3:12). These two factors tip the balance in favor of Matthew showing closer affinity with OT than Hellenistic writing. It may be suggested that these two factors do not amount to a lot of evidence. If we increased the amount of Matthean text examined beyond the dream narratives and included the story of the Magi, we would have examples of antithesis.[367] This highlights the difficulty caused by the small amount of text which we are examining. Nevertheless, it was right to restrict ourselves to the dream narratives so that we were comparing like with like. Are we then claiming OT affinity with only a slim amount of evidence? There is further support in Matthew's use of *inclusio*, when compared with the frequency of usage in other writers, especially OT and Josephus. There is also some support for it in Matthew's use of repetition. Although examples of reasonable length were found in five works of Jewish origin[368] and two of Greek origin,[369] we saw above how several of them differed from Matthew in their use of repetition to express command and obedience. When these are laid aside, cases which came closest to Matthew's length of eleven to nineteen words were Herodotus and OT, the latter having significantly more examples. We may draw more support from Matthew's use of typology. Although this is unique as a mnemonic technique in the narratives examined, the analogy drawn is with the life of Moses, an OT character. When all is told, Matthew appears to have closer affinity with OT.

Is there any particular OT book or single narrative on which Matthew's sources based the dreams? Soares Prabhu suggests that Gen 46:2-4 in its Septuagintal form was used,[370] while Gnuse advocates all the patriarchal

---

367. There is a contrast between the use of βασιλεύς (Matt 2:1) to refer to Herod and its use in the phrase ὁ τεχθεὶς βασιλεὺς τῶν Ἰουδαίων (Matt 2:2) to refer to Jesus. We have further antithesis in the contrast between the expressed intention of Herod in his words to the Magi, "that I too may come and worship him" (Matt 2:8) and his actual action in which "he sent and killed all the male children" (Matt 2:16). The second reference takes us into one of the dream narratives. There is also a contrast between the Magi and Herod, both of whom express the intention to pay homage (προσκυνέω at Matt 2:2, 8), but only the Magi actually do it (Matt 2:11). There is, however, no use of the μέν . . . δέ . . . construction in the Magi narrative.

368. OT; Josephus, *War*; *Ant.*; Pseudo-Philo, LAB; *Testament of Naphtali*; *Genesis Apocryphon*.

369. Herodotus and Longus.

370. Prabhu, *Formula Quotations*, 223.

dreams in Genesis.[371] The evidence from memory techniques does not allow us to be so precise as to name a particular OT book.

### Table 9: Old Testament Books

| | OT-Heb | Genesis | Numbers | Judges | 1 Samuel | 1 Kings | Daniel |
|---|---|---|---|---|---|---|---|
| Dreams | 23 | 13 | 1 | 1 | 1 | 2 | 5 |
| Acrostic | 0 | 0 | 0 | 0 | 0 | 0 | 0 |
| Alliteration | 4 | 1 | 0 | 0 | 0 | 1 | 2 |
| Anaphora | 0 | 0 | 0 | 0 | 0 | 0 | 0 |
| Antithesis | 3 | 3 | 0 | 0 | 0 | 0 | 0 |
| Association | 0 | 0 | 0 | 0 | 0 | 0 | 0 |
| Assonance | 3 | 3 | 0 | 0 | 0 | 0 | 0 |
| Chiasmus | 2 | 1 | 0 | 0 | 0 | 1 | 0 |
| Formulaic Expressions | Frequent 3 Types | 16 | 0 | 1 | 0 | 4 | 4 |
| Inclusio | 6 | 3 | 0 | 0 | 0 | 0 | 3 |
| Key Word | 9 | 4 | 0 | 0 | 0 | 1 | 4 |
| Metre | 0 | 0 | 0 | 0 | 0 | 0 | 0 |
| Numerical Aids | 2 | 2 | 0 | 0 | 0 | 0 | 0 |
| Onomatopoeia | 1 | 0 | 0 | 0 | 1 | 0 | 0 |
| Order | 0 | 0 | 0 | 0 | 0 | 0 | 0 |
| Parallelism | 5 | 1 | 0 | 0 | 0 | 4 | 0 |
| Repeated Blocks | 11 | 6 | 1 | 0 | 1 | 1 | 2 |
| Typology | 0 | 0 | 0 | 0 | 0 | 0 | 0 |

Our evidence would suggest that Genesis is unlikely to have been Matthew's only source for the dream narratives. As far as typology is concerned, the affinities of Matthew's dream narratives lie with Exodus as well as, and to a greater extent than, Genesis. Other memory patterns and points of style

371. Gnuse, "Dream Genre," 97.

also point beyond Genesis. Although there are six cases of extensive repetition in Genesis, there are another five elsewhere in OT. Ultimately six of the eleven cases are particularly pronounced.[372] We may overlook "symbolic" dreams, even although they generally employ the same memory devices as "message" dreams, for they follow a different structure and ultimately that is a memory technique too. This means that we also rule out the five dreams in Daniel, for they are all symbolic.[373] Balaam's experience in Numbers 22 looks hopeful because his dialogue with God echoes information already given to the reader in verses 4 and 5, just as the angel does in telling Joseph about Mary's conception through the Holy Spirit, but it is debatable whether this counts as a dream narrative, for it has no dream formula. In 1 Kings 19, Elijah obeys the command given by the angel, just as Joseph does, and then the incident is repeated, the command and obedience occurring twice, just as the angel reappears to Joseph with fresh commands. However, this is not strictly a dream, but two waking experiences, what are sometimes referred to as *Wecktraümen*.[374] In 1 Samuel 3, there are echoes between Samuel's statement and Eli's response and between Eli's commands and Samuel's action which can be related to the angel's command and Joseph's obedience. However, for a case of semantic parallelism, similar to what we find in Matthew, we need to look to 1 Kings 3:5–15. The reality is that Matthew's usage could have been picked up anywhere in OT, most likely from a poetic text, for parallelism is regarded as the characteristic of Hebrew poetry. Similarly, other devices may have been learned from a variety of OT books. At this stage we return to Daniel, not discussed in any detail, but dismissed with a general comment above. There we find *inclusio*, formulaic expressions, key words and extensive repetition, all of which are used in Matthew, but absent is parallelism which plays a significant part in Matthew. We know that Matthew was familiar with Daniel and although he may not have modeled his dreams on Daniel's, he may have been influenced by Daniel in his use of devices, as with other parts of the OT. We conclude that the OT influence is most likely to have been of a general nature, although the Pentateuch would undoubtedly be an important factor for Matthew.

He seems to have been steeped in the OT scriptures through reading them or listening to them. He may even have been scribally trained. However, when he came to compose the birth narratives, he chose to draw upon

---

372. Gen 41:5–8, 22–24, 25–31; Num 22:9–13; 1 Sam 3:2–15; 1 Kgs 19:5–7; LXX Dan 4:7–9, 10–13, 17–18, 20.

373. We concede that Dan 8:1–14, which narrates the dream of the ram and goat, has elements of an auditory message dream (Dan 8:13–14), but it is essentially a symbolic dream.

374. Flannery-Dailey, *Dreamers, Scribes, and Priests*, 43, 154.

this knowledge and write in a biblical register. This was in line with his frequent quotations from OT, designed to show continuity with the OT story and particularly to portray Jesus as the fulfillment of OT hopes.

If we put OT aside, does Matthew have striking affinities with any other writers? There are similarities between Matthew and Herodotus, particularly in their use of *inclusio* and blocks of repetition, but we found only one case of parallelism in Herodotus's fourteen dream narratives, whereas Matthew has five examples in his three narratives.[375] We may therefore ignore the parallelism, but we need to take account of the *inclusio* and repetition. These may be explained in terms oral sources, used by each of them. If we compare Matthew with Longus, there were eight examples of parallelism in the latter which, although it is syntactical, compares favorably with the former's six. However, Longus makes less use of *inclusio* and extensive repetition. The usage in Longus is to be explained in terms of rhetoric rather than oral sources. If we take the Greco-Roman writers as a block, *inclusio* is fairly popular, as is parallelism, and although we do find repetition, it is not usually extensive. These shared features may be explained, as suggested above, in terms of a common cultural background.

We consider where Josephus lies in relation to OT and Greco-Roman authors, knowing already that he is a Hellenistic Jew and likely to be subject to both influences. With seven cases of *inclusio* in thirty-three dreams Josephus is closer to OT which has six instances in twenty-three narratives than he is to the classical authors who have eighteen instances out of one hundred and eighty opportunities. With five repeated blocks, he remains proportionately closer to OT which has eleven as against the classical thirteen. However, he does not engage in as much extensive repetition as OT. We may guess that he is less concerned than OT writers to have his readership remember the detail of what he wrote or that he and his assistants regard verbatim repetition as contrary to the kind of style they wish to achieve. When it comes to antithesis, he is very much closer to the classical group with his twenty five and their one hundred and two, while OT has only two. *Inclusio* placed Josephus closer to OT, while antithesis placed him decidedly closer to the Greco-Romans, with repeated blocks slightly more evenly balanced. His Jewish and Hellenistic mix seems to be borne out by these findings.

---

375. The tables featuring Matthew list five dreams, of which three are narrated in full and two simply referred to.

Table 10: Old Testament – Josephus – Jewish – Classical Writers

|  | OT–Heb | LXX | Josephus | Jewish | Classical |
|---|---|---|---|---|---|
| Dreams | 23 | 23 | 33 | 22 | 180 |
| Acrostic | 0 | 0 | 0 | 0 | 0 |
| Alliteration | 4 | 7 | 3 | 0 | 8 |
| Anaphora | 0 | 0 | 0 | 0 | 0 |
| Antithesis | 3 | 3 | 25 | 11 | 102 |
| Association | 0 | 0 | 0 | 0 | 0 |
| Assonance | 3 | 2 | 1 | 0 | 7 |
| Chiasmus | 2 | 2 | 3 | 1 | 9 |
| Formulaic Expressions | Frequent 3 Types | Frequent 3 Types | Most | 0 | Artemidorus |
| Inclusio | 6 | 6 | 7 | 5 | 18 |
| Key Word | 9 | 9 | Yes | 7 | 40 |
| Metre | 0 | 0 | 0 | 0 | 6 |
| Numerical Aids | 2 | 2 | 2 | 0 | 0 |
| Onomatopoeia | 1 | 1 | 0 | 1 | 0 |
| Order | 0 | 0 | 0 | 0 | 0 |
| Parallelism | 5 | 5 | 0 | 2 | 17 |
| Repeated Blocks | 11 | 11 | 5 | 3 | 13 |
| Typology | 0 | 0 | 0 | 0 | 0 |

We compare Greco-Roman writers with those of OT, acknowledging that the spectrum of devices is to be found in both groups.[376] Chiasmus (OT displaying two and Greco-Roman eight) and key words (OT nine, Greco-Roman forty) are fairly evenly balanced. *Inclusio* is proportionately more prevalent in OT with its six cases and Greco-Roman eighteen. Likewise OT has proportionately more cases of parallelism with five compared to seventeen among the Greco-Romans. When the latter group is broken down, we have eight examples in Longus and three in Valerius Maximus. With repeated blocks of texts OT has the edge with eleven against thirteen in

---

376. There were 23 twenty-three dreams narratives examined in OT and 180 in classical writings.

classical works. Again the break down proves interesting with two lengthy examples in Herodotus, more like OT, and shorter instances elsewhere. However, what really marks OT and the classical writers out as different is the use of antithesis, with three in the former and one hundred and two in the latter. What emerges is that although OT and Greco-Roman writers use the same devices, there is a discernible difference in the frequency with which they use particular types, especially *inclusio*, parallelism, repeated blocks and antithesis. This difference is not due to a particular author displaying many examples, because we need to relate these examples to the number of dreams which he narrates. Nor does it depend ultimately upon a single author, for we recognize that there can be variation of style from one writer to another and so we look for the typical usage of a particular group. However, just as we have noted a device such as semantic parallelism which is culturally specific, so frequency of usage can also reveal literary traits which distinguish a specific culture.

We now compare the other Jewish sources, excluding the OT and Josephus, already examined, with the classical authors. Proportionately they have roughly the same usage of antithesis, key words and parallelism. However, they differ to the extent that the Jewish writers, in relative terms, make greater use of *inclusio* and repeated blocks of text. The greater Jewish use of *inclusio* and repetition is in line with OT practice. What is surprising is the Jewish use of antithesis which is closer to Greek writers. We may wonder to what extent this can be attributed to the availability of the μέν . . . δέ . . . construction for Jews writing in Greek. In fact of the eleven examples cited only one uses this construction (Acts 22:9) and the two examples from Pseudo-Philo are in Latin. No doubt antithesis, along with the other features common to Jewish and Classical authors, is to be explained by the multicultural state of Jewish society.

### Table 11: Greek Authors

|              | Herodotus | Plutarch | Longus | Artemidorus |
|--------------|-----------|----------|--------|-------------|
| Dreams       | 14        | 21       | 6      | 46          |
| Acrostic     | 0         | 0        | 0      | 0           |
| Alliteration | 0         | 1        | 0      | 1           |
| Anaphora     | 0         | 0        | 0      | 0           |
| Antithesis   | 6         | 14       | 10     | 24          |

|  | Herodotus | Plutarch | Longus | Artemidorus |
|---|---|---|---|---|
| Association | 0 | 0 | 0 | 0 |
| Assonance | 0 | 0 | 1 | 2 |
| Chiasmus | 0 | 0 | 1 | 5 |
| Formulaic Expressions | 1 | 0 | 0 | 0 |
| Inclusio | 3 | 2 | 1 | 6 |
| Key Word | 2 | 5 | 4 | 4 |
| Metre | 1 | 3 | 0 | 1 |
| Numerical Aids | 0 | 0 | 0 | 0 |
| Onomatopoeia | 0 | 0 | 0 | 0 |
| Order | 0 | 0 | 0 | 0 |
| Parallelism | 1 | 1 | 8 | 3 |
| Repeated Blocks | 2 | 0 | 1 | 7 |
| Typology | 0 | 0 | 0 | 0 |

Finally we consider the relationships between the Greek authors. We have already noted that there is minimal use of devices in the narratives examined from Polybius, Diodorus, Dionysius and Appian. The same is largely true of Philostratus and Chariton. This means that the big players are really Herodotus, Plutarch, Longus and Artemidorus. All four display an abundance of antithesis.[377] Although it is used in other cultures,[378] this is a popular Greek device.[379] These authors also use *inclusio* and key words which cross cultures.[380] Each of them engages in parallelism with Longus having the most examples.[381] Herodotus, Longus and Artemidorus show some evidence of lengthy repetition.

These four writers share some common ground in their use of rhetorical devices in a way that those discounted do not, although Plutarch

377. This was also true of Polybius, Diodorus, Dionysius, Philostratus, and Chariton.

378. There are many examples in the Hebrew Bible, Proverbs 19 displaying several by itself (e.g., Prov 19:4, 12, 14, 16, 21, 25).

379. Overall we found 78 examples in 129 Greek narratives examined and we note again that the Greek language provides a unique way of expressing it with the μέν . . . δέ . . . construction.

380. The discounted writers all have key words and Dionysius and Philostratus have *inclusio*.

381. Chariton has one example.

would not usually be thought of as embracing an embellished style in the *Lives*.[382] Despite common features, they each belong to a different genre, representing history, biography, fiction and dream interpretation. The first three are engaged in literature, while Artemidorus serves a more practical goal. Herodotus belongs to an earlier era and deals with oral sources, while Longus may be regarded as a 'sophistic' writer. Although we recognize similarities among these writers, it would be going too far to suggest any common influence other than Greek literary practice.

## Conclusion

The examination of memory patterns carried out for this study confirms the intermingling of Jewish and Hellenistic cultures. This is the environment in which Matthew and any source functioned. Nevertheless, we can detect in the Matthean dream narratives a slight cultural bias away from Hellenism in the lack of antithesis, so popular among Greek writers, and towards Judaism in the example of semantic parallelism, as evidenced in OT. Further support for bias towards Judaism is to be found in repetition where Matthew's usage is more comparable to that of OT than other literature, in *inclusio* where the frequency in Matthew is more like that of OT and Josephus and in typology where Matthew uses OT "types," such as Moses or Israel. Given that certain patterns are built into the memory of the infancy narratives and given that memory is closely related to the identity of people, we conclude that Matthew and any person who may have transmitted the dream narratives to him use memory patterns in much the same way as OT story-tellers.

To this we need to add features which emerged in the Dreams chapter and in the Matthew chapter, something we shall do in our next chapter where we seek to draw all our threads together.

382. Schmitz, "Plutarch and the Second Sophistic," 32–33.

# 8

# Conclusion

## Drawing Threads Together

THE AIM OF THIS study has been to discern whether Jewish or Hellenistic literary culture had a stronger influence upon Matthew. At the outset we noted that Matthew wrote in Greek, frequently quoted from OT, used the LXX, but deviated from it when it did not suit his purpose, following the Hebrew text or another translation of it.[1] These factors suggest both Greek and Jewish influences at work.

In the Dreams chapter we set Matthew's narratives alongside other ancient texts. What we noticed was how they differed from those of ANE and the classical world in that his dreams do not come from the realm of the dead and do not show any evidence of healing or incubation. This distances Matthew from certain aspects of Hellenistic influence. Since his dreams involve no description of the angel of the Lord, they are more like OT dreams which do not describe God.[2] This places Matthew closer to Jewish influence. On the other hand, Matthew's dreams do resemble the message type of ANE which come to royal families. We also observed a resemblance between the dreams narrated by Matthew and those Josephus attributes to Amram and Pseudo-Philo to Miriam. This again points to Jewish influence.

In the Matthew chapter we observed how the genre of gospel most closely resembles that of encomiastic biography, a literary form found in the Greco-Roman world. However, we also noted Matthew's use of Semitisms.[3]

---

1. See his handling of Hosea 11:1 (Matt 2:15).

2. This is not meant to suggest that angels should be equated with God, but simply to draw a parallel. There are times in the OT when angels are described, although God never is.

3. We highlighted an example where Joseph is told καλέσεις τὸ ὄνομα αὐτοῦ Ἰησοῦν (Matt 1:21). This involves a biblical expression, the Septuagintal form of קרא + שם + proper name.

As a result, the overall picture remains complicated and shows multi-cultural facets. When we looked at Matthew's use of memory patterns, we found an example of parallelism at 1:24 which we argued was semantic, sharing affinity with OT practice, and we noted the lack of antithesis, a popular Greek device. These two factors suggest that the Jewish or OT influence was somewhat stronger than the Greek.

When we set Matthew's set of memory patterns against the examples found in the dream narratives of other literature, we found that Matthew is unique in his use of typology. When we bear in mind that the types which the First Gospel uses for Jesus are Moses and Israel, we detect OT influence. However, we also found that when Matthew employs formulaic expressions, *inclusio*, key words, syntactical parallelism and repetition, he is drawing upon techniques which are common to Greek, Roman and Jewish writers and so cross the cultural divide. Since the time of Hengel it has been a given of modern scholarship that in the first century CE there was an intermingling of Judaism and Hellenism. Without wishing to contradict this cultural overlap, we may press the evidence we gained from our comparisons. The extent of *inclusio* in the First Gospel is more in line with the frequency of usage in OT and Josephus than other writers. Similarly with repetition, Matthew's length of eleven to nineteen words came closest to Herodotus and OT, the latter having significantly more examples. Although Matthew's parallels with OT are undeniable, we were unable to link his usage with any particular OT book.

There is no simple answer to the question with which we set out, for Matthew participates in both Jewish and Hellenistic literary cultures or rather the amalgam of the two. However, in the final analysis he does appear to come a little closer to OT practice. It should be noted that we are saying OT practice rather than Jewish. For Matthew is not fully in step with contemporary Jewish writers such as Josephus or Pseudo-Philo. They may have been more influenced by Hellenistic practice. They also seem to be engaged in a different sort of activity from Matthew, sometimes retelling OT dreams in their own words, often altering them substantially, to serve their own purposes.[4] The result is that they lack many of the memory patterns present in the original OT narrative. Where they do have devices, they have inserted them themselves.

We can say that Matthew seems to have been steeped in the OT scriptures through reading them himself or hearing them read by others. Consequently, when he came to write the birth narratives, he drew upon

---

4. *Genesis Apocryphon* 21:8–22 gives us a second dream experienced by Abram. It consists of an elaboration on Gen 13:14–18, where there is in fact no dream, only a speech made by the Lord to Abram.

this knowledge and composed them in a biblical register. We may question whether this is enough to allow us to describe Matthew's cultural background as Jewish. After all, Luke employs a Septuagintal style without scholars concluding that he is Jewish. While it is true that Matthew writes in Greek and quotes from LXX, he also deviates from LXX when it does not suit his purposes, as in his quotation of Hosea 11:1. Although we cannot be sure that he knew Hebrew or translated the Hosea text himself, he was certainly aware of this version, which differed from LXX, and chose to use it. At the very least it seems likely that he was mingling with people who did know Hebrew and the following other factors suggest he may well have known Hebrew himself. When he uses ἐγερθείς with the imperative παράλαβε, he is following the Hebrew construction קוּם + imperative. This idiom is usually rendered by the LXX as ἀναστὰς + imperative. Although Matthew has the same construction as LXX, he is using a different verb for "rise" which suggests that he was not rigidly tied to LXX. He quotes the Hebrew name Immanuel (1:23), providing a translation. However, at 1:21 we have a Hebrew wordplay on Jesus's name, but no explanation is offered of how popular etymology associated the name with the Hebrew words for "save" and "salvation." These factors would suggest a more Semitic background than would be gained from LXX alone. We suggest that Matthew's apparent access to Hebrew does make a difference and supports the claim that he belonged to a Jewish background in which the Hebrew scriptures played an important part.

The outcome of this research should not surprise us when we bear in mind the frequency with which Matthew quotes from OT. There appear to be five direct quotations in the first two chapters of the gospel,[5] possibly drawing from different versions of the OT.[6] We have also seen how Matthew's infancy narratives reveal Moses typology, with aspects of Jesus's life reflecting experiences of Moses[7] and the wording of 2:20 echoing Exodus 4:19 (LXX).[8] Overall it would be fair to say that Matthew has a close textual

---

5. Matt 1:23 quotes Isa 7:14; Matt 2:6 quotes Mic 5:2; Matt 2:15 quotes Hos 11:1; Matt 2:18 quotes Jer 31:15. Matt 2:23 is difficult to locate in OT.

6. The quotation from Isa 7:14 comes largely from LXX, whereas with Hosea 11:1, Matthew avoided LXX, using the Hebrew text or a Greek version which followed it more closely.

7. The infant Jesus was in danger from Herod, as the baby Moses was from Pharaoh. The holy family escaped to Egypt, where the adult Moses had escaped from Egypt to Midian.

8. Matthew's words τεθνήκασιν γὰρ οἱ ζητοῦντες τὴν ψυχὴν τοῦ παιδίου resemble LLX's τεθνήκασι γὰρ πάντες οἱ ζητοῦντές σου τὴν ψυχήν.

familiarity with OT.[9] The memory patterns embedded in his dream narratives also suggest such OT familiarity.

We, therefore, suggest that when Matthew came to write the dream narratives, he deliberately used OT memory patterns and other stylistic traits which were very familiar to him because he wanted to achieve a biblical register. This, alongside his OT quotations and typology, portrayed Jesus as the continuation and fulfillment of Israel's history, recorded in OT.

## Progress Made by this Study

It would be fair to ask where this study has taken us beyond what we already know of Matthew's interest in OT. It has enabled us to redress the balance with those who write about Hellenistic influence on Matthew's writing.[10] We do not deny such influence. Indeed, as we have seen, the data which emerges from our search for memory patterns points to a mixed culture. However, our data, which also shows Matthew sharing some affinity with OT practice, modifies the stress we place on Hellenism. It suggests a Jewish origin for Matthew and those with whom he was associating.

Where does this conclusion stand in relation to the work of other scholars, particularly those we considered in the first chapter? Soares Prabhu thinks that Matthew based his writing on the Elohist dreams of Genesis, particularly that of Jacob at Beersheba in 46:2-4,[11] while Gnuse argues that all the patriarchal dreams in Genesis lie behind Matthew's narrative.[12] Brown suggests that the dreams may have been inspired by the Joseph dreams in Genesis 37, 40-41.[13] We do not propose any particular OT text or set of texts as the basis for the format of Matthew's dream narratives. Just as Matthew and any around him were influenced by OT memory patterns, so he may well have been influenced by the form and content of OT dreams in the way they narrated their tales, but only in a general way. We found eleven examples of extensive repetition from across OT. Although there were seven cases in Genesis, there were also four examples drawn from Numbers, 1 Samuel, and Daniel. Furthermore, Matthew possibly has a case of semantic

---

9. France describes the first book of NT as "a scripturally-based Gospel," pointing out that while all the gospels contain frequent quotations and allusion to OT, this feature is more pronounced in Matthew (France, *Matthew*, 22).

10. Kennedy, *New Testament Interpretation*; Dodson, *Reading Dreams*; Talbert, *Matthew*; Kinney, *Hellenistic Dimensions*.

11. Prabhu, *Formula Quotations*, 223.

12. Gnuse, "Dream Genre," 97.

13. Brown, *Birth of the Messiah*, 111-13.

parallelism and to find an example of that in a prose dream narrative we need to look to 1 Kings, but more likely the usage in Matthew was picked up from a non-dream narrative and even from poetry rather than prose. Consequently, we have suggested that the OT influence is most likely to have been of a general nature.

With regard to scholars who see Matthew as being strongly influenced by the Hellenistic world, Dodson concerns himself with the literary function of the dreams in the First Gospel and how they correspond to the script of dreams in Greco-Roman literature, concluding that Matthew's writing conforms to the expectations of Gentiles of Greco-Roman background.[14] Dodson is concerned with the audience Matthew is seeking to address, whereas I am interested in the nature of the community which may have provided Matthew with any source material for the dream narratives and, more importantly, the community which gave him a grounding in the Hebrew scriptures.

What conclusion do we reach? As far back as 1915 McNeile said of the infancy narratives that "no theory is probable which assigns a pagan origin to narratives which are Jewish to the core."[15] Various discoveries since McNeile's day, Qumran, the Palestinian Targum to the Pentateuch and apocalyptic literature, reveal that Judaism of the first century CE was a complex phenomenon. We have encountered possible evidence of this in the dream narratives. We saw, for example, in the dream chapter how the angel of the Lord shared some points of resemblance with the *oneiros* figure and this may have come to Matthew indirectly through the Hellenistic influence on the appearance of angels in Daniel. Nevertheless, the comment made by Brown in 1993 still stands that Jewish sources, such as OT, midrash and folk lore, coupled with Jesus tradition and theological reflection, are sufficient to account for Matthew's writing.[16] This theory remains valid provided that we do not create too sharp a Jewish and Greco-Roman dichotomy. The two worlds are not separate, having considerable overlap, for it was a multicultural society. The pattern of dream reporting testifies to this, as does the use of dreams in literature which is similar throughout the Mediterranean, the biblical lands and further east. As Oppenheim says of message dreams, "Accounts of this dream type are found in literary texts, from the Sumerian and Egyptian royal stelae to the Gospel of Matthew, from the Iliad to Ptolemaic Egypt, and throughout the literary products of Western civilization

---

14. Dodson, *Reading Dreams*, 227–29.
15. McNeile, *Gospel according to St. Matthew*, 23.
16. Brown, *Birth of the Messiah*, 580.

as far as the classical tradition exercised its sway."[17] As already noted, some of the evidence from memory patterns points to a multi-cultural situation. Nevertheless, the contribution of this study has been to reaffirm the Jewish background of the dream narratives. I acknowledge that this is not an entirely new discovery. However, its significance lies in striking a balance with those who, like Dodson, emphasize Greco-Roman literary conventions. I do not deny that Matthew may have been aware of these conventions. Given the multi-cultural environment in which he was living, he could easily have read Greco-Roman texts or listened to them being read. His education may also have included basic tuition in rhetoric. However, his affinity with OT in its use of memory patterns coupled with OT quotations and allusions suggests that Jewish influence was more dominant.

## The Appearance of Matthew's Dream Narratives

Beyond this conclusion, we are now able to say why Matthew's narratives appear the way they do. We have already noted that the dreams recorded in Matthew are different from the way people report their dreams today. We can now say that they came to be framed this way because of a dream structure which was widely used throughout ANE, a structure which was discerned by Oppenheim. However, there are other factors at work as well. In the Matthew chapter we established that the memory patterns which are present in his narratives. The presence of these memory aids explains why Joseph's dreams are related the way they are. Indeed we can go further and state that Matthew's dream accounts stand out from many contemporary dream narratives for the prominence of these patterns. In the final analysis we can say that Matthew narrates Joseph's dreams as he does because of the way people remembered traditions, and because of the way they expressed those memories in an oral or semi-literate culture.

## The Methodology

It is arguable that the most significant aspect of this study has been the methodology employed. I have devoted a chapter to the theory and processes, for, as far as I am aware, no one else has used memory patterns to try and establish cultural identity. The approach was grounded in social memory theory because of the way memory is formed and preserved in a social group. We recognized that it is in a social context that individuals

17. Oppenheim, "Mantic Dreams," 347.

become familiar with the rules of narrativization, which in an oral or semi-literate society would include patterns of memory. In outlining this theory we often drew directly on what the ancients themselves had to say about rhetorical devices. In a bid to establish which cultural background had a stronger influence on the formation of Matthew's dream narratives, we looked out for features which were peculiar to one particular culture and, more commonly, we took into account typical usage in OT, Jewish, and Greco-Roman writing compared to Matthew's text.

This methodology could now be applied more widely. The exercise which would come closest to the work of this study would be an examination of the memory patterns in Matthew's miracle narratives,[18] for these could be compared with what is to be found in the other gospels and we also have similar narratives in Jewish and Hellenistic literature.

We have found an abundance of memory patterns displayed in the dream narratives. In attempting a case for the oral transmission of these narratives, the use of *inclusio* in the Sermon on the Mount was also examined and found to be extensive. The whole of the First Gospel could be searched for mnemonic devices. Once found, they may enable us to make more extensive claims regarding sources for parts of the gospel beyond the dream narratives and how Matthew has handled these. This might ultimately feed into the debate with Robert MacEwen and Alan Garrow in regard to the claim that Matthew has used Luke[19] and also discussions about Matthew's level of rhetorical education.

The one gospel which displays clear evidence of an oral approach is Mark's. Dewey has drawn attention to this by showing how eleven of the thirteen scenes which are introduced in Mark 1–2 begin with the connective καί.[20] It may be worthwhile searching for memory patterns in the Second Gospel. If this search proves fruitful, a comparison could then be made in the other two Synoptics where the same event is narrated—parallel passages in the text of John could also be included. The comparison would be similar to the techniques of redaction criticism, but used to establish whether memory patterns have been preserved, abandoned, altered or added. What emerges from such examination may be able to tell us something about the preservation of oral material concerning the life of Jesus.

---

18. Kahl has already worked on the miracle stories using a form-critical approach (Kahl, *New Testament Miracle Stories*). He concludes that those in Matthew have a closer affinity with a Jewish background, while Mark's lie more closely to a Greco-Roman background.

19. MacEwen, *Matthean Posteriority*; Garrow, "Streeter's 'Other' Synoptic Solution."

20. Dewey, "Oral Methods," 32–44.

## CONCLUSION

We have noted the amount of repetition in the dream narratives. We saw verbatim repetition varying from single words through short phrases to nineteen words and also repetition of the basic structure of the three narrated dreams. Anderson has also drawn attention to the repetition to be found throughout Matthew's Gospel.[21] Birger Gerhardsson has written of the way in which the rabbis of the Tannaitic and Amoraic periods taught by requiring their students to memorize.[22] The word *mishnah* itself means *repetition* as well as *instruction*. Tannaitic rabbis may well have been around when Matthew's Gospel was produced, for they are reckoned to have flourished between 70 CE and 220 CE. Research could be done into such questions as how widespread was the use of repetition in Jewish teaching and what evidence of it can be found earlier than 70 CE. The research conducted for this study has shown that OT made more extensive use of repetition than classical literature and in Daniel, particularly in the LXX version, there is some evidence of lengthy repetition. Further research needs to be done for the first century. This in turn would lead on to issues of how likely it was that Jesus taught by repetition and with what degree of accuracy his teaching has been transmitted to us. Such research may also throw light on Matthew and any who may have supplied him with tales of Joseph's dreams, particularly whether they had connections with the rabbis.

The study of memory patterns and rhetorical devices could be pursued also by classical scholars. While they have written extensively about other aspects of the style employed by Greco-Roman authors, few have focused attention on the kind of techniques examined here.[23]

Although others have already written about the use of mnemonic devices in NT,[24] the methodology used in this study is novel. As we become ever more attuned to the ways in which people functioned in oral and semiliterate societies, there is scope for the methodology to be applied elsewhere and for new avenues to be explored.

---

21. Anderson, *Matthew's Narrative Web*.

22. Gerhardsson, *Memory and Manuscript*.

23. One of the exceptions would be Moles, *Plutarch*, 13, who notes the ring composition in Plutarch.

24. E.g., Achtemeier, "*Omne verbum sonat*," 3–27.

# Bibliography

À Lapide, Cornelius. *The Great Biblical Commentary*. Translated by Thomas W. Mossman. 4th ed. London: Hodges, 1890.
Achtemeier, Paul J. *"Omne verbum sonat:* The New Testament and the Oral Environment of Late Antiquity." *JBL* 109 (1990) 3–27.
Albl, Martin C. *"And Scripture Cannot Be Broken": The Form and Function of the Early Christian Testamonia Collections*. NovTSup 96. Leiden: Brill, 1999.
Alexander, Loveday C. A. "New Testament Narrative and Ancient Epic." In *Acts in Its Ancient Literary Context: A Classicist Looks at the Acts of the Apostles*, by Loveday C. A. Alexander, 165–82. LNTS 289. London: T. & T. Clark, 2005.
Alford, Henry. *The Four Gospels*. Vol. 1 of *Greek Testament Critical Exegetical Commentary*. 5th ed. London: Rivingtons & Deighton Beel, 1863.
Allen, Willoughby Charles. *The Gospel according to S. Matthew*. ICC. Edinburgh: T. & T. Clark, 1907.
Allison, Dale C., Jr. *The New Moses: A Matthean Typology*. Edinburgh: T. & T. Clark, 1993.
Alter, Robert. *The Art of Biblical Narrative*. 2nd ed. New York: Basic, 2011.
———. *The Art of Biblical Poetry*. 2nd ed. New York: Basic, 2011.
Anderson, Graham. *The Second Sophistic: A Cultural Phenomenon in the Roman Empire*. London: Routledge, 1993.
Anderson, Janice Capel. *Matthew's Narrative Web: Over, and Over, and Over Again*. JSNTSup. Sheffield: JSOT, 1994.
Anonymous. *Ad C. Herennium*. Libri IV. Translated by Harry Caplan. London: Heinemann, 1954.
Anonymous. *Genesis Apocryphon*. Translated by Daniel A. Machiela. Leiden: Brill, 2009.
Anonymous. *Geneva Study Bible*. 1599. Online. http://www.biblestudytools.com/commentaries/geneva-study-bible/matthew/matthew-1.html.
Anonymous. *Testament of Naphtali*. Greek. Edited by Robert Henry Charles. Oxford: Clarendon, 1908.
Anselm of Laon. *Bibliorum Sacrorum Cum Glossa Ordinaria*. Tomus Quintus. Venice, 1603.
Appian. *Punic Wars, Syrian Wars, Civil Wars*. Edited by L. Mendelssohn. Translated by Horace White. LCL. Cambridge: Harvard University Press, 1913.
Aquinas, Thomas. *Catena Aurea—Gospel of Matthew*. Translated by William Whiston. Grand Rapids: Christian Classics Ethereal Library, 1842.

Aristotle. *Parva Naturalia (including De Memoria et Reminiscentia)*. Greek text with English translation. Translated by W. S. Hett. LCL. Cambridge: Harvard University Press, 1957.

Artemidorus. *Oneirocritica*. Greek. Edited by Roger A. Pack. Leipzig: Teubner, 1963.

Aserinsky, Eugene, and Nathaniel Kleitman. "Regularly Occurring Periods of Eye Motility, and Concomitant Phenomena, During Sleep." *Science* NS 118 (1953) 273–74.

Assmann, Jan. "Ancient Egyptian Antijudaism: A Case of Distorted Memory." In *Memory Distortion*, edited by D. Schachter, 365–76. Cambridge: Harvard University Press, 1995.

———. "Collective Memory and Cultural Identity." *New German Critique* 65 (1995) 125–33.

———. *Religion and Cultural Memory*. Translated by Rodney Livingstone. Stanford: Stanford University Press, 2006.

Baddeley, Alan, et al. *Memory*. 2nd ed. New York: Psychology, 2015.

Bailey, D. R. Shackelton, ed. *Valerius Maximus: Memorable Doings and Sayings*. Translated by D. R. Shackelton Bailey. Vol. 1. Cambridge: Harvard University Press, 2000.

Bailey, Kenneth E. "Informal Controlled Oral Tradition and the Synoptic Gospels." *Asia Journal of Theology* 5 (1991) 34–51. Reprinted in *Themelios* 20 (1995) 4–11.

———. "Middle Eastern Oral Tradition and the Synoptic Gospels." *Expository Times* 106 (1995) 363–67.

Bakker, Egbert J. "The Syntax of Historie: How Herodotus Writes." In *Cambridge Companion to Herodotus*, edited by Carolyn Dewald and John Marincola, 92–102. Cambridge Companions to Literature. Cambridge: Cambridge University Press, 2006.

Bar-Ilan, Meir. "Illiteracy in the Land of Israel in the First Centuries CE." In *Essays in the Social Scientific Study of Judaism and Jewish Society*, edited by S. Fishbane, et al., 46–61. Vol. 2. New York: Ktav, 1992.

Barclay, William. *Educational Ideals in the Ancient World*. London: Collins, 1959.

Bartlett, F. C. *Remembering: A Study in Experimental and Social Psychology*. 1932. Reprint, Cambridge: Cambridge University Press, 1995.

Bauckham, Richard. "Eyewitnesses and Critical History: A Response to Jens Schröter and Craig Evans." *Journal for the Study of the New Testament* 31 (2008) 221–35.

———. "For Whom Were Gospels Written?" In *The Gospels for All Christians: Rethinking the Gospel Audiences*, edited by Richard Bauckham, 9–48. Grand Rapids: Eerdmans, 1998.

———. "In Response to My Respondents: *Jesus and the Eyewitnesses*." *Journal for the Study of the Historical Jesus* 6 (2008) 225–53.

———. *Jesus and the Eyewitnesses: The Gospels as Eye Witness Testimony*. Grand Rapids: Eerdmans, 2006.

Bäuml, Franzh. "Oral and Written Traditions in the Middle Ages." *New Literary History* 16 (1984) 31–49.

Bengel, Johann A. *Gnomon of the New Testament*. Edited by Ernest Bengel and J. C. F. Steudel. Translated by James Bandinel. Edinburgh: T. & T. Clark, 1877.

Berlin, Adele. *The Dynamics of Biblical Parallelism*. Bloomington: Indiana University Press, 1984.

Blomberg, Craig L. "Review of *The Gospels for All Christians.*" *Denver Seminary Review* 1 (1998). Online. http://www.denverseminary.edu/article/the-gospels-for-all-christians-rethinking-the-gospel-audiences.
Bloomer, W. Martin. *Valerius Maximus & the Rhetoric of the New Nobility*. London: Duckworth, 1992.
Bloomfield, S. T. *The Greek Testament with English Notes*. Vol. 1. 9th ed. London: Longman, Brown, Green, 1855.
Boomershine, Thomas E. "Audience Address and Purpose in the Performance of Mark." In *Mark as Story: Retrospect and Prospect*, edited by Kelly R. Iverson and Christopher W. Skinner, 115–42. Atlanta: Society of Biblical Literature, 2011.
———. "Jesus of Nazareth and the Watershed of Ancient Orality and Literacy." *Semeia* 65 (1994) 7–36.
Bornkamm, Günther. *Jesus of Nazareth*. Translated by Irene and Fraser McLuskey, with James M. Robinson. London: Hodder & Stoughton, 1960.
Brayford, Susan. *Genesis*. Septuagint Commentary Series. Leiden: Brill, 2007.
Brodersen, Kai. "Appian." In *The Oxford Companion to Classical Civilization*, edited by Simon Hornblower, et al., 59. 2nd ed. Oxford: Oxford University Press, 2014.
Brown, Raymond E. *The Birth of the Messiah: Commentary on the Infancy Narratives in the Gospels of Matthew and Luke*. Updated ed. New York: Doubleday, 1993.
Bultmann, Rudolf. *Jesus and the Word*. Translated by Louise P. Smith and Erminie H. Lantero. New York: Scribner, 1934.
Burridge, Richard A. "About People, By People, For People: Gospel Genre and Audiences." In *The Gospels for All Christians: Rethinking the Gospel Audiences*, edited by Richard Bauckham, 113–46. Grand Rapids: Eerdmans, 1998.
———. *What are the Gospels?: A Comparison with Graeco-Roman Biography*. 2nd ed. Cambridge: Cambridge University Press, 2004.
Buttrick, George A. "Matthew: Exposition." In *The Interpreter's Bible*, edited by George Arthur Buttrick, 7:250–62. New York: Abingdon, 1951.
Byrskog, Samuel. *Story as History—History as Story: The Gospel Tradition in the Context of Ancient Oral History*. WUNT 123. Tübingen: Mohr/Siebeck, 2000.
Calvin, John. *Commentary on a Harmony of the Evangelists*. Translated by William Pringle. Grand Rapids: Christian Classics Ethereal Library, 1845.
Carter, Warren. "Matthew 1–2 and Roman Political Power" In *New Perspectives on the Nativity*, edited by Jeremy Corley, 77–90. New York: T. & T. Clark, 2009.
———. *Matthew and Empire: Initial Explorations*. Harrisburg, PA: Trinity, 2001.
———. *Matthew: Storyteller, Interpreter, Evangelist*. Peabody, MA: Hendrickson, 1996.
Cayton, Mary Kupiec. "Review of Michel de Certeau's *The Writing of History*." *Church History* 62 (1993) 454–55.
Chariton. *Chaereas and Callirhoe*. Edited by Rudolf Hercher. Leipzig: Teubner, 1859.
Charles, R. H.. *The Greek Versions of the Testaments of the Twelve Patriarchs*. 1908. Reprint, Eugene, OR: Wipf & Stock, 2008.
Cicero. *De Inventione*. Translated by H. M. Hubbell. LCL. London: Heinemann, 1968.
———. *De Oratore*. Translated by E. W. Sutton and H. Rackham. Vol. 2. LCL. London: Heinemann, 1939.
Clarke, Adam. *Commentary on the Whole Bible*. 1810–1826. Online. http://www.studylight.org/com/acc/view.cgi?book=mt.
Coleman, Janet. *Ancient and Medieval Memories*. Cambridge: Cambridge University Press, 1992.

Cooper, Alan. "Two Recent Works on the Structure of Biblical Hebrew Poetry." *Journal of the American Oriental Society* 110 (1990) 687–90.
Costa, Desmond. *Lucian: Selected Dialogues Translated with an Introduction and Notes.* Oxford: Oxford University Press, 2005.
Cousin, Jean. *Études sur Quintilien.* Vol. 1. Paris: Boivin, 1936.
Cribiore, Raffaella. *Gymnastics of the Mind: Greek Education in Hellenistic and Roman Egypt.* Princeton: Princeton University Press, 2005.
Daube, David. "The Earliest Structure of the Gospels." *NTS* 5 (1959) 174–87.
Davies, W. D., and Dale C. Allison, Jr. *A Critical and Exegetical Commentary on the Gospel according to Saint Matthew.* Vols. 1 and 3. ICC. Edinburgh: T. & T. Clark, 1988.
Davis, Casey Wayne. *Oral Biblical Criticism: The Influence of the Principles of Orality on the Literary Structure of Paul's Epistle to the Philippians.* JSNTSup 172. Sheffield: Sheffield Academic, 1999.
Davis, Charles Thomas. "Tradition and Redaction in Matthew 1:18—2:23." *JBL* 90 (1971) 404–21.
De Certeau, Michel. *The Writing of History.* Translated by Tom Conley. New York: Columbia University Press, 1988.
Dewey, Joanna. "Mark as Interwoven Tapestry: Forecasts and Echoes for a Listening Audience." *Catholic Biblical Quarterly* 53 (1994) 221–36
———. "Oral Methods of Structuring Narrative in Mark." *Interpretation* 43 (1989) 32–44.
———. "Textuality in An Oral Culture: A Survey of the Pauline Traditions." *Semeia* 65 (1994) 37–65.
Diodorus Siculus. *Bibliotheca Historica.* Translated by C. H. Oldfather, et al. Vols. 4–8. LCL. Cambridge: Harvard University Press, 1989.
Diogenes Laertius. *Lives of Eminent Philosophers.* Edited and translated by R. D. Hicks. LCL. Cambridge: Harvard University Press, 1925.
Dionysius Halicarnassus. *Antiquitatum Romanarum quae supersunt.* Translated by Earnest Carey. Vols. 1–4. LCL. Cambridge, MA: Harvard University Press, 1937–40.
Dodds, E. R. *The Greeks and the Irrational.* Berkeley: University Press of California, 1951.
Dodson, Derek S. "Reading Dreams: An Audience Critical Approach to the Dreams in the Gospel of Matthew." PhD diss., Baylor University, 2006. https://beardocs.baylor.edu/handle/2104/5006.
Dunn, James D. G. *Jesus Remembered: Christianity in the Making.* Vol. 1. Grand Rapids: Eerdmans, 2003.
———. "Kenneth Bailey's Theory of Oral Tradition: Critiquing Theodore Weeden's Critique." *JSHJ* (2009) 44–62.
———. *A New Perspective on Jesus: What the Quest for the Historical Jesus Missed.* Grand Rapids: Baker Academic, 2005.
———. "On History, Memory and Eyewitnesses." *JSNT* 26 (2004) 473–87.
Edwards, Catherine. *Lives of the Caesars / Suetonius.* Oxford: Oxford University Press, 2000.
Edwards, Richard A. *Matthew's Story of Jesus.* Philadelphia: Fortress, 1985.
Enslin, Morton S. "The Christian Stories of the Nativity." *JBL* 59 (1940) 317–38.

Erll, Astrid. "Cultural Memory Studies: Introduction." In *Media and Cultural Memory* 8, edited by Astrid Erll and Ansgar Nünning, in collaboration with Sara B. Young, 1–18. New York: de Gruyter, 2008.

———. "Literature, Film, and the Mediality of Cultural Memory." In *Media and Cultural Memory* 8, edited by Astrid Erll and Ansgar Nünning, in collaboration with Sara B. Young, 389–98. New York: de Gruyter, 2008.

Eve, Eric. *Behind the Gospels: Understanding the Oral Tradition.* London: SPCK, 2013.

———. "Orality Is no Dead-End." *JSHJ* 13 (2015) 3–23.

———. *Writing the Gospels: Composition and Memory.* London: SPCK, 2016.

Farrar, Frederic W. *Life of Christ.* Vol. 1. 1874. Online. http://www.preteristarchive.com/Books/1874_farrar_christ_index.html.

Farris, Stephen. *The Hymns of Luke's Infancy Narratives.* New York: Bloombury Academic, 2015.

Feld, Steven. "Wept Thoughts: The Voicing of Kaluli Memories." In *South Pacific Oral Traditions*, edited by Ruth Finnegan and Margaret Orbell, 85–108. Voices in Performance and Text. Indianapolis: Indiana University Press, 1995.

Feldman, Louis H. *Flavius Josephus: Judean Antiquities 1–4: Translation and Commentary.* Vol. 3. Leiden: Brill, 2000.

Fentress, James, and Chris Wickham. *Social Memory.* Oxford: Blackwell, 1992.

Finkelberg, Margalit. "Elitist Orality and the Triviality of Writing." In *Politics of Orality*, edited by Craig Cooper, 293–306. Mnemosyne 280. Leiden: Brill, 2007.

Finnegan, Ruth. *Oral Literature in Africa.* Rev. ed. Cambridge: Open Book, 2012.

———. *Oral Poetry: Its Nature, Significance, and Social Context.* Cambridge: Cambridge University Press, 1977.

Flannery-Dailey, Frances. *Dreamers, Scribes, and Priests: Jewish Dreams in the Hellenistic and Roman Eras.* JSJSup 90. Leiden: Brill, 2004.

Flory, A. Stewart. *The Archaic Smile of Herodotus.* Detroit: Wayne State University Press, 1987.

Fohrer, Georg, ed. *Hebrew and Aramaic Dictionary of the Old Testament.* Translated by W. Johnstone. London: SCM, 1973.

Foley, John Miles. *The Singer of Tales in Performance.* Indianapolis: Indiana University Press, 1995.

———. "What's in a Sign?" In *Signs of Orality: The Oral Tradition and Its Influence in the Greek and Roman World*, edited by E. Anne Mackay, 1–27. Mnemosyne 188. Leiden: Brill, 1999.

———. "Words in Tradition, Words in Text." *Semeia* 65 (1994) 169–177.

Ford, Andrew. "From Letters to Literature: Reading the 'Song Culture' of Classical Greece." In *Written Texts and the Rise of Literate Culture in Ancient Greece*, edited by Harvey Yunis, 15–37. Cambridge: Cambridge University Press, 2003.

Foster, Paul. "Memory, Orality, and the Fourth Gospel: Three Dead-Ends in Historical Jesus Research." *JSHJ* 10 (2012) 191–227.

Fox, Matthew, and Niall Livingstone. "Rhetoric and Historiography." In *A Companion to Greek Rhetoric*, edited by Ian Worthington, 542–561. Blackwell Companions to the Ancient World. Malden, MA: Blackwell, 2007.

France, R. T. *Matthew.* TNTC. Leicester: InterVarsity, 1985.

Frenschkowski, Marco. "Traum und Traumdeutung im Matthäusevangelium: Einige Beobachtungen." *JAC* 41 (1998) 5–47.

Fuller, Lois K. "The 'Genitive Absolute' in New Testament/Hellenistic Greek: A Proposal for Clearer Understanding." *Journal of Graeco-Roman Christianity and Judaism* 3 (2006) 142–67.

Gamble, Harry Y. *Books and Readers in the Early Church: A History of Early Christian Texts*. New Haven: Yale University Press, 1995.

Gargarin, Michael. "The Orality of Greek Oratory." In *Signs of Orality: The Oral Tradition and Its Influence in the Greek and Roman World*, edited by E. Anne Mackay, 163–80. Mnemosyne 188. Leiden: Brill, 1999.

Garrow, Alan. "Streeter's 'Other' Synoptic Solution: The Matthew Conflator Hypothesis." *NTS* 62 (2016) 207–226.

Gedi, Noa, and Yigal Elam. "Collective Memory—What Is It?" *History and Memory* 8 (1996) 30–50.

Gerhardsson, Birger. *Memory and Manuscript: Oral Tradition and Written Transmission in Rabbinic Judaism and Early Christianity*. Lund: Gleerup, 1961.

Gibbs, Jeffrey. *Concordia Commentary on Matthew 1:1–11:1*. St. Louis: Concordia, 2006.

Gignac, Francis Thomas. *A Grammar of the Greek Papyri of the Roman and Byzantine Periods*. Vols. 1–2. Milano: Istituto Editoriale Cisalpino-La Goliardica, 1976–81.

Gill, John. *Exposition of the Bible*. 1746–48. Online. http://www.biblestudytools.com/commentaries/gills-exposition-of-the-bible/matthew.

Gilliard, Frank D. "More Silent Reading in Antiquity: *Non Omne Verbum Sonabat*." *JBL* 112 (1993) 689–94.

Gleaves, G. Scott. *Did Jesus Speak Greek?: The Emerging Evidence of Greek Dominance in First-Century Palestine*. Eugene, OR: Pickwick, 2015.

Gnuse, Robert Karl. *Dreams and Dream Reports in the Writings of Josephus: A Traditio-Historical Analysis*. Arbeiten zur Geschichte des antiken Judentums und des Urchristentums 36. Leiden: Brill, 1996.

———. "Dream Genre in the Matthean Infancy Narratives." *NovT* 32 (1990) 97–120.

Goffman, Erving. *Frame Analysis: An Essay on the Organization of Experience*. New York: Harper & Row, 1974.

Goodwin, Philip. *The Mystery of Dreames, Historically Discoursed*. London: A. M. for Francis Tyton, 1658.

Gowing, Alain M. *Empire and Memory*. New York: Cambridge University Press, 2005.

Gowler, David B. Review of *A New Perspective on Jesus*. *CBQ* 68 (2006) 141–42.

Grant, Robert, and David Tracy. *A Short History of the Interpretation of the Bible*. 2nd ed. Philadelphia: Fortress, 1984.

Green, H. Benedict. *Matthew, Poet of the Beatitudes*. JSNTSup 203. Sheffield: Sheffield University Press, 2001.

Griffiths, Alan. "Stories and Storytelling in the Histories." In *Cambridge Companion to Herodotus*, edited by Carolyn Dewald and John Marincola, 130–44. Cambridge Companions to Literature. Cambridge: Cambridge University Press, 2006.

Grotius, Hugo. *Annotations on the New Testament*. Vol. 1. 1641–44. Online. http://www.preteristarchive.com/StudyArchive/g/grotius-hugo.html.

Grubber, Mayer I. "The Meaning of Biblical Parallelism: A Biblical Perspective." *Prooftexts* 13 (1993) 289–93.

Gundry, Robert H. *Matthew: A Commentary on his Literary and Theological Art*. Grand Rapids: Eerdmans, 1982.

Hagner, Donald A. *Matthew 1–13*. WBC 33A. Dallas: Word, 1993.

Halbwachs, Maurice. *On Collective Memory.* Translated by Lewis A. Coser. Chicago: University Press of Chicago, 1992.

Halverson, John. "*Oral and Written Gospel:* A Critique of Werner Kelber." *NTS* 40 (1994) 180–95.

Hammond, N. G. L., and H. H. Scullard, eds. *The Oxford Classical Dictionary.* 2nd ed. Oxford: Oxford University Press, 1970.

Hanson, John S. "Dreams and Visions in the Graeco-Roman World and Early Christianity." In *ANRW* 2/23.2 (1980) 1395–427.

Harrington, Daniel J. *The Gospel of Matthew.* Sacra Pagina 1. Collegeville, MN: Liturgical, 1991.

Harris. William V. *Ancient Literacy.* Cambridge: Harvard University Press, 1989.

———. *Dreams and Experience in Classical Antiquity.* Cambridge: Harvard University Press, 2009.

Harrison, Juliette Grace. "Cultural Memory and Imagination: Dreams and Dreaming in the Roman Empire 31 BC—AD 200." PhD diss., University of Birmingham, 2009. http://www.etheses.bham.ac.uk/469.

Havelock, Eric A. *Preface to Plato.* Oxford: Blackwell, 1963.

Haydock, George Leo. *Catholic Bible Commentary.* 1859. Online. http://haydock1859.tripod.com.

Hearon, Holly E. "From Narrative to Performance: Methodological Considerations and Interpretive Moves." In *Mark as Story: Retrospect and Prospect*, edited by Kelly R. Iverson and Christopher W. Skinner, 211–32. Atlanta: Society of Biblical Literature, 2011.

Hengel, Martin. *The 'Hellenization' of Judaea in the First Century after Christ.* Translated by John Bowden. London: SCM, 1989.

———. *Judaism and Hellenism: Studies in their Encounter in Palestine during the early Hellenistic Period.* Vol. 1. Translated by John Bowden. London: SCM, 1974.

Henrichs, Albert. "Writing Religion: Inscribed Texts, Ritual Authority, and the Religious Discourse of the Polis." In *Written Texts and the Rise of Literate Culture in Ancient Greece*, edited by Harvey Yunis, 38–58. Cambridge: Cambridge University Press, 2003.

Henry, Matthew. *Matthew to John* Vol. 5 of *Commentary on the Whole Bible.* Grand Rapids: Christian Classics Ethereal Library, 1708–1710.

Herodotus. *Histories.* Translated by G. C. Macaulay. New York: Macmillan, 1890.

Hezser, Catherine. *Jewish Literacy in Roman Palestine.* TSAJ 81. Tübingen: Mohr/Siebeck, 2001.

———. "Private and Public Education." In *The Oxford Handbook of Jewish Daily Life in Roman Palestine*, edited by Catherine Hezser, 466–79. Oxford Handbooks in Classics and Ancient History. Oxford: Oxford University Press, 2010.

Hilgard, Ernest R., et al. *Atkinson and Hilgard's Introduction to Psychology.* 6th ed. New York: Harcourt Brace Jovanovich, 1975.

Homer. *Iliad.* Edited by D. B. Oxford: Clarendon, 1884–1897.

———. *Odyssey.* Edited by W. B. Stanford. London: MacMillan, 1967.

Howatson, M. C., ed. *The Oxford Companion to Classical Literature.* 3rd ed. Oxford: Oxford University Press, 2011.

Humphrey, J. H., ed. *Literacy in the Roman World.* Journal of Roman Archaeology Supplementary Series 3. Ann Arbor: Journal of Roman Archaeology, 1991.

Hurtado, Larry W. "Greco-Roman Textuality and the Gospel of Mark: A Critical Assessment of Werner Kelber's *The Oral and the Written Gospel*." *Bulletin for Biblical Research* 7 (1997) 91–106.

———. "Oral Fixation and New Testament Studies? 'Orality,' 'Performance,' and Reading Texts in Early Christianity." *NTS* 60 (2014) 321–40.

Husser, Jean-Marie. *Dreams and Dream Narratives in the Biblical World*. Translated by Jill M. Munro. BibSem 73. Sheffield: Sheffield Academic, 1999.

Hymes, Dell. "Ways of Speaking." In *Explorations in the Ethnography of Speaking*, edited by Richard Bauman and Joel Sherzer, 433–51, 473–74. 2nd ed. Studies in the Social and Cultural Foundations of Language 8. Cambridge: Cambridge University Press, 1989.

Iverson, Kelly R. "Orality and the Gospels: A Survey of Recent Research." *Currents in Biblical Research* 8.1 (2009) 71–106.

Jacobson, Howard. *A Commentary on Pseudo-Philo's Liber Antiquitatum Biblicarum*. Vol. 1. Arbeiten zur Geschichte des antiken Judentums und des Urchristentums 31. Leiden: Brill, 1996.

———, ed. and trans. *The Exagoge of Ezekiel*. Cambridge: Cambridge University Press, 1983.

Jaffee, Martin S. "Writing and Rabbinic Oral Tradition: On Mishnaic Narrative, Lists and Mnemonics." *Journal of Jewish Thought and Philosophy* 4 (1995) 123–46.

Jamieson, Robert et al. *Commentary Critical and Explanatory on the Whole Bible*. 1871. Online. http://www.biblestudytools.com/commentaries/jamieson-fausset-brown/matthew/matthew.html.

Jevons, F. B. "Dreams." In *A Dictionary of the Bible*, edited by James Hastings, 1:622–23. Edinburgh: T. & T. Clark.

Johnson, Sherman E. *Matthew Exegesis*. In *The Interpreter's Bible*. Vol. 7. New York: Abingdon, 1951.

Josephus. *Antiquitates Judaicae*. Edited by B. Niese. Greek. Berlin: Weidmann, 1892.

———. *The Complete Works*. Translated by William Whitson. 1895. Reprint, Nashville: Nelson, 1998.

———. *De Bello Judaico*. Edited by B. Niese. Greek. Berlin: Weidmann, 1895.

———. *Josephi Vita*. Edited by B. Niese. Greek. Berlin: Weidmann, 1890.

Jousse, Marcel. *Le Parlant, la Parole, et le Souffle*. Paris: Gallimard, 1978.

Kahl, Werner. *New Testament Miracle Stories in their Religious-Historical Setting: A Religionsgeschichtliche Comparison from a Structural Perspective*. FRLANT 163. Göttingen: Vandenhoeck & Ruprecht, 1994.

Kee, Howard Clark. "Matthew." In *The Interpreter's One-Volume Commentary on the Bible*, edited by Charles M. Layman, 609–612. New York: Abingdon, 1971.

———, trans. "Testaments of the Twelve Patriarchs: A New Translation and Introduction." In *The Old Testament Pseudepigrapha*, edited by James H. Charlesworth, 1:775–81. New York: Doubleday, 1983.

Keith, Chris. *Jesus's Literacy: Scribal Culture and the Teacher from Galilee*. London: T. & T. Clark, 2011.

Kelber, Werner H. "Jesus and Tradition: Words in Time, Words in Space." *Semeia* 65 (1994) 139–67.

———. "*The Oral and the Written Gospel*: Fourteen Years Afterward." In *Imprints, Voiceprints and Footprints of Memory*, edited by Werner H. Kelber, 167–86. Atlanta: Society of Biblical Literature, 2013.

———. *The Oral and the Written Gospel: The Hermeneutics of Speaking and Writing in the Synoptic Tradition, Mark, Paul, and Q.* Philadelphia: Fortress, 1983.
Kennedy, George A. *The Art of Persuasion in Greece.* London: Routledge & Kegan Paul, 1963.
———. *Classical Rhetoric and its Christian and Secular Tradition from Ancient to Modern Times.* Chapel Hill: University Press of North Carolina, 1980.
———. *New Testament Interpretation through Rhetorical Criticism.* Chapel Hill: University Press of North Carolina, 1984.
———. *Progymnasmata: Greek Textbooks of Prose Composition and Rhetoric.* Atlanta: Society of Biblical Literature, 2003.
Kilpatrick, G. D. *The Origins of the Gospel according to St. Matthew.* Oxford: Clarendon, 1946.
Kingsbury, Jack Dean. *Matthew as Story.* Philadelphia: Fortress, 1986.
Kinney, Robert S. *Hellenistic Dimensions of the Gospel of Matthew: Background and Rhetoric.* WUNT 2/414. Tübingen: Mohr/Siebeck, 2016.
Kirk, Alan. "Review of *Memory, Jesus and the Synoptic Gospels*." *Review of Biblical Literature* 15 (2013) 307.
———. "Social and Cultural Memory." In *Memory, Tradition, and Text: Uses of the Past in Early Christianity*, edited by A. Kirk and T. Thatcher, 1–24. SBL Semeia Studies 52. Atlanta: Society of Biblical Literature, 2005.
Kirk, Alan, and Tom Thatcher. "Jesus Tradition as Social Memory." In *Memory, Tradition, and Text: Uses of the Past in Early Christianity*, edited by A. Kirk and T. Thatcher, 25–42. SBL Semeia Studies 52. Atlanta: Society of Biblical Literature, 2005.
Knox, Wilfred L. *Some Hellenistic Elements in Primitive Christianity.* London: Oxford University Press, 1944.
———. *The Sources of the Synoptic Gospels.* Cambridge: Cambridge University Press, 1957.
Koet, Bart J. "Review of *The Dreams of Matthew 1:18—2:23: Tradition, Form, and Theological Investigation*." *Review of Biblical Literature* 67.1 (2015) 1–5.
Kugel, James L. "A Feeling of Déjà Lu." *JR* 67 (1987) 66–79.
Kümmel, Werner Georg. *Introduction to the New Testament.* London: SCM, 1965.
Lambrecht, Jan. *The Sermon on the Mount.* GNS 14. Wilmington, DE: Michael Glazier, 1985.
Landy, Francis. "Recent Developments in Biblical Poetics." *Prooftexts* 7 (1987) 163–78.
Lang, Mabel L. *Herodotean Narrative and Discourse.* Cambridge: Oberlin College by Harvard University Press, 1984.
Lange, Johann Peter. *Theologisch-homiletisches Bibelwerk.* Translated by Philip Schaff. New York: Scribners, 1865.
Le Donne, Anthony. *Historical Jesus.* Cambridge: Eerdmans, 2011.
———. *The Historiographical Jesus.* Waco, TX: Baylor University Press, 2009.
Lee, Margaret Ellen, and Bernard Brandon Scott. *Sound Mapping the New Testament.* Salem, OR: Polebridge, 2009.
Lewis, Charlton T., and Charles Short. *A Latin Dictionary.* Oxford: Oxford University Press, 1879.
Liddell, H. G., et al. *A Greek-English Lexicon.* 9th ed. Oxford: Oxford University Press, 1968.

Lightfoot, John. *Commentary on the Gospels*. 1859. Online. http://www.preteristarchive.com/Books/1658_lightfoot_talmud-hebraica.html.
Locke, John. *An Essay Concerning Human Understanding*. London: Mory, 1690.
Lohr, Charles H. "Oral Techniques in the Gospel of Matthew." *CBQ* 23 (1961) 403–435.
Longus. *Daphnis et Chloe*. Edited by Rudolf Hercher. Greek. Leipzig: Teubner, 1858.
Lord, Albert B. *The Singer of Tales*. Cambridge: Harvard University Press, 1960.
Lounsbury, Richard C. *The Arts of Suetonius: An Introduction*. New York: Lang, 1987.
Lucian. *De morte Peregrini*. Edited by A. M. Harmon. Translated by F. G. Fowler and H. W. Fowler. Cambridge: Harvard University Press, 1936. http://www.sacred-texts.com/cla/luc/wl4/wl420.htm.
Luraghi, Nino. "Meta-*historie*: Method and Genre in the *Histories*." In *Cambridge Companion to Herodotus*, edited by Carolyn Dewald and John Marincola, 76–91. Cambridge Companions to Literature. Cambridge: Cambridge University Press, 2006.
Luz, Ulrich. *A Commentary on Matthew 1–7 and 21–28*. Translated by James E. Crouch. Hermeneia. Minneapolis: Fortress, 2007.
MacEwen, Robert K. *Matthean Posteriority: An Exploration of Matthew's Use of Mark and Luke as a Solution to the Synoptic Problem*. LNTS 501. London: Bloomsbury T. & T. Clark, 2015.
Machiela, Daniel A. *The Dead Sea Genesis Apocryphon: A New Text and Translation with Introduction and Special Treatment of Columns 13–17*. STDJ 79. Leiden: Brill, 2009.
Mack, Burton L. *A Myth of Innocence: Mark and Christian Origins*. Philadelphia: Fortress, 1988.
Maldonado, Juan. *St. Matthew's Gospel, Chapters I to XIV*. Vol. 1 of *A Commentary on the Holy Gospels*. Translated by George J. Davie. 2nd ed. London: John Hodges, 1888.
Malina, Bruce J. "The Literary Structure and Form of Matthew 28:16–20." *NTS* 17 (1970) 87–103.
Marincola, John. "Herodotus and the Poetry of the Past." In *Cambridge Companion to Herodotus*, edited by Carolyn Dewald and John Marincola, 13–28. Cambridge Companions to Literature. Cambridge: Cambridge University Press, 2006.
Marrou, H.-I. *Histoire de l'Éducation dans l'Antiquité*. 6th rev. ed. Paris: Seuil, 1995.
Martzavou, Paraskevi. "Dream, Narrative, and the Construction of Hope in the 'Healing Miracles' of Epidauros." In *Unveiling Emotions: Sources and Methods for the Study of Emotions in the Greek World*, edited by Angelos Chaniotis, 177–204. Heidelberger althistorische Beiträge und epigraphische Studien 52. Stuttgart: Steiner, 2012.
Mason, Steve. *Josephus and the New Testament*. Peabody, MA: Hendrickson, 1992.
———. *Judean War 2: Translation and Commentary*. Vol. 1b of *Flavius Josephus*. Leiden: Brill, 2008.
McCail, Ronald. *Longus: Daphnis and Chloe: A New Translation*. Oxford: Oxford University Press, 2002.
McGing, Brian C. *Polybius's Histories*. Oxford: Oxford University Press, 2010.
McIver, Robert K. *Memory, Jesus, and the Synoptic Gospels*. Atlanta: Society of Biblical Literature, 2011.
McKnight, Scot. "Review of *Matthew's Narrative Web*." *JBL* 115 (1996) 141–43.

McNeile, Alan Hugh. *The Gospel According to St. Matthew: The Greek Text with Introduction, Notes, and Indices.* London: MacMillan, 1915.
Meier, Carl Alfred. "The Dream in Ancient Greece and Its Use in Temple Cures (Incubation)." In *The Dream and Human Societies*, edited by G. E. von Grunebaum and Roger Caillois, 303–320. Berkeley: University Press of California, 1966.
Meier, John P. *Matthew.* NTM. Dublin: Veritas, 1980.
Metzger, Bruce M. *A Textual Commentary on the Greek New Testament.* London: United Bible Societies, 1971.
Meyer, E., ed. *Pausanias: Beshchreibung Griechelands.* Zürich: Artemis, 1954.
Meyer, Heinrich. *Matthew.* Vols. 1–2 of *Kritisch-exegetischer Kommentar zum Neuen Testament.* Edited by Frederick Crombie and William Stewart. Translated by Peter Christie. 6th ed. New York: Funk & Wagnalls, 1884.
Miller, George A. *Psychology: The Science of Mental Life.* Harmondsworth, UK: Penguin, 1977.
Moles, J. L. *Plutarch: The Life of Cicero, with an Introduction, Translation, and Commentary.* Warminster, UK: Aris & Phillips, 1988.
Moore, Stephen D. *Literary Criticism and the Gospels: The Theoretical Challenge.* New Haven: Yale University Press, 1989.
Morgan, Teresa. *Literate Education in the Hellenistic and Roman Worlds.* Cambridge Classical Studies. Cambridge: Cambridge University Press, 1998.
———. "Rhetoric and Education." In *A Companion to Greek Rhetoric*, edited by Ian Worthington, 303–319. Blackwell Companions to the Ancient World. Malden, MA: Blackwell, 2007.
Moseley, Nicholas. "Pius Aeneas." *Classical Journal* 20 (1925) 387–400.
Moulton, R. G. *The Literary Study of the Bible.* London: Isbister, 1896.
Murray, Oswyn. *Early Greece.* Sussex, UK: Harvester, 1980.
———. "Herodotus and Oral History." In *The Greek Sources: Proceedings of the Groningen 1984 Achaemenid History Workshop*, edited by Heleen Sancisi-Weerdenburg and Amélie Kuhrt, 16–44. Vol. 2 of *Achaemeid History.* Leiden: Nederlands Instituut voor het Nabije Oosten, 1987.
Mussies, G. "Parallels to Matthew's Version of the Pedigree of Jesus." *NovT* 28 (1986) 32–47.
Neill, Stephen. *The Interpretation of the New Testament 1861–1961.* London: Oxford University Press, 1964.
Nicholas of Lyra. *Postillae Perpetuae in Universam Sanctam Scripturam.* Rome: n.p., 1471.
Nicholson, E. W. *Jeremiah 26–52.* Cambridge Bible Commentary. Cambridge: Cambridge University Press, 1975.
Nimis, Stephen A. "Ring-Composition and Linearity in Homer." In *Signs of Orality: The Oral Tradition and Its Influence in the Greek and Roman World*, edited by E. Anne Mackay, 65–78. Mnemosyne 188. Leiden: Brill, 1999.
Noegel, Scott B. "Review of Flannery-Dailey's *Dreamers, Scribes, and Priests: Jewish Dreams in the Hellenistic and Roman Eras.*" *JHS* 5 (2005). Online. http://www.jhsonline.org/reviews/review202.htm.
Nora, Pierre. *Realms of Memory: Rethinking the French Past.* New York: Columbia University Press, 1996.

Oakley, S. P. "Style and Language." In *The Cambridge Companion to Tacitus*, edited by A. J. Woodman, 195–211. Cambridge Companions to Literature. Cambridge: Cambridge University Press, 2009.

O'Connor, M. *Hebrew Verse Structure*. Winona Lake, IN: Eisenbrauns, 1980.

Olsen, Mari Broman. "The Koine Greek Verb: Tense and Aspect." Paper presented at Byzantine and Modern Greek Studies: The Next Wave, Fourth Interdisciplinary Conference, Ohio State University, October 1994.

Olshausen, Hermann. *Kommentar über sämmtliche Schriften des Neuen Testaments*. Translated by H. B. Creak. 4th ed. Edinburgh: T. & T. Clark, 1871.

Ong, Walter J. *Orality and Literacy: The Technologizing of the Word*. New York: Methuen, 1982.

Oppenheim, A. Leo. "The Interpretation of Dreams in the Ancient Near East." *Transactions of the American Philosophical Society* 46 (1956) 179–373.

———. "Mantic Dreams in the Ancient Near East." In *The Dream and Human Societies*, edited by G. E. von Grunebaum and Roger Caillois, 341–50. Berkeley: University Press of California, 1966.

Papanikolaou, A. D. *Chariton-Studien: Untersuchungen zur Sprache und Chronologie der griechischen Romane*. Hypomnemata 37. Göttingen: Vandenhoeck & Ruprecht, 1973.

Parker, Pierson. *The Gospel before Mark*. London: Cambridge University Press, 1953.

Parry, Milman. *The Making of Homeric Verse*. Oxford: Clarendon, 1971.

Pausanias. *Hellados Periegesis*. Translated by W. H. S. Jones. Loeb. Cambridge: Harvard University Press, 1918–35.

Pearce, T. E. V. "Epic Regression in Herodotus." *Eranos* 79 (1981) 87–90.

Perrin, Bernadotte. *Plutarch's Lives, with an English Translation*. London: Heinemann, 1914.

Philo. *De Somniis: I–II*. Translated by F. H. Colson and G. H. Whitaker. Vol. 5. LCL. Cambridge: Harvard University Press, 1934.

———. *De Vita Mosis: I*. Translated by F. H. Colson. Vol. 6. LCL. Cambridge: Harvard University Press, 1935.

Philostratus the Athenian. *Vita Apollonii*. Edited by Carl Ludwig Kayser. Translated by F. C. Conybeare. New York: MacMillan, 1912.

Pillemer, David B. *Momentous Events, Vivid Memories*. Cambridge: Harvard University Press, 1998.

Pizzuto, Vincent A. "The Structural Elegance of Matthew 1–2: A Chiastic Proposal." *CBQ* 74 (2012) 712–37.

Plato. *Theaetetus*. Translated by Harold N. Fowler. Loeb. Cambridge: Harvard University Press, 1921.

Plummer, Alfred. *An Exegetical Commentary on the Gospel according to S. Matthew*. London: Stock, 1909.

Plutarch. *Parallel Lives*. Edited and translated by Bernadotte Perrin. Vols. 2–4, 7–9. LCL. London: Heinemann, 1914–26.

Polybius. *Histories*. Translated by Evelyn S. Shuckburgh. New York: Macmillan, 1889.

———. *Histories*. Edited by Theodorus Büttner-Wobst after L. Dindorf. Leipzig: Teubner, 1893.

Poole, Matthew. *Annotations upon the Holy Bible*. Vol. 3. New York: Carter, 1852.

Porter, Stanley E. "Did Jesus Ever Teach In Greek?" *TynBul* 44 (1993) 199–235.

Poulakos, Takis. *Speaking for the Polis: Isocrates's Rhetorical Education.* Columbia: University Press of South Carolina, 1997.
Powell, Mark Allan. "Narrative Criticism: The Emergence of a Prominent Reading Strategy." In *Mark as Story: Retrospect and Prospect*, edited by Kelly R. Iverson and Christopher W. Skinner, 19–43. Atlanta: Society of Biblical Literature, 2011.
Prabhu, George M. Soares. *The Formula Quotations in the Infancy Narratives of Matthew.* Analecta Biblica 63. Rome: Biblical Institute, 1976.
Pretzler, Maria. "Pausanias and Oral Tradition." *Classical Quarterly* 55 (2005) 235–49.
Pseudo-Philo. *Liber Antiquitatum Biblicarum.* Translated by M. R. James. London: n.p., 1917. Online. http://www.sacredtexts.com/bib/bap/index.htm.
Pula, James S. "Tadeusz Kościuszko: A Case Study in Constructed Historical Symbolism." *Polish Review* 53 (2008) 159–82.
Quintilian. *Institutio Oratoria.* Translated by H. E. Butler. LCL. London: Heinemann, 1921.
Rawlinson, Graham E. "Reibadailty." *New Scientist* 162 (1999) 55.
Rawson, E. *Intellectual Life in the Late Roman Republic.* London: Duckworth, 1985.
Redman, Judith C. S. "How Accurate Are Eyewitnesses? Bauckham and the Eyewitnesses in the Light of Psychological Research." *JBL* 129 (2010) 177–97.
Reimarus, Hermann Samuel. *Fragments.* Translated and edited by Charles Voysey. London: Williams & Northgate, 1879.
Renan, Ernest. *Vie de Jésus.* Translated by William G. Hutchison. London: Scott, 1897.
Robbins, Vernon K. "Oral, Rhetorical and Literary Cultures." *Semeia* 65 (1994) 75–91.
———. "Rhetoric and Culture: Exploring Types of Cultural Rhetoric in a Text." In *Rhetoric and the New Testament: Essays for the 1992 Heidelberg Conference*, edited by Stanley E. Porter and Thomas H. Olbrict, 443–63. JSNTSup 90. Sheffield: JSOT, 1993.
Robinson, Bernard P. "Matthew's Nativity Stories: Historical and Theological Questions for Today's Readers." In *New Perspectives on the Nativity*, edited by Jeremy Corley, 110–31. New York: T. & T. Clark, 2009.
Robinson, T. H. *Matthew.* Moffatt New Testament Commentary. London: Hodder & Stoughton, 1928.
Rodríguez, Rafael. *Oral Tradition and the New Testament: A Guide for the Perplexed.* Guides for the Perplexed. London: Bloomsbury, 2014.
———. *Structuring Early Christian Memory: Jesus in Tradition, Performance, and Text.* LNTS 407. London: T. & T. Clark, 2010.
Rose, H. J. *A Handbook of Greek Literature.* London: Methuen., 1960.
Rose, Steven. *The Future of the Brain: The Promise and Peril of Tomorrow's Neuroscience.* Oxford: Oxford University Press, 2005.
Rubin, David C. *Memory in Oral Traditions: The Cognitive Psychology of Epic, Ballads, and Counting-out Rhymes.* Oxford: Oxford University Press, 1995.
Ruge-Jones, Philip. Review of Werner H. Kelber and Samuel Byrskog, eds., *Jesus in Memory: Traditions in Oral and Scribal Perspectives.* *CBQ* 73 (2011) 666.
Sale, W. Merritt. "Homer and Avdo: Investigating Orality through External Consistency." In *Voice into Text: Orality and Literacy in Ancient Greece*, edited by Ian Worthington, 21–42. Mnemosyne 157. Leiden: Brill, 1996.
Schmitz, Thomas A. "Plutarch and the Second Sophistic." In *A Companion to Plutarch*, edited by Mark Beck, 32–42. Blackwell Companions to the Ancient World: Literature and Culture. Malden, MA: Wiley Blackwell, 2014.

Schröter, Jens. "The Gospels as Eyewitness Testimony? A Critical Examination of Richard Bauckham's *Jesus and the Eyewitnesses*." *JSNT* 31 (2008) 195–209.

———. "Jesus and the Canon: The Early Jesus Traditions in the Context of the Origins of the New Testament Canon." In *Performing the Gospel: Orality, Memory, and Mark*, edited by Richard A. Horsley et al., 104–146. Minneapolis: Fortress, 2006.

Schudson, Michael. "Dynamics of Distortion in Collective Memory." In *Memory Distortion: How Minds, Brains, and Societies Reconstruct the Past*, edited by David L. Schacter, 346–64. Cambridge: Harvard University Press, 1995.

Schwartz, Barry. "Where There's Smoke, There's Fire: Memory and History." In *Memory and Identity in Ancient Judaism and Early Christianity: A Conversation with Barry Schwartz*, edited by Tom Thatcher, 7–37. Semeia Studies 78. Atlanta: Society of Biblical Literature, 2014.

Schweizer, Eduard. *The Good News according to Matthew*. Translated by David E. Green. London: SPCK, 1975.

Scodel, Ruth. "Social Memory in Aeschylus's Oresteia." In *Orality, Literacy, and Memory in the Ancient Greek and Roman World: Orality and Literacy in Ancient Greece*, edited by E. Anne Mackay, 115–41. Leiden: Brill, 2008.

Scott, Bernard Brandon. "Blowing in the Wind." *Semeia* 65 (1994) 181–91.

Scott, Thomas. *The Holy Bible, Containing the Old and New Testaments According to the Authorized Version; with Explanatory notes, Practical Observations, and Copious Marginal References*. New York: Dodge & Sayre, 1816.

Simonetti, Manlio, ed. *Ancient Christian Commentary on Scripture: Matthew 1–13*. Downers Grove, IL: InterVarsity, 2001.

Slusser, Michael. "Reading Silently in Antiquity." *JBL* 111 (1992) 499.

Small, Jocelyn Penny. *Wax Tablets of the Mind: Cognitive Studies of Memory and Literacy in Classical Antiquity*. London: Routledge, 1997.

Smith, Edward E., et al. *Atkinson and Hilgard's Introduction to Psychology*. 14th ed. Belmont, CA: Wadsworth/Thomson Learning, 2003.

Smith, Southwood. "Lectures on Forensic Medicine." *London Medical Gazette*, January 20, 1838.

Spence, Jonathan D. *The Memory Palace of Matteo Ricci*. London: Faber & Faber, 1984.

Stanford, W. B. *Commentary on The Odyssey of Homer*. Vol. 1. London: MacMillan, 1967.

Stendahl, Krister. "Matthew." In *Peake's Commentary on the Bible*, edited by Matthew Black and H. H. Rowley, 769–72. Sunbury-on-Thames, Middlesex: Nelson, 1962.

———. "Quis et Unde? An Analysis of Matthew 1–2." In *Judentum, Urchristentum, Kirche*, edited by Walther Eltester, 94–105. Berlin: Töpelmann, 1960.

Strauss, David. *Das Leben Jesu*. Translated by George Eliot. 2nd ed. London: Swan Sonnenschein, 1892.

Subash, William J. *The Dreams of Matthew 1:18–2:23: Tradition, Form, and Theological Investigation*. Studies in Biblical Literature 149. New York: Lang, 2012.

Suetonius. *De Vita Caesarum*. Translated by Alexander Thomson. Philadelphia: Gebbie, 1889.

Tacitus. *Annales*. Edited by Charles Dennis Fisher. Oxford: Clarendon, 1906.

———. *Annales*. Translated by Alfred John Church and William Jackson Brodribb. London: Macmillan, 1895.

———. *Historiae*. Edited by Charles Dennis Fisher. Oxford: Clarendon, 1911.

———. *Historiae*. Translated by Alfred John Church and William Jackson Brodribb. London: Macmillan, 1873.
Talbert, Charles H. *Matthew*. Paideia Commentaries on the New Testament. Grand Rapids: Baker Academic, 2010.
Tarrant, Harold. "Orality and Plato's Narrative Dialogues." *Voice into Text: Orality and Literacy in Ancient Greece*, edited by Ian Worthington, 129–47. Mnemosyne 157. Leiden: Brill, 1996.
Taylor, Vincent. *The Formation of the Gospel Tradition*. London: MacMillan, 1933.
Teffeteller, Annette. "Orality and the Politics of Scholarship." In *Politics of Orality*, edited by Craig Cooper, 67–86. Mnemosyne 280. Leiden: Brill, 2007.
Thackeray, H. St. J., trans. *The Jewish Antiquities, Books I–IV*. Vol. 4 of *Josephus*. London: Heinemann, 1930.
———. *The Jewish War, Books I–III*. Vol. 2 of *Josephus*. London: Heinemann, 1927.
Thatcher, Tom. "Why John Wrote a Gospel: Memory and History in an Early Christian Community." In *Memory, Tradition, and Text: Uses of the Past in Early Christianity*, edited by Alan Kirk and Tom Thatcher, 79–97. SBL Semeia Studies 52. Atlanta: Society of Biblical Literature, 2005.
Thomas, Rosalind. "Herodotus's Histories and the Floating Gap." In *The Historian's Craft in the Age of Herodotus*, edited by Nino Luraghi, 198–210. New York: Oxford University Press, 2001.
———. *Literacy and Orality in Ancient Greece*. Key Themes in Ancient History. Cambridge: Cambridge University Press, 1992.
———. *Oral Tradition and Written Record in Classical Athens*. Cambridge Studies in Oral and Literate Culture 18. Cambridge: Cambridge University Press, 1989.
———. "Prose Performance Texts: Epideixis and Written Publication in the Late Fifth and Early Fourth Centuries." In *Written Texts and the Rise of Literate Culture in Ancient Greece*, edited by Harvey Yunis, 162–88. Cambridge: Cambridge University Press, 2003.
Thurén, Lauri. "On Studying Ethical Argumentation and Persuasion in the New Testament." In *Rhetoric and the New Testament: Essays for the 1992 Heidelberg Conference*, edited by Stanley E. Porter and Thomas H. Olbricht, 464–78. JSNTSup 90. Sheffield: JSOT, 1993.
Tilg, Stefan. *Chariton of Aphrodisias and the Invention of the Greek Love Novel*. Oxford: Oxford University Press, 2010.
Turner, Paul. *Daphne & Chloe—Longus: A New Translation with an Introduction*. Harmondsworth, UK: Penguin, 1956.
———. *Penguin Classics Introduction to Daphnis and Chloe by Longus*. London: Penguin, 1989.
Valerius Maximus. *Factorum ac dictorum memorabilium libri IX*. Edited and translated by D. R. Shackleton Bailey. LCL. Cambridge: Harvard University Press, 2000.
Van der Stockt, Luc. "Compositional Methods in the Lives." In *A Companion to Plutarch*, edited by Mark Beck, 321–32. Blackwell Companions to the Ancient World: Literature and Culture. Malden, MA: Wiley Blackwell, 2014.
Vansina, Jan. *Oral Tradition as History*. Wisconsin: University Press of Wisconsin, 1985.
———. *Oral Tradition: A Study in Historical Methodology*. 2nd ed. Translated by H. M. Wright. New Brunswick, NJ: Transaction, 2006.
Verdegen, Simon. *Plutarch's Life of Alcibiades: Story, Text, and Moralism*. Plutarchea Hypomnemata. Leuven: Leuven University Press, 2010.

Viljoen, Francois P. "The Significance of Dreams and the Star in Matthew's Infancy Narrative." *Hervormde Teologiese Studies* 64 (2008) 845–60.
Wagar, W. Warren. "Review of Michel de Certeau's 'The Writing of History.'" *American Historical Review* 95 (1990) 452–53.
Wainwright, Elaine M. "Review of *Matthew's Narrative Web*." *CBQ* 58 (1996) 146–47.
Walker, Norman. "The Alleged Matthean Errata." *NTS* 9 (1963) 391–94.
Walsh, John A. "The Dream of Joseph: A Jungian Interpretation." *Journal of Psychology & Theology* 11 (1983) 20–27.
Wansbrough, Henry. "The Infancy Stories of the Gospels since Raymond E. Brown." In *New Perspectives on the Nativity*, edited by Jeremy Corley, 4–22. London: T. & T. Clark, 2009.
Watson, Francis. *Gospel Writing: A Canonical Perspective*. Grand Rapids: Eerdmans, 2013.
Watson, J. S. *Cicero on Oratory and Orators*. Carbondale: Southern Illinois University Press, 1986.
Watson, Wilfred G. E. *Classical Hebrew Poetry: A Guide to its Techniques*. JSOTSup 26. Sheffield: JSOT, 1984.
Webb, Ruth. "Rhetoric and the Novel: Sex, Lies and Sophistic." In *A Companion to Greek Rhetoric*, edited by Ian Worthington, 526–41. Blackwell Companions to the Ancient World. Malden, MA: Blackwell, 2007.
Weeden, Theodore J. "Kenneth Bailey's *Theory of Oral Tradition*: A Theory Contested by Its *Evidence*." *JSHJ* 7 (2009) 3–43.
Weldon, Mary Susan. "Remembering as a Social Process." In *The Psychology of Learning and Motivation: Advances in Research and Theory*, edited by Douglas L. Medin, 67–120. San Diego: Academic, 2000.
Weldon, Mary Susan, and Krystal D. Bellinger. "Collective Memory: Collaborative and Individual Processes in Remembering." *Journal of Experimental Psychology: Learning, Memory, and Cognition* 23 (1997) 1160–75.
Wesley, John. *Notes on the Whole Bible*. 1754–65. Online. http://www.biblestudytools.com/commentaries/wesleys-explanatory-notes.
Whibley, Leonard, ed. *A Companion to Greek Studies*. New York: Hafner, 1968.
White, Robert J. *The Interpretation of Dreams: Oneirocrotica by Artemidorus: Translation and Commentary*. Park Ridge, NJ: Noyes, 1975.
Williams, James D., ed. *An Introduction to Classical Rhetoric: Essential Readings*. Malden, MA: Wiley-Blackwell, 2009.
Willis, John T. "The Juxtaposition of Synonymous and Chiastic Parallelism in Tricola in Old Testament Hebrew Psalm Poetry." *VT* 29 (1979) 465–80.
Wordsworth, Christopher. *New Testament of LSJC in Original Greek with Notes*. London: Rivingtons, 1856.
Worthington, Ian. "Greek Oratory and the Oral/Literate Division." In *Voice into Text: Orality and Literacy in Ancient Greece*, edited by Ian Worthington, 165–77. Mnemosyne 157. Leiden: Brill, 1996.
Wright, D. S., et al. *Introducing Psychology: An Experimental Approach*. Harmondsworth, UK: Penguin, 1972.
Yates, Frances A. *The Art of Memory*. Chicago: University of Chicago Press, 1966.
Yerushalmi, Yosef Hayim. *Zakhor*. Seattle: University Press of Washington, 1983.

Yunis, Harvey. "Why Written Text?" In *Written Texts and the Rise of Literate Culture in Ancient Greece*, edited by Harvey Yunis, 1–14. Cambridge: Cambridge University Press, 2003.

Zerubavel, Y. "The Historical, the Legendary and the Incredible: Invented Tradition and Collective Memory in Israel." In *Commemorations: The Politics of National Identity*, edited by J. R. Gill, 105–125. Princeton: Princeton University Press, 1995.

# Author Index

Achtemeier, Paul J, 37n154, 41–43, 41n175, 42n178, 82, 82n18, 87n42, 229n24
Alford, Henry, 108n41
Allen, Willoughby Charles, 33, 33n136
Allison, Dale C., Jr., 4n11, 82n19, 85, 85n32, 92, 92n72, 104n25, 116, 116n84, 117, 117n86, 117n88, 117n89, 128n58, 209n338
Alter, Robert, 91, 91n68, 91n69, 92, 92n70, 92n71, 141, 141n98, 141n99, 141n102, 155, 155n38, 172, 172n143, 210, 211
Anderson, Graham, 199n291
Anderson, Janice Capel, 31, 31n130, 87, 87n47, 107n40, 129n61, 134, 134n79, 135n80, 229, 229n21
Aquinas, Thomas, 103n16
Assmann, Jan, 48, 64–66, 64n72, 64n73, 65n74, 65n75, 65n76, 66n77, 68, 72, 75

Baddeley, Alan, 60, 60n58, 61n59, 61n61, 84n26
Bailey, Kenneth E., 57n49, 73–75, 73n115, 74n116, 74n117, 74n119, 74n120, 74n122, 184
Bakker, Egbert J., 176, 176n150, 176n151, 177, 177n167
Bar-Ilan, Meir, 11n1
Bartlett, F. C., 60–61, 60n56
Bauckham, Richard, 48, 67–69, 67n87, 68n88, 68n91, 68n92, 69, 69n93, 74, 74n118, 75

Bengel, Johann A., 142, 142n105
Berlin, Adele, 90, 90n62
Bloomer, W. Martin, 184n209, 184n211
Boomershine, Thomas E., 14, 14n19, 14n25, 14n26, 15n27, 15n31
Brayford, Susan, 150n15, 151, 151n16, 151n17, 154n37
Brown, Raymond E., 3–4, 3n7, 3n8, 4n10, 28, 28n117, 28n118, 41n173, 71, 71n102, 71n103, 71n104, 72, 103, 103n20, 116, 116n83, 164n85, 168n111, 225, 225n13, 226, 226n16
Burridge, Richard A., 120, 120n2, 121n3, 121n4
Byrskog, Samuel, 24n87, 24n90, 40, 40n168

Coleman, Janet, 49n2, 49n4, 50n11
Cousin, Jean, 94n84
Cribiore, Raffaella, 44n184, 79n8

Davies, W. D. & Dale C. Allison, Jr., 2n4, 28n119, 90, 90n57, 90n59, 103, 103n22, 104n25, 107, 121n8, 122n13, 122n14, 122n16, 122n17, 123n25, 123n26, 124, 124n28, 124n29, 124n32, 124n33, 127n54, 141, 141n100
Davis, Casey Wayne, 13n11, 13n12
Dewey, Joanna, 13n17, 14n20, 15n31, 29, 29n120, 37n151, 39n162, 41, 42, 228, 228n20
Dodds, E. R., 100, 100n3

## AUTHOR INDEX

Dodson, Derek S., ix, 3, 3n7, 5–9, 5n21, 6n22, 7n31, 8n34, 8n35, 106, 106n36, 148, 148n9, 177n162, 225n10, 226, 226n14, 227
Dunn, James D.G., 39n162, 48, 57–58, 57n46, 57n47, 57n49, 66–67, 67n81–86, 68, 69–70, 69n94, 70n95, 73, 74, 74n117, 75

Edwards, Catherine, 193, 193n263
Edwards, Richard A., 129n62
Enslin, Morton S., 27, 28n116
Erll, Astrid, 54n36, 55n41, 66, 66n78
Eve, Eric, 15, 15n33, 15n34, 52n24, 55, 55n39, 57n46, 57n49, 59n52, 63, 63n70, 74, 74n121, 83n25, 121, 121n10

Farris, Stephen, 96n90
Feld, Steven, 15n31, 19, 19n60
Feldman, Louis H., 162n75, 166n101
Fentress, James and Chris Wickham, 62n66, 84n30
Finnegan, Ruth, 15n31, 16, 16n36, 16n40, 19, 19n57, 19n58, 21n71, 30–31, 31n126, 213, 213n363–6
Flannery-Dailey, Frances, 7n28, 101n9, 102n14–5, 106n37, 109n46, 111, 111n60, 112, 112n62, 113n69, 113n72, 114n73, 114n75, 115, 115n79–80, 216n374
Foley, John Miles, 40–41, 40n171, 41n172, 52n25, 147, 147n2–5
Foster, Paul, 15, 15n32, 73n114
Fox, Matthew and Niall Livingstone, 45n194, 45n197–8, 180n182, 181n190, 182n192, 195n276
France, R. T., 2n16, 62n68, 117n86–7, 122n13, 124n27, 124n33, 127n55, 225n9
Fuller, Lois K., 34n140, 107n38, 132n75

Gamble, Harry Y., 11n1
Garrow, Alan, 123n23, 228, 228n19
Gedi, Noa and Yigal Elam, 55n40
Gerhardsson, Birger, 22, 22n74–75, 229, 229n22

Gibbs, Jeffrey, 118, 118n90, 122n13, 122n15, 123n22, 127n55
Gill, John, 103, 103n19
Gilliard, Frank D., 42n178
Gnuse, Robert Karl, 3, 3n7, 4–5, 4n13, 5n16, 33, 33n137, 38, 38n158, 101n9, 105–6, 105n30–31, 105n33, 109n50, 110, 110n54, 163n76, 164n 86–7, 214–15, 215n371, 225, 225n12
Goffman, Erving, 85, 85n37
Green, H. Benedict, 22n78
Griffiths, Alan, 24, 24n92–3, 28, 31, 31n131, 32
Gundry, Robert H., 122n13, 122n16, 123n22, 123n24, 127n56, 141, 141n101

Hagner, Donald A., 103, 103n21, 120n1, 122n13, 122n16, 123n24–5, 127n56
Halbwachs, Maurice, 56, 56n43–4, 63, 64, 65, 84n29
Hanson, John S., 6, 6n23, 6n26, 101n9, 106, 106n35
Harrington, Daniel J., 122n13–14, 123n25, 124n33
Harris. William V., 11n1, 70, 70n97, 70n100, 84, 84n29, 100, 100n2, 101n7, 101n9
Harrison, Juliette Grace, 72–73, 72n107–8, 73n113
Havelock, Eric A., 82n17
Hengel, Martin, 1, 1n1, 122–23, 123n19, 212, 212n357, 223
Hezser, Catherine, 11n1, 14, 14n21, 125, 125n37, 126–27, 127n52
Hilgard, Ernest R., et al., 53n26, 53n29–30, 54n33, 130n68–9
Husser, Jean-Marie, 106n37, 109, 109n44, 109n49, 110n55–6, 111n57, 111n59, 112, 112n63, 112n66–7, 114n77
Hymes, Dell, 147, 147n2

Jacobson, Howard, 95n85, 168n110
Jaffee, Martin S., 13, 13n16, 14, 14n22
Jousse, Marcel, 82n17

Kahl, Werner, 228n18
Kee, Howard Clark, 170n123
Keith, Chris, 14n25, 57n46
Kelber, Werner H., 13, 13n14, 15,
    15n30–31, 20, 20n61, 22,
    22n72–73, 59, 59n53
Kennedy, George A., 1n2, 22, 22n77,
    45n195–96, 47n204, 80n11–12,
    81n15, 82, 82n21, 83, 83n22,
    94n77, 121n12, 125, 125n36,
    125n38, 126n45, 126n51,
    127n53, 130, 130n71, 225n10
Kingsbury, Jack Dean, 142n104
Kinney, Robert S., 1n2, 121, 121n9,
    122n18, 123n20, 126, 126n47,
    126n50, 225n10
Kirk, Alan, 57n46, 58, 58n51
Knox, Wilfred L., 27, 27n115
Kugel, James L., 90, 90n61, 91n63,
    92, 92n70, 139, 139n94, 141,
    141n98, 210
Kümmel, W. G., 123n23

Lambrecht, Jan, 37, 37n152
Landy, Francis, 90, 90n62, 91n64
Lange, Johann Peter, 115
à Lapide, Cornelius, 115, 115n78
Le Donne, Anthony, 57, 57n46, 57n48,
    58, 59n54, 63, 63n69, 85n34–35
Lee, Margaret Ellen and Bernard
    Brandon Scott, 11n2, 13n13,
    13n18, 27n112, 46n203, 129–33,
    129n64, 130n72–3, 132n74
Locke, John, 66, 66n79
Lord, Albert B., 15n31, 17–19, 17n44,
    18n49–50, 18n54, 20, 20n62,
    21, 21n68, 22, 30n124, 31, 42,
    70, 86, 98, 98n106, 137, 137n85,
    147, 147n1
Luraghi, Nino, 23n83–4, 23n86, 24,
    24n91, 24n94, 25, 25n97
Luz, Ulrich, 31, 31n127–8, 32, 31n132,
    88, 88n49, 90, 90n58, 121,
    121n4–5, 122n13–4, 122n16,
    123, 123n24, 124n27, 138,
    138n92, 163n75

MacEwen, Robert K., 123n23, 228,
    228n19
Machiela, Daniel A., 171n129
Mack, Burton L. 95, 95n87
Maldonato, Juan, 103, 103n18
Marincola, John, 22n76
Marrou, H.-I., 125n37
Mason, Steven N., 160n58, 167n109
McCail, Ronald, 200, 200n307, 201,
    201n309
McGing, Brian C., 180, 180n183
McIver, Robert K., 18, 18n52, 62n67
McNeile, Alan Hugh, 226, 226n15
Meier, Carl Alfred, 102n11
Metzger, Bruce, 38n157, 134n78,
    173n145
Meyer, E., 26n107
Miller, George A., 54n32, 54n35, 54n37
Moles, J. L., 36n149, 190n244, 191,
    191n250, 229n23
Morgan, Teresa, 45n191, 79n8, 125,
    125n35, 125n37
Moseley, Nicholas, 29n121
Moulton, R. G., 89n52

Nicholson, E. W., 118n91
Noegel, Scott B., 102n14
Nora, Pierre, 56, 56n45

Oakley, S. P., 186, 186n224, 186n228
O'Connor, Michael, 90, 90n
Olsen, Mari Broman, 107n40
Ong, Walter J., 12, 12n5, 12n8, 16,
    16n35, 16n37, 18n53, 40n166,
    42, 42n201, 81–82, 81n16,
    82n17, 83, 87n42, 178n169
Oppenheim, A. Leo, 8n33, 70n96,
    101–6, 101n8, 101n10, 104n27,
    105n28–9, 105n32, 108, 109n45,
    109n47, 110n55, 112, 113,
    114n74–6, 119, 131, 144, 212,
    213n358, 226, 227, 227n17

Papanikolaou, A. D., 198n282
Parry, Milman, 15n31, 17–19, 17n44–5,
    17n48, 20, 20n64, 21, 22, 29, 30,
    30n124, 31, 42, 86, 88n50, 137
Perrin, Bernadotte, 190n241–42

Pillemer, David B., 61, 61n62, 62, 62n65
Pizzuto, Vincent A., 41, 41n174, 63–4n71, 134, 134n77, 142, 142n103, 142n105–6
Plummer, Alfred, 103, 104n23
Porter, Stanley E., 63n71
Prabhu, George M. Soares, 3, 3n7, 4–5, 4n12, 33, 33n138, 214, 214n370, 225, 225n11
Pretzler, Maria, 25n102, 26, 26n107–110
Pula, James S., 86, 86n40–1

Rawlinson, Graham E., 53n28
Rawson, E., 125n37
Redman, Judith C.S., 53n27, 68n90
Robbins, Vernon K., 12, 12n6, 15, 15n28–9, 95, 95n86–87
Rodríguez, Rafael, 16, 16n38–39, 39–40, 39n161–64, 40n169–70, 57n46, 58, 58n51
Rose, H.J., 45n192–93, 80n13
Rose, Steven, 62, 62n67
Rubin, David C., 84, 84n28, 130, 130n66–67

Schmitz, Thomas A., 36n148, 191, 191n248–9, 221n382
Schröter, Jens, 57n46, 58, 58n50, 68n89
Schudson, Michael, 59–60, 59n55, 61, 61n63, 62n64, 149n14
Schwartz, Barry, 55, 55n42, 58, 85–86, 85n36–38, 86n39
Schweizer, Eduard, 122n16, 123n25, 127n55
Slusser, Michael, 42n178
Small, Jocelyn Penny, 50n14, 51n18, 52n23
Smith, Edward E., 53n26, 53n29–30, 54n33, 130n68–9
Smith, Southwood, 71, 71n105, 72n106

Stanford, W.B., 137n87
Stendahl, Krister, 104, 104n24
Strauss, David, 40, 40n165, 40n167

Talbert, Charles H., 2n4, 37, 37n152–53, 38n155–56, 121n11, 122n17, 126n46, 127n54, 142n104, 225n10
Teffeteller, Annette, 17n42, 20–21, 20n63, 20n65–6, 21n67, 29, 30, 30n123–4, 88n50, 137, 137n86
Thackeray, H. St. J., 161n62–3, 161n65
Thatcher, Tom, 57n46, 58–59, 58n51
Thomas, Rosalind, 15n31, 18, 18n55, 19n56, 29n122, 31, 31n129
Tilg, Stefan, 198, 198n282
Turner, Paul, 200–201, 201n308, 201n310

Vansina, Jan, 213, 213n359–62
Verdegen, Simon, 191n250

Walsh, John A., 100n5
Watson, Francis, 123n23
Watson, J.S., 79n3
Watson, Wilfred G. E., 87, 87n45, 89, 89n51–53
Webb, Ruth, 45, 46n200, 196, 196n277–8, 198, 198n281, 199n291
Weeden, Theodore J., 74, 74n120, 74n122
Weldon, Mary Susan, 68n90
White, Robert J., 203n312, 206n331–2
Williams, James D., 43, 43n179–80
Worthington, Ian, 34, 34n141–2, 38, 38n159, 39, 39n160, 177n166

Yates, Frances A., 50n8

Zerubavel, Y., 85n34

# Subject Index

alliteration, ix, 9, 42, 83, 86–87, 95–97, 119, 133, 144, 146, 149–52, 157, 163, 165, 165n96, 174, 187–89, 191, 195–96, 202, 206–7, 213, 215, 218–19

anaphora, 82, 87, 87n43, 96, 96n92, 97, 133, 144, 146, 157, 174, 187–88, 196, 202, 207, 215, 218–19

antithesis, 78, 80n11, 87, 93–94, 97–99, 133, 144–47, 153, 157, 166–70, 172n137, 173–75, 177–78, 180–82, 185–86, 186n228, 187–89, 191, 194–96, 198–99, 201–2, 205–8, 208n334, 208n337, 213–14, 214n367, 215, 217–21, 223

Apocrypha, 110, 148, 156–58

artificial memory, 19n59, 50, 52, 79, 83

art of rhetoric, 46, 184

Asiatic style, 45, 80

assonance, ix, 9, 83, 87, 95–96, 98, 133, 144, 146, 149–51, 157, 165, 175, 185–88, 193, 195–96, 198, 202, 206–7, 213, 215, 218, 220

Atticism, 45, 198, 198n282

Atticistic, 161, 167

authorship, 123, 123n22, 124n33

biblical register, 92, 148, 156, 174, 217, 224, 225

chiasmus, 35, 37, 41, 89, 142–46, 152–53, 158, 175, 178, 185, 187–88, 193, 196, 202, 205–7, 215, 218, 220

classification of dreams, 101–4

collective memory, 48, 52, 55–59, 55n38, 64, 65, 68n91–92, 84n29, 85, 86

cultural background, ix, 1, 2, 2n6, 9, 43, 46, 86, 90, 95n87, 96, 98n105, 99, 122, 135, 145, 186, 203, 207, 209, 212–13, 217, 224, 228, see also cultural setting

cultural imagination, 72–73

cultural leanings, 40, 99, 169, 198, 214

cultural memory, 48, 64–66, 71–73, 75, 76

cultural setting, ix, 43, 77, see also cultural background

cultural traditions, 1, 65

culturally specific, ix, 9, 78, 96, 98, 99, 210, 219

culture, 1, 7, 12, 13, 14, 15, 16, 19, 44, 46, 54n37, 60n57, 95, 95n87, 97, 98, 99, 123, 126n51, 149, 175, 219, 222, 225, 227, 228

Dead Sea Scrolls, 170, see also Qumran Scrolls

definition of memory patterns, 81–86

divine self-identification, 4, 106, 163

dream books, 101n10, 109

Epic of Gilgamesh, 109, 109n45

extensive repetition, 152, 152n20, 155–56, 166–67, 174, 186, 191, 195, 212, 216, 217, 225

folklore, 24, 32, see also folktale

## SUBJECT INDEX

folktale, 24, 31, see also folklore
formulaic expression, 17–18, 20–21, 24, 28–29, 33, 39, 41, 77, 79, 81, 86, 97–98, 133, 137–38, 143–47, 152–54, 165, 175–78, 188, 196, 202, 207, 209, 212, 216, 220, 223

genitive absolute, 6, 34n140, 107, 107n38, 132n75
genre, 17, 17n43, 19, 106n37, 120–21, 123, 144, 191, 212, 221–22
Greco-Roman, 6, 8, 15, 21, 25, 46, 90–93, 95, 99, 106, 108n43, 121, 125–26, 141, 144–45, 175, 196, 208, 217–19, 222, 226–28, 228n18, 229

Hellenism, 1, 7, 99, 122, 123, 149, 210, 212. 221, 223, 225
Hellenistic audience, ix, 163n76
Hellenistic culture, 7, 9, 123, 158, 160, 221
Hellenistic influence, 1, 6, 126, 152, 156, 187, 222, 225–26
Hellenistic Judaism, 7, 106n37, 115
historicity, 69–70, 76
Homeric, 12, 17–20, 22, 31, 82n17, 111, 119, 129n63, 137, 147, 212

illiterate, 11, 13, 14
image, ix, 9, 59n54, 62n64, 62n66, 84, 85, 86, 133
inclusio, 30, 33–35, 36n147, 37, 37n154, 38, 38n156, 39, 39n162, 81–82, 86–87, 89–90, 97–99, 131, 133, 134–35, 143–47, 149–54, 157–58, 162–63, 167–69, 171–79, 181, 185–88, 190–91, 194–96, 199, 202, 205–7, 209–10, 210n343, 212–20, 220n380, 221, 223, 228, see also ring composition
incubation, 8, 113–14, 114n73, 114n75, 115, 119, 222
individual memory 48, 52–54, 56, 57, 59, 64, 66, 67–68
infancy narratives 3, 4, 4n11, 29, 33, 36, 38, 48, 64, 65, 69–70, 71–73, 76, 115, 116n84, 127–28, 135, 164, 168, 208, 221, 224 226
intermingling of Judaism and Hellenism 1, 149, 212, 223

Jewish
  background, 9, 117, 119, 224, 227, 228n18
  influence ,25, 119, 210, 211, 222, 227
Judaism, 1, 7, 99, 106n37, 115, 122, 123, 149, 210, 212, 221, 223, 226

keying, 85–86, 118–19
key word, 28, 31, 39, 67, 87, 88–89, 98, 138–39, 143, 144–46, 152–54, 157–58, 160, 162, 166–67, 169–70, 172, 172n141, 173–76, 178, 182, 185–86, 188, 196, 202, 204, 207, 209–10, 212–13, 215–16, 218–20, 220n380, 223

literacy, 9, 11n1, 12–14, 14n25, 15, 40, 43, 82n17
  levels of, 9, 11n1, 14; see also literate
literary
  convention, 5, 7, 8, 227
  practice, ix, 1, 1n2, 41, 146, 157, 221
  style, 38, 161, 167
literate, 11n1, 12–14, 16, 29, 45–46, 52, 125
  literate culture, 14, 227; see also literacy
LXX, xii, 2, 2n3, 107n39, 108n41, 124, 127n57, 148n8, 149–51, 152, 152n23–4, 152n26, 153n35–6, 154, 155, 156, 157, 157n40, 158, 159, 159n52, 162, 162n75, 166n101, 167n109, 216n372, 218, 222, 224, 224n6, 229; see also Septuagint

Matthew's source, ix, 27, 63, 214
memorization, 11, 46, 83, 88
memory
  device, 46, 77, 78–81, 157, 216;
  distortion, 48, 53n29, 59–64

pattern, ix, 9, 25, 35, 40–41, 46, 48,
    54–55, 73, 75–78, 81–86, 86–94,
    95, 96, 97, 98, 99, 103, 107, 108,
    110, 118, 119, 120, 133–44, 145,
    146–221, 223, 225, 227, 228, 229
technique, 156, 174, 215, 216
message dreams, 7, 62, 70, 70n96,
    70n100, 102, 103, 106, 106n37,
    108, 110–11, 111n58, 114n76,
    119, 129, 138, 155, 165, 171,
    177, 181, 216, 226
methodology x, 9, 60, 76, 77–99,
    110n52, 118, 133, 138, 141,
    141n99, 146–47, 155, 159n54,
    206, 208n335, 208n337, 209–10,
    210n345, 227–29
mnemonic purpose, 43, 46, 48, 52, 80
Moses, 4, 25, 27, 32, 32n132, 41, 65,
    70n101, 73, 82n19, 92, 97n104,
    115–16, 116n85, 117–19, 123,
    127, 127n58, 141, 164, 209n338,
    214, 221, 223–24, 224n7
multi-cultural, 99, 145, 223, 227

numerical aids, 144, 152, 158, 165, 175,
    188, 196, 202, 207, 215, 218, 220

oneiros, 7, 7n28–9, 89, 113, 209n339,
    226
onomatopoeia, 144, 152, 158, 175, 188,
    196, 202, 207, 215, 218, 220
oral
    oral communication, 15, 16, 30,
        40, 81
    oral composition, 16, 17–20, 21, 29,
        34, 42, 46, 137
    oral culture, 13, 16, 16n37
    oral-derived text, 201
    oral performance, 16, 30, 67, 81
    oral tradition, 15, 19, 22, 24, 25, 26,
        31, 39, 41n172, 52, 57, 59, 66,
        67, 73, 74, 75, 82n17, 88
    oral societies, ix, 9, 16, 17, 22,
        129n65, 213
    oral transmission, 15, 16, 19, 20–21,
        28, 30, 31, 32, 38, 39, 41, 46, 48,
        59, 66, 67, 73, 75, 76, 81, 88, 108,
        136, 144, 161, 162, 180, 201,
        203, 206, 228
orality, x, 9, 10, 11–47, esp. 15–16,
    86, 125, 137, 201

parallelism, 20, 21, 24, 28, 30–31, 33,
    39, 41, 46, 77, 81, 82, 87, 88n50,
    90–93, 97–99, 133, 139–47,
    149–50, 152–56, 158, 172–75,
    177–79, 185–86, 186n228, 187–
    91, 195–98, 200–202, 206–7,
    209–21, 223, 226
pattern of dream reports, 104–8
premeditated, 17, 17n42, 18n50, 19, 20,
    21, 137,
Pseudepigrapha, 110

quest for the historical Jesus, 48, 66–69,
    75
Qumran Scrolls, 1, 14, 110, 122; *see also*
    Dead Sea Scrolls

register, 41, 92, 147–48, 156, 174, 217,
    224–25
repetition, 18, 20, 21, 24, 28–30, 33, 36,
    38–39, 39n162, 41, 42, 46, 77,
    78, 80–81, 86–89, 96n89, 98,
    107, 111, 119, 126n48, 129–30,
    132–33, 135–38, 143, 145–47,
    149–50, 152, 152n20, 153,
    153n36, 155–57, 160, 162, 164–
    71, 171n129, 172–74, 177–87,
    190–92, 194–95, 197–201, 204–
    6, 209, 211–14, 216–17, 219–21,
    223, 225, 229
rhetoric, 9, 10, 43–46, 50–51, 79n4,
    95n87, 96, 99, 121, 125–26,
    180–81, 182n192, 183–84, 208,
    217, 227
rhetorical devices, 40, 41–43, 77, 79,
    81, 147, 151, 161–63, 175, 180,
    183, 193–94, 196, 198, 200, 201,
    203, 203n312, 204, 208, 220,
    228–29
rhetorical education, 44–45, 120,
    125–26, 201, 228
rhythm, ix, 9, 44, 83, 133, 155, 210

## SUBJECT INDEX

ring composition, 33, 34, 34n141, 35, 36, 39, 89, 97, 177, 177n166, 178, 191, 229n23, see also inclusio

schema/schemata, 53n29, 60–61, 61n60, 83–84, 84n27, 86, 89, 104, 118
   schema-based error, 53n29, 60–61, 84n27
script, 60–61, 84, 84n29, 86, 104, 112, 119, 146, 226
semantic parallelism, 91–93, 99, 140–41, 141n99, 143, 147, 155, 172–74, 206–7, 211, 213–14, 216, 219, 221
semi-literate, ix, 9, 12, 17, 26, 48, 82, 213, 227
semi-literate societies, ix, 9, 17, 213
Semitic background, 141, 224
Septuagint, xii, 2, 8, 116, 148, 149–51, 159, 208, see also LXX
social memory, 48, 55–59, 62n66, 64, 66–67, 68, 75, 86, 227
sophistic, 45n199, 196–99, 199n291, 201, 203, 221
sound mapping, 129–33
sources, ix, 9, 16–17, 20, 22–28, 31, 32, 34, 34n140, 35, 43, 67, 71, 99, 104, 106, 114n73, 119, 123n23, 127, 148, 160, 167, 169, 176, 179, 187, 198, 201–3, 207, 214, 217, 219, 221, 226–28
specification, 92, 141, 141n99, 143, 154, 155, 156, 211
structure, ix, 9, 13, 20, 24, 30, 34, 39, 39n162, 42, 47, 61, 65, 67, 74, 79, 84, 84n26, 86–87, 90, 103, 105, 107, 119, 125, 127, 127n56, 129–33, 135, 139–40, 142, 142n104, 146–47, 178, 190, 191n250, 209, 216, 227, 229
style, 14, 28, 33–39, 42, 43n182, 44–47, 63n71, 77, 79–83, 92, 99, 112, 137, 147, 156, 161, 161n65, 165, 167, 172n137, 173–75, 180–82, 184, 186, 190–91, 191n250, 193, 196, 200–201, 208, 215, 217, 219, 221, 224, 229
stylistic purpose, 43, 79, 81, 163, 201
symbolic dreams, 70n96, 102, 103, 104, 109n45, 159, 170, 177, 197, 216
syntactical parallelism 91, 91n67, 141, 147, 172, 186, 197, 200, 206, 210, 212, 223

translation distortion 48, 63, 63n71, 64, 149, 149n14, 150, 151, 155
typology 3, 27, 32, 70n101, 82, 85, 86, 92–93, 97, 98, 102n11, 117–19, 127, 133, 144, 146, 158, 154, 175, 188–89, 196, 202, 207, 209, 214, 215, 218, 220, 221, 223–25

verbatim
   verbatim repetition, 18, 135, 137, 143, 155, 166–67, 170, 174, 211, 217, 229
   verbatim transmission, 22
vision 5n20, 77, 100, 102n13, 110, 112, 159, 159n54, 160, 166–67, 171, 171n134, 172, 172n137, 173, 178, 186

# Ancient Document Index

## Old Testament /Hebrew Bible

### Genesis

| | |
|---|---|
| 4:18 | 12n7 |
| 4:23 | 91 |
| 13:14–18 | 223n4 |
| 15:1–21 | 114n77 |
| 15:12–21 | 149, 149n13, 152n23, 152n26–7 |
| 15:12 | 149–50, 152n30, 154 |
| 15:13 | 149–50 |
| 15:14–15 | 150, 154 |
| 15:16 | 150 |
| 15:17 | 149, 154 |
| 15:18 | 150 |
| 16:7–12 | 5n17 |
| 18:27 | 96n89 |
| 19:30 | 151n16 |
| 20:1–8 | 149n12, 151, 152n23–4, 152n26, 153n33 |
| 20:1 | 151 |
| 20:2 | 151, 151n16 |
| 20:3–8 | 4, 4n14, 5, 105n34 |
| 20:3–7 | 129 |
| 20:3 | 151, 152n30, 153n31 |
| 20:4 | 166n4 |
| 20:6 | 151 |
| 20:8 | 108n43, 151, 152n30, 154 |
| 22:11–12 | 5n17 |
| 26:23–25 | 8 |
| 26:24 | 149n13, 152n30 |
| 28:10–22 | 8, 149n13, 152n20–3, 152n26, 162, 212n355 |
| 28:10–17 | 114n77 |
| 28:11–12 | 152n30 |
| 28:11 | 154n37 |
| 28:12–16 | 4n14, 105n34 |
| 28:12–15 | 159n44 |
| 28:12 | 4, 151n17, 162n25 |
| 28:13 | 4 |
| 28:16 | 154n37 |
| 28:17 | 154n37 |
| 28:18 | 152n30, 162n25 |
| 28:19 | 154n37, 162n25 |
| 28:22 | 162n25 |
| 31:1–13 | 105n34 |
| 31:10–13 | 4n14, 5, 149n13, 152n20, 152n22, 152n24, 212n355 |
| 31:10 | 4, 152n30, 154 |
| 31:11–13 | 159n44 |
| 31:24 | 4, 4n14, 149n13, 105n34, 152n30, 153n31 |
| 35:22–26 | 3 |
| 37–50 | 151n17 |
| 37:5–7 | 149n13, 152n28 |
| 37:5 | 152n30, 153n31 |

## Genesis (continued)

| | |
|---|---|
| 37:6 | 152n30 |
| 37:7–9 | 149n13 |
| 37:7 | 159, 159n49 |
| 37:9 | 152n30, 153n31, 159n49 |
| 37:25–28 | 3n9 |
| 40:9–13 | 149n13, 152n21 |
| 40:9–11 | 159n49 |
| 40:9 | 152n30 |
| 40:16–19 | 149n13, 152n21 |
| 40:16–17 | 159n49 |
| 40:16 | 152n30 |
| 41:1–7 | 153n33 |
| 41:1–4 | 149n13 |
| 41:1 | 152n30 |
| 41:5–8 | 149n13, 152n22, 212n355, 216n372 |
| 41:5 | 152n30 |
| 41:7 | 167n109 |
| 41:14–45 | 149n13 |
| 41:17–24 | 159n49 |
| 41:17–21 | 152n22, 212n355 |
| 41:18 | 159n52 |
| 41:22–24 | 152n22, 212n355, 216n372 |
| 41:25–31 | 152n21–2, 212n355, 216n372 |
| 41:26 | 154 |
| 41:27 | 154 |
| 46:1–8 | 149n13, 152n22–4, 152n26, 212n355 |
| 46:1–4 | 114n77 |
| 46:2–4 | 4, 4n14, 5, 105n34, 214 |
| 46:2 | 152n30, 153n31 |

## Exodus

| | |
|---|---|
| 4:19–20 | 127n57 |
| 14:10–31 | 117 |
| 16:1–17:7 | 117 |
| 19:1–23:33 | 117 |
| 33:1–23 | 117 |
| 34:29–35 | 117 |

## Numbers

| | |
|---|---|
| 22:8–13 | 105n34 |
| 22:9–13 | 149n13, 77n1, 152n22, 212n355, 216n372 |
| 22:20–21 | 149n13, 77n1, 105n34 |
| 22:31–35 | 77n1 |
| 33:9–37 | 12n7 |

## Deuteronomy

| | |
|---|---|
| 31:7–9 | 117 |

## Joshua

| | |
|---|---|
| 1:1–9 | 117 |

## Judges

| | |
|---|---|
| 2:1–4 | 5n17 |
| 6:11–22 | 5n17 |
| 7.13–14 | 149n13 |
| 7:13 | 152n30 |
| 13:3–5 | 5n17 |
| 13:20–25 | 5n17 |

## 1 Samuel

| | |
|---|---|
| 3:1–21 | 8, 114n77, 156, 169, 216 |
| 3:2–15 | 149n13, 152n22, 152n24–5, 152n29, 212n355, 216n372 |
| 21:1–6 | 15 |

## 1 Kings

| | |
|---|---|
| 3:1–15 | 8 |
| 3:3–15 | 149n13 |
| 3:4–15 | 114n77, 129 |
| 3:5–15 | 105n34, 152n21, 152n24, 152n27–8, 163 |
| 3:5 | 152n30, 153n31 |
| 3:6–7 | 154 |
| 3:8 | 154 |

| | | | |
|---|---|---|---|
| 3:12–13 | 154–55 | 8:15–26 | 5n20, 149n13, 152n26 |
| 3:12 | 154, 155, 214 | | |
| 9:1–9 | 163 | 9:20–27 | 5n20 |
| 19:5–7 | 77n1, 149n13, 216n372 | 9:21 | 6n25, 7n32, 113 |

## Hosea

| | |
|---|---|
| 11:1 | 2, 117, 128n59, 134, 148n8, 222n1, 224, 224n5–6 |

## Psalms

| | |
|---|---|
| 22:1 | 143 |

## Isaiah

| | |
|---|---|
| 7:14 | 2, 2n3, 127, 143, 148n8, 224n5–6 |
| 8:8 | 2n3 |
| 8:11 | 2n3 |

# Apocrypha

## Esther

| | |
|---|---|
| 10:4–8 | 157n41 |
| 11:2–12 | 157n39 |
| 11:4 | 157 |
| 11:5 | 157 |
| 11:7 | 157 |

## Jeremiah

| | |
|---|---|
| 31:15–22 | 118n91 |
| 31:15 | 118, 142, 224n5 |

## 2 Maccabees

| | |
|---|---|
| 15:12–16 | 157 |
| 15:11 | 157 |
| 15:14 | 157 |
| 15:16 | 157 |
| 15:17 | 157 |

## Daniel

| | |
|---|---|
| 2:31–35 | 149n13, 152n21, 152n23–4 |
| 2:31 | 152n30 |
| 2:36–45 | 149n13, 152n26 |
| 4:5–15 | 149n13, 152n21, 152n26 |
| 4:5 | 152n30 |
| 4:7–9 | 155, 216n372 |
| 4:10–13 | 155, 216n372 |
| 4:16–24 | 149n13 |
| 4:17–18 | 155, 216n372 |
| 4:20 | 155, 216n372 |
| 4:25–34 | 149n13, 152n22, 212n355 |
| 7:1–10 | 152n29 |
| 7:1–8 | 149n13 |
| 7:1 | 152n30 |
| 7:9–14 | 149n13, 152n21 |
| 7:15–27 | 149n13, 152n22, 212n355 |
| 8:1–14 | 149n13, 152n21, 152n24, 216n373 |
| 8:1 | 152n30 |
| 8:13–14 | 216n373 |
| 8:15–27 | 7n32 |

# Pseudepigrapha

## Testament of Naphtali

| | |
|---|---|
| 5:1–8 | 170n122 |
| 5:1 | 170n124 |
| 5:2 | 170, 170n124 |
| 5:3 | 170, 170n124 |
| 5:4 | 170:124, 170n125 |
| 5:5 | 170 |
| 5:6–7 | 170n126 |
| 5:6 | 170 |
| 5:9 | 170n125 |
| 6:1–10 | 170n122 |
| 6:4–5 | 170n126 |
| 6:6 | 170n126 |
| 6:7–8 | 170n126 |

## New Testament

### Matthew

| | |
|---|---|
| 1:1—4:16 | 127 |
| 1:1—2:23 | 127 |
| 1:1-18 | 133 |
| 1:1-17 | 111 |
| 1:1 | 128, 131, 134 |
| 1:16 | 3, 128 |
| 1:18—2:23 | 28, 111, 130, 138 |
| 1:18—2:1 | 133 |
| 1:18-25 | 41n173, 131 |
| 1:18-23 | 142 |
| 1:18-21 | 116 |
| 1:18-19 | 132 |
| 1:18 | 34, 107n38, 131, 132, 133, 134, 140 |
| 1:19 | 33, 132 |
| 1:20-25 | 2, 28, 33, 135n84 |
| 1:20-24 | 28 |
| 1:20-21 | 128, 135 |
| 1:20 | 30, 64, 100n1, 107n38, 107, 107n40, 108, 108n42, 129, 132, 133, 137, 139, 140, 210 |
| 1:21 | 30, 103n16, 108, 108n42, 112n65, 116, 124, 129, 134, 139, 140, 141, 144, 210, 222n3 |
| 1:22-23 | 127, 137n88 |
| 1:22 | 29, 103n18-9, 131, 137 |
| 1:23 | 112n65, 124, 127, 128, 129, 131, 140, 140n96, 143, 148n8, 224n5 |
| 1:24-25 | 135, 138, 141 |
| 1:24 | 133, 138, 139, 140, 141, 143, 169, 212 |
| 1:25 | 112n65, 134, 140, 141 |
| 2:1-12 | 133, 142 |
| 2:1-6 | 131, 132 |
| 2:1 | 33, 34, 107n38, 128, 131, 132, 133, 134, 214n367 |
| 2:2 | 128, 208, 214n367 |
| 2:3 | 33 |
| 2:4 | 33, 128, 128n60 |
| 2:5-6 | 137, 137n88 |
| 2:5 | 131 |
| 2:6 | 131, 224n5 |
| 2:7-15 | 131, 132 |
| 2:7 | 30, 33, 131 |
| 2:8 | 214n367 |
| 2:11 | 214n367 |
| 2:12-23 | 41n173, 133 |
| 2:12-13 | 135 |
| 2:12 | 2, 29, 30, 33, 34, 115n78, 128, 132, 133, 134, 135n84, 138 |
| 2:13-23 | 142 |
| 2:13-15 | 2, 133, 135n84 |
| 2:13-14 | 28, 116, 128 |
| 2:13 | 7, 29, 30, 33, 34, 64, 100n1, 107n38, 107, 107n40, 108n41-2, 128, 129, 132, 133, 136, 138, 139, 208, 209n342 |
| 2:14-15 | 127 |
| 2:14 | 133, 136, 139 |
| 2:15 | 29, 108n41, 117, 128, 128n59, 129, 131, 134, 137, 137n88, 142, 148n8, 222n1, 224n5 |
| 2:16-18 | 116, 127, 131, 133 |
| 2:16 | 30, 128, 131, 214n367 |
| 2:17-18 | 137n88 |
| 2:17 | 29, 131, 137 |
| 2:18 | 142, 224n5 |
| 2:19-23 | 131, 133, 142 |
| 2:19-21 | 2, 28, 135n84 |
| 2:19-20 | 128, 136 |
| 2:19 | 7, 33, 64, 107n38, 107, 107n40, |

| | | | | | |
|---|---|---|---|---|---|
| | | 127n57, 131, 132, 133, 134, 138 | 7:16 | 37, 38 |
| | | | 7:20 | 37, 38 |
| 2:20–21 | | 133 | 7:21–27 | 126 |
| 2:20 | | 100n1, 108n42, 129, 136, 139 | 7:24–27 | 126 |
| | | | 8:1 | 37 |
| 2:21 | | 133, 136, 139 | 8:3 | 135 |
| 2:22 | | 2, 30, 33, 34, 128, 133, 134, 135, 135n84, 138, 209n342 | 8:17 | 9, 137n88 |
| | | | 8:29 | 128n60 |
| | | | 9:18–26 | 124n31 |
| | | | 9:24 | 33 |
| 2:23 | | 29, 122n16, 127, 129, 131, 133, 137, 137n88, 224n5 | 9:27 | 128n60 |
| | | | 9:32 | 33 |
| | | | 10:2 | 124n30 |
| | | | 11:2 | 128n60 |
| 3:1 | | 33 | 11:25–30 | 117 |
| 3:5 | | 33 | 12:3–4 | 15 |
| 3:11 | | 208n336 | 12:15 | 33 |
| 3:13–17 | | 117 | 12:17–21 | 137n88 |
| 3:13 | | 33 | 12:17 | 29 |
| 3:17 | | 128n59 | 12:23 | 128n60 |
| 4:1–11 | | 117, 127n58, 128n59 | 12:25 | 33 |
| | | | 12:40 | 117n86 |
| 4:3 | | 128n60 | 12:45 | 33 |
| 4:6 | | 128n60 | 12:49 | 135 |
| 4:14–16 | | 137n88 | 13:8 | 208n336 |
| 4:14 | | 29 | 13:35 | 29 |
| 4:24 | | 122n16 | 13:55 | 111n61 |
| 5–7 | | 36, 117 | 14:13–21 | 135 |
| 5:1–2 | | 127n58 | 14:13 | 33 |
| 5:1 | | 37 | 14:31 | 135 |
| 5:3–16 | | 125 | 14:33 | 128n60 |
| 5:3–12 | | 126 | 15:21 | 33 |
| 5:3 | | 37 | 15:22 | 128n60 |
| 5:10 | | 37, 37n154 | 15:32–38 | 135 |
| 5:11–12 | | 37n154 | 16:16 | 128n60 |
| 5:13 | | 126 | 16:20 | 128n60 |
| 5:17–20 | | 126, 126n44 | 16:21 | 135 |
| 5:21–7:20 | | 126 | 17:1–9 | 117 |
| 5:21–48 | | 126 | 17:1 | 33 |
| 5:29–30 | | 126 | 17:5 | 33 |
| 5:46–47 | | 126 | 17:24–27 | 122n16 |
| 6:1–18 | | 126 | 18:16 | 33 |
| 6:11 | | 126 | 20:17–19 | 135 |
| 6:16–18 | | 37n151 | 20:17 | 33 |
| 6:25–34 | | 38 | 20:30–31 | 128n60 |
| 6:25 | | 37, 38 | 21:1 | 167n109 |
| 6:31 | | 37, 38, 38n157 | 21:4–5 | 137n88 |
| 6:34 | | 37, 38 | 21:4 | 29 |

## Matthew (continued)

| | |
|---|---|
| 21:9 | 128n60 |
| 21:15 | 128n60 |
| 21:35 | 208n336 |
| 21:37 | 128n60 |
| 22:7 | 122n13 |
| 22:42–45 | 128n60 |
| 23:10 | 128n60 |
| 23:21 | 33 |
| 24:40–41 | 33 |
| 26:37 | 33 |
| 26:57 | 128 |
| 26:63 | 128n60 |
| 26:68 | 128n60 |
| 27:1 | 128 |
| 27:9–10 | 137n88 |
| 27:9 | 29 |
| 27:11 | 128, 128n60 |
| 27:17 | 128n60 |
| 27:19 | 2, 33 |
| 27:20 | 128 |
| 27:22 | 128n60 |
| 27:27 | 33 |
| 27:29 | 128, 128n60 |
| 27:37 | 128n60 |
| 27:42 | 128n60 |
| 27:43 | 128n60 |
| 27:46 | 143 |
| 27:54 | 128n60 |
| 28:11 | 33 |
| 28:16–20 | 117 |
| 28:19 | 128 |
| 28:20 | 127, 128n60 |

## Mark

| | |
|---|---|
| 1–2 | 228 |
| 2:1—3:6 | 73n114 |
| 2:18–20 | 37n151 |
| 2:23 | 167n109 |
| 3:8 | 122n16 |
| 3:17 | 124, 124n30 |
| 5:22–43 | 124, 124n31 |
| 11:20–25 | 37n151 |
| 15:34 | 143n107 |

## Luke

| | |
|---|---|
| 1:1–4 | 23n83 |
| 1:6 | 6n24 |
| 1:26–38 | 5n20 |
| 1:26 | 5n18 |
| 1:52–53 | 96n90 |
| 1:63 | 42n176 |
| 3 | 12n7 |
| 4:16–20 | 14n25 |
| 6:1 | 167n109 |
| 6:17 | 122n16 |

## Acts

| | |
|---|---|
| 8:30 | 42n177 |
| 9:3–17 | 110 |
| 9:3–9 | 77n1, 171n134, 172, 172n136 |
| 9:4 | 173 |
| 9:5 | 173n144 |
| 9:6 | 172 |
| 9:7 | 172n140 |
| 9:8 | 172 |
| 9:10–17 | 77n1, 171n134, 172 |
| 9:11 | 172, 173 |
| 9:12 | 173 |
| 9:17 | 173 |
| 9:18 | 173 |
| 10:1–8 | 110 |
| 10:3–8 | 77n1, 171n134, 172n136, 173 |
| 10:5 | 173 |
| 10:7 | 173 |
| 10:8 | 173 |
| 10:9–16 | 77n1, 171n134, 172n135, 172n136, 173 |
| 10:9–10 | 110 |
| 10:11 | 172n142, 173n146 |
| 10:13 | 173n147 |
| 10:15 | 173n148 |
| 10:16 | 172n142 |
| 10:30–33 | 172n136 |
| 11:4–11 | 172n136, 172n141, 173 |

| | |
|---|---|
| 11:5 | 172n142, 173n146 |
| 11:7 | 173n147 |
| 11:9 | 173n148 |
| 11:10 | 172n142 |
| 16:6–10 | 171n133, 172 |
| 16:6 | 172n137 |
| 16:9 | 110 |
| 16:10 | 172n137 |
| 18:9–11 | 171n133 |
| 18:9 | 110, 172n138 |
| 22:6–11 | 172n136, 173 |
| 22:7 | 173 |
| 22:9 | 172n137, 219 |
| 22:17–21 | 77n1, 171n134 |
| 23:11 | 110, 171n133, 172, 172n139, 211 |
| 26:12–18 | 172n136, 172n141, 173 |
| 26:14 | 173 |
| 27:23–26 | 171n133 |
| 27:23 | 110, 172, 172n139, 211 |
| 27:24 | 172, 172n139, 211 |

## Dead Sea Scrolls

### Genesis Apocryphon (1QapGen)

| | |
|---|---|
| 13–15 | 170n127, 171 |
| 19:14–21 | 170n127, 171 |
| 20:22 | 170n127, 171, 171n128 |
| 21:8–22 | 170n127, 171 |
| 21:8 | 171 |
| 21:10 | 171 |
| 21:13–14 | 171 |
| 21:15 | 171 |

## Rabbinic Writings

### Mishnah

| | |
|---|---|
| Tamid 3:7–9 | 14n23 |
| ʿErub. 10:10–14 | 14n23 |
| Pesaḥ. 2:5–6 | 14n23 |

## Other Jewish Writings

### Josephus

*Antiquities*

| | |
|---|---|
| 1–14 | 161n65 |
| 1.5 | 161n66 |
| 1.208–9 | 165n92, 166n101, 166n103 |
| 1.279–84 | 162, 165n92, 166n103 |
| 1.279 | 161n69, 162n71, 165n95 |
| 1.280 | 162n73 |
| 1.284 | 162n68, 162n70, 162n72, 162n74, 165n95 |
| 1.313–14 | 165n92 |
| 1.331–34 | 165n92 |
| 2.10–17 | 165n92 |
| 2.12 | 166n102 |
| 2.17 | 166n102 |
| 2.63–73 | 165n92 |
| 2.63 | 166n102 |
| 2.66 | 166n102 |
| 2.68 | 166n102 |
| 2.69–70 | 166n102 |
| 2.72 | 166n102 |
| 2.73 | 166n102 |
| 2.75–86 | 165n92, 166n104 |
| 2.75 | 166n102 |
| 2.76 | 166n102 |
| 2.80 | 166n102 |
| 2.81 | 166n102 |
| 2.83 | 166m102, 167n109 |
| 2.86 | 166n102 |
| 2.171–76 | 165n92 |
| 2.212–17 | 164, 164n84, 165n92 |
| 2.212 | 164, 164n88 |
| 2.214 | 164, 164n89–90 |
| 2.216 | 164 |
| 2.217 | 164n86, 164n91 |
| 5.215–16 | 165n92 |
| 5.218–22 | 165n92, 166n105 |
| 5.218 | 166n108 |
| 5.277–78 | 165n92 |

## Antiquities (continued)

| | |
|---|---|
| 5.348–50 | 165n92 |
| 6.37–40 | 165n92, 166n100 |
| 7.92–93 | 165n92, 166n100 |
| 8.22–25 | 163n77, 165n92 |
| 8.22 | 165n95 |
| 8.25 | 165n95 |
| 8.125–29 | 163n77, 165n92 |
| 8.125 | 165n95 |
| 8.127–28 | 165n96 |
| 8.128 | 165n96 |
| 8.129 | 165n95–6 |
| 10.194–211 | 165n92, 166n106 |
| 10.195 | 166n102 |
| 10.199 | 166n102 |
| 10.200 | 166n102 |
| 10.204 | 166n102 |
| 10.207 | 166n102 |
| 10.208 | 166n102 |
| 10.210 | 166n102 |
| 10.216–17 | 165n92 |
| 10.217 | 166n102 |
| 10.218 | 161n67 |
| 10.269–77 | 165n92, 166n107 |
| 10.269 | 166, 165n95 |
| 10.269 | 166n102 |
| 10.270 | 166, 166n102 |
| 10.272 | 165n95, 166n102 |
| 10.277 | 165n95 |
| 11.326–28 | 165n92 |
| 1.333–35 | 165n92 |
| 12.112 | 165n92 |
| 13.332 | 165n92 |
| 15–19 | 161n65 |
| 17.345–48 | 163n78, 165n92 |
| 17.345 | 165n93 |
| 17.346 | 163n81, 165n96 |
| 17.348 | 165n93 |
| 17.349–53 | 163n78, 165n92, 166n99 |
| 17.349 | 165n94 |
| 17.352 | 165n98 |
| 20.18–19 | 165n92 |
| 20.18 | 165n97 |
| 20 | 161n65 |

## Contra Apionem

| | |
|---|---|
| 1.47–49 | 161n59 |
| 1.50 | 161n64 |
| 1.53–56 | 161n61 |

## Jewish War

| | |
|---|---|
| 2.11 | 163n82 |
| 2.112–13 | 163n78, 165n92 |
| 2.112 | 163n82, 167n109, 165n95 |
| 2.113 | 163n80, 165n95–6 |
| 2.114–16 | 163n78, 165n92, 166n99, 166n103 |
| 2.114 | 165n94, 165n95, 165n98 |
| 2.116 | 163n83, 165n95, 165n98 |

## Vita

| | |
|---|---|
| 208–210 | 165n92 |
| 208 | 165n95 |
| 210 | 165n95 |
| 342 | 161n61 |
| 358 | 161n61 |
| 364–67 | 161n60 |

# Philo

## De Somniis

| | |
|---|---|
| 1.1–2 | 101n9 |
| 1.2–3 | 159n43 |
| 1.189 | 159n44 |
| 2.1–3 | 101n9 |
| 2.6 | 159n45, 159n50 |
| 2.78 | 159n51 |
| 2.159 | 159n47 |
| 2.206 | 159n46 |
| 2.216–218 | 159n48 |
| 2.216 | 159n52 |

## De Vita Mosis

| | |
|---|---|
| 1.273–274 | 77n1, 159n53 |
| 1.273 | 160n55 |
| 1.274 | 160n56 |

## Pseudo-Philo

*Liber Antiquitatum Biblicarum*

| | |
|---|---|
| 8:10 | 168, 168n112 |
| 9:10 | 168n112, 169n118–120, 212n352 |
| 18:3–9 | 168n112, 169n117, 169n118 |
| 23:3–14 | 168n112, 168n114, 169, 169n117, 212 |
| 28:4–5 | 168n112, 169n117 |
| 42:2–3 | 6n25 |
| 53:1–13 | 168n112, 169n115, 169n117, 212n353 |

## Greco-Roman Writings

### Appian

*Bella Civilia*

| | |
|---|---|
| 1.11.97 | 182n195–6 |
| 1.12.105 | 182n195–6 |
| 2.16.115 | 182n195–6 |
| 4.14.110 | 182n195–6, 183 |

*Historia Romana*

| | |
|---|---|
| 8.1.1 | 182, 182n195 |
| 8.20.136 | 182n195, 182n198, 183n200 |
| 11.9.56 | 182n195, 182n198–9 |
| 12.2.9 | 182n195–6 |
| 12.4.27 | 182n195–6 |

### Aristotle

*Ars Rhetorica*

| | |
|---|---|
| 3.1403b | 43n182 |

*De Memoria et Reminiscentia*

| | |
|---|---|
| 1:449b24 | 49n6 |
| 1:450a | 32, 49n5 |
| 2:451a 18f | 50n7 |
| 2:451b 6–18 | 50n9 |
| 452a12–425a25 | 50n13 |

### Artemidorus

*Oneirocritica*

| | |
|---|---|
| 1.2 | 102n12–3, 203n315 |
| 1.31 | 203n315 |
| 1.32 | 203n315 |
| 1.64 | 203n315 |
| 1.67 | 203n315 |
| 1.79 | 203n315 |
| 2.9 | 203n315 |
| 2.14 | 203n315 |
| 2.34 | 203n315 |
| 2.44 | 203n315 |
| 2.66 | 203n315 |
| 3.28 | 203n315 |
| 4.23 | 203n315 |
| 4.48 | 203n315 |
| 4.65 | 203n315 |
| 4.66 | 203n315 |
| 5.2 | 204n319 204n322, 205n325 |
| 5.3 | 204n318–9 |
| 5.5 | 204n319, 206 |
| 5.9 | 203n317, 204n319, 204n322 |
| 5.12 | 89n55, 204n319, 205, 205n328, 209n341 |
| 5.13 | 204n319, 204n321 |
| 5.20 | 204n319 |
| 5.23 | 204n319, 205n325 |
| 5.24 | 204n319 |
| 5.26–31 | 204n319 |
| 5.26 | 204 |
| 5.27 | 204n322 |
| 5.28 | 205n328 |
| 5.29 | 204 |
| 5.30 | 204, 205n325. 205n327 |
| 5.33 | 204n319 |
| 5.35 | 204n319 |
| 5.37 | 91n67, 204n319, 206, 206n329 |
| 5.39 | 204n319, 205, 205n325, 205n328, 206 |
| 5.42 | 204n319, 205n325 |

| Oneirocritica (continued) | | 4.13–34 | 78n2 |
|---|---|---|---|
| 5.43 | 204n319, 206 | 4.13.18 | 82n20, 96n92 |
| 5.47–49 | 204n319 | 4.15 | 94n79 |
| 5.47 | 91n67, 205, 205n327, 206, 206n329 | 4.17 | 81n14 |
| | | 4.58 | 94n80, 94n83 |
| 5.48 | 203n317 | | |
| 5.51 | 204n319, 204, 204n322 | | |

## Chariton

### Chaereas and Callirhoe

| 5.55 | 203n317 | 1.12.5 | 197n280, 198n283 |
|---|---|---|---|
| 5.56–58 | 204n319 | 1.12.10 | 197n280, 198n283 |
| 5.57 | 204n320 | 2.1.2 | 197n280, 198n284–5 |
| 5.58 | 205n327 | | |
| 5.63–65 | 204n319, 205n328 | 2.3.5 | 197n280, 198n286 |
| 5.64 | 205n325, 205n327, 206n329 | 2.9.1–6 | 197n280, 198n286–7 |
| 5.65 | 205n325, 206 | 3.7.4 | 187n280, 198n285–6 |
| 5.67 | 204n319 | | |
| 5.69–71 | 204n319 | 4.1.1–3 | 197n280, 198n283 |
| 5.71 | 205n325 | 5.5.5–7 | 197, 197n280, 198n288 |
| 5.72 | 203n317 | | |
| 5.74 | 204n319, 205n325 | 6.2.2 | 197n280, 198n283 |
| 5.75 | 204n319, 205n328 | | |
| 5.78 | 203n317, 204n319, 204n322, 205, 205n325 | | |

## Cicero

### De Inventione

| | | 1:7 | 51n19 |
|---|---|---|---|
| 5.79 | 203n317, 204n319, 204n322, 205 | 1:9 | 51n19 |

### De Oratore

| 5.82 | 204n319 | 2.350–60 | 79n7 |
|---|---|---|---|
| 5.84–87 | 204n319 | 2.351–54 | 51n15 |
| 5.84 | 206 | 3.206–8 | 78–79 |
| 5.85 | 205, 205n325, 205n328 | 3.207 | 85n31 |
| | | 3.208 | 80n9 |
| 5.92 | 203n317, 204m319, 204n322, 205, 205n325 | | |

## Diodorus Siculus

### Bibliotheca Historica

| 5.94 | 203n317, 204n319, 205n325 | 13.97.6 | 181n189, 181n191 |
|---|---|---|---|
| | | 16.33.1 | 181n189 |
| | | 17.103.7 | 181n189 |

## Auctor ad C. Herennium

## Dionysius of Halicarnassus

| 3 | 51n16 | | |
|---|---|---|---|
| 3.12 | 51n20 | *De Compositione Verborum* | |
| 3.16.29–3.19.32 | 51n17 | 4.110 | 180n184 |

## ANCIENT DOCUMENT INDEX

*Antiquitates Romanae*
| | |
|---|---|
| 1.1.3 | 181 |
| 1.56.5 | 181n186 |
| 1.57.4 | 181n186 |
| 3.67.3 | 181, 181n186 |
| 5.54.2 | 181n186 |
| 7.68.3–6 | 181, 181n186 |
| 20.12.1–2 | 181n186 |

## Herodotus

*Histories*
| | |
|---|---|
| 1.1.1 | 24n92 |
| 1.34 | 176n152, 177n160–1 |
| 1.107–8 | 176n153, 177n160 |
| 1.107.2 | 32n133, 73n110 |
| 1.209 | 176n153, 177n160–1, 212n354 |
| 1.209.1 | 178n172 |
| 1.209.4 | 178n173 |
| 2.55.1 | 23n81 |
| 2.91.3–5 | 24n89 |
| 2.123.1 | 23n80 |
| 2.139 | 176n152, 176n157, 178n168, 89n54, 90n56 |
| 2.141 | 176n152, 176n155, 176n157, 177n161, 178n168 |
| 3.30 | 176n152, 177n161 |
| 3.124 | 176n153, 177n160–1 |
| 3.149 | 176n154 |
| 4.14 | 24n89 |
| 5.56 | 176n152, 176n156, 176n158, 177n161, 177n163 |
| 6.75.3 | 25n95 |
| 6.8 | 25n96 |
| 6.107 | 176n153, 177n160–1, 178n170 |
| 6.118 | 176n154 |
| 6.131 | 176n153 |
| 6.137.1–2 | 24n88 |
| 7.12–14 | 176n152, 176n155, 177n161, 148n12 |
| 7.12 | 176n156, 177n162 |
| 7.14 | 177n159, 177n164 |
| 7.17–18 | 176n152, 176n157 |
| 7.17 | 178n168 |
| 7.19 | 176n153, 177n160–1, 178n171, 148n12 |
| 7.152.3 | 23n85 |
| 8.38 | 23n82 |

## Homer

*Iliad*
| | |
|---|---|
| 1.206 | 17n46 |
| 2.1–41 | 111n58, 177 |
| 2.20 | 7n27, 113 |
| 2.41–42 | 108n43 |
| 5.429 | 206n330 |
| 10.494–97 | 111n58 |
| 10.496–97 | 7n27, 113n68 |
| 23.58–107 | 111n58 |
| 23.62ff | 7n27 |
| 23.62–101 | 113n68 |
| 24.677–95 | 111n58 |
| 24.682–89 | 7n27, 113n68 |

*Odyssey*
| | |
|---|---|
| 1.44 | 17n47 |
| 1.136–43 | 137n87 |
| 2.1 | 97n97 |
| 4.354–55 | 190n239 |
| 4.794–841 | 111n58 |
| 4.795–841 | 113n68 |
| 4.795ff | 7n27 |
| 6.15–50 | 111n58 |
| 6.19–49 | 113n68 |
| 6.19ff | 7n27 |
| 14.482–98 | 111n58 |
| 15.1–56 | 111n58 |
| 19.535–81 | 111n58 |
| 19.562–67 | 101n9 |
| 20.30–55 | 111n58 |
| 24.12 | 113n70 |

## Longus

*Daphnis and Chloe*

| | |
|---|---|
| 1.2.3–1.3.1 | 35n144 |
| 1.5.3 | 35n145 |
| 1.7.1–1.8.2 | 198n290, 199n292, 199n295, 199n298–9 |
| 2.10.1 | 198n290, 199n295, 200n302 |
| 2.23.1—2.24.1 | 35, 198n290, 199n292–5 |
| 2.26.5—2.28.1 | 198n290, 199n298, 198n300, 200–1, 200n302–3 |
| 2.27.1 | 200n304 |
| 2.27.2 | 200n305 |
| 2.27.3 | 200n306 |
| 2.34.1–3 | 35 |
| 2.34.1 | 36n146 |
| 2.34.3 | 36n146 |
| 3.22–23 | 35n143 |
| 3.27.1—3.28.1 | 198n290, 199, 199n292, 199n295–6, 199n298, 199n300 |
| 3.29 | 35n143 |
| 4.29 | 35n143 |
| 4.34.1–3 | 198n290, 199, 199n298, 199n301, 200n302 |

## Philostratus the Athenian

*Vita Apollonii*

| | |
|---|---|
| 1.5 | 194n268, 194n271 |
| 1.9 | 194n268, 194n270–1 |
| 1.10 | 194n268, 194n270–1 |
| 1.23 | 194, 194n268, 194n270–1, 194n274 |
| 1.29 | 194, 194n268, 194n271 194n273 |
| 4.11 | 198n268–9 |
| 4.34 | 194n268, 194n271–2 |
| 8.7.5 | 194n268–9 |
| 8.12 | 194n268, 194n270 |

## Plato

*Meno*

| | |
|---|---|
| 81 C-D | 49n3 |

*Phaedo* 49

*Protagoras*

| | |
|---|---|
| 324d | 112n64 |
| 332e | 112n64 |

*Respublica*

| | |
|---|---|
| 333c | 112n64 |
| 383a | 112n64 |
| 476c | 151n18 |
| 572b | 151n18 |

*Sophista*

| | |
|---|---|
| 266b | 151n18 |

*Theaetetus*

| | |
|---|---|
| 191 C-D | 49n1 |

## Plutarch

*Parallel Lives*

*Alcibiades*

| | |
|---|---|
| 39.1–2 | 189n230, 189n236 |

*Alexander*

| | |
|---|---|
| 2.2–3 [2] | 189n230, 189n236, 190n243 |
| 18.4 | 189n230, 189n236 |
| 24.3–5 [3] | 189n230, 190n243 |
| 26.3 | 189n231, 189n236, 190n238–9 |

*Anthony*

| | |
|---|---|
| 16.3 | 189n230, 189n233 |
| 22.2 | 189n232–4 |

*Aristides*

| | |
|---|---|
| 11.5 | 189n231, 189n233 |
| 19.2 | 189n231, 189n233, 189n235 |

*Caesar*

| | |
|---|---|
| 32.6 | 189n230, 190n243 |
| 63.5–7 | 189n323, 189n236, 190, 190n246 |
| 68.2–3 | 189n230, 189n236 |

*Cimon*

| | |
|---|---|
| 18.2–4 | 189n230, 189n236, 190n238, 190, 190n240 |

*Eumenes*

| | |
|---|---|
| 6.4–7 | 36, 189n230, 189n236, 190, 190n240, 190n243, 190n245 |

*Pericles*

| | |
|---|---|
| 3.2 | 189n230, 189n233 |
| 13.8 | 189n231, 189n237 |

*Themistocles*

| | |
|---|---|
| 26.2–4 | 189n230, 190n238 |
| 30.1–3 | 189n231, 190n243, 191, 191n247 |

## Polybius

*Histories*

| | |
|---|---|
| 5.108.5 | 179n175–6 |
| 10.4.4–10.5.6 | 179n175 |
| 10.4.6 | 179n178 |
| 10.5.1 | 180n179 |
| 10.5.3 | 179n178 |
| 10.11.5–8 | 179n175 |
| 10.11.6 | 180n180 |
| 10.11.8 | 180n180 |

## Quintilian

*Institutio*

| | |
|---|---|
| 1.3.1 | 44n185 |
| 1.4.6–1.7.35 | 44n186 |
| 1.10.7 | 46n203 |
| 2.4.2–4 | 44n187 |
| 2.4.2 | 44n190 |
| 2.4.18 | 44n188 |
| 2.4.20 | 44n189 |
| 4.5 | 126n44 |
| 9.1–3 | 78n2 |
| 9.3.2 | 83n23 |
| 9.3.28 | 87n44 |
| 9.3.66 | 83n24 |
| 9.3.81 | 94n78 |
| 10.3.3–6 | 12n9, 19n59 |
| 10.3.19 | 13n10 |
| 11 | 19n59, 51n16 |
| 11.2, 23–26 | 52n21 |
| 11.2, 32–33 | 52n22 |

## Suetonius

*De Vita Caesarum*

*Augustus*

| | |
|---|---|
| 91.1 | 192n254, 192n256, 193n258, 193n260 |
| 91.2 | 192n253, 192n256 |
| 94.4 [2] | 192n252, 192n256 |
| 94.5 | 192n252, 192n255 |
| 94.8 [2] | 192n252, 193n257, 193n259 |
| 94.9 | 192n252, 192n255 |

*Caligula*

| | |
|---|---|
| 57.3 | 192n252, 193n260 |

*Domitianus*

| | |
|---|---|
| 15.3 | 192n252, 192n255 |
| 23.2 | 192, 192n252 |

*Galba*

| | |
|---|---|
| 4.3 | 192n253, 192n255 |
| 9.2 | 192n254–5 |
| 18.2 | 192n253, 192n255 |

*Julius*

| | |
|---|---|
| 7.2 | 192n252, 192n255 |
| 81.3 [3] | 192n252, 193n261 |

*Nero*

| | |
|---|---|
| 7.1 | 192n254–5 |
| 46.1 | 192n252, 192n255 |

*Otho*

| | |
|---|---|
| 7.2 | 192n254, 193n262 |

*Tiberius*

| | |
|---|---|
| 74 | 192n253, 192n255 |

*Vespasianus*

| | |
|---|---|
| 5.5 | 192n252, 192n256 |
| 7.2 | 192n253, 193n260 |
| 25 | 192n252 |

## Tacitus

*Annals*

| | |
|---|---|
| 1.65 | 186n222, 186n225–7 |
| 2.14 | 186n222, 186n226 |
| 11.4 | 186, 186n222, 186n227 |
| 12.13 | 186n222, 186n227 |

*Germania*

| | |
|---|---|
| 27.1 | 186n228 |

*Histories*

| | |
|---|---|
| 4.83 | 186n223, 186n227 |

## Valerius Maximus

*Factorum ac dictorum*

| | |
|---|---|
| 1.7.1 | 184, 184n207, 185n216 |
| 1.7.2 | 184n208, 185n218 |
| 1.7.3–7 | 184n207 |
| 1.7.3 | 185, 185n218, 185n220 |
| 1.7.4 | 185n216 |
| 1.7.7 | 184 |
| 1.7.8 | 184n208 |
| 1.7, ext.1–6 | 185n218 |
| 1.7, ext.1–3 | 184n207 |
| 1.7, ext.1 | 185n220 |
| 1.7, ext.4–7 | 184n208 |
| 1.7, ext.4 | 185, 185n214 |
| 1.7, ext.5 | 185, 185n213 |
| 1.7, ext.6 | 185, 185n213–5, 185n219–220 |
| 1.7, ext.7 | 185n217 |
| 1.7, ext.8 | 184n207, 185n213–4, 185n218 |
| 1.7, ext.9 | 184n208, 185n216 |
| 1.7, ext.10 | 184, 184n207, 185n213, 185n218–9 |